RETAILING
Sixth Edition

JAY DIAMOND, Professor
Marketing, Retailing, Fashion Department
Nassau Community College

GERALD PINTEL, Professor Emeritus
Accounting and Business Administration Department
Nassau Community College

Prentice Hall, Upper Saddle River, New Jersey 07458

Library of Congress Cataloging-in-Publication Data

Diamond, Jay.
    Retailing / Jay Diamond, Gerald Pintel. — 6th ed.
        p. cm.
    Pintel's name appears first on the earlier edition.
    Includes index.
    ISBN 0-13-448384-7
    1. Retail trade—Management.   2. Retail trade—Vocational
guidance.   I. Pintel, Gerald.   II. Title.
HF5429.P57   1996
658.8′7—dc20   95-22285
                                               CIP

Acquisitions Editor: **Don Hull**
Editorial /production supervision: **Tele-Composition, Inc.**
Production Coordinator: **Lynne Breitfeller**
Associate Managing Editor: **Carol Burgett**
Marketing Manager: **John Chillingsworth**
Buyer: **Vincent Scelta**
Editorial Assistant: **John Larkin**

© 1996 by Prentice Hall, Inc.
A Simon & Schuster Company
Upper Saddle River, New Jersey 07458

Printed in the United States of America

10 9 8 7 6 5 4 3 2 1

ISBN   0-13-448384-7

Prentice-Hall International (UK) Limited, *London*
Prentice-Hall of Australia Pty. Limited, *Sydney*
Prentice-Hall Canada Inc., *Toronto*
Prentice-Hall Hispanoamericana, S.A., *Mexico*
Prentice-Hall of India Private Limited, *New Delhi*
Prentice-Hall of Japan, Inc., *Tokyo*
Simon & Schuster Asia Pte. Ltd., *Singapore*
Editora Prentice-Hall do Brasil, Ltda., *Rio de Janeiro*

Contents

Chapter 3
Franchising   44

Chapter 4
Consumer Behavior   62

Part 2 Organization, Management, and Operational Functions

Chapter 5
Store Organization   78

Chapter 6
Human Resources Management

Chapter 7
Store Location and Layout

Chapter 8
Merchandise Handling

Chapter 9
Loss Prevention

Part 3 Buying and Merchandising Concepts

Chapter 10
The Buying Function   188

Chapter 11
Resident Buying Offices
and Other Market Consultants   206

Chapter 12
Merchandise Pricing   224

Part 4 Building and Maintaining the Retail Clientele

Chapter 13
Advertising and Promotion   242

Chapter 14
Visual Merchandising   280

Chapter 15
Direct Retailing   312

Part 5 Retail Information Systems, Functions, and Controls

Chapter 16
Personal Selling   332

Chapter 17
Accounting Procedures and Operational Controls   348

Chapter 18
Credit and Customer Services   374

Chapter 19
Research 394

Preface

Although the last edition of *Retailing* is just a few years old, a sufficient number of changes have taken place in the field to make it a very different place in which merchants operate their businesses. Department stores continue to play a less important role, while discounters and value-oriented retailers have captured the attention of the consumer. Shoppers are no longer restricted to the few traditional shopping districts that they once had to patronize for their purchases, but are able to buy in newer environments, or remain at home to satisfy their needs.

The sixth edition of *Retailing* addresses the changes that confront today's practitioners and examines the future that they face. In such a competitive field as retailing, only the fittest will be able to survive and bring a profit to their stores.

Although many of the practices and principles adhered to today are different from those of the past, many older ones are still being successfully followed by merchants around the globe. These, featured in the previous editions, coupled with the new, make this most recent edition one that will benefit everyone who reads it. The additions to this text are numerous. Included at the beginning of each chapter is a vignette enhanced with a full-page photograph that explores a pertinent aspect of contemporary retailing. Each chapter also features a section on Trends that concisely lists the directions that retailers are taking in specific areas. The chapter on Store Location and Layout has been expanded to include the exciting new retail environments such as festival marketplaces, megamalls, the "mills" outlet centers, and other places that consumers may opt to go to for their purchases. A wealth of new artwork has been added, as well as the updating of materials.

In order to make this edition more suitable for one-semester courses or those taught on the quarter system, the subject matter has been realigned into 19 chapters in five units, offering every aspect of retailing needed by those entering the field or others who are already making it their careers.

The typical elements such as Learning Objectives, Action For The Independent Retailer, Important Points In The Chapter, and Review Questions have been retained, and a bank of updated questions is included in the Instructor's Manual.

A new, exciting teaching tool has been developed. A video series, paralleling the text, has been produced to provide reinforcement and better comprehension for the students. Areas such as Retailing Classifications and Environments, Careers, Buying and Merchandising, Promotion, and Customer Services are illustrated by in-store and market footage and by interviews with leaders in the field.

Successful Retailers Participate in Such Activities As . . . .

Selecting the Best Shopping Districts for their Stores . . . .

Fifth Avenue, New York: A Downtown Shopping District
Photograph: Ellen Diamond

The Fashion Mall at Plantation: An Upscale Mall
Courtesy: Melvin Simon Associates, Inc.

The Mills: Enclosed Outlet Centers
Courtesy: Western Development Corporation

Designing Environments that Serve Their Needs ....

Hanna Barbera: Specialty Children's Retailer
Courtesy: Space Design International

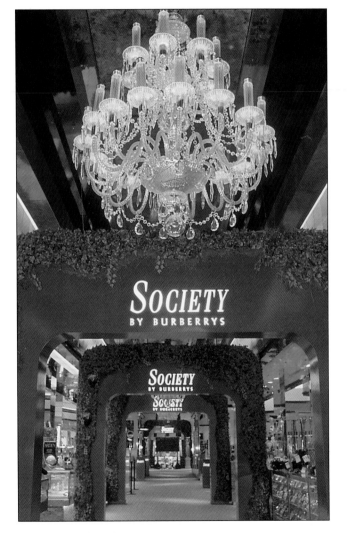

Entrance: Society by Burberrys
Courtesy: Bloomingdale's, Chicago

Choosing Merchandise that Suits Their Customers . . . .

Shoppers Viewing Merchandise on Display
Photograph: Ellen Diamond

An Assortment of Children's Clothing
Photograph: Ellen Diamond

Girl's Merchandise Presented in Self-Serve Cases
Photograph: Ellen Diamond

Arousing Attention Through Promotion and Visual Merchandising . . . .

The Thanksgiving Day Parade
Courtesy: Macy's

Shoppers Examining Merchandise
in Display Window
Photograph: Ellen Diamond

RETAILING

Chapter 1
The Nature of Retailing

Photographs by Ellen Diamond

LEARNING OBJECTIVES

Upon completion of this chapter, the student should be able to:

1. Write a brief essay on the evolution of retailing in America, including the reasons for the changes.
2. Discuss six different types of retailing institutions (such as chain stores and department stores).
3. Describe the operations of six major American retailers.
4. Explain the reasons for department store spinoffs.
5. Discuss the success of the warehouse clubs.

SUCCESS AGAINST ALL ODDS . . .

In the late 1960s, Leslie Wexner believed he had the right formula to achieve success in specialty store retailing. At that time, department stores were moving full speed ahead with significant branch openings. With a family in the department store business, expansion would be simple to achieve. Wexner, however, had another plan. He would embark upon a path that would eventually catapult him to unparalleled fame in retailing.

His concept involved the opening of a few specialty units that would limit his merchandise offering to a specialized assortment for women. He chose the name The Limited, which would immediately signal a restricted merchandise assortment. In 1971, the chain expanded to eight stores, a considerable accomplishment in so short a time frame. With total sales at $4 million, Wexner was on his way to a goal that had been but a dream.

Not one to rest with this modest achievement, Wexner quickly opened unit after unit, and The Limited became a major player in specialty store retailing.

Recognizing the need for other stores with slightly different focuses, Wexner next charted the course for another group of stores, Express. With a target market that was a little younger than The Limited shopper, Express stores soon began to appear everywhere. Another star was added to what would eventually become the Wexner retailing empire.

Through expansion and acquisition, what was originally a modest entry into retailing was now the major player in the field. Lerner New York, a chain whose customer base was low income women, was purchased and restructured to become more fashion oriented. Victoria's Secret, a British-based intimate apparel store, was acquired and brought to the United States. It quickly became the store for others in that specialization to imitate. Large-sized women soon found a newly enhanced Lane Bryant organization that featured fashions similar to those The Limited offered, only in sizes they could wear. This happened when Wexner bought the company and upgraded it to a more fashionable operation. Stores like The Limited Woman, also for women with fuller figures; Limited Too for children; Structure for men; Cacique, another intimate apparel salon; Abercrombie & Fitch, an old-world retailer with emphasis on conservative dress; Bath and Body Works, a chain that specializes in care for the body; and Henri Bendel, by most standards the epitome of high fashion for the discerning shopper became members of The Limited's dynasty.

With more than 4,000 stores in the organization, Wexner's retailing presence is felt in every major mall and fashionable shopping area in the United States. It is hard to find a location where The Limited hasn't set up shop.

As one observes the different types of retail environments available to satisfy the merchandise needs of consumers, regional shopping centers, mega-malls, discount arenas, downtown central shopping districts, flea markets, and power centers, it is quite obvious that retailing is an enormous industry. As we move toward the close of the twentieth century it should be understood that there are more than 1.4 million retail establishments in the United States that employ 20 million workers. That is, one in five Americans works in some aspect of retailing! In 1994, sales in the United States exceeded $2 trillion. Retailing has certainly come a long way since the fur trappers and farmers of the fifteenth century exchanged or bartered their goods.

A look at retailing's history will help us understand the route it has taken to bring it to today's practices.

HISTORICAL DEVELOPMENT

Retailing had its meager beginning in the early fifteenth century at the *trading post*. At that time, currency was not used to make purchases; instead, goods from European markets were exchanged for the pelts of fur trappers and produce grown by farmers.

In the mid-eighteenth century, this first retail institution began to expand its operation to better serve the needs of the American colonists. A greater variety of merchandise was needed by the settlers, and the trading post gave way to the *general store*. This retail store operated on a cash basis, a departure from the barter system of the earlier retailer. The merchandise assortment was extensive, with offerings of foodstuffs, yard goods, feed for cattle, manufactured goods from the Old World, shoes, and such animal supplies as harnesses. The merchandise was not carefully organized as it is in retail stores today. A haphazard nondepartmentalized arrangement was typical. The general store is still in evidence today in rural areas.

In the middle of the nineteenth century there was a great variety of goods being produced in the United States, so much so that the general store was unable to carry the unlimited offerings of manufacturers. This necessitated the beginning of specialization in retailing and the introduction of the *limited line store*. This store carried a wide variety of one classification of merchandise. Shoe stores, ladies' specialty shops, jewelry stores, and groceries are examples of limited line stores. Today the limited line store, or specialty store, as it is commonly referred to, still enjoys an important place in retailing. The early specialty shops were generally individual proprietorships (individually owned). Many of them have grown into large, well-known retail empires and enjoy the distinction of having started the chain organization. A number of these great merchants will be discussed later in this chapter.

The *chain organization,* the first venture into large-scale retailing in the United States, began in the latter part of the nineteenth century. A chain organization is generally defined as two or more stores, similar in nature and having common ownership. Many of these operators of successful limited line stores opened second, third, and more units in other areas. Among the early chain organizations were J. C. Penney Co.; A & P, the food giant; and F. W. Woolworth Co., the "5 & 10 cent store."

At the end of the nineteenth and the beginning of the twentieth century the *department store,* a departmentalized retail store carrying a wide variety of hard and soft goods, became popular. Essentially, the department store is the bringing together of many limited line operations under one roof, with common ownership. This institution differed from the general store in that it presented an orderly arrangement of many types of merchandise, in contrast to the disorganized presentation of goods in the general store. The offerings of the department store—in addition to the typical hard goods such as furniture, appliances, and tools, and the soft goods such as wearing apparel, clothing accessories, and piece goods—often include departments specializing in financial services, gourmet foods, pets, optics, travel arrangements, entertainment information and sales, and so on. The luxury of one-stop shopping is available to the department store customer. Branch stores, smaller units of the department store that carry a representation of the main store's offerings, have become popular as much of the population has moved to the suburbs. Today in the retail field few new department stores are being established; instead we are witnessing a great expansion of the established stores through additional branches.

In an effort to better serve the needs of those people unable to patronize the existing retail institutions, either because of their distance from the stores or their lack of time to buy in person, the *mail order retailer* began to attract attention. At first, in the late nineteenth century, little was available to the mail order customer. Extensive catalogs, which since then have enjoyed great popularity, were prepared and sent to customers, and the mail order business became an important part of retailing. Montgomery Ward & Co. and Sears, Roebuck and Co. were early mail order houses. Today, even with mass transportation, the extensive chain organization, and the branch store, mail order retailing, now known as direct marketing or direct retailing, flourishes as never before. Its importance to today's retailing is explored in Chapter 15.

Supermarkets, large departmentalized food stores, became popular in the late 1930s. In addition to the large variety of foodstuffs, they carry an abundance of miscellaneous items such as drugs; toys; men's, women's, and children's accessories; plants; and hardware. As the department store provides one-stop shopping for the consumer, similarly the supermarket affords the luxury of purchasing all one's food needs at one location instead of making separate trips to the grocer, butcher, baker, and produce dealer. Although the great majority of supermarkets are chain organizations, many independent markets also are in operation.

The 1950s were a time for yet another retailing innovation. It was a period when *discount operations* were springing up all over the country. Unlike the conventional retail store with all of its services, the discounter offers limited service in exchange for lower prices. This method of merchandising is not restricted to one type of retailing organization but is found in chain, department, and specialty store operations.

Although retailing has gone through significant changes since the trading post era, most of the other types of retail organizations are still in operation. Some of course are less popular than they once were, whereas others have gained in importance. Throughout this text we will explore all of today's retail operations, including such innovative operations as off-price stores, closeout stores, warehouse clubs, and manufacturer-owned retail outlets.

MAJOR CLASSIFICATIONS OF RETAILERS

The era of the trading post belongs to history, but the other types of retail institutions that have been organized since that time are very much in evidence today. Except for the general store, they are all flourishing throughout the United States.

Retailers may be classified in many ways. As examples, they can be grouped according to their merchandising activities (the activities in the buying–selling cycle), the merchandise they carry, their dollar volume, or the number of people they employ. Although the study of each classification may be valuable, we can get a complete overview of retailing institutions by investigating small retailers and large retailers as separate categories, with further expansion into the variety of large retailers

The Small Retailer

The small retail business as defined here grosses under $500,000 annually. Typically, there is little job specialization. The store owner is generally responsible for the overall management and merchandising tasks. The owner buys, sells, sets work schedules, plans sales promotions, secures personnel, and so forth. The "larger" small retailer, doing business at the $500,000 level, has more specialized personnel working in the organization. There might be a person responsible only for merchandising duties, which include the entire buying–selling cycle. A part-time trimmer might be hired for window displays. A store manager would be responsible for the management of the physical layout of the store and supervision of personnel. But in stores of smaller gross sales it is obvious that the owner must perform all activities.

The majority of small retail stores are individual proprietorships; however, included in the group are partnerships and corporations. The general store and the specialty store are two types of small stores, with the latter accounting for almost all small retailing institutions.

In addition to the typical small conventional retail establishments, the general and specialty stores, retailing on a small scale is still in evidence throughout the United States. Flea markets, both outdoor and indoor, are succeeding and are providing opportunities for those who wish to sell at retail but have chosen not to take the traditional "store" route.

Boutiques, which carry exclusive merchandise, thrive in affluent areas and cater to a small group of sophisticated shoppers. In the food industry, specialists who feature gourmet foods and other items are capturing the attention of the consumer. Kiosks and pushcarts offer still another small retail opportunity.

The General Store

The age of specialization, the success of the chain organization, movement to urban and suburban communities, the automobile, and the continued growth of the mail order house are some factors that have contributed to the decline of the general store.

In rural areas the general store, which features a wide variety of unrelated merchandise, is still in operation. Management of the operation is generally haphazard. The sophisticated tools and aids of today's modern retailers are rarely employed. The proprietor engages in purchasing merchandise that is so varied as to include cracker barrel goods and ready-made apparel. The knowledge of such proprietors in any single area is so limited that they lack the ability necessary to make the right decisions. How can one individual have the product knowledge for so diversified an inventory? The limited floor space doesn't allow for a wide assortment within each merchandise classification. The general store has the questionable distinction of being the most mismanaged type of retail organization. Retailers, although reluctant to agree on many things, usually concede that the general store will never regain its popularity. Figure 1–1 shows a picture of a general store currently operating in New England.

Figure 1–1   New England general store. Photograph by Ellen Diamond

The Specialty Store

The limited line store or specialty store, as it is usually referred to today, is an establishment that carries one line of merchandise. Stores specializing in jewelry, furs, shoes, hardware, groceries, baked goods, and broader classifications, such as women's clothing or men's accessories, are examples of the specialty or limited line store. Some of those, which may be found all over the country, are The Limited, Structure, Express, Casual Corner, Ups 'N Downs, Radio Shack, and Lerner New York. The greatest number of successful small retailers operate specialty stores. Some of the factors that have led to the success of this type of organization are:

1. Personalized service
2. Wide assortment of merchandise in a limited classification
3. Knowledgeable buying—the buyer must be educated only in certain lines of merchandise

The chain organization is the major competitor of the small specialty store. The chain is actually a retail organization with many units carrying specialty merchandise. The chain's ability to offer lower prices due to greater buying power and its wide advertising to the consumer pose the greatest threat to the small retailer.

In an attempt to meet the "unfair" competition of the chain, some small merchants have united informally. The combining of small orders to qualify for quantity discounts, particularly in groceries, small hard goods, and staple menswear such as shirts and other accessories, has enabled the small merchant to become more competitive by lowering prices. Lately advertising, an area that the small retailer often avoids because of the costs involved, has become popular as a group activity. Where one merchant would spend a large sum for promotion, the group now shares the costs. A complete listing of all the stores involved in the advertisement indicates to the consumer those offering the advertised merchandise. In both group-buying and group-advertising activities, noncompeting stores are generally involved.

More formalized groups of small retailers are evidenced by the *voluntary chain* or the *cooperative chain*. The former is usually organized by a wholesaler who enters into contractual arrangements with the individual retailers, requiring that all purchases be made from that wholesaler. In addition, promotional plans, point-of-purchase display arrangements, advertising materials, merchandising advice, counter and shelf arrangements, and location selection are typical aids provided by the wholesaler. The *cooperative chain* differs in that the retailers join together and operate their own warehouse. They too are involved in many group activities that tend to lower the cost of individual operations and increase individual efficiency.

In retailing today, with the giant chain and department store organizations, small retailers can more effectively compete through group activities such as group buying and advertising, which reduce costs to the individual member. Of paramount importance in the field is knowledgeable advice on management and merchandising. Whereas the large retailer can afford the luxury of specialists, the small merchants, through their combined efforts, can avail themselves of an exchange of ideas. One store owner may be expert in designing the best store layout, another might excel in the buying activity; still another might have a talent for preparing advertising copy. This exchange of information and ideas provides the special knowledge so necessary for success in retailing. Because the merchants are not direct competitors, this free exchange can be open and beneficial to all.

Since the nature of some small stores dictates a different type of management, retailing today still includes completely independent retailers who are not involved in any group arrangement. Others find this type of arrangement well suited to their needs.

The Flea Market Stall

In years gone by, flea markets were established as places where people were able to dispose of the "treasures" they accumulated over a period of time. Once having accomplished this, they usually were out of business. Today, however, the flea market is not an arena for this purpose, but a regular format for individuals to conduct retail businesses. For a modest fee, approximately $40 a day, an individual can set up shop. This format has become so successful that acquiring a space has been as difficult as gaining a desirable location in a traditional shopping area. Stalls are generally leased for a one-year period.

Flea markets, which were once limited to rural areas, may be found today in the biggest cities. Locations are no longer limited to the backroads, as pictured in Figure 1–2, but to parking lots of drive-in movies and racetracks, and to indoor facilities that once housed major retail operations. Figure 1–3 shows an example of one of America's largest flea markets in a suburb of Ft. Lauderdale, Florida that uses a drive-in movie parking lot as its sales arena.

Price is the major attraction offered by flea market operators. Because of the minimal expense involved in the business' operation, the markup on merchandise is significantly less than that of dealers who operate at regular store locations. The merchandise offered runs the gamut from clothing for every member of the family and household items to food specialties and antiques. The hours of operation are generally limited to two or three days a week, and the service provided is almost nonexistent. It should be noted that some flea market operators, however, do make exchanges and even offer to take such credit cards as Mastercard and VISA.

So successful have many of these operations been that they have caused considerable problems for nearby operators of conventional stores. Where it has been fair game for the chains and department stores to have an edge over the small retailer, "foul" is begin echoed by the giants in retailing when threatened by the pricing strategies of the flea market operators who price similar or identical merchandise below what they sell it for.

Figure 1–2   Backroad flea market. Photograph by Eileen Diamond

A RETAILING FOCUS   *The Swap Shop*

One need only observe the daily traffic jams leading to the parking lots that accompany one of the South's few remaining drive-in movies in Sunrise, Florida to realize that a crowd-pleasing attraction is the cars' destination. It is not the movies that take center stage when darkness comes, but the daytime activity that captures the attention.

Housed in permanent structures, some of which are two stories, and outside stalls, more than 1,000 vendors hawk everything from household goods to fashion merchandise. It is the famous Ft. Lauderdale Swap Shop, second only in size to one in San José, California. Flea markets, or swap meets, as they are often called, are not new to the retail scene. This one, however, has the distinction of being truly unique.

The areas are set up according to the merchandise offered. That is, watch vendors co-exist in one area, sunglasses merchants in another, handbag sellers in yet another, and so forth. There is a semblance of order, atypical of flea markets. The difference does not stop there.

Amusement and entertainment attractions help bring in the crowds. A professional circus performance, complete with elephants, lions, trapeze artists, clowns, and production numbers, is presented throughout the day without cost to the observer. Internationally acclaimed performers such as country singers Willie Nelson and The Gatlin Brothers regularly grace center stage. This too is free of charge. The food arena is comparable to anything found at the malls, and parking is plentiful. Each feature is a major reason why the Swap Shop is such a winner.

A measure of the success of this market is the price vendors are willing to pay for their locations, some of which are considerably better than others. In addition to the standard rental fees found at such retail environments, merchants wishing to operate in the best spots enter into an auction for the space for a year. It is reported that as much as $50,000 has been bid for the privilege of setting up shop in one of the choice places!

Figure 1–3 Swap Shop, the second largest flea market in America. Photograph by Ellen Diamond

Boutiques

An area in retailing that has afforded an individual the opportunity for self-employment has been "boutique" merchandising. These generally high-priced establishments are somewhat similar to small specialty stores, but the merchandise assortment is not restricted to a particular classification of goods, and the items are not stocked in any depth. In fact, where most small specialty retailers feature a range of sizes within its styles, the boutique is more apt to specialize in "one of a kind" items. The boutique is a small venture in which the female shopper (it is almost always a women's store) can purchase the highest fashion in select clothing and accessories. Many boutiques feature items that are in-house creations. The emphasis of boutiques is exclusivity, and it is for this reason that they are becoming extremely popular with people who are not price conscious.

Stores of this nature are popping up all over the country in fashionable areas and are proving to be excellent outlets for producers of unique merchandise. Figure 1–4 features a typical boutique.

Food Specialists

All across the country specialty food retailers are beginning to open stores that concentrate a narrow assortment of items rather than the vast merchandise mixes of the supermarkets. They might concentrate exclusively on delicacy items for entertainment needs, prepared foods that require only reheating and serving, gourmet baked goods, or produce of the highest quality. One of the reasons for this specialization is that it enables the shopper with limited time to make quick selections and attend to other responsibilities. The return of women to the workplace in record numbers has accounted significantly for the growth of the food specialists.

Kiosks and Pushcarts

In festival marketplaces like Quincy Market in Boston and South Street Seaport in New York City, and in regional shopping malls, discount centers and other shopping

Figure 1–4   Boutiques are small, high-priced specialty stores. Photograph by Ellen Diamond

environments, kiosks, "shops without walls," and pushcarts are in evidence. They are an alternative way in which merchandise may be sold without the need for considerable expense such as high rents and fixturing.

The Large Retailer

Today retailing is dominated by the large organization. The department store, chain organization, supermarket, catalog store, manufacturer's outlet, warehouse club, general merchandise discounter, and mail-order house provide the majority of retail sales.

The Department Store

The department store is a departmentalized retail institution that offers a large variety of hard goods and soft goods, provides numerous customer services, has large sales volume, and employs a great number of people specializing in various tasks. Its organization will be discussed in a later chapter.

The merchandise assortment varies depending on the size of the store. Organizations such as Macy's, Marshall Field, or Jordan Marsh offer enough types of merchandise in a range of prices for a consumer family to satisfy just about any of its needs. Such offerings as men's, women's, and children's clothing, apparel accessories, musical instruments, sporting equipment, toys, furniture, hardware, cosmetics, gourmet foods, liquor, floor covering, bedding, draperies, and appliances are among those in the inventory. A Macy's shopper can buy anything from a computer to a painting, a set of luggage to fresh beluga caviar. In many stores, optical goods, beauty salon services, precious jewelry, religious articles, meat and poultry, silverware, and other commodities are available through *leased departments*. These departments are operated by independent retailers or independent chain owners, generally because the nature of the goods or services warrants unusual specialized ability. The department is usually leased on a square foot rental or a percentage of sales. Department stores have found that they can realize a greater profit for the store in this way than if they operated these departments themselves. An important reason for offering these specialized goods and services is to provide the customer with one-stop shopping.

The greatest variety of services offered in retailing is found in the department store. Free delivery, gift wrapping, charge accounts, return privileges, extended credit plans, and the provision of meeting rooms for clubs are among the usual services. Unusual ones include personal shoppers, baby-sitting while parents are shopping, special hours for children shoppers before holidays, and the procurement of tickets for theatrical and sporting events.

Department stores may be individually owned or belong to ownership groups. With the trend of company mergers and acquisitions, today's department store ownership groups are always changing.

Branches and Spinoffs.   With the increase in the number of families moving from the cities to the suburbs, the almost hopeless traffic congestion, the shortage of adequate parking facilities, and the development and growth of shopping malls, department stores have opened additional units away from cities. The branch is a store, usually smaller than the main store, carrying a representation of the parent store's merchandise. It is geared to the needs of the community in which it is located. Some branch stores have exceeded the sales volume of the main store.

Spinoffs or twig stores, once relatively rare in modern retailing but gaining in importance, are very small units belonging to a department store, which, unlike the branch, carry only one classification of merchandise. Aeropostale and Charter Club stores were developed by Macy's and are now part of the Macy's-Federated Stores empire. Figure 1–5 features a spinoff operation.

The Chain Store

The chain store may be defined as a centrally owned and managed organization with two or more similar units each carrying the same classification of merchandise. The merchandiser categories include drugs, hardware, shoes, restaurants, jewelry, variety goods, groceries, baked goods, and more. For example, F. W. Woolworth is a variety chain; A & P is a supermarket chain; J. C. Penney is a general merchandise chain; Lerner New York is a women's fashion chain, and The Home Depot is a "do-it-yourself" chain. Each unit in these chains is similar in nature to the others. The department store has the main store as its base of operations and it plans its purchases there, whereas the chain organization operates from central headquarters, a location that houses merchandisers, buyers, personnel administrators, advertising executives, and so on. Large chains have regional offices in addition to central headquarters. The units of the chain are generally charged with the responsibility of selling merchandise, while the central team is the decision-making body of the organization. Store managers do not formulate policy; instead, they carry out the policies of the central staff.

In addition to the typical merchandising and management responsibilities carried out in central headquarters, some chains centrally plan their stores' visual presentations. Williams-Sonoma, for example, creates its visual plans at a central location in California and disseminates them to each store for copying. In Chapter 14, Visual Merchandising, the concept is fully explored.

Figure 1–5   Aeropostale—a Macy's spinoff store. Photograph by Ellen Diamond

A RETAILING FOCUS   *The Home Depot*

The Home Depot was founded in 1978 in Atlanta, Georgia. It is a do-it-yourself warehouse retailer that currently operates 335 warehouse outlets in the United States and 13 in Canada. Its growth has been astounding in such a short period of time.

While retailers in the do-it-yourself home center industry are not new, none has made such an impact in the industry as has The Home Depot. Among the many factors that have contributed to the company's success are:

- installation in 1983 of computerized checkout systems that eliminated the necessity for item pricing. Not only did this reduce costs of inventory marking, but it also enabled cashiers to move the lines of customers quickly through the cash register areas.
- computer-assisted ordering put in place in 1984 helped to maintain inventory levels of staple merchandise automatically.
- entry into the "super-size" store market with the opening of stores of 140,000 square feet or more. This enabled the company to enter into new merchandise markets.
- low everyday price policy established in 1987, which helped achieve an even sales volume every day. Many similar stores subscribe to periodic sales, which tend to make customers wait to buy their goods at the temporarily reduced prices.
- development of a Universal Product Code system for its stores in 1987.
- implementation of satellite communications in all of its stores in 1988.

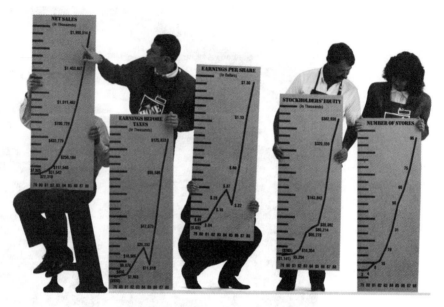

Figure 1–6   Ten years of growth at The Home Depot. *Courtesy:* The Home Depot

The stores now carry more than 30,000 individual items including lumber, kitchen and bath fixtures, building materials, wall and floor coverings, paint, plumbing, electrical supplies, hardware, unfinished furniture, tools, and seasonal merchandise. In outside areas, they sell gardening and landscaping supplies in 10,000 to 15,000 square feet of space.

Not only has its embracing of the latest technologies propelled The Home Depot into the favorable position it now enjoys, but its commitment to personal customer service has made the warehouse outlets places where shoppers can satisfy their consumer needs and get excellent one-on-one assistance. The selling floors are filled with scores of employees, easily identified by their orange aprons, each of whom is a specialist in a particular product. Salespeople stationed in the vast kitchen cabinet areas will spend considerable time assisting in the planning of customers' kitchens. Courtesy seems to be a major concern of management, no matter how large or small the purchase.

The company has been compared to other kinds of successful retailers who have captured large consumer markets: Toys "Я" Us, the toy leader; Nordstrom, the high-fashion specialty retailer whose forte is customer service; and Wal-Mart, the leader in everyday low pricing for general merchandise. The Home Depot has done what retailers have found to be almost impossible today: achieve significant levels of customer loyalty.

The Home Depot is on the move and expects to add sixty new units to its chain in the next five years. From all indications it will more than likely achieve that goal. Figure 1–6 shows ten years of growth at The Home Depot.

There is a growing trend in the United States for chain organizations to diversify and develop groups of stores within the structure, each emphasizing a different merchandising approach. For example, Edison Brothers, which made its mark in retailing as a shoe chain, has expanded its operation to include a separate chain of stores, Jeans West, that features apparel.

Supermarkets

The supermarket is a large departmentalized, self-service organization selling primarily food. The merchandise assortment has grown from the usual grocery, meat, poultry, and produce categories to include hardware, toys, hosiery, drugs, books, greeting cards, and so on. A supermarket may be independently owned, belong to a voluntary or cooperative chain, or be part of a regular chain organization. The greatest number of supermarkets belongs to the third category. Emphasis on lower prices, parking facilities for customers, and the luxury of one-stop food shopping are some of the more important factors that lead to their success.

A RETAILING FOCUS   *Bockwinkel's*

For many years, the United States has witnessed enormous growth in one segment of the retail food industry: the supermarket. All across the country, supermarkets have grown into "superstores" that stock much more than food items. Customers are able to satisfy their needs with a host of non-food items ranging from small appliances to records and tapes. While this form of retailing continues to grow, more specialized food markets are cropping up in many places. These entrepreneurs have recognized that not every food customer enjoys supermarket shopping, nor do they need the vast assortment of merchandise offered in these establishments. While the assortment is plentiful, the attention to service and other amenities are minimal.

There is a growing segment of the population that prefers to purchase foods that are better than the typical variety stocked in the supermarkets, and to be afforded the luxuries of shopping in specialty stores. One of the food markets that has paid attention to these customers' needs is Bockwinkel's, which advertises itself as "the chain store alternative."

The company currently operates several stores in the Chicago area, and is planning to expand to other out-of-state markets. Its success has been attributed to offering an appropriate merchandise mix, which includes premium, fresh, quality products, specialty prepared food items, and regular grocery items, in a setting that emphasizes personal services and customer amenities.

As it opens each store, the company pays more attention to store design to make the customer's shopping experience more pleasurable. In their entry in Burr Ridge, Illinois, the customer is greeted by a column-flanked, skylit vestibule that allows natural sunlight to adorn an eight-foot waterfall. The flower department surrounds the waterfall, bringing fragrance, color, and freshness to the entranceway. Not only is this an unusual manner in which to greet customers, it also motivates many to purchase the flowers. Exquisite fixturing is obvious with the extensive use of brass and mahogany trim. The salad bar fixturing dominates the produce section and enhances the fresh items it displays. Curved casework allows for the exceptional displays of bakery products and gourmet specialty items. Instead of the standard signs that tell of each aisle's offerings, Bockwinkel's uses festive banners that ultimately guide the shoppers to the checkout counters. At the checkout area, there is a large customer service area that is highly visible and clearly identified. Since service is its forte, the store gave this station considerable attention in terms of design. The epitome of customer service is evident in the conveyor system which moves the groceries from the checkout counter to the sidewalk where they are loaded into the customers' cars.

It is stores like Bockwinkel's that emphasize that not every customer fits the mold assumed by supermarkets. A Bockwinkel's store is shown in Figure 1–7.

The Direct Marketing Retailer

Selection of merchandise from a catalog and ordering through the mail or by phone are the major characteristics of the direct marketing retailer. The merchandise offering of some companies is so large and diversified that rarely can one find as wide an assortment in a "merchandise-stocking" store. In addition to those retailers that sell exclusively by mail, a large percentage of the total sales of department and specialty stores can be attributed to this method of retailing. Spiegel and Horchow are two lead-

Figure 1–7   Bockwinkel's, the chain store alternative to the supermarket. *Courtesy:* Schafer Associates, Inc.; Photograph by Les Boschke Photography

ing direct marketers who sell exclusively through the mail. Their offerings include a vast assortment of both hard and soft goods.

Although the chain has moved retail stores closer to the people and has perhaps made buying through catalogs not as necessary as it was in earlier times when farmers and others in isolated areas depended heavily on mail order for merchandise, this method of doing business continues to be important. The large number of women in the workforce results in less time for shopping and encourages mail order purchasing. As is evidenced by the great sales volume of mail order houses, this form of retailing is more important than ever.

The Catalog Store

A companion business to the direct marketing retailer is the catalog store. This method of retailing involves the stocking of merchandise in "warehouse" stores where customers may come in for immediate receipt of goods or may order, by way of catalog, from their homes. The catalog store has grown significantly and has become another method of large scale retailing. The main feature of catalog retailing is price. At considerably lower prices than traditional retailers charge, consumers can purchase appliances, precious jewelry, housewares, cameras, and so on. One such company that is a giant in the field is Service Merchandisers, with stores throughout the United States. Like the traditional retailers, it offers such services as charges, gift certificates, refunds, and exchanges.

Through a combination of in-store purchases and mail order, the catalog store is continuing to grow, becoming a major force in large-scale retailing.

Off-price Merchants

The term "off-price" refers to those retailers who buy goods at prices well below the original wholesale price, and sell them to the consumer at lower than the regular price. Originally the idea of Frieda Loehmann, who began such an operation in her home in Brooklyn in 1921, off-price is a type of retailing that has grown considerably. Loehmann's

Figure 1–8   Marshalls is a major off-price retailer. Photograph by Ellen Diamond

concept was to scout the fashion markets of New York City's garment center for overruns, one-of-a-kind samples, slow sellers, and other items manufacturers were eager to quickly eliminate from their inventories. The early success eventually led to the store's becoming one of the nation's leading off-price retailers with approximately 100 stores in 28 states.

The Loehmann's plan ultimately caught the fancy of other retailers, who also jumped on the off-price bandwagon. Today, retail empires bear names such as T.J. Maxx, Hit Or Miss, Burlington Coat Factory, Symms, Today's Man, and Marshall's (Figure 1–8).

Manufacturers' Outlets

No matter how carefully a manufacturer plans his or her production, a certain number of items do not sell as well as anticipated. They might be styles that didn't capture the consumer's attention, colors that were less successful than expected, "broken-sizes," or merchandise that carried prices that were higher than the shopper was willing to pay.

Many manufacturers dispose of these items by selling them to the aforementioned off-price merchants. Others, however, have taken to opening their own merchandise outlets. In centers such as Freeport, Maine, North Conway, New Hampshire, Harriman, New York, and Secaucus, New Jersey, a host of these producers have set up their own retail outlets. Names like DKNY, Calvin Klein, Mikasa, Gucci, Liz Claiborne, and Ralph Lauren quickly dispose of their unwanted merchandise without the need to sell to off-price retailers to do it for them (Figure 1–9).

Warehouse Clubs

In cavernous spaces, retail operations such as Sam's Wholesale Club, The Price Club, and Pace attract patrons whose goal is to buy merchandise at the lowest possible prices. Shoppers must become members of the club, for a fee of approximately $30.00

Figure 1–9 Manufacturer's outlets are operated to dispose of slow sellers. Photographs by Ellen Diamond

per year in order to enter the vast shopping arenas. Offered are a variety of foods and household products, some clothing, electronics, and anything else that the merchant might buy at a good price. The purchases are generally of the bulk variety. For example, twenty-four rolls of paper towels that have been prepacked, is commonplace. Service is at a minimum. Customers are often required to do their own packing and to pay cash for their purchases. In some cases, such as at The Price Club, shoppers may use the Discover card to pay their bills.

General Merchandise Discounters

One need only to go to most cities throughout the United States to come upon such discounters as Wal-Mart, Kmart and Caldor (Figure 1–10). In these stores, consumers

Figure 1–10. Wal-Mart is the largest of the general merchandise discounters. Photograph by Ellen Diamond.

are able to avail themselves of a great assortment of merchandise, including clothing for the family, home furnishings, electronics, beauty aids, food, toys, sporting goods, and pharmaceuticals. The key to the success of these stores is price. Vendors buy in large quantities and pass the savings on to their customers.

TRENDS

Retailing is constantly reinventing itself. Many practices that were once commonplace have changed owing to customer demand and more sophisticated technological advances. There are trends that are in evidence today and others that may appear in the future. Those of a general nature are presented in this chapter, whereas others, with specific applications and orientations, will be featured in their appropriate places throughout the text.

International Expansion

With the success of Toys "Я" Us on foreign shores, other retailers are taking similar routes. Mexico, for example, has become a prime destination for Wal-Mart, which will soon have approximately 65 units in that country, and J. C. Penney, which has seven major branches on the drawing board. Building supply retailers such as Home Depot and Payless Cashways also are entering the Mexican arena. Dillards is another entrant, as is Burlington Coat Factory.

Other foreign shores that are witnessing an invasion of American retailers are Canada with 120 Wal-Mart stores and a major Home Depot unit; Asia with Kmart units; Great Britain with its first membership warehouse, Price-Costco, and the specialty chain, Talbots; Paris with the arrival of The Gap; Japan and Germany, also with The Gap; and Russia with franchised Radio Shack operations in Moscow.

Some companies place even greater emphasis abroad than at home. Foot Locker, for example, is opening more units overseas than in America, in such places as Australia, Mexico, Hong Kong, and China.

Large Store Dominance

Each year fewer and fewer small retailers are opening stores because of the growth of the giants in the industry. Through vast expansion programs, companies like The Gap, Limited Corporation, Home Depot, Wal-Mart, Kmart and the many wholesale membership clubs like Price-Costco have taken over specific merchandise markets. Merger and acquisition such as the combining of The Federated Stores with the Macy's empire have left little room for anyone to begin a new department store venture.

Subspecialization

More and more companies that restrict their merchandise offering to one, narrow classification are becoming dominant players in retailing. The Knot Shop (Figure 1–11), for example, sells only ties, whereas Coach limits its assortment primarily to handbags and related leather items. The reason for this trend is that the consumer has less time to shop and is able to satisfy a specific need in a relatively brief period of time.

Expansion of the Off-pricers

Stores like Burlington Coat Factory, Marshall's, Filene's Basement, Symms, and T.J. Maxx continue to find new markets. A large segment of the population indicates that price rather than service is the primary reason for patronizing a store, and the off-price merchant fits the bill. Off-price merchants are expanding both here in the United States and also overseas; for example, T.J. Maxx has opened stores in England using the name T.K. Maxx and Burlington Coat Factory has opened units in Mexico.

Designer-Owned and -Operated Stores

Names like Armani, DKNY, Ralph Lauren, Calvin Klein, and Liz Claiborne now grace store entrances as well as labels on the garments they produce. Some, such as Ralph Lauren, operate full-service specialty shops as well as clearance outlets. Others, like Armani, offer different shops for different merchandise groups. For example, at the Giorgio Armani stores, the haute couture collection is featured, whereas at the A/X Exchange the assortment is leisure oriented and at lower price points.

Whatever the arrangement, these designers believe that by limiting the merchandise to their own brands, competition from others will be eliminated.

Nontraditional Stores

In what was once a field dominated by traditional retailers, new concepts are catching fire. *Closeout stores* that feature manufacturer's leftovers, *one-price stores* that sell merchandise at only one price such as Georgia Girl where every item is $10.00, and *warehouse clubs* like Price-Costco that require memberships before purchases may be made, are expanding all across the country.

Other trends, including merchandise protection systems, direct retailing, new methods such as the screening of potential applicants, the expansion of private label programs, and so forth, will be discussed later.

Figure 1–11   The Knot Shop is a subspecialty retailer. *Courtesy:* The Knot Shop. Sadin Photo Group, Ltd. © Copyright 1991, Don Broff

ACTION FOR THE INDEPENDENT RETAILER

Too often, retailing textbooks and discussions by educators and practitioners alike focus on large-scale retailing. While it is true that the vast majority of retailing operations are the large organizations and that many of their practices may be adapted to the smallest in the industry, the small independent retailer and the problems associated with being an independent are usually glossed over or totally ignored by the professionals.

As we have learned in this chapter, the small retailer is still in evidence in all parts of the country. While the popularity and success of the general store have declined, and the specialty store has remained somewhat of a vehicle for small retailers, flea markets and boutiques are flourishing.

For these reasons, each chapter will feature a concluding section, *Action for the Independent Retailer,* which will highlight those areas in which even the smallest could benefit. For example, the computer is looked upon as a tool for big business. The small independent can make limited use of such technology at modest expense, which will enable the conducting of a more efficient operation. In areas such as merchandising, buying, and personnel, attention will be paid to the small retail organization.

IMPORTANT POINTS IN THE CHAPTER

1. The growth of retailing in America can be traced from colonial trading posts, where barter was used as the process for exchange, to the retailing giants of the present day.

2. The history of retailing parallels the growth of American consumer demand. As the society became wealthier and more sophisticated, retailers responded by offering a greater variety of goods and increasing the size and the number of locations at which such goods could be purchased.

3. To satisfy today's consumer, goods are presently offered at retail in a great variety of stores featuring an enormous range of goods and services.

4. Large-scale retailing has seen the growth of the catalog store, which is a companion business to the direct marketing retailer. It offers immediate receipt of merchandise in housewares, precious jewelry, appliances, and so forth at lower prices than those of the traditional store.

5. Small-scale retailing is in evidence with the success of flea markets. Those wishing to operate independent "stalls" can do so in these sales arenas with a minimal investment. Other ventures include boutiques and food specialists.

6. The single largest women's clothing chain is The Limited, Inc., with divisions such as The Limited Stores, Express, Victoria's Secret, Lane Bryant, Lerner New York, Henri Bendel, and Abercrombie & Fitch.

7. Do-it-yourself warehouse outlets, such as The Home Depot, are finding tremendous markets in the United States.

REVIEW QUESTIONS

1. What form of retailing was the direct outgrowth of the trading post? What was the reason for its origin?

2. Contrast the general store with the specialty store. In which would the independent retailer more likely be successful?

3. What are the differences between voluntary and cooperative chains?

4. Briefly discuss the independent retailer's opportunity in the flea market.

5. What is a boutique?

6. What alternatives to traditional stores are offered by small retailers?

7. How does the department store method of management differ from chain store management?

8. Define: branch store, spinoff store.
9. In what way has the catalog store expanded upon the direct marketing concept?
10. Describe the unique operation of The Home Depot.
11. Discuss the reasons why manufacturers' outlets have grown.
12. Why do warehouse clubs appeal to consumers?
13. In what way did Frieda Loehmann's merchandising concept affect present-day retailing?
14. Discuss some of the reasons for success of The Limited Stores.
15. Besides food items, supermarkets have expanded their merchandising into different lines. What are they?
16. Even with improved transportation facilities, direct marketing retailing continues to grow. How do you explain this?
17. Why have some department stores failed?
18. Discuss the attraction of overseas expansion for American merchants.
19. How has The Gap expanded its operation?

CASE PROBLEM

For the last ten years, American tourists have flocked to the studio of the French designer, Chantrel Picard, to purchase her exclusive merchandise. Unique designs in sportswear, gowns, shoes, and accessories have captured the hearts of her devoted fans. While the prices for the merchandise are at the top of the scale, customers seem to be willing to pay.

At the present time, Madame Picard is considering possible expansion of her operation. Among the issues that have been discussed are the following:

1. The company could move to larger quarters in the area where all of the exclusive designers have their headquarters. A facility that is available would provide double the amount of space, enabling Picard to feature a greater assortment of merchandise.
2. Many established major department stores, in Europe and the United States, have proposed to Madame Picard that she give them exclusive distribution of her designs. Each would open a separate department in its store and maintain the prices that Picard now charges in her own studio.
3. Madame Picard's assistant believes that expansion of the company is best suited to the opening of boutiques that would bear her name. These shops would be located in fashion centers in different cities in the United States and abroad.

While the cost is considerable, several backers have indicated that they would be willing to finance such an expansion program.

Questions

1. What factors should Madame Picard and her company consider before making a decision?
2. Which choice would you suggest she make? Why?

Chapter 2
Careers

Photograph by Ellen Diamond

```
┌─────────────────────────────────────────────────────────────────────┐
│                        LEARNING OBJECTIVES                          │
│                                                                     │
│   Upon completion of this chapter, the student should be able to:   │
│       1. Describe the personal qualities and qualifications for     │
│          employment.                                                │
│       2. Discuss the advantages and disadvantages of ownership of a │
│          retail business.                                           │
│       3. Classify career opportunities according to the four main   │
│          divisions of a large retail organization.                  │
│       4. Prepare an outline of the main criteria in choosing the    │
│          best job.                                                  │
│       5. Produce a resume.                                          │
└─────────────────────────────────────────────────────────────────────┘
```

STRIKING IT RICH IN SALES . . .

When Nordstrom first opened its doors as a shoe operation in Seattle in 1901, no one imagined that it would eventually achieve international status as a prestige merchant. Its selection was limited to footwear until 1963, when the company expanded its offerings and also carried clothing; however, the mark it made on the public was essentially due to its service orientation. Now with 77 stores in the United States, and many more stores in the development state, Nordstrom is fast becoming the best known specialized department store in the country.

While Nordstrom offers high-quality merchandise, so do other stores such as Bloomingdale's, Macy's, Saks Fifth Avenue, Bergdorf Goodman, and Henri Bendel. What makes Nordstrom different from the rest, however, is the company's demand for excellence in selling. At a time when shoppers have become accustomed to lackluster treatment by sales associates in even the most upscale stores, the "Nordies," as the salespeople are often referred to, deliver service that is unparalleled anywhere in retailing.

The salespeople are always cheerful, ready to meet just about any customer request, and are willing to go to extremes to make the sale that sellers in other stores would not think of. One story will give insight into the dedication of the employees: a salesperson was called by a frantic shopper whose luggage was lost on an arriving flight; the sales associate made his way to the caller's hotel to deliver a wardrobe that consisted of a suit, shirt, tie, shoes, and socks just a few hours before they were needed for an important business engagement. Not only did the sales associate bring the merchandise within an hour, but he arranged for a tailor to accompany him to make immediate alterations on the garments that needed them. This is just one of the hundreds of acts of service that has made Nordstrom famous, and its sales associates among the highest earners in retail sales.

The reason given for this unusual dedication is a compensation system that is entirely based upon commission. Associates are not guaranteed an hourly wage, which is commonplace in retailing, but are rewarded with earnings that far exceed what is typically expected for a salesperson. Nordies are often the beneficiaries of incomes that are in the neighborhood of $90,000 a year, significantly more than many people in retail management earn. By making every shopper feel like he or she may have just about any service delivered, the sales tend to soar.

Although those interested in retailing careers are generally enthralled with careers in buying and merchandising or management, the road to success in those areas is often long and tedious. When success is finally achieved, and even with such success those who earn more than the aforementioned $90,000 are few and far between. For an associate with a positive attitude, dedication to service, and a willingness to go the extra mile, a career in sales at a Nordstrom facility is one that will bring financial success.

As retailers expand their operations, the need for personnel at all levels continues to grow. One need only examine the classified advertisements in newspapers throughout the country and abroad or pay a visit to an employment agency to become aware of the wide range of retailing opportunities that are available to qualified individuals.

While many industries are geographically concentrated in specific regions, retailing is alive and well all over the world. Where there are people, there are stores to serve their needs. Whether the retailing community is "downtown" based, thriving in suburban malls, or made up of neighborhood clusters, the number of stores offering employment seems to keep growing.

Unlike most other industries, retailing doesn't trap an individual in specific parts of the country, neither does it offer a limited range of jobs. It affords the individual a broad spectrum of positions that are as varied in responsibility as they are in the salaries paid and the personal rewards offered.

College students will find the field is one in which opportunities lie in big business, small stores, self-employment, and fields directly related to retailing, such as resident buying offices and the reporting services. Retailing is a world that promises excitement, challenges, and financial rewards for those willing to enter.

PERSONAL QUALITIES AND QUALIFICATIONS FOR EMPLOYMENT

No discussion of career opportunities would be complete or meaningful without dealing with the necessary personal qualities leading to success. Those who are responsible for recruitment generally attempt to select individuals whose qualities are commensurate with what the retailing occupations will demand. Most personnel directors and employment managers believe that those candidates for retail careers who show initiative and who are imaginative, enthusiastic, and intelligent have the greatest potential. While these qualities are often difficult to discern during an interview, they are the ones possessed by successful merchants.

It is generally agreed that, in addition to these qualities, those entering the field should have specific technical knowledge in the areas of mathematics and product information. For example, those who follow a merchandising path will constantly be called upon either to compute or interpret markup, markdown, open to buy, and so on (all of which will be discussed in detail), or to evaluate a variety of products in terms of their production, material content, price, and so on. While these skills can be learned on the job, the individual who demonstrates such knowledge at the interview will probably beat out the other candidate for the job.

Preparation in terms of formal education is far less rigid than in most fields. While it is generally agreed that formal education is of paramount importance and essential for mid-management level positions at most retail organizations, the level of study required is not as stringent or restrictive as in other fields. Careers in such fields as accounting, engineering, medicine, teaching, law, and so on demand significantly more formal education than does retailing. In addition, many of these require licensing or certification for entry into the field.

Many of those responsible for hiring for store positions report that the associate's degree often satisfies the need for entry-level positions which could eventually lead to management. That is not to say that a candidate with a bachelor's degree would not receive even more favorable consideration for many positions.

There are no shortcuts to success in retailing. It is the individual who possesses the positive traits and puts them to productive use who will be successful.

Before deciding upon a specific retailing career, the individual should carefully explore all of the available opportunities in the field. Will the larger store be better for learning the basics? Will the small store provide more "personal attention"? Is self-employment a viable alternative to working for someone else? The answers to these questions, as well as others, can be found in the material that follows.

SELF-EMPLOYMENT

While the American dream for a majority of people has been self-employment, the climate of our country indicates one should tread with caution before making the jump. It is certainly evident that numbers of Americans successfully begin retail operations each year, and many will continue to do so in the future, but success is not guaranteed. An examination of important statistics, relevant to business failure, shows that approximately 90 percent of the failures are attributed to insufficient capital and inexperience, both of which often plague the hopeful retailer wishing to start his or her own business. Coupling these startling facts with the opportunities afforded by the major retailers to great numbers of individuals wanting to enter the field seems to make self-ownership less than fulfilling. With all of this negativism, there is some room for those who still feel the pot of gold at the end of the rainbow is within their reach. Cautious optimism is perhaps an appropriate outlook.

Having outlined the pitfalls of establishing one's own retail outlet, there are some areas for potential success. Some are finding self-employment in franchising, where for an outlay of capital individuals can open their "own" retail operations and have the benefit of large company recognition, training, advice, and the basic necessities to, hopefully, gain success. Many believe that all of the advantages and disadvantages of this type of ownership, to be discussed in a later chapter, provide the safest route to being in one's own business.

Where franchising is somewhat restrictive—and this varies from one franchise organization to another, as does the cost for ownership—"starting from scratch" is another route to take. With the enormous competitive edge enjoyed by the large retailers across the United States, it should be understood that this is risky business. Having weighed the costs and the time commitment involved, it is wisest to establish an operation that capitalizes on a degree of expertise "owned" by the prospective retailer and the inability of the giants in the field to compete. For example, the small retailer who wishes to operate a boutique that is filled with "customized" designs of the owner will probably achieve more success than the one who carries a merchandise line available at many stores. Similarly, if a small merchant operating from a less costly location than other retailers can establish a clientele based upon discount prices, he or she might be successful. Flea markets all across the country are offering individuals the opportunity to own their own retail outlets. While this might not be the "dream" operation, it *is* self-employment.

It is unlikely that individuals will be able to begin their own operation at any location where a major retailer wants to open. For example, examination of any mall immediately indicates that 95 percent of the stores are part of large chain organizations. Why would a realtor want to rent to the small independent retailer, if the giants of the industry, with greater capital and expertise, are better risks? The giant retailer is the dominant force in the retail industry.

Bearing in mind all of the negatives associated with self-employment, many individuals will still want to satisfy that irresistible urge of ownership. In that case, it is appropriate to speak to the "professionals." The Small Business Administration, Chambers of Commerce, and operators of successful small stores are sources of counsel for people before they get started.

OPPORTUNITIES IN SMALL STORES

Working for a small retail operation severely limits one's opportunities. Not only have the numbers of small retailers been declining, but those who are operating a business are generally unable to meet the salary requirements of the knowledgeable individual, and certainly cannot match the salaries paid by large organizations.

Most small retailers are their own decision makers. Many are unwilling to permit others to share in decision making and insist on handling such tasks as merchandising, buying, management, and so on. In such an environment, it is not unlikely to find that business is transacted today exactly as it was done twenty-five years ago. Typically, small merchants are unwilling to make changes that employ today's technology or are unable to afford the investment that change often requires.

Employment in a small store is generally limited to selling. In some situations, there is limited opportunity as the store's manager or assistant manager. Rarely can one expect to go past that level. If it is a career that one envisions, with appropriate financial rewards, it is the large store organization that provides this opportunity.

OPPORTUNITIES IN LARGE RETAIL ORGANIZATIONS

Today's retailing headlines are proof that stores are expanding their operations in record numbers. The department stores, through branch openings, and the chain store organizations, through the continuous opening of units, provide significant opportunities all over the country. No matter where one lives, there is a mall or a downtown area that is being developed or revitalized. As the population increases, retailers are determined to meet the needs of the consumers, and they are making enormous dollar commitments to gain their share of the market.

Whether in managing personnel, purchasing merchandise, promoting new lines, directing warehouse operations, changing displays, coordinating fashion concepts, or managing a department or a store, the challenge is there.

Each major company has its own list of career titles and its own approach to filling these positions with qualified individuals. In the progressive larger department store organizations, there are executive development programs that train qualified individuals for merchandising or management level careers. The better programs provide both classroom and on-the-job training.

Figure 2-1 shows the career path and job description of those individuals who are hired as trainees and are pursuing a merchandising career at Macy's. The time spent at each level or position depends upon the individual's ability and is not just a prescribed period of time. Thus it enables those who show promise to advance quickly, enabling others to achieve the appropriate amount of "seasoning" before moving on.

The arrows in the illustration indicate the movement from trainee to buyer and the stops along the way. Not every organization uses the Macy's system. Each company provides the appropriate route for the goals that have been established by management. Stores have other routes or paths that lead to store management, personnel management, and so forth.

In many chain organizations, such as The Limited, with about 4,200 stores in all of its divisions across the country, the situation is different. The store manager has the training responsibility, which is generally limited to on-the-job training. Assistant managers are "coached" so that they can eventually make the transition to store manager. Successful store managers of chains eventually become district managers and then regional managers.

Whether it is the department store with its formal training or the chain with its on-the-job learning concept, the opportunities are enormous for the talented individual.

JOB CLASSIFICATIONS

The major retailers offer a host of different opportunities to individuals. Some are merchandising oriented, some are concerned with the management of the store, some are artistic in nature, and others are analysis-oriented. In order to provide a meaningful overview of the field, we have arranged the different career titles into categories that most closely parallel the manner in which many large retail companies are organized. It should be understood that different stores use different organizational structures (to be explored in a later chapter) and job titles that might be different than the ones used in the following illustrations.

The categories into which the jobs are classified are based upon the main functions of most retail operations: merchandising, store management, advertising and sales promotion, and control. In addition to analyzing the specific careers, we will explore the retail advisory organizations. Following each category will be an overview to provide further insight into specific careers.

Merchandising

Few would argue with the statement that the buyer is the lifeblood of the retail organization. Couple this with a projection from the United States Labor Department's Bureau of Labor Statistics that buyers' positions will increase through the 1990s, and you will see that a buying career is an excellent bet for anyone who is oriented in this direction. Buyers or purchasing agents, as they are often referred to, work for stores or resident buying offices. The buyer's career being explored here is the one directly involved in employment at the retail level. Resident buyer opportunities will be explored later in the chapter.

It should be understood that it is the rare situation that enables the recent college graduate to enter retailing as a buyer. This is the eventual goal for purchasing-oriented individuals. Most people must first prove themselves as executive trainees or assistant buyers. Watching their work in these positions, merchandising managers (the buyer's supervisors) can best evaluate the buying potential of each employee. Through close scrutiny of the work of the assistant buyer, which may involve merchandise selection

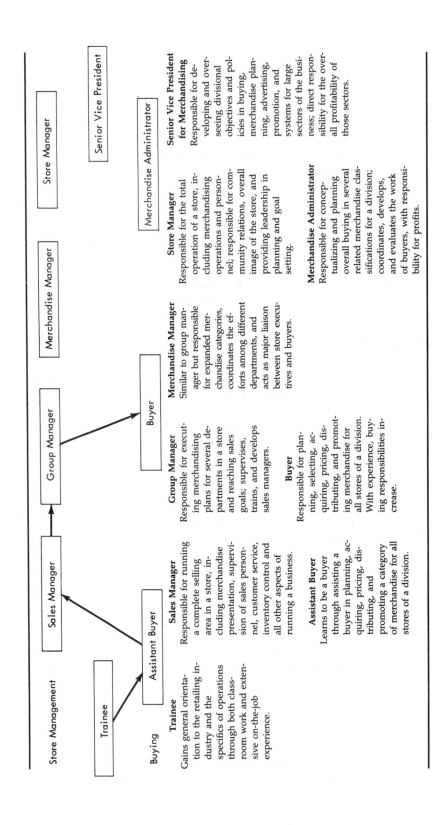

Figure 2–1 Macy's Career Path and Job Descriptions. *Courtesy*: Macy's.

(usually limited to staples), following up of orders, vendor relationships, product knowledge, and so on, managers can make decisions on promotion to buyer.

Store buyers' salaries and responsibilities usually vary according to the nature of the merchandise classification for which they purchase, the merchandising structure of the company, the volume of the department for which they are purchasing, and the variety of buyer-related responsibilities performed. For example, some companies still hold the buyer responsible for the department's sales force.

A significant fact that should be emphasized is the virtual freedom from discrimination in retail buying. Few fields could boast the large number of women in executive positions. Many retailers, in fact, report that there are more female buyers in their organization than male counterparts. Another plus that motivates people to become professional purchasers is the time necessary to achieve the level of buyer. On average, it takes only four to seven years to become a store buyer. In what other career can you reach an executive-level position in such a short period of time, and at a salary often better than that in most fields?

The ultimate achievement for most buyers is to reach the level of merchandise manager. Examination of the table of organization of any large retail organization shows two levels of merchandisers. The top position is that of the general merchandise manager, or GMM, with the divisional merchandise managers directly under the supervision and authority of this individual. Since the actual number of a store's merchandisers is small by comparison with the buyers and assistant buyers, the likelihood of rising to this position is low. Attaining these positions most often requires a significant number of years as a buyer. In reality, rising to the level of a divisional merchandise manager usually demands many years as a buyer, with experience as general manager and divisional manager.

The career of the top merchandising manager, the GMM, is most demanding. The position is one of policy maker as well as operating officer. The GMM is a member of the store's top management team and is directly responsible for meeting management's objectives in merchandising and enforcing the company's policies. He or she is directly involved in policy matters concerning price lines, image, quality levels, and style emphasis. The position is one of the most powerful in the store.

Next in command are the divisional merchandise managers (DMM). Each is responsible for a separate merchandise classification and for the number of buyers in the specific division. For example, the DMM for menswear might be responsible for individual buyers who purchase for such departments as clothing, furnishings, sportswear, shoes, and so forth. The role includes coordinating the efforts of the buyers, evaluating and informing buyers of particular merchandising trends concerning color, fabrication, style, and so on, overseeing unit control systems, keeping track of open-to-buys, planning major purchases with the buyer, recommending promotional ideas, and overseeing the entire division. Where the GMM's role is one of overall merchandising management, the DMM operates specifically within his or her division, always bearing in mind the policies established by the senior merchandiser, the GMM.

Where retailing once gave the opportunity for reaching the level of merchandiser to anyone in the organization who showed merit, today the career of merchandising manager is generally restricted to the individual with advanced formal education as well as store experience. Such a person needs analytical know-how to survive the demands made on a top-level manager, and it is unlikely that anyone less prepared could capably meet the position's challenges.

Figure 2-2 shows a composite of selected merchandising careers with a brief statement on responsibilities.

Figure 2–2   Merchandising Careers: A Composite of Selected Job Titles

Job Title	Responsibilities
General Merchandise Manager	Head store's merchandising function or division and is chief merchandising decision maker.
Divisional Merchandise Manager	Responsible for a particular division's merchandise planning. Supervises buyers in the division.
Buyer	Selects merchandise from vendors and prices it for resale. In some stores, manages the department's sales staff.
Assistant Buyer	Aids the buyer with purchasing of new merchandise, places reorders and special orders, purchases "staples."
Unit Control Manager	Individual responsible for keeping track of the "units" sold.
Fashion Coordinator	Advises on fashion trends, arranges fashion shows, coordinates "fashion emphasis" among departments.

Store Management And Operations

In any retail organization, the primary functions are divided among the merchandising division and the ones classified as store management and operations. The former concerns itself primarily with the buying functions while the latter two are chiefly responsible for such duties as staffing, management of the individual departments, procurement of supplies, security, merchandise handling, and the other responsibilities that are neither publicity nor control oriented.

With the enormous expansion being witnessed in retailing today, and the bright outlook in the field, those wishing to pursue management and operations careers will find the doors wide open. One need only go from one mall to the next to see the vast number of opportunities available. Relocation is not necessary. Individuals can generally drive within five to ten miles of their homes to discover retail centers abounding with career opportunities.

Assistant department managers, as the title indicates, help to manage a specific department. Involvement in such duties as scheduling, handling complaints, selling on the floor, rearranging stock, and so on, are commonplace to the job. Most companies promote from within in the case of department managers. An assistant who proves most reliable on the job is often promoted to manager. The manager usually runs the department and is responsible for management of the department's selling staff. Many stores treat department managers as individuals who are running their own businesses with incentive bonuses paid for achievement.

Personnel or human resources departments have the responsibility of supplying the store with capable workers. People in personnel often have educational backgrounds that include psychology, testing, and management courses. Dealing on a regular basis with recruitment, training, evaluation, and so on, the personnel department constantly deals with employer–employee relations. With the high rate of employee turnover experienced by retailers, this is an area where good people are needed.

For the very best middle management employees, the ultimate goals are branch manager, store manager, regional manager, or personnel director. While it should be recognized that the careers at the upper end of the ladder are certainly less plentiful than those at the lower end or middle, the opportunity to reach the top is there. If room is not available at one's own company, there is always another company willing to bring someone aboard if he or she has demonstrated a solid foundation. Unlike some jobs that may be dead end, management has a bright future.

All stores today have in their employ individuals whose primary responsibility is to make shopping easier and to satisfy the customer's needs. The service manager,

Figure 2–3   Store Management and Operations Careers: A Composite of Selected Job Titles

Job Title	Responsibilities
Store Manager	Oversees and directs the operational function of the store.
Department Manager	Takes responsibility for management of a specific department; sets employee schedules; organizes merchandise.
Human Resources Manager	Directs personnel operations and oversees such aspects as recruitment, labor relations, evaluation, and so on.
Customer Service Manager	Assumes complete responsibility for management and direction of services offered to customers.
Purchasing Agent	Buys the supplies that are necessary to run the store.
Receiving Manager	Manages and controls all aspects of the receiving department.
Traffic Manager	Directs the flow of merchandise from the receiving to the selling areas.
Security Chief	Manages security staff, implements plans for safeguarding merchandise.
Training Director	As part of personnel management team, establishes training program for employees.
Adjustment Manager	Handles customer adjustment and manages return department.

for example, is usually called upon to handle customers' complaints or problems that haven't been solved elsewhere in the store. This job requires a high level of patience and an ability to make the customer feel satisfied. Personal shoppers are also becoming more important to many of the top-level organizations. These people have the responsibility to act in the particular shopper's best interest and serve them to make purchasing easier. Macy's in New York, goes so far as to employ "interpreters," personal shoppers who cater to non-English–speaking people.

From the various services which will be explored in a later chapter, it will be quite evident that this is a career choice offering experiences that are often totally customer-oriented.

Figure 2-3 features a list of typical job titles and responsibilities that are usually associated with store management divisions. It should be noted that in some stores the department manager position belongs in the merchandising division.

Sales Promotion

In order to promote the store's image and to capture its share of the consumer market, large retail organizations participate in a wide variety of promotional activities. The career opportunities are specifically in advertising, special events, display, and other areas of promotion.

The career path for those interested in advertising and sales promotion is unlike the route that is followed for merchandising and management. Individuals who enter this field have usually undertaken specializations in school that are not necessarily retail oriented, and they probably have an artistic or creative flair. Those with the ability to capture the attention of the consumer through imaginative and motivational writing and who are capable of presenting ideas visually through drawing or photography would be prepared for a career in this specialization.

One need only consider consumer newspapers, magazines, direct mail brochures, television, radio, and the numerous special promotions and store events that are presented to us every day to comprehend the enormity of the advertising and sales promotional responsibilities of retailing. A quick look at the table of organization for most large retailers would turn up such job titles as copywriter, typographer, proofreader, layout artist, merchandise artist, advertising manager, special events director, publicity manager, and so forth. In order to meet and beat the competition, stores must employ large staffs of people to help their advertising and promotional messages reach the marketplace and motivate purchasing.

With particular emphasis for most retailers today on direct mail catalogs, to appeal to the individual who doesn't have time to visit the store, there is expansion of advertising departments.

It should be noted that individuals seeking these creative oriented positions must often have more than a positive interview. Where all of the other retailing divisions may base their selection of personnel on interviews, testing, references, past experience, or any combination of these factors, the person seeking employment in advertising will be called upon to submit a portfolio. This might include a variety of materials indicative of the candidate's ability. Writing, layout, drawings, photographs, special event creations, and so on would be appropriate for advertising portfolios. Anyone pursuing such a career should carefully prepare the presentation under the direction of a professional since this, more than likely, will be the key to employment.

Visual merchandisers are individuals whose job it is to show the store and its merchandise to the best possible advantage. Whetting the customer's appetite, so that purchases will be consummated, is the sum total of the visual merchandiser's task.

A career in display is not a typical goal for one who sets out for a life in retailing. While a knowledge of the store organization and its merchandising classifications is helpful, it is not one of the chief requirements for the visual merchandising hopeful. Of paramount importance is a working knowledge of color theory and coordination, lighting techniques, the specifics of balance, special arrangements, and so forth. In essence, those seeking opportunities in visual merchandising should be artistically oriented. If one is, the possibility of a career in visual merchandising is bright.

There are different paths to follow in visual merchandising. One is to work for a major retail organization that has its own display department. Apprentice positions that require individuals to prepare windows for displays, dress mannequins, and refresh "tired" props are often available in these stores. The size of the retail operation and its commitment to visual merchandising dictate the number of different types of available positions for visual merchandisers. Some companies have specialists in a particular narrow area, while others prefer "jacks of all trades." For example, the very large retailer will employ an individual expressly for the purpose of preparing signage cards or one whose sole responsibility is to change interior counter displays. At the head of the visual merchandising department is the manager or director who usually reports to the director of publicity or sales promotion. These two individuals have the ultimate responsibility for setting the tone and image of the store's windows and interiors. Their subordinates create backgrounds, change mannequins, "dress" windows, prepare copy, and so on.

Figure 2–4 is a listing of special promotional type jobs accompanied by the responsibilities of each position.

Control

People who prepare for careers in control are not generally students specializing in merchandising or retail management programs. Those who serve in the control division of a store usually come from backgrounds which are more associated with accounting, finance, budgeting, credits, and collections.

In this division, three specific departments—accounting, control, and credit— have the vast majority of the jobs. Proper accounting procedures assure that the retailer will take the appropriate discounts on invoices, prepare payrolls, plan inventory procedures, write financial reports, prepare statements, and so on. In the control

Figure 2–4   Sales Promotion Careers: A Composite of Selected Job Titles

Job Title	Responsibilities
Advertising Manager	Oversees all aspects of advertising campaigns and is responsible for entire advertising staff.
Copywriter	Prepares the written message which accompanies both print and broadcast advertisements.
Layout Artist	Arranges the artwork and copy in a workable format.
Production Manager	Is responsible for technical aspects of advertisement creation.
Visual Merchandising Director	Takes charge of all visual merchandising and is responsible for window and interior display coordination.
Signmaker	Prepares signs, display copy cards, price tags, and so on for use in displays.
Special Events Manager	Is responsible for special events concepts which carry out store's image, promotions, sales, and so on.
Fashion Scout	Researches fashion trends and directions and advises key personnel of the "latest" in fashion.
Publicity Manager	Keeps the store's name "alive" by getting media to cover and report on store's activities and promotions.

sector, attention is paid to the control of expenses, audit of sales figures, and reports concerning statistical information on merchandise.

Since charge account customers are becoming the most important patrons of many retailers in terms of dollars spent, the credit department has a variety of tasks to perform. The credit manager, the head of the department, must have a number of years of experience at lower levels involving credit. The people in his or her department are involved in responsibilities such as interviewing prospective charge customers, analyzing loans, setting limits on customers' accounts, keeping credit records, billing, and pursuing collection of unpaid debts. The tasks are, for the most part, clerical in nature, except, of course, for those that are interview oriented.

Figure 2–5 is a representation of the typical jobs and responsibilities of those who are in the control division of a store.

Retail Advisory Organizations

Not directly involved in the store's day-to-day operations are individuals who nonetheless play a vital role in assisting retailers with their merchandise decision making. The careers afforded in these retail advisory organizations are many, and should be carefully explored by those who want to enter a market that is not directly retailing, but that is similar in terms of preparation needed for retailing careers.

Figure 2–5   Control Careers: A Composite of Selected Job Titles

Job Title	Responsibilities
Accounting Manager	In charge of accounting department personnel and is responsible for formulating procedures and practices.
Accounts Payable	Is responsible for paying bills, checking for discounts, anticipations, terms, and so on.
Payroll Administrator	Administers payroll procedures and practices.
Inventory Controller	Is responsible for methods and procedures used in inventory taking.
Merchandise Statistician	Works on statistical analysis used in merchandising reports.
Credit Manager	In charge of credit department, is responsible for employees in credit and credit procedures.
Credit Authorizer	Makes recommendations pertaining to customers' lines of credit.
Credit Interviewer	Interviews prospective credit customers for store's charge accounts.

Those who study retailing and fashion should be aware that enormous opportunity lies in areas that serve the retailer but that are separate business entities. The most significant are the independent resident buying offices. Their job titles are numerous and the roles the individuals play are often preparatory for careers in management positions in stores.

Resident buying offices rarely require bachelor's degrees, thus giving the holders of associate degrees or certificates an opportunity for exciting careers. Typically, the entry-level position is at the assistant buyer level, with promotion to buyer achievable as quickly as the individual's performance merits. Often, the movement from assistant to buyer takes two to three years. As in retailing, the next levels are divisional merchandise manager, and ultimately merchandising vice president. One particular advantage of careers in buying offices is the work schedule. Unlike retailing, where hours include evenings and weekends, the resident office typically operates from 9:00 to 5:00 on a weekday schedule.

Reporting services, clipping services, fashion consulting companies, and the like are other organizations where careers are available. Like the resident offices, there are regular business hours and the requirements for employment are generally less stringent than in retail management. It should be understood, however, that there are considerably fewer of these companies than of resident buying offices, and thus there is less chance for a career.

Finally, please note that both the resident buying offices and the other retail advisory services employ more women than men. They are certainly fields of equal opportunity employment.

Figure 2–6 shows the organization chart of a large resident buying office. Close examination will indicate the vast number of opportunities afforded the individual who chooses this type of organization for a career.

CHOOSING THE BEST COMPANY AND THE RIGHT JOB

After studying the careers that are available in store organizations and in the retail advisory organizations, one sees that much opportunity exists for the qualified individual. This question is often raised: "What route should I take to enter the field?" We cannot give a simple answer to this important question. Those wishing to enter the field must carefully explore all that is available as well as the particular retail organizations that offer these opportunities.

One approach is to investigate each opportunity in terms of specific criteria. Some of the following questions can help an individual determine whether or not the job in question is suitable:

1. Does the company offer a formal training program?
2. Is the company policy for filling upper-level positions based upon promotion from within?
3. Will advancement require relocation to another part of the country?
4. Is the starting salary competitive with that of other companies?
5. What is the company's image, and is it compatible with one's personal beliefs?
6. Is there a prescribed time framework for moving to a higher position?
7. Are the benefits satisfactory?
8. Does the work environment provide an atmosphere that will enhance the employee's effort?
9. How large is the company, and will its size deter chances for advancement?
10. What are the expansion plans for the company?

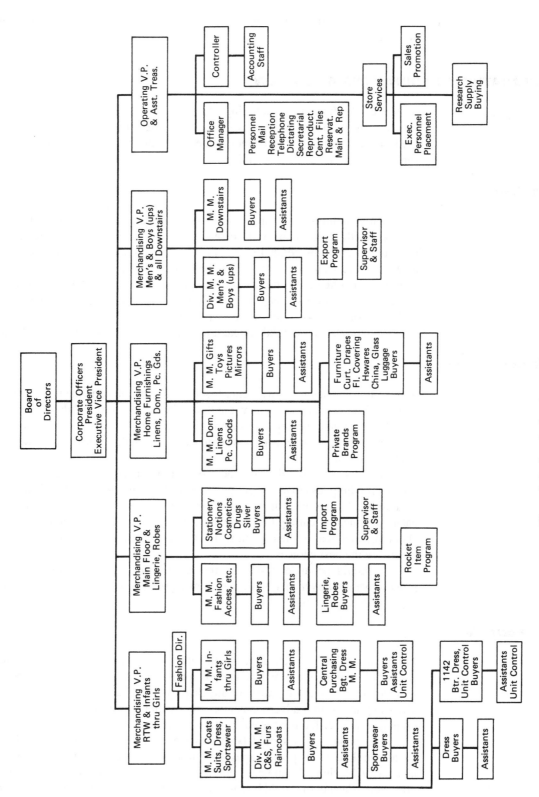

Figure 2-6 Organization chart—resident buying office.

Once these questions can be answered to the applicant's satisfaction, it is up to the individual to select the job that most closely satisfies his or her needs.

PREPARATION FOR OBTAINING A POSITION

No matter which avenue of retailing one chooses to enter, careful preparation is necessary to achieve the goal. This involves developing a resume and a cover letter that is used to accompany it, understanding the essentials of a favorable interview, and, for some positions, creating a portfolio.

The Resume

When those in human resources or personnel departments, or management positions that deal with recruitment wish to select the most capable workers for their companies, they generally begin by examining each prospect's resume. This document gives the reader an overview of the candidate's history and a means of determining whether or not he or she will meet the requirements of the position. A resume may be constructed by individuals with the aid of many books on the subject or with the assistance of a professional resume writer. In either case, it should carefully spell out why a candidate's credentials make him or her worthy of an interview (Figure 2–7).

The Cover Letter

Simplicity is the key to a cover letter that is used to accompany the resume (Figure 2–8). It should briefly state one's interest in the position, how the candidate selected the company to investigate, perhaps the mention of a name of someone with whom the reader will be familiar, such as a present employee, or anything else that will motivate the reader's interest.

It is essential that the document be grammatically perfect, and free of spelling errors. Anything less than perfection tends to discredit the candidate. The letter should be addressed to an individual, and not merely to "personnel director." The names are easily obtained by calling the company. Finally, the stock on which the letter is typed should be identical to the one on which the resume has been printed. White or cream colors are the best choices.

It should be understood that this is generally the only way to convince the prospective employer that he or she should give you the opportunity to discuss your capabilities in person.

The Portfolio

For some positions, such as those in retail advertising or visual merchandising, a scrapbook or portfolio of your creations serves as a means of motivating the viewer to grant an interview. Photographs of any displays, for example, or drawings that eventually were turned into advertisements, or copy that was used in a catalog will give the employer a better feeling for your creative abilities.

The photographs should be professionally taken to show the work to its best advantage. Lackluster photographs serve little purpose and might present your work in an unfavorable light. A number of different exhibits should be used to show the variety of your work. Each item should be carefully mounted and arranged in an attractive folder.

Just as there are professional resume writers, there are people who are available to assist in the development of a portfolio.

JENNIFER MURRAY
3930 Stanton Street
Chicago, IL 60616

EDUCATION: Bradley Community College   Chicago, IL
              AAS Fashion Merchandising, June 1995
              Honors: Magna Cum Laude

SPECIAL
EXPERIENCE: Participated in an internship with Printemp in
              Paris as an personal shopper.

COLLEGE
ACTIVITIES: Fashion show coordinator
              President, Retailing club
              Freshman orientation advisor

WORK
EXPERIENCE:
6/92 - 8/92   BOOGIE'S DINER. Selling and inventory management.
              Oak Street, Chicago, IL.
5/93 - 9/93   THE GAP. Selling and visual merchandising.
              Water Tower, Chicago, IL.
6/94 -
present   LORD & TAYLOR. Personal shopper and interpreter.
              Assisted customers with their selections, and
              ultimately developed my own clientele.

INTERESTS: Travel, theater, skiing, aerobics.

REFERENCES: Will be furnished upon request.

Figure 2–7   Resumes present an overview of the job applicant.

Interview Preparation

The taking of an interview requires planning. Individuals need to understand the importance of appearance and the ability to communicate, and they should become familiar with the company to which they are applying for a position.

First and foremost is appearance. When you open the door to the interviewer's office, it is that first impression that counts. If appropriate dress is not obvious, it may be learned by reading books on the subject, meeting with a specialist in that area, or visiting the company to study the employees' dress.

The proper use of language will immediately indicate whether or not you have the ability to communicate, and how well your manner of speech will fit with the company's image. Taking communication courses and listening to yourself on tapes will help you to improve your communication skills.

Use of role playing techniques, in which you act as the interviewee and someone else plays the interviewer, will enable you to go through a simulated interview session. Questions that you have difficulty with may be re-addressed and the answers refined so that you create a better impression during the real interview.

During the interview, you should ask questions about the company. Much of the time, interviewers will be favorably impressed if a candidate expresses some knowledge of the company. This information can be easily obtained through literature that some companies make available or by reading business journals and newspapers.

With careful preparation, the candidate is more likely to make a better impression and get the job.

3930 Stanton Street
Chicago, IL 60616
December 19, 1995

Ms. Emily Winters
Human Resources Manager
Lord & Taylor
1525 Fifth Avenue
New York, NY 10007

Dear Ms. Winters:

At the suggestion of Mr. Anthony Finch, Director of Executive
Development at Lord & Taylor in Chicago, I am writing to you
about possible employment as a personal shopper in your New
York City flagship store.

I completed my two-year degree in Fashion Merchandising in
June, 1995, and am currently anticipating enrollment at the
Fashion Institute of Technology in New York for a bachelor's
degree. The program is given in the evening which will enable
me to work full time.

The time spent at your company's Chicago store enabled me to
apply what I learned in college to the real world of retailing
It was an excellent experience.

Enclosed is a copy of my resume which should give you some
background information about me.

Sincerely,

Jennifer Murray

Figure 2–8   A cover letter that accompanies the resume.

TRENDS

Today's retail scene offers significantly more retail opportunities than ever before, primarily owing to the growth of chains, catalog operations, home shopping outlets, and warehouse outlets.

Management Positions

With companies such as The Limited and The Gap expanding all over the country, there is a greater need for managers. These two companies alone have more than five thousand units; they provide excellent opportunities for careers.

Companies like Price Club and Sam's Club, giants in the warehouse concept, also provide enormous possibilities for managers. In addition to the top positions of warehouse manager, many assistants and section heads are needed to run the operations.

International Opportunity

Many American retailers are rapidly entering foreign markets. In order to bring expertise to these stores, they usually require a nucleus of the employees to come from their stores in the United States. Because of this, those interested in an off-shore experience will find more and more management level positions available to them in international settings.

Nontraditional Careers

With the enormous expansion of catalog offerings and the advent of shopping via cable television, a host of different opportunities is now available, including copy writers, artists, buyers, merchandisers, and sellers.

Personal Shoppers

More upscale department stores are improving their customer services in order to compete favorably in the marketplace. Many are emphasizing personal shopping services in which customers are made more comfortable in making their purchases. The income for a personal shopper is generally based upon some form of commission in addition to a salary, making these positions highly prized. In companies like Bergdorf Goodman, long an advocate of personal shopping, employees earn as much as $75,000 a year.

ACTION FOR THE INDEPENDENT RETAILER

The focus of this chapter is primarily upon the career opportunities in large retail organizations. As shown, although not significantly stressed in the preceding material, there is opportunity in independent organizations.

The independent owner should understand that there is a wealth of talent flowing from the college campuses each year. Too often, the independent neglects this market and concentrates on the "seasoned" retail employee. A great deal can be learned from the larger organization. Big business is willing to invest in new talent, and it does so through formal training programs. Once having molded the "recruits," the organization has solid employees who perform in a manner required by the company. While the independent can't structure a formal training program, it can develop talent that shows promise in a less formal structure. The college graduate can bring new technical training as well as an enthusiasm to perform. Independents can gain much by "breaking in" an apprentice and reaping the rewards which come as a result of the relationship.

Too often, the smaller store frowns upon the recent graduate. If the large organization can benefit, what's to stop the independent from doing the same?

IMPORTANT POINTS IN THE CHAPTER

1. Success in retailing careers depends upon such personal qualities as initiative, enthusiasm, and intelligence. Given these qualities, an individual has potential for success.
2. While self-employment in a retail operation is the dream of many people, cautious optimism is the appropriate attitude. Countless numbers of small retail operations fail due to inexperience and insufficient capital.
3. Employment opportunity in small stores is often limited to selling. Few small retailers have the funds necessary or the willingness to train individuals seeking positions that will afford anything more than routine duties.
4. In the large retail organizations, opportunity for achievement is available in executive training programs. These programs are usually formally structured, and afford the individual the opportunity to explore a wide variety of positions through classroom and on-the-job training.
5. Most large retail companies provide career opportunities in merchandising, store management and operations, advertising and sales promotion, and control.

6. Because of their nature and size, the store management and operations divisions offer individuals the most career opportunities.

7. Before accepting a particular job offer, the candidate should consider such factors as the availability of a formal training program, promotion policies, store size and location, salary structure, benefits, and expansion potential of the company.

8. A professionally prepared resume, and if appropriate to the position, an exciting portfolio, are necessities for securing the better positions.

REVIEW QUESTIONS

1. Describe two advantages of a retailing career as compared to other careers.
2. What are four essential personal qualities one should possess for a successful career?
3. Is a formal education required for a retailing career?
4. Discuss the potential for self-employment in retailing.
5. Can one find a successful career in a small store?
6. List the stages in the career path at Macy's.
7. Indicate the various positions in the merchandising division and discuss the realistic potential for most people in that division.
8. What is the job of assistant department manager?
9. Why is the career path for those interested in advertising and sales promotion different from the route that is followed in merchandising and management?
10. Why are the chances for advancement more likely in management and operations than in merchandising?
11. Describe the role of the publicity manager.
12. Why is the credit manager's job becoming increasingly more important?
13. Name two types of retail advisory organizations. Which provides a more direct service to the retailer?
14. How does one "scientifically" select the better retail job?
15. Why is a resume an important part of the job search?

CASE PROBLEMS

Case Problem 1

Jane Peters, a retailing major, is graduating from a two-year college. She is a C+ student and has many extracurricular activities, including being the vice-president of DECA (Distributive Education Clubs of America). Her work experience has been as a part-time salesperson in the men's college shop at a local department store since entering college, and as a stock person in a supermarket during her last year in high school.

During the past two weeks, Jane was interviewed on campus by representatives of three retail organizations for possible employment after graduation. The offers were as follows:

1. The first opportunity is placement in the executive training program at a well-known department store with several branches. Training would be for approximately six months on a job rotational plan in the main departments of the store, coupled with classroom

instruction. Her salary would be $450 per week for that period. At the end of six months a permanent assignment would be made, with an increase in salary to $500 per week.

2. The personnel director of a giant supermarket chain offered Jane an assistant manager's job in a local unit of the chain. She would work directly under the store manager, assisting him with employee scheduling, purchase requisitions, handling of complaints, and so forth. The salary is $400 per week the first year, $450 per week for the second year, and as a store manager, $475 per week the third year.

3. The third opportunity is in a large shoe chain with 600 stores throughout the country. One year of selling shoes is a requirement of all new employees, at a salary of $200 per week plus three percent commission. After that period there is assignment as an assistant store manager at a salary of $275 per week plus three percent commission on all shoes she sells. Her other duties would be to assist with window displays and reorder merchandise, to be responsible when the manager is away, and so on. After two or three years as an assistant manager, assignment as manager is given to qualified individuals at an annual salary of $30,000 per year, plus a bonus based on the store's sales.

Questions

1. What aspect of the jobs should Jane carefully consider before making a final determination?
2. Considering the important factors, which job would you advise Jane to take?

Case Problem 2

Paul Matthews has worked for the past five years at the Elegant Lady, a fashionable, large specialty shop. After one year as an assistant department manager and two as a department manager, he was promoted to assistant buyer of active sportswear, a position he still holds at an annual salary of $30,000. Three months ago Paul inherited $100,000. He has always dreamed of owning his own retail store and now, with the money he has, he might be able to realize his dream. After some investigation, these two propositions, both fitting his finances, seem most appealing:

1. A small store located in a small active shopping center is available to lease for the purpose of opening a ladies' specialty shop. The store is equipped with air conditioning but requires counters, wall cases, and so forth. Currently the shopping center does not have the type of operation envisioned by Matthews. The workday is flexible in that the other stores in the center do not have uniform hours. The number of employees needed, the price range of merchandise to be carried, the store policies, and so forth, will be established by Matthews. He will be his own boss and can finally operate in a manner that pleases him.

2. "Petite Lady," a franchise organization specializing in clothing for short women, has a new location available in the city's downtown shopping area. There are 70 similar units in the organization, which began its operation five years ago. They expect to complete an additional 75 stores within the next five years. The stores are all open daily from 9:30 A.M. to 6:00 P.M. and two evenings until 9:30 P.M. All merchandise is purchased from the franchiser, and the rules and regulations set forth by the company must be followed. For the first two years, a minimum of $2,000 a month is expected by the individual owner; after that the earnings will probably increase, as they have for many other stores in the group.

Questions

1. What are the advantages and disadvantages of both situations?
2. How do the opportunities of ownership compare with his present job?
3. Which course of action should Paul Matthews take?

Chapter 3
Franchising

Courtesy: Radio Shack

LEARNING OBJECTIVES

Upon completion of this chapter, the student should be able to:

1. Define franchising and give examples of franchising operations.
2. Identify seven different types of franchises.
3. List and discuss eight advantages of franchising to the franchisee.
4. List and discuss six disadvantages of franchising to the franchisee.
5. List and discuss four benefits of franchising to the franchiser.
6. Write an essay explaining areas of conflict between franchiser and franchisee.

IT AIN'T JUST RADIOS . . .

When Tandy Corporation purchased an obscure nine-unit chain in Boston in 1963, who would have realized the potential it had to become one of the largest retail organizations in the world. Unlike most companies, which are either traditional chain operations, in which the company owns and operates all of the units, or franchised organizations that enable individuals to purchase specific locations, Radio Shack uses a combination of both arrangements. More than 2,000 of the company's 7,000 units are franchises, enabling people to realize their dreams of retail ownership.

When we read about the significant failure rate in franchising, one must stop to wonder why Radio Shack enjoys its status as the fifth largest franchiser in the United States. Its success is measured not only in size, but also in profitability. There are many reasons for Radio Shack's position in the field of retailing.

Many franchised operations pay little attention to the improvement of their businesses and the protection of their franchisees, once the initial "start-up" fee has been collected. Not so with Radio Shack. They provide several services to their franchisees to ensure continued growth.

- An on-going training program is in place to make certain that product knowledge is enhanced and sales techniques are constantly refined.

- Monthly fliers are mailed to over 217 million households annually, and ads in newspapers and magazines are regularly placed to target regular and potential customers.

- A computerized point-of-sale system cuts the time needed to process a purchase. This enables today's shopper, who has less time to spend in the store, to be satisfied quickly.

- Products are added to inventories only after they have been analyzed to show consumer need. This reduces the amount of "dead" inventory a store carries.

- Each product meets the standards established by the Federal Communications Commission and Underwriter's Laboratories, guaranteeing customer satisfaction.

- Numerous repair centers are in operation to make certain that customers are satisfied when their products fail. For their computer customers, Radio Shack maintains a telephone support program at the company's headquarters in Ft. Worth, Texas, which provides immediate technical assistance.

- Regular analysis takes place to determine which products may be unique to specific geographical locations. In this way, each store has the appropriate mix necessary to satisfy its customers.

The success of the company can best be summarized with the following:

- One out of every three households in the United States buys a Radio Shack product every year.
- Approximately 70 percent of the customers return to make another purchase from Radio Shack within a 12-month period.
- The average dollar amount of a sales ticket in a typical Radio Shack outlet has increased an average of 9.6 percent since 1985.

With such a success story, who says franchising isn't a viable method of retailing?

In each chapter of the text there is a discussion on the application of the principles involved to the small independent retailer. Franchising, the subject matter of this chapter, is almost exclusively concerned with small business. The possibilities for an individual to become involved in franchising are so varied that a deal can be made for as little as $5,000 initial outlay to as much as several million dollars. Even the more expensive possibilities can be heavily mortgaged, bringing down the capital requirements considerably.

There is nothing new in the concept of franchising. It is likely that this type of agreement existed in America during colonial times. Rapid growth began after World War II, when industry grew to enormous proportions. In large part this expansion was due to the returning servicemen, some with accumulated savings, many taking advantage of the financing available through the Veterans Administration. They were eager, after years of rigid army discipline, to be their own bosses.

The major problem faced by these young people was their lack of business experience. Their few mature years had been spent in the service, and most of them had never held full-time jobs. To tap this huge sum of money and vast store of ambition, many established business organizations undertook the franchising of their products. They offered proven products, big business "know-how," and financial help in return for a considerable expansion of their profits. The result has been a continuing boom in franchised sales that has increased in volume each year. Approximately 3,000 companies use franchising in more than 65 industries, with in excess of 500,000 locations. Since 1989, 96.9 percent of the franchises opened are still in operation, with over 85.7 percent still being run by the original owner. Overseas, more than fifty countries have American franchises.

Most individuals think of Carvel's, McDonald's, and other fast food establishments when the word "franchising" is used. While it is true that the bulk of the retail oriented franchisers are food related, there are significant indications that the franchising world is spreading its wings and is going to other types of products.

A look into the pages of the *Franchise Opportunities Handbook* will show that expansion of clothing companies is happening via the franchise route. One of the first companies to franchise was Benetton, which was one of the fastest growing franchised organizations in the 1980s. Today it has several hundred stores in the United States. Other retail franchises include hardware, variety stores, furniture, opticals, and specialty goods.

Not every franchise boasts the success of a McDonald's. Many fail! To proceed with caution when making an investment in a franchise is sound advice.

DEFINITION OF FRANCHISING

Because of the great variety of franchising agreements, it is difficult to define a franchise. It is estimated that there are between 2,000 and 8,000 companies offering franchising deals, and each company's contract is different. The broadest definition is the one given by the Small Business Administration:

> *A franchise contract is a legal agreement to conduct a given business in accordance with prescribed operating methods, financing systems, territorial domains, and commission fees. It holds out the offer of individual ownership while following proven management practices. The holder is given the benefit of the franchiser's experience and help in choice of location, financing, marketing, record keeping, and promotional techniques. The business starts out with an established product or service reputation. It is organized and operated with the advantage of "name" and standardization.*

This definition contains the great amount of information that a textbook definition should. However, all franchising agreements do not include every item mentioned. For example, many franchisers make their profit by selling the product to the franchisee; others profit by charging a commission on all franchisee sales. Only careful examination of the particular contract will indicate the agreements therein.

TYPES OF FRANCHISE ARRANGEMENTS

Conventional

This type of arrangement is usually broken down into two types, both involving varying degrees of geographical coverage.

The *territorial franchise* gives the holder the privilege of enjoying an "override" on sales of all the units within a particular area. The area might be confined to a large city, an entire state, or even a section of the country. Frequently the holder also assumes the responsibility of training and setting up the various operators of subfranchisees within the given area, which may encompass several counties or states. It is not unusual for the operating franchisee never to come in direct contact with the parent organization, but rather to deal entirely with the owner of the territorial franchise. Tastee Freeze and Service Master are typical of territorial franchises. A recent entry into the territorial arrangement is Warehouse, a London-based company. (See Figure 3–1.)

The *operating franchise* is held by the independent operator within any given territory who runs his or her own business within the given area allotted by the franchise (often conferred by the territorial franchiser). The operator deals either directly or indirectly with the parent organization. Such units as McDonald's and Kenny Rogers offer this type of arrangement. (See Figure 3–2.)

Figure 3–1   Interior of a Warehouse franchise. *Courtesy:* Images & Details

A RETAILING FOCUS   *Warehouse*

Warehouse, a London-based fashion specialty retailer, has burst upon the streets of the United States. In 1984, the off-beat retail chain opened its doors in Paramus, New Jersey, and what appears to be a very successful venture for two seasoned American retailers began.

Kathy Deane and Richard Krantz both risked successful careers to become the exclusive franchisers of Warehouse in the United States. Both had worked for Macy's. Deane was a dress buyer who came from a family that was involved in the fashion world. Krantz, who started his retail career as a trainee in 1976, joined Macy's in 1978 as a group manager, was promoted to junior sportswear buyer and then to a counselor at Macy's in Stamford, Connecticut. When he left Macy's he was vice president of merchandise administration for better juniors.

When they approached Jeff Banks, the London designer and founder of Warehouse, he told them he had been asked numerous times to grant franchising rights in the United States but never felt the right people had approached him. When he met Deane and Krantz he felt that these two entrepreneurs could take the Warehouse concept and make it a profitable venture in the United States. What appealed to the Americans was the fact that Warehouse was a vertical operation, one which included designing, manufacturing, and retailing, and that the company had continually been a trendsetter in the missy and contemporary markets.

Once the deal was consummated, location of the first unit was considered to be one of the most important decisions for the American operation. Many locations including New York City, Chicago, San Diego, and Boston, tempted them, but they sought a place that would be most profitable for the pilot store. The Paramus Park mall in New Jersey was chosen because their research indicated that this mall had the highest sales per square foot of any suburban mall in the United States. Since Paramus offered one of the country's most diverse customer bases, they felt that if the Warehouse could do well there, it could do well anywhere.

Once they had decided on the first location, they carefully examined the company's merchandise offerings. Although the designs proved to be huge successes in London,

Figure 3–2   Kenny Rogers—A conventional franchise. Photograph by Ellen Diamond

Deane and Krantz believed that they had to edit the collection for the American market. While the line is designed by a British team, the American stores go deeper into the looks that are important for the American market. Being seasoned merchants, Deane and Krantz believed they knew the market well enough to make the necessary changes.

Merchandise is manufactured all over the world, including the United States, which produces the cotton knitwear and jeans. In terms of the merchandise mix, it is wearable clothing, nothing extreme.

To date there are seven Warehouse stores in New York and New Jersey, most in high volume shopping malls. In the very near future Deane and Krantz expect to try their first venture into Manhattan. Their customer market ranges from the 16 year old to the 60 year old, with enough style variation to please both groups.

They believe this is only the beginning and with their present success in America and the continued recognition of Jeff Banks as an international designer, the American counterpart of the business should continue to grow.

While most Americans think of McDonald's and Carvel when franchising is mentioned, Deane and Krantz, now married, expect to open 20 stores in the Northeast in the next few years, and ultimately to make Warehouse a famous American franchise. An American franchise of Warehouse is shown in Figure 3–1.

A RETAILING FOCUS   McDonald's

The story of franchising in the United States, or in the world for that matter, would be incomplete without a chapter on the fabulously successful franchise empire, McDonald's.

With a market share of approximately 20 percent, close to 11,000 units, and sales that are in the vicinity of $16 billion, McDonald's is a business that warrants exploration. Who would have believed, when Ray Kroc opened his first unit in 1955 in Des Plaines, Illinois, that more than 22 million people a day worldwide would be feasting on the company's offerings.

In 1955 Ray Kroc was a 52-year-old salesman when he acquired the franchise rights to the company from Dick and Mac McDonald. Many doubted that a national chain that featured low-priced hamburgers would capture the hearts and pocketbooks of Americans. They certainly were wrong. Kroc's enthusiasm and ability to motivate people, a skill he developed in sales, helped make McDonald's the leading franchise in the United States.

It should be understood, however, that Kroc's early skills were not the only reasons for the company's extraordinary success. Utilizing the most imaginative marketing tools, the company has surpassed all of its competitors. It always pays close attention to the needs of consumers and delivers what they want. When breakfast wasn't really a consideration for companies of this type, McDonald's forged ahead and stole the breakfast crowd from many of the traditional restaurants. For just a small amount, it enabled senior citizens to swell the ranks of those who ate breakfast away from home, not to mention others who had to "eat on the run." When Americans turned to salads as a mainstay in their diets, McDonald's was right there with a tempting array.

McDonald's is no longer just an American adventure. Franchises are found in more than 50 countries throughout the world with such unlikely places as Russia joining the roster.

Although the company is an American institution which sponsors many noteworthy charitable ventures (such as the Ronald McDonald houses for families with critically ill children), not everyone is enthralled with the company's presence. Some criticize the restaurants—"eyesores that encourage loitering for the purpose of drug deals" and the food—"meals are laden with fats that clog arteries." McDonald's, to its credit, rarely turns a deaf ear to its critics. It has altered some of its recipes to lower the fat content and has tried to make its units rid themselves of those who seem to loiter. At the company headquarters in Oak Brook, Illinois, the McDonald's business philosophy is directed. In addition to its home for its top management team, "Hamburger University" is located there. It is at this training center where the franchisees learn how to operate their franchises successfully. The strict formula carried out here earns most of the credit for the company's success. Each year about 3,500 individuals participate in the training sessions. The "student body" includes corporate employees, prospective franchisees, and potential suppliers. Nothing is left to chance. In an industry where Burger King is a distant second place and such companies as Kentucky Fried Chicken and Wendy's are even further behind, McDonald's, with all of its imaginative marketing skills, is still the winner.

Mobile

The mobile franchise usually involves the same arrangement as the conventional franchise except that the franchisee dispenses a product or service from a moving vehicle. This vehicle is either owned by the franchisee or leased from the parent company. Tastee Freeze, a franchiser of soft ice cream stands, had such an arrangement but discontinued it after heavy losses were incurred. However, such companies as Mister Softee have found this arrangement very successful. (See Figure 3–3.)

Distributorship

Under this arrangement, the franchisee takes title to the various types of goods and further distributes them to subfranchisees. The distributor usually has exclusive coverage of a rather wide geographical area and acts as a supply house for the units that carry the company's product(s). Many firms in the appliance field operate on this basis. Eureka and the Nissen Trampoline Company operate distributorships.

Figure 3–3   Mister Softee—A mobile franchise. *Courtesy:*
Mister Softee

Coownership

Coownership occurs where a large capital outlay is needed. The franchiser and franchisee share in the investment and then divide the profits. Many firms in the food service industry use such plans, including Denny's Restaurants and Houlihans.

Comanagement

In the case of comanagement, the franchiser usually controls the major part of the investment. The investor-manager is allowed to share proportionately in the profits. An increase in sales volume increases the owner-manager's share. This acts as an incentive to further promote the firm's business. Several motel chains operate on this basis. Travelodge and Holiday Inn are examples.

Lease

In a lease arrangement, the franchiser either backs up or takes out a lease on a satisfactory location, often receiving a profit on the rental income paid by the franchisee. Though this plan is seldom representative of the total franchise package, it is often used in conjunction with other stipulations. Many of the franchisers within the food service industry incorporate this plan into their overall formula.

Licensee

This again represents an arrangement often used in conjunction with others. Under this plan the franchisee is allowed to use the franchiser's trademarks, business techniques, advertising layouts, and so forth. Normally, however, the company does not provide the product but instructs the franchisee as to where it might be obtained. Often, the franchiser has an agreement with a national supplier who will supply the various products to the franchisee at a specific price.

Manufacturing

In this arrangement, a parent company will franchise a firm to manufacture its product(s) using prescribed techniques and materials. Often, distance and shipping costs necessitate this arrangement. The franchisee not only manufactures but also distributes the product, using the marketing techniques of the parent firm.

Service

Here, the franchiser sets forth prescribed patterns by which a franchise will supply a professional service. Employment agencies and any number of other service businesses fall within this category. An example of a service franchise is Lawn-A-Mat, a lawn preparation company.

It should be noted that many franchising firms do not fall within one specific category. Indeed, most firms offer more than one type of arrangement and exhibit a great degree of flexibility according to the situation. Counteroffers by prospective franchisees are not unusual, especially with regard to the more expensive franchises involving large capital outlays. In addition, some firms are in a constant state of reorganization in adapting their plans to the needs of the market.

An analysis of the various franchising techniques is made even more difficult in view of the increasing number of new firms that are entering the industry.

COSTS OF FRANCHISING

The cost of getting into a franchising operation varies as widely as the number of franchising possibilities available. It may run from about $5,000 for a start-up company to more than $750,000 for McDonald's.

HOW TO FIND A FRANCHISER

Finding a franchise deal is relatively simple. With the growth of the franchising industry, there is considerable competition among franchisers in finding interested franchisees. This has led to a great deal of advertising, as evidenced by the business opportunities section of most newspapers, which contain ads for many types of franchises. In addition, various organizations run franchise shows at which prospective franchisees are given an opportunity to discuss deals with a wide variety of possible franchisers. The *Franchise Annual,* a trade publication, lists scores of shows in major cities throughout the country, as does the *Franchise Opportunities Handbook,* published by the United States Department of Commerce.

HOW TO FIND A FRANCHISEE

Finding the right franchisee is a serious problem for the parent company. The success of the parent company depends upon the success of the outlets. Finding a person who will be successful is much more difficult than signing a contract.

The careful screening process that is required to ensure success can be expensive. For example, a large food chain placed a $14,000 advertisement to recruit franchisees. Of the 50 responses, 38 prospects were interviewed. Final contracts were signed by just two people. The cost of advertising alone was $7,000 per franchisee!

QUALIFICATIONS AND CONSIDERATIONS FOR THE FRANCHISEE

Before going into a franchising contract, prospective franchisees should consider their own qualifications. The Small Business Administration suggests that prospects ask themselves such questions as the following:

1. Am I qualified, in terms of the capital and special qualifications needed, for the deal?
2. Am I willing to accept the franchiser's supervision and to abide by the rules and regulations that the franchiser requires? These can be real problems for independent-minded people who are in business for themselves.
3. Why would I want a franchised business rather than one I can start entirely on my own? Essentially, the franchisee splits the profits with the franchiser. Moreover, expansion possibilities are strictly limited by some franchisers.
4. Can I afford to be without income during the training and setting-up period? Going into business is a giant step. Selecting the correct format for oneself adds to the complications.

THE FRANCHISE CONTRACT

Franchise contracts vary according to the franchiser. In many cases, it is not a fixed document but one that is changed to fit each situation. The contract is a binding legal agreement that may be very complicated to the uninformed, and since the success and happiness of the franchisee depend in large part upon the content of the document, the contract must never be signed without legal advice. Before the contract is approved the franchisee must consider the following vital areas:

Nature of the Company

1. Has the firm been in business long enough to determine its successfulness?
2. Does it have the financial capability to stand behind its outlets?
3. Is it selective in choosing its franchisees? The more selective the firm, the better the chances that one will succeed by associating with it.
4. What are the reactions of the other franchisees to having committed themselves?
5. How many of the outlets are company owned?

The Product

1. To what extent is it available and where?
2. What is its present status in the market?
3. To what degree is it unique?
4. Is it a repeat item?
5. Who manufactures it?

6. What is its legal status?

7. Where is it sold?

8. Is it patented?

9. Is it seasonal and to what degree?

10. Is it highly perishable?

11. What is the time element involved in getting it into a saleable state?

The Territory

1. Is it a growing market area?

2. Is it completely and accurately defined?

3. Does it assure exclusive representation?

4. Is it subject to seasonal fluctuations?

5. Is it a highly competitive area?

6. Is it above or below the statewide average per capita income level?

7. What kind of people make up the majority of the population?

The Contract

1. Are there any prior verbal agreements that failed to show up in the written contract?

2. Is it renewable and is there a fee involved?

3. Can it be terminated? Sold? Transferred?

4. Does it assign responsibility with regard to any lawsuits that might result involving the product?

5. Does it specify all the financial conditions of the arrangement? Fee? Royalty? Is this amount fixed?

6. Is there a quota clause with regard to sales?

7. Is there a purchase clause with regard to the parent company's products?

8. Does it allow any outside business interests?

9. Does it have a return privilege permitting the holder to return unsaleable merchandise?

10. Does it provide that the holder pay part of promotional costs?

11. Is it beneficial to both parties?

Assistance

1. Is there a comprehensive training program?

2. Will the franchiser aid in such things as site selection and lease arrangements? Is there a fee involved?

3. Will guidance be given with advance planning for store opening?

4. Will you receive merchandise buying and inventory control training?

5. Will you be assisted with financing arrangements?

6. Will follow-up counseling and financial statement analysis be rendered?

In view of the preceding questions, it is evident that evaluating a franchise offer is a difficult task. The disclosure rule that the Federal Trade Commission put into effect in 1979 goes a long way in answering some of these questions. The disclosure rule will be discussed later in this chapter.

BENEFITS OF FRANCHISING

The concept of franchising is one which affords benefits and opportunity to both the franchisee and the franchiser. Each has a specific goal in mind, with financial profit being the prime motivation for both. Before either takes this route, each should consider the risks involved and the reasons for embarking upon such an arrangement.

The Franchisee's Viewpoint

While the American dream is for self-employment, the franchising route to achieve this end has disadvantages as well as advantages. Both should be carefully examined and evaluated.

Advantages

1. Franchise training programs, which run from several days to several weeks, provide business know-how to prospective franchisees. This permits the franchisee to go into a business with no previous experience.
2. Since the success of the franchised outlet is to the benefit of the parent company, the franchisee can expect support in almost every possible way.
3. A franchised business generally requires less original cash investment for fixtures and equipment than a conventional business, thanks to the credit help available from the franchiser.
4. Operating cash requirements are less since franchise inventories are less diversified than nonfranchised inventories, and the terms under which such merchandise is purchased are generally liberal.
5. The vast purchasing power of the parent company results in lower costs and higher gross profits for the franchisee. (Some franchisees will argue this point.)
6. The advertising and promoting done by large franchisers offer benefits far in excess of those available to conventional businesses.
7. Prepared displays, kits, and other up-to-date merchandise assistance are constantly being prepared by the home office and distributed to its outlets.
8. The parent company, keenly aware of competition, maintains a constant program of research and development aimed at improving its product or service.
9. Constant assistance in the form of periodic visits by experts is available to the franchiser for normal business advice or special problems.
10. The large size of the franchising organization frequently results in savings in such areas as insurance, hospitalization, and retirement.
11. Help in record keeping, tax advice—in short, assistance in the multitude of areas that frequently plague the small business—are available at no cost.
12. Many franchisers offer scientific help in site selection.

While it is not the purpose of this book to go into detail in any of the areas of parent company help, the following illustration will indicate the depth of the location analysis performed by Mister Donut. It is part of a five-page preliminary investigation, called the "survey report."

Location Analysis

1. The main street
2. The number of lanes in the adjacent highway
3. Whether there are dividers

4. Speed limits
5. Stop signs and stop lights
6. One-way streets
7. Traffic count
8. Anticipated highway changes
9. Foot traffic, heavy? Light?
10. Does traffic back up at peak hours? When?
11. Proportion of women in cars
12. Trucks
13. Proportion of local versus long-distance or out-of-state cars
14. Other businesses in the area
15. Schools
16. Religions, by denomination
17. Population data
18. Housing data
19. Income data
20. Nearest competition
21. Summary of zoning regulations
22. Real estate taxes, on land alone? With building? Anticipated?
23. Utilities available
24. Visibility of the location from all directions; hills; corners
25. Position of neighboring buildings, feet of setback
26. Space for Mister Donut signs

It should be pointed out that this is merely the preliminary location report and by no means the total amount of data on which the location decision is based. Remember, the success of the franchiser depends upon the success of its outlets.

While the advantages to be derived from operating a franchise are considerable, the franchisee must in one way or another pay for them. The following are some of the major disadvantages expressed by many franchisees:

Disadvantages

1. The costs are too high. Many franchisees feel that the fees, prices for supplies, and other required charges are exorbitant. In many instances it is felt that profits could be increased if the franchiser could be eliminated. This logic is questionable since it rarely takes the advantages of the system into account.
2. Many complaints center around the decisions made in far-off home offices with little or no understanding of the conditions at the local outlets. Thus, policies that benefit the majority of the outlets may be harmful to a few locations. As with many large centralized organizations, rigidity can be a serious problem.
3. Although franchisers know that their ultimate success depends upon the success of their franchisees, they question the amount of success. There is, after all, a certain amount of profit to be divided up between franchiser and franchisee. How that pie is divided is largely in the hands of the franchiser. Consequently, decisions that affect the profit generally favor the franchiser.
4. The franchising contract is the source of many complaints. This document is frequently long, complicated, and not fully understood by the franchisee. One of the principal problems is termination of the franchise. Some franchisees complain that their contract can be terminated for two reasons. One, as expected, is failure. The other is success, in which

case the franchiser might wish to take over a lucrative location to run it as a company-owned unit. Even in cases in which the contract states that termination can only be affected for "good cause," the problem of defining good cause is difficult. What constitutes late payment? One day? One week? What about poor management? Who is to decide? Some states have passed legislation to control termination, but efforts to pass a national law through Congress have failed. Since no legislation can specifically cover all possible causes of termination, it is likely that the courts will continue to be an important factor in this area.

The Franchiser's Viewpoint

As is the case with the franchisee, the parent company benefits from a franchise operation in many important aspects.

The franchiser, by supplying a large amount of the capital needed for building new units, permits rapid expansion without decreasing the ownership of the company (as would be the case if capital were to be raised by the sale of stock), or its working capital. The latter is true because of the financing supplied by the franchisee.

A serious problem faced by expanding companies is finding management with the proper ambition, incentive, and motivation. In franchising, all unit managers are in business for themselves with their own capital to protect and future to insure; thus, each manager is vitally interested in success and anxious to operate efficiently and profitably to protect the cash investment.

The chance of success of an outlet owned by a local person is greater than one owned by a distant, impersonal corporation. The community is more likely to accept a product sold to them by one of their own.

An example of the economic advantage available to the franchiser is the fact that, in the first three years in which Kentucky Fried Chicken published its quarterly earnings, every quarter showed an increase of 80 to 100 percent over the same period of the preceding year.

SAFEGUARDS FOR PROSPECTING FRANCHISEES

All businesses, particularly those in the process of rapid growth, attract a wide variety of charlatans and fast dealers. The franchising industry is no exception. Out-and-out fraud, exaggerated advertising, and hidden costs are not unusual in franchisee recruiting. However, this sort of dishonesty, though frequently well publicized, is not widespread. It is unfair to criticize an entire industry because of a small dishonest group.

Anyone interested in becoming a franchisee should take advantage of the available safeguards. As has been mentioned previously, the contract must be negotiated with the help of a capable attorney. Other available methods of checking the reputation of a franchiser are the Better Business Bureaus, the International Franchise Association, and any one of the many franchise consultants that are available.

Because of the many complaints by franchisees, the Federal Trade Commission requires that a disclosure document be presented by the franchiser at least ten days prior to the signing of the contract. The FTC rule requires detailed information in such areas as the business experience of the franchiser and its principal executives, as well as its bankruptcy and litigation history; the cost required to commence operations and the continuing expenses to be paid to the franchiser; a list of the persons and products that the franchisee will be required to deal with and any affiliation between them and the franchiser and its principals; information on the renewal and termination features in the contract and statistical information about the rate of termination in the past; financial information about the franchiser; and standards for making earnings claims. This last is very important. Franchisers can no longer select their most successful units and offer these as examples of profitability.

The FTC's disclosure rule offers few problems for the large, successful franchisers. They already provide most of the information to their prospective clients. The rule is aimed chiefly at the sharpshooters who have been attracted to the franchising industry.

Unfortunately, the FTC is plagued by low budgets and limited manpower. It simply lacks the resources to perform effectively as a policing body.

TRENDS

Franchising today is more than just for fast food businesses. The opportunities are there in a variety of retail formats.

Hardware Operations

Of the top ten grossing retail franchises, two are hardware oriented. True Value, with approximately 7,000 units, and Ace Hardware with more than 5,000 units lead the pack.

Variety Stores

Companies like Ben Franklin continue to add to their numbers, as does Dollar General, making this another classification suitable for potential franchisees to consider.

Furniture

Ethan Allen, once strictly a traditional chain, is expanding via franchising and setting the tone for others in the furniture industry to follow. Colortyme now has the vast majority of its units as franchises, as do Expressions, Jennifer Convertibles, and USA Baby/Baby's Room.

Sporting Goods

More and more sporting goods companies are going the franchising route. In the top 50 retail franchises, four feature this type of arrangement. A total of 650 outlets in companies like Nevada Bob's, Pro Golf Discount, Las Vegas Discount Golf, and Merle Harmon's FanFare are franchises.

ACTION FOR THE INDEPENDENT RETAILER

Since the beginning of the twentieth century, America has witnessed a slow but constant trend toward big business. Small businesses have gradually been replaced by industrial giants. Since the close of World War II, the pace has been accelerated. Many of us have witnessed the replacement of the mom-and-pop grocery store by a large supermarket, and the neighborhood drugstore by a unit of a large chain. Franchising, by encouraging individuals to start independently owned businesses and by providing the expertise to compete successfully, may be reversing the trend toward big business.

If so, it is not only good for individuals who want to "be in business for themselves"; it also benefits our society as a whole by safeguarding the future of the middle class.

IMPORTANT POINTS IN THE CHAPTER

1. Franchising is an arrangement wherein an organization (the franchiser) that has developed a successful product or service sells to an individual (the franchisee) the right to engage in the business provided that individual follows an established pattern of operations.
2. The growth of the franchising idea during the last thirty-five years has been enormous. Retail sales made by franchised dealers are an important part of the total national retail sales.
3. Franchise opportunities are available in almost all areas of retailing at costs ranging from a few thousand dollars to more than $1 million.
4. By helping the individual with "know-how" and capital, franchising permits people with limited funds and no prior experience to go into business for themselves.
5. The principal advantages of franchising to the franchiser are an opportunity to expand with less capital than is normally required and no problems in finding hardworking, ambitious people to manage their units.
6. Some franchisees complain that their costs of conducting a franchised business are unnecessarily high. In addition, they feel that they are too rigidly controlled.
7. Franchisers are faced with the high cost of finding franchisees and the limitation on expansion brought about by the limited number of franchise locations available.
8. As with all rapidly growing industry, franchising has attracted many disreputable people. Proper safeguards should be taken before an individual enters a franchising agreement.
9. Current trends in franchising include expansion of the franchising concept, more competition among fast-food franchises, more company-operated units, and multiunit franchisees.
10. The FTC's disclosure requirements are an attempt to safeguard the interests of prospective franchisees.

REVIEW QUESTIONS

1. Discuss the causes of the rapid expansion in the franchising industry at the close of World War II.
2. Indicate some of the factors that may be found in a franchising contract that will benefit the franchisee.
3. Compare a territorial franchise with an operating franchise. Which is apt to be more successful economically?
4. Differentiate between franchise coownership and comanagement. When are these types of franchises preferable to outright ownership?
5. What problems does a franchiser face in the recruitment of franchisees?
6. The franchiser generally makes a profit as soon as the franchise contract is signed. Mention several reasons for which a financially able prospect may be turned down.

7. What factors relating to the franchiser are important to the prospective franchisee?
8. Before accepting the territory offered by the parent company, the prospective franchisee should check out certain facts. List as many points as you can.
9. Discuss the most important items that every good franchise contract should contain.
10. Explain the benefits of the franchise deal to the franchiser.
11. Discuss the data that should be found in a comprehensive location survey. Is a franchisee likely to investigate a site as thoroughly as the franchiser might?
12. Since the franchiser frequently finances part of the franchisee's investment, how can franchising be considered an inexpensive means of expanding?
13. Compare the operation of a franchised store with a store operated by a manager.
14. Explain the mutual importance of the franchiser–franchisee relationship.
15. Discuss the effect of competition among franchisers in the fast-food industry.
16. Why are franchisers running out of territories? How will this affect the individual franchisee? The prospective franchisee?
17. How does a franchiser protect its outlets from failure?
18. Discuss the effect of franchisee failure upon the franchiser.
19. To be successful, a franchiser must be flexible. Why is this true?
20. Discuss the provisions of the FTC's disclosure rule.

CASE PROBLEMS

Case Problem 1

Kwik-Snak, Inc. has been franchising fast-food shops for the past seven years. Its products such as hamburgers and franks have won wide customer approval. This fact, coupled with alert, intelligent management, has made Kwik-Snak a great success. At present the company is financially stronger than ever and aggressively interested in expansion. Unfortunately, thanks to the rapid expansion of the past few years, there are no prime locations left.

A careful analysis of the existing locations revealed that many of the franchisees, though successful, are doing considerably less business than projections indicate should be done. A case in point is a site in the suburb of a large Southwestern city that is grossing $300,000 a year, in an area that the company feels should yield $500,000 per year. A location doing $200,000 of business a year is considered prime, and the wording of the contract is such that a new location could be established in the area.

Several members of the board of directors of Kwik-Snak, who realize that a major part of their success has been due to the excellent franchiser–franchisee relationship, oppose this move. Another group of directors feels that a company that stops expanding will lose its aggressiveness and spirit to the eventual disadvantage of existing franchisers.

Questions

1. Discuss the situation from the viewpoint of a stockholder of the parent company.
2. What are the points of view of the members of the board of directors? Take one point of view and defend it.
3. How would a franchisee feel about this? Why?

Case Problem 2

The franchisees of a large, successful soft ice cream franchiser have formed an association at which they discuss problems of mutual interest. They feel that in cases of franchiser–franchisee conflicts of interest, the united front presented by the association strengthens their position with the home office.

The dispute in question involves buying supplies from the home office. The association agrees that the product must be bought from the home office to insure consistency among the various outlets. The product is unique and successful, and since the home office was the developer, it is entitled to profit from it.

The purchase of paper goods (napkins, cups, and so forth) is another matter. Paper goods are not manufactured by the home office. There is nothing unusual about them, and they could be bought locally (meeting home office specifications) much more cheaply.

It is the position of the home office that it is unfair of the franchisees to favor only those areas favorable to the franchiser. The franchisees are successful and the home office is entitled to a fair share of all the profits.

Questions

1. Discuss from the point of view of the franchiser.
2. Discuss from the point of view of the franchisee.
3. What would you suggest is the best solution for all concerned?

Chapter 4
Consumer Behavior

Photograph by Ellen Diamond

```
┌─────────────────────────────────────────────────────────────┐
│                     LEARNING OBJECTIVES                       │
│                                                               │
│  Upon completion of this chapter, the student should be able to:│
│     1. Discuss the psychological steps involved in decision   │
│        making.                                                │
│     2. Write a short essay on learning, including the         │
│        importance of drive, cues, response, and reinforcement.│
│     3. Differentiate between rational and emotional motives.  │
│     4. Discuss attitudes and habits, giving examples of each. │
│     5. Understand the importance of the family life cycle to  │
│        successful retailing.                                  │
│                                                               │
└─────────────────────────────────────────────────────────────┘
```

WHAT A DIFFERENCE AN AGE MAKES . . .

In hoping to determine who the likely candidates would be for their products, DuPont undertook what is called a "cohorts" study, or a study of groups. Consumers were segmented into ten specific categories, beginning with those who were the World War I babies and concluding with the youngest group whom they called "Mature Boomlets."

DuPont's findings, summarized in this vignette, indicated that people in different groups spend differently, which can impact upon the various retailers they patronize.

World War I Babies. Born during the "Great Depression," these people suffered hardships that have influenced the rest of their lives. Purchases, therefore, are not generally made on a whim or for impractical purposes, but rather for necessities. They usually seek bargains and make purchases at chains or discounters that give them value for the dollar.

Roaring Twenties Babies. Like the members of the World War I group, Roaring Twenties babies too are cautious spenders. Fashion is usually of little importance; money spent for clothing is often spent at discount operations, warehouse outlets, and off-price centers. Necessities are their primary goals.

Depression Babies. Although they were born during a down period in this country, the effects of that period don't deter them from being good customers for retailers. They are interested in luxury items and status merchandise, which makes them excellent consumers for upscale department and specialty stores. They seek designer merchandise.

World War II Babies. Although they are excellent fashion merchandise consumers and users of prestige merchandise, World War II babies do not have the time necessary to spend shopping in the traditional department stores. Many opt for smaller boutiques for fashion items, and often use numerous catalogs to satisfy their needs. Those with lesser incomes sometimes shop at off-price outlets where they may obtain fashion items at greatly reduced prices.

Mature Boomers. Raising families often cuts into the amount these 40- to 45-year-olds spend for fashion merchandise and luxury items. Function is generally more important than fashion. Purchasing is usually done at chain organizations, department stores, and off-price outlets.

Mid-Boomers.   Falling somewhere in the 33- to 39-year age category, mid-boomers are generally bent on making fashion and prestige statements. They, therefore, are excellent candidates for boutiques, high-fashion specialty stores, and department stores where their appetites are easily satisfied.

Young Boomers.   The members of this classification (age 26 to 32 years) earn less than the mid-boomer group, but also spend effortlessly. They are "trendy" shoppers, choosing items that indicate newness. The specialty chain is their territory.

Mature Busters.   Since they have lower incomes, 20- to 25-year-olds have little need for quality merchandise. They do buy a great deal of lower priced goods, making them excellent prospects for low-end chain organizations.

Young Busters.   With limited incomes that come from part-time employment, those who are from 14 to 19 years of age are less able to spend large sums of money. They usually depend on parents for many of their needs. They seek out trendy items at low-price specialty chains.

Mature Boomlets.   The youngest category, surprisingly, is a great group for fashion merchandise and items such as high-priced sneakers. They are often indulged by their parents, and manage to buy items that many consider outlandishly expensive.

When merchants carefully consider the makeup of their clientele in terms of age, they are better able to stock their stores with assortments that will have greater appeal to them.

At its essential core, success in retailing depends upon customer satisfaction. Consequently, all of the functions of retailing must be targeted to that goal. Site selection, store layout, merchandising, services offered, and in fact every instance where retailers have options, must be resolved in favor of the choice that will maximize overall customer satisfaction. That is to say, even if a retailer decides against a particular customer service, the decision will be based upon the expectation that the reduced prices that result from the savings will improve overall customer satisfaction. Those stores that are best able to satisfy customers will make the sales. Consumers who are satisfied with their purchases are likely to become loyal repeat customers.

It is obvious that the more a retailer knows about the customer, the greater the chance for success. The study of consumer behavior—the why, where, how, and when consumers buy—is of crucial importance. For example, studies show that children's shoes are bought by mothers. Since more and more mothers work, children's shoe stores need to be open on Sundays. Similarly, automobiles and major appliances are bought by husbands and wives together. Retailers of that type of merchandise must be open in the evening and on weekends when both spouses are available.

Most successful retailers make decisions in this area based upon intuition, and their success indicates that they are usually correct. Whether they are aware of it or not, these people are unconscious students of consumer behavior. Like many other professionals, they have been able to learn their trade effectively through insight and trial and error. Similarly, like other professionals, they could improve their performance through the formal study of the principles that are the basis for their intuition.

In this chapter, we shall discuss the psychology and sociology of consumer behavior. It should be noted that in the field of research there are many theories to explore.

CONSUMER PSYCHOLOGY

This section of the chapter will focus on the internal thought process of an individual consumer—that is, the influence of the buyer's own personality rather than the influence of the social group to which the consumer belongs.

Decision Making

Consumer buying is a matter of decision making. Therefore, it is important to understand the internal working of the decision-making process. This process involves the following steps: stimulus and problem recognition, information gathering and selection, and finally, purchase and evaluation. An understanding of each of these steps and their application to successful retailing are necessary.

Stimulus and Problem Recognition

Decision making, like all instances of problem solving, starts with an awareness of the problem. Some stimulus is necessary to bring the problem to the attention of the future buyer. The initiation of the idea can come from a variety of sources, each of which will turn the consumer's thoughts toward resolving the problem. For example:

- *Self:* I have a headache, I need an aspirin.
- *Friend:* Let's see a movie tonight.
- *Business Advertisement:* All designer jeans 10 percent off.

Whatever the source of the stimulation, it serves to begin the decision-making process by focusing attention on the need. Of particular interest to retailers is the fact that advertising and other promotional devices, such as counter and window displays, can provide the stimulus if they are properly conceived.

Of course, the stimulus will not lead to a problem until a need arises. For example, the person with the headache who needs an aspirin will take one if it is available, and, thus, the decision about whether or not to buy is hastened. If, on the other hand the response to the stimulus, "I have a headache; I need an aspirin," is, "I took the last one in the bottle last week," then the problem is recognized and the decision-making process goes on. Similarly, if the response to the friend's suggestion is, "I have too much homework," or to the advertisement is, "I have all of the jeans I need," then there is no problem. If, however, the response to the stimulus is positive, then the decision-making process continues.

Information Gathering and Selection

In the event that the problem recognized is of sufficient importance to the consumer to require a solution, the next step in the decision-making process is gathering information and making the selection. Even in the simplest case, many decisions must be made. "Shall I buy an advertised, popular brand of aspirin or the generic brand, which is cheaper and, I'm told, just as good?" "Shall I buy the one advertised on TV as stronger or my own brand?" "Shall I stop in the next drugstore I come to or wait until I get to my neighborhood drugstore?"

As the intended purchase becomes more expensive and complicated, the information gathering becomes more intensive. For example, a person needing a new car must first decide on standard size, compact, or subcompact. Then, having decided on a compact, two-door or four-door? Blue or gray? Automatic or shift? Which maker?

The list is endless and the complications so great that outside help is frequently needed. For such expensive purchases people usually visit many showrooms, have discussions with friends who have made similar purchases, and consult literature such as *Consumer Reports* magazine before making a decision.

Retailers, in order to turn the information-gathering phase of the decision-making process to their best advantage, must be prime providers of information. Advertising, visual presentations, and knowledgeable sales personnel are of great importance in getting the message across. The consumers, after all, are faced with alternatives and must be convinced that the retailer's product is more likely to satisfy their needs than is the product of a competitor.

Purchase and Evaluation

After the prospective purchaser has evaluated the information that has been gathered, the next step in the decision-making process is the actual purchase. It is at this point that the retailer's involvement is most intense because the decision to purchase a product involves the selection of the specific store from which the purchase is to be made. The buying decision may have had as a stimulus an advertisement stating, "All designer jeans 10 percent off," but that does not mean that the purchase will be made from that particular advertiser. All that the ad did was start a reaction that resulted in a consumer's decision to buy a pair of jeans. Among the information gathered was: Is a 10 percent deduction enough, or is another store offering more? What is the store's image? Convenience? Return policy? and so on.

The availability of the required merchandise is another important factor to the retailer at this time. Once the decision to purchase a particular item is made, the purchaser wants the goods to be available in the selected store. If the merchandising of that particular store has not anticipated the customer's desire, not only will the sale be lost, but also the selection of that particular store in the future is jeopardized.

The decision-making process does not end with the purchase. There is still the problem of satisfaction. The satisfied purchaser may be an immediate customer for accessories. The shirt buyer may select a tie; the woman who bought a handbag may be interested in matching shoes. In addition, the contented customer may become a loyal repeater, and that is the bottom line of successful retailing.

On the other hand, a dissatisfied customer can be a serious problem. Not only is the future business of the dissatisfied customer lost; also endangered is the business of friends who may hear the story. How does a retailer guard against dissatisfaction? For one thing, no high-pressure selling should be used; for another, follow-up calls or letters on expensive items such as automobiles and high-priced appliances help. Honest advertising and liberal merchandise return policies are steps in the right direction. Finally, money-back guarantees if the consumer is not satisfied are offered by many large retailers who recognize that an unsatisfied customer is worse than a lost sale.

Learning

Basically, decision making is a learning process. Having made the buying decision by the steps indicated previously and achieved satisfaction, the consumer is likely to repeat the purchase when the need arises again. Decision making, then, is a response to a stimulus. Some years ago Ivan Pavlov, a Russian psychologist, found that with the proper conditioning, he could teach a subject to respond in a particular way to a given stimulus. In other words, he could guide the learning procedure. His work was simple: each time he fed a dog, he would ring a bell. After repeated trials, the dog would salivate at the sound of the bell, without the presence of food. He had taught the dog to salivate on cue. This work is the foundation of learning theory and provides the basis of much of today's retail advertising and sales promotion.

Modern behavioral scientists have refined Pavlov's work by breaking it down into four steps: drive, cues, response, and reinforcement.

Drive

The first step in the learning process is a drive. By definition, a drive is an individual's awareness of an internal tension that is caused by a need from within. Basic drives may be to satisfy needs for humor, shelter, or warmth. Other drives may be to obtain a new tie, hair style, or sweater. The drive creates a tension in the individual, which will only be appeased by taking action. If the drive is strong enough, the individual will seek to satisfy it.

Cues

The manner in which an individual responds to the drive depends upon cues that he or she has been made aware of. These are ideas and other bits of information that have been stored in memory. Advertising is an example of an important generator of cues. An individual who is interested in buying a pair of slacks may remember a recent advertisement for just the sort of merchandise that will be suitable. Another, anxious to satisfy a drive for food, may remember a Chinese restaurant or Burger King nearby. Advertising, window displays, conversations with friends, and store decor are all cues of sorts.

Response

A positive action taken, as a result of cues, to satisfy a drive is called a response. This would be the actual making of the purchase that will ease the tension caused by the drive. Purchasing the slacks or ordering the food would be examples of responses in the illustrations just given.

Reinforcement

When the response to the drive proves satisfying, reinforcement occurs. When a similar need arises in the future, the reinforced response is likely to return as an important cue for future satisfaction. Those who enjoy McDonald's hamburgers return again and again. Popular brands are established through positive reinforcement, as is store loyalty.

It may seem a long jump between Pavlov's dogs and successful retailing, but consider the worker who glances at a clock at 12:00 and becomes hungry for lunch. Is that response unlike the salivating dog's? How about the individual who is deluged by television commercials for designer jeans? Isn't that an effective way to start a drive and suggest a brand name as a cue?

Buying Motives

The more retailers know about their customers, the more likely they are to satisfy the customers' needs. One major piece of information is why people buy and what motivates them. Different people buy for different reasons. Consider this: An individual decides to buy a car. The alternatives from which the selection is to be made are enormous. To understand the reason for a particular choice, we must first understand why the decision to buy the car was made in the first place. Has the old car broken down?

Does it look tacky? Is it in the repair shop too often? Is it a gas-guzzler? If we can understand the motivation for the purchase, we can direct our total sales pitch, including advertising, merchandising, personal selling, and other promotion, in that direction.

Rational versus Emotional Motivation

One common way of classifying motives is by differentiating between rational and emotional buyers.

Rational buyers do their homework. In the case of the car buyer, comparative data will be obtained on the cost of the automobile, gas mileage, frequency of repair, estimated life, and so on. The actual purchase will be based upon the outcome of careful study.

In contrast, the emotional buyer bases the buying decision on style, pride of ownership, romance, and so on.

For example, any jacket will provide warmth. The rational buyer will select the product that provides the best construction, durability, and economy. The emotional buyer will buy the high-fashion, designer-labeled jacket that looks best. It should be pointed out that we are discussing buying motives, not intelligence. The rational buyer may gather the wrong information, interpret it incorrectly, and for any of a number of reasons make a totally irrational purchase.

It must be understood that the borderline between rational and emotional motives is frequently crossed. That is, some individuals, usually rational buyers, take an occasional flyer for an emotional product that strikes their fancy. Moreover, an individual who buys clothing on an emotional basis might put considerable research into the purchase of a lawn mower.

The point for retailers is that when selling products that appeal to emotional purchasers, use an emotional sales pitch. One does not, for example, use the same advertising and sales promotion for a Cadillac as one would use for a Hyundai. Also, alert retailers must change their messages as their products move from one category to another. Consider Volkswagen advertising over the years. Originally the automobiles were offered as low-cost, efficiently operating machines, ideally suited to the rational buyer. In recent years costs have increased, styling has improved, and the stripped-down version is hard to find. The down-to-earth advertising has changed to one with snob appeal. The cars now appear outside of mansions, fancy country clubs, and expensive art galleries. The ads are peopled by cultured, wells-spoken individuals, who can well afford a Cadillac or a Mercedes-Benz. The focus is no longer targeted to the down-to-earth rational buyer, but to the status-seeking, prestige-conscious, emotional buyer.

Maslow's Hierarchy of Needs

Abraham Maslow proposed an order in which needs are fulfilled, which has become an important part of the literature of motivation. His proposal provides a listing of the relative importance of each motivating need in relation to other needs. The following explains his view of motivational needs in order of their importance:

Necessities for Survival.   Obviously, these needs that are required for survival are more important than any other type of motivation. People who need food, water, shelter, or sleep will not be motivated to satisfy any other needs until those are satisfied. In affluent societies, such as ours, motivations to ensure survival are rarely an important factor.

After the basic survival needs have been satisfied, an individual turns to the satisfaction of a need for the safety and protection of self, family, and friends. This drive for self-preservation is often capitalized upon by retailers of such products as vitamin pills, security devices, and the like. Consider the advertising for smoke detectors that provide safety for the family, or the automobiles that provide the greatest safety in the event of an accident. The need for safety and security is basic, and the retailer must bear that in mind when making product selections, making advertising and sales promotion decisions, and planning the training of sales staff.

Social Motivation.   Next in Maslow's order of importance is social motivation. Man is by nature a social animal. That is, happiness depends upon a successful adjustment to society. An individual must love and be loved by a family and be an accepted member of a group. Included in this motive is the need to attract a mate and care for a family. We are constantly bombarded by advertisements that offer satisfaction of this need. Cosmetics, clothing, and furniture, as well as membership in organizations and home entertaining, are appeals to the satisfaction of this motive.

Self-Esteem.   The need for self-esteem and recognition by society is next in Maslow's order of importance. The longing for status and recognition is frequently satisfied by the ownership of certain products that are the proof of success. The sale of expensive cars and furs, the choice of the "right" school for one's children, shopping in high-image stores, and having the "right" label on one's clothes are examples of attempts to satisfy the need for self-esteem. When Ford Motors advertises, "Step Up to a Lincoln Continental," this is exactly what we are talking about.

Self-Actualization.   This is Maslow's final level of motivation. It refers to the development of one's self by realizing one's full potential for understanding and gracious living. Books, records, objects of fine art, and colleges offering cultural courses to nontypical students are examples of the products sold to satisfy the need for self-actualization.

When Maslow theorized his hierarchy of needs, he did not intend it as a hard and fast rule. In fact, some people buy expensive cars before fully satisfying all of the previous needs outlined. However, Maslow's categories provide a good rule of thumb to retailers. Stores, or departments within stores, by understanding the underlying purpose behind a consumer's buying decision, can focus their efforts toward satisfying that particular need by adjusting their offerings and sales pitch to a specific area.

Attitudes

An attitude is an individual's feeling toward a particular object. These preconceived opinions are often crucial to a store's success. Attitudes are learned; they are the result of, for example, an individual's experience, conversations with friends, and reactions to advertising and sales promotion. The importance of attitude to retailing success can be illustrated. For example, an individual has several friends who have had negative experiences with the return policies of a particular store. As a result, the individual may never try the store. A positive attitude can result if the experiences with a particular retailer are good. Attitudes can be shaped from a wide variety of sources. Even such information as the personal life of the store's owner can have an effect on a prospective customer toward a store. Attitudes can rarely be changed. For example, the perception of Sears has always been that of an organization that gives value, and the store's emphasis has been on hardware, housewares, and appliances. An ongoing attempt to include fashion clothing as part of the store's image has met with only fair success. Or consider the perception that small, independently owned retailers do not accept returned goods easily. It is doubtful that a small retailer that advertises a liberal return policy would change many consumers' perceptions.

A retailer's image (the way that it is perceived by customers and potential customers) is vital and difficult to alter. Consequently, every effort must be made to minimize customer discontent. The slogan, "The Customer Is Always Right" has a more beneficial effect on the store than it does on the customer.

Habits

Another important factor in consumer behavior is the buying habits of the retailer's market. When, where, and how much will be purchased are pieces of information that the successful retailer must blend effectively if customer satisfaction is to be achieved.

Conforming to the customer's "time" habit—that is, when the consumer buys—requires that the retailer have the merchandise on hand, the staff available, and the advertising geared to consumer wants. Christmas tree ornaments must be available in December, and bathing suits, in the spring and early summer. Advertising must inform customers of the availability of the goods, and the store's operation must be geared to handle peak loads whenever necessary. In the case of supermarkets, whose peak day is Friday, advertising usually appears in the Thursday newspapers and the shelves are fully stocked by Friday morning.

Another aspect of the "time" habit concerns the time of day or week that shopping is done. This habit has undergone considerable change in recent years, as more and more women have entered the workforce. To adjust to these changes shops have had to alter their operations. An example of this can be found in the operation of Adrien Arpel. They operate small (10×12 feet is adequate) skin care units in major department stores (Macy's, Bloomingdale's, Foley's of Houston, etc.). Their principal product is a 20-minute facial that busy working women can use on a drop-in rather than a pre-appointment basis. The fact that there is a large market for quick beauty treatment, as opposed to hours spent in a traditional beauty salon, is evidenced by the rapid spread of Adrien Arpel units throughout the country.

Satisfying the "time" habit is usually learned quickly and conformed to easily. It is not a habit that can easily be changed. The "where" habit, the store from which a consumer buys a particular item, is another matter. In recent years, this habit has been changed. Supermarkets now carry a line of nonprescription drugs, large drugstores display housewares and small appliances, and even prestigious men's shops carry women's ready-to-wear. This is not to indicate that the "where" habit is easily changed. It requires a considerable investment in inventory, promotion, and patience. But it can be done.

The quantity habit is easily adjusted to. It depends upon the area that the retailer services. In suburban areas where shoppers travel by automobile, supermarket shoppers buy in huge quantity. Not so in urban areas, where supermarket purchasers must hand-carry the goods. They shop more frequently and buy smaller quantities. Similarly, in economically deprived areas, food marketers must be prepared to sell eggs individually rather than by the dozen.

Conforming to customers' behavioral habits is relatively easy. However, many retailers do not seem to realize that these habits are in a constant state of change and that frequent adjustments may be necessary. For example, the growing number of working women has resulted in a change in buying habits. For one thing, since shoppers who work are not able to shop during the day, evenings and Sundays have become increasingly important for shopping. Also, the unavailability of working women during shopping hours has increased the number of men shoppers for goods that have traditionally been the responsibility of their wives. Promotional displays, merchandise, and sales presentations that had been successful with women must be adjusted to this new breed of customer. Where people shop is another changing habit.

For example, the success and continued growth of the flea market has been causing serious problems to traditional retailers. As more people get into the habit of buying at these low-overhead, cut-price retailers, the competition is forced to adjust to this new threat by means such as carrying different lines of merchandise or lowering prices.

CONSUMER SOCIOLOGY

Understanding another influence on consumer behavior, which gives insight into their buying habits, requires the study of individuals as members of groups. We have already discussed the psychological influences on buyer motivation. These were the individual, internal thought processes of a person that result in a particular behavioral pattern. They are not the whole story. Individuals are also influenced by the groups to which they belong. This is the work of sociologists. These behavioral scientists are concerned with the influences that family, friends, and groups have on an individual's activities.

Similar people tend to congregate together. The similarity can be based upon economic success, educational achievement, religion, ethnic background, and a host of other factors. Since people within a group have a tendency to act in a similar fashion, it is worthwhile to study these groupings. Retailers generally focus their efforts on a particular segment of the market. Understanding the characteristics of this segment or group, its likes, dislikes, needs, motivations, and buying patterns, will improve the retailer's ability to ensure customer satisfaction.

The problem with sociological grouping is that there are simply too many ways to define the boundaries of groups and there may be serious overlaps. One generally accepted system of classifications is based upon economics and similarity of outlooks, goals, and attitudes.

Upper-Upper

Members of the upper-upper group are the socially elite, who comprise 1 percent of the population. Their great wealth is inherited and is used to purchase mansions in exclusive neighborhoods, summer homes, education in the "best" schools, and so on.

Cost is not an important factor in their purchases. They are conservative in dress and inconspicuous in spending habits. Since traveling takes much of their time, a considerable amount of their purchasing is done abroad. People in this class are the targets for the advertisement in Figure 4–1.

A RETAILING FOCUS   Tiffany & Co.

If there was ever a place for people in the upper-upper class to satisfy their jewelry appetites, Tiffany & Co. is it. Since its opening in 1837, the store has become one of the most prominent retailers of precious gems. Charles Tiffany was a gifted and innovative entrepreneur who exhibited a flair for the sensational. He catered to the whims of his customers by offering them any extravagance that they were willing to pay for.

Throughout history, the most prominent members of American society were and still are frequent Tiffany customers. J. P. Morgan, the financier, ordered gold and silver services; Diamond Jim Brady was a regular purchaser of jewelry; Lillian Russell and Sarah Bernhardt, theatrical legends, indulged themselves with Tiffany purchases; and even President Lincoln purchased a seed pearl necklace there for his wife, Mary.

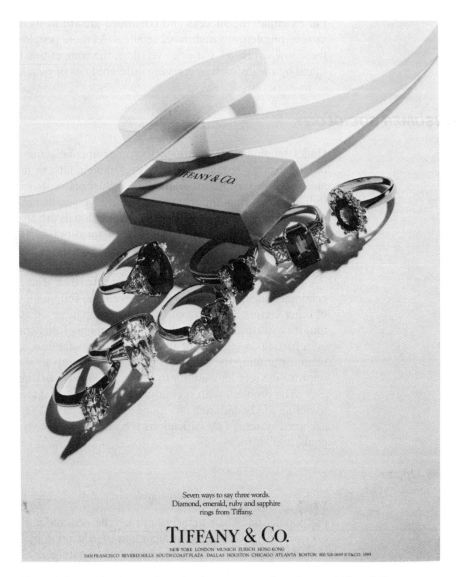

Seven ways to say three words.
Diamond, emerald, ruby and sapphire
rings from Tiffany.

TIFFANY & CO.

NEW YORK LONDON MUNICH ZURICH HONG KONG
SAN FRANCISCO BEVERLY HILLS SOUTH COAST PLAZA DALLAS HOUSTON CHICAGO ATLANTA BOSTON 800-526-0649 ©T&CO. 1989

Figure 4–1   An advertisement directed at the upper-upper class. *Courtesy:* Tiffany & Co.

Throughout its existence, the store has regularly gained notice from the world through a variety of endeavors. Among them were:

- recognition at the Paris Exposition in 1878 as first place recipient for gold and silver craftsmanship.
- introduction in 1870 of the now famous six pronged "Tiffany setting" for diamonds.
- discovery of the world's largest and finest canary diamond in the Kimberly mines.
- establishment of special collections exclusively for Tiffany & Co. by such world renowned designers as Jean Schlumberger, Elsa Peretti, and Paloma Picasso.
- serving as the "location" for the movie *Breakfast at Tiffany's*.

In addition to jewelry, the company features silver, china, crystal, timepieces, stationery, leather accessories, scarves, and fragrance.

For over 150 years, Tiffany & Co. has been an American institution with an international reputation for quality, craftsmanship, and exceptional merchandise design. Today, in addition to the landmark store located on Fifth Avenue in New York City, Tiffany & Co. operates branches in Atlanta, Beverly Hills, Boston, Chicago, Costa Mesa, Houston, San Francisco, and Philadelphia. Internationally, Tiffany has shops in London, Munich, Hong Kong, and Zurich and sells its products through Faraone shops in Milan and Florence and through Mitsukoshi in Japan and Hawaii.

Lower-Upper

These are the newly rich. They amount to 2 percent of the population. They are professionals, executives of large corporations, or owners of successful businesses. They are active in social affairs and free and conspicuous spenders.

Members of the lower-upper class are wealthy people who do not worry about costs. Labels are important to them, so they shop in exclusive shops and high-image department stores. They own boats, swimming pools, and large homes. They are proud of their wealth and enjoy displaying it.

Upper-Middle

This group consists of 12 percent of the population. They are the best educated in the society, career oriented, and concerned with status. They are frequently professionals, middle-level executives, or owners of successful businesses.

At this level of income, the cost of purchases begins to be important. They are careful, rational buyers. They buy quality merchandise and although they are conspicuous spenders, they try not to appear that way. Their goal is a "gracious" way of life.

Lower-Middle

This group of white-collar and highly paid blue-collar workers consists of about 30 percent of the population. These "typical Americans" are respectable, conscientious, and conservative. They are do-it-yourself homeowners and respectable churchgoers.

Members of the lower-middle class are very price-conscious. They are careful, rational shoppers who buy from a wide variety of nonexclusive stores.

Upper-Lower

This is the largest segment of our population, consisting of about 35 percent of the population. They generally hold blue-collar jobs and are not well educated. Job security is more important to them than upward mobility.

These are impulsive, emotional buyers who are very susceptible to advertising and loyal brand users. They shop at low-end stores where credit is available. Being uninformed shoppers, they frequently overpay.

Lower-Lower

This class of poorly educated, unskilled workers comprise 20 percent of the population. They are present oriented and generally disinterested in upward mobility. They populate slum areas and are frequently welfare recipients.

Members of this class shop locally where credit is available. They are impulsive buyers who frequently overpay. An unusually large proportion of their income is spent to improve their personal appearance.

Family Life Cycle

Another way to categorize individuals into groups is according to their stage in the family life cycle. Newly married couples or couples with young children usually have similar needs and motivations for their purchases. (See Figure 4–2.)

TRENDS

The manner in which the consumer behaves, in terms of purchasing, changes from time to time. A consumer's buying power is influenced by economic conditions and other factors. Some of the trends in consumer behavior follow.

Catalog Purchasing

With more women in the workplace who have less time for traditional in-store purchasing, catalog shopping has become a necessity for satisfying the needs of many consumers. Many retailers are reporting a decrease in the number of shoppers who frequent their stores.

Figure 4–2   Family Life Cycle

Stage	Distinguishing Features	Buying Patterns
Single	Low earnings. Small financial responsibilities. Interested in romance and recreation.	High-fashion clothing. Automobiles, vacations, cosmetics, furniture and electronics. Entertainment.
Newlywed	Two earners. Small financial responsibilities. Free spenders.	Durable goods for new home. Vacations, entertainment. Clothing.
Full Nest I; youngest child under 6	One or two earners. If wife works, a considerable sum goes to child care. Tight financial position. Desire home ownership.	Careful spenders. Practical housewares and appliances; durability and safety are prime factors.
Full Nest II; youngest child over 6	Improved financially. One or two incomes. Less advertising influence. Concerned with future.	Home buyers. Child-oriented products and vacations. Savings. Some luxuries.
Full Nest III: grown children still home	High income level. Financial independence. Skeptical of advertising.	Quality replacement in durable goods. Vacations and retirement homes. Travel. Boats. Books.
Empty Nest I; still working	Financially secure. One spouse may be retired.* Children independent.	Retirement home. Luxuries. Travel. Recreation. Self-education. Gifts. Clothing.
Empty Nest II; retired	Cut in income. Worry about future finances. Keep homes but cut spending.	Medical care and other health improvements. Few luxuries. Price conscious. Travel, inexpensive recreation.
Sole Survivor I; employed	Good income. Present oriented. Active in job. Friends. Often sells homes.	Health services. Travel. Clothing. Recreation.
Sole Survivor II; retired	Poor income. Depressed.	Health. Security. Careful shopping. Join social groups.

*In more and more situations, wives don't retire until the husband retires, which provides for highest level of family incomes.

Rational Purchasing

The expansion of such value discount operations as WalMart and Kmart and the warehouse outlets like Price Club indicate that Americans are turning toward rational purchases. Price has become an extremely important factor. Although much merchandise, particularly that with a fashion orientation, is bought based upon emotional appeal, the rational shoppers are increasing in number.

ACTION FOR THE INDEPENDENT RETAILER

It is likely that understanding consumer behavior and capitalizing on that knowledge is more important to the small retailer than to the giant competitor. For one thing, the small retailer can less afford to lose a sale.

Small retailers generally suffer from limited amounts of space and capital. These assets, therefore, must be used with care and accuracy. Only the largest stores have the space and financial ability to carry goods that will appeal to a wide variety of customers. Because of these limitations, the small retailer must aim at a relatively small, specialized segment of the market. To try to do otherwise will result in too narrow an inventory in any one category of goods to be effective. Once having decided which section of the population to service, small retailers will increase their chance of success by learning as much as possible about that class of individuals. Failure to do so might result in so impossible a situation as locating a children's shoe store in a neighborhood peopled by retired individuals. The large store, of course, faces a far less severe problem. Space and sufficient financial strength to enable the store to carry a huge inventory permit them to appeal to broad classes of individuals, which allows their thrust to be broader and less subject to error. In brief, behavioral scientists have much to say to the small retailer, who would be wise to pay attention.

In conclusion, it should be noted that, sociologically speaking, there are many ways in which consumers with similar habits and motivations can be grouped. Race, religion, ethnic background, earnings, and educational achievement are only a few ways in which people with similar characteristics and, of importance to retailers, similar buying habits and motivations can be grouped. Moreover, people with similar characteristics tend to live in the same neighborhood. Small retailers must understand as much as possible about their clientele. They all do it by trial and error, but one wonders if they don't miss something. Some research or formal study in this area might be of considerable value.

IMPORTANT POINTS IN THE CHAPTER

1. Customer satisfaction, the key to successful retailing, depends in large part upon the retailer's understanding of the psychological and sociological elements of the consumer's buying decision.

2. Consumer psychology deals with the effects of customers' personalities on their buying decisions.

3. Decision making can be broken down into the following steps: stimulus and problem recognition, information gathering and selection, and purchase and evaluation.

4. The steps in the learning process are drive, cues, response, and reinforcement. A satisfactory purchase provides reinforcement and leads to repeated purchases.

5. A rational purchase is one based on a study of cost efficiency. Emotional purchases are based on pride, romance, style, and so forth.

6. Maslow theorizes that needs are satisfied in the following order: first, necessities for survival; then, social motives.

7. An attitude is an individual's feeling toward a particular object. Attitudes are more easily learned than changed.

8. Retailers must adjust their operation to comply with their customers' buying habits.

9. Sociologists have found that consumers can be grouped into broad categories that have similar habits and motivations.

REVIEW QUESTIONS

1. Why might a retailer, aware of the importance of customer satisfaction, decide on an "all sales final" policy?

2. Discuss the types of stores that benefit greatly from being open on Sundays and those that can remain closed.

3. One of the steps in decision making is stimulus and problem recognition. Define and give examples.

4. How does a consumer gather information for the buying decision? How can a retailer get involved in that process?

5. Discuss the importance of post-purchase evaluation.

6. Define the use of the word "drive" in the learning process. Give examples.

7. How does Pavlov's work with dogs relate to retailers?

8. Define the term *reinforcement* as it relates to the learning process. Provide examples that indicate its importance to the retailer.

9. Define rational motivation. Give examples.

10. Define emotional motivation. Give examples.

11. You are selling ski jackets. Differentiate between the presentation that you would make to a rational buyer and that you would make to an emotional buyer.

12. Explain the theory of Maslow's hierarchy of needs and list them in proper order.

13. What is an attitude? How may it be learned? How changed?

14. Give examples of the effect of the how, why, and where of consumer habits on retailers.

15. What information can sociologists provide to retailers?

16. Discuss the buying motivations of the upper-middle class.

17. Describe the upper-lower class. How can a retailer reach members of this group?

18. Discuss newlyweds as customers.

19. What are the buying interests of a middle-aged couple with independent children?

20. Is the understanding of the sociological makeup of the area important to the small retailer? Why?

CASE PROBLEMS

Case Problem 1

John Sawyer, age 42, has a fine job with a major firm of stockbrokers. He earns in excess of $100,000 per year and his prospects for advancement, both in earnings and position within the firm, are excellent.

The Sawyers live in a house in a distant, middle-class suburb of New York City. John commutes to work by car. The house is small and unspectacular. The Sawyers and their children, aged 16, 12, and 8, find it quite crowded and have decided to sell the house and move to larger quarters.

After a great deal of searching, the Sawyers have decided upon a house in an exclusive suburb, which costs $600,000. This is more expensive than the Sawyers can afford, but Mr. Sawyer, thanks to the excellent banking connections he has developed at work, can raise an unusually high mortgage that will swing the deal. Although he realizes that he cannot really afford the house, John Sawyer plans to go ahead with the deal for these reasons:

1. The whole family loves the house.
2. If he can hang on for a few years, promotions and salary increases will make everything come out satisfactorily.
3. Entertaining both his business superiors and customers in the new house will have a favorable effect on his future earnings.
4. New friends from the new affluent neighborhood may prove to be valuable customers.
5. The new friends his children will make will have a positive effect on their future.

Questions

1. Are these rational or emotional motives? Why?
2. Which of Maslow's hierarchy of needs does this purchase satisfy? Discuss.
3. To what social class do the Sawyers belong?
4. Discuss the purchase in terms of the decision-making process.

Case Problem 2

Younglife Builders, Inc. is in the process of completing a large apartment complex in a nearby suburb of San Francisco. The complex has been designed to attract young singles and newlyweds. The apartments are of one, two, and three rooms and are designed to appeal to the prospective clientele. Included in the plans are tennis courts, jogging tracks, and other athletic facilities. There will also be public rooms for social activities and small gymnasiums and saunas. Because of the unique appeal of the proposal, the apartments have all been rented prior to completion and there is a waiting list to cover cancellations. Naturally, the rents are quite high.

Centralized within the complex is a large shopping center that will be operated by the builders. Because of the size of the complex and the distance to competing stores, it is a "can't miss" location for retailers. As a result, the builders are in the enviable position of having long lists of fully qualified applicants to choose from.

Leases for this sort of situation frequently include clauses under which the rental is based, in part, upon the tenant's gross income. Therefore, Younglife Builders, Inc. will increase its profits by selecting from the retail applicants the stores that will be most successful. Another consideration to be taken into account is that the apartment renters must have all of their reasonable buying needs satisfied by the shopping center.

Questions

1. What types of stores (in terms of specific merchandise carried) should be selected?
2. Why?

Chapter 5
Store Organization

Photograph by Ellen Diamond

DECENTRALIZATION WORKS FOR THEM . . .

At a time when the key to most chain and department stores' organizational philosophy is to centralize most of its decision-making operations, a major player, J. C. Penney, goes the other way in merchandising their units. Just about every company with many stores makes purchasing the full responsibility of the buying and merchandising team. That is, from some central location such as a flagship store or corporate headquarters, buyers and merchandisers sit in their ivory towers making decisions on merchandise acquisition for all of their outlets. Although this approach does guarantee a degree of uniformity for inventory for an entire company, and savings are realized because just a few individuals are involved in the decision-making process, it nonetheless doesn't take into account the different needs of some stores in the organization. Organizations with stores in different climate zones and in areas that have different needs because of income variations, for example, often require a more tailor-made inventory than that which often comes from uniform decisions made at the home office.

J. C. Penney, operator of more than 1,600 outlets, uses a different approach. The individual store managers have a great deal of leeway in deciding much of the merchandise that will enter their doors. The Penney's system involves the development of a catalog by the buyers in which photographs and merchandise descriptions are inserted. The buyer, having selected the items he or she believes appropriate for the company's stores, leaves much of the final selection of merchandise to the discretion of the individual store managers. Not every item is merchandised in this manner. Some items must be accepted into every store's product mix. The remainder of the product mix is determined by each manager. With stores in every corner of the country, catering to different classes of consumers, Penney's believes this is the best arrangement. In cases in which a manager might pass up a "hot item," the buyer has the right to require that merchandise be carried.

Shipments are carefully scrutinized because they must come from a central warehouse. Only on rare occasions may a store manager deal directly with a vendor.

Although this decentralization technique is generally frowned upon by most companies, J. C. Penney believes it is one of the reasons for its success.

Any human effort that must be done by more than one person will be accomplished more effectively if it is organized. If all individuals involved have a clear idea of their duties and responsibilities, there will be less chance of duplication of work, or tasks being omitted. A small luncheonette run by a husband and wife must have organization. If there is no clear understanding of who is responsible for making the egg salad, there will be days in which twice the amount of required egg salad is made and other days in which none is made. Of course a very small enterprise needs no formal organization. Where there are few people involved, each person's tasks and responsibilities are quickly and easily understood. An enterprise involving thousands of employees is another matter.

The organization of a retail store is accomplished by the identification and separation of all of the similar functions (activities) of the enterprise, and the assignment of the responsibility for the performance of these functions to specific groups of individuals. The lines of authority and control must be clearly established and thoroughly understood by every worker in the organization. In other words, all individual workers in the organization must know what their jobs are, what people they supervise, and to whom they are responsible.

THE USE OF CHARTS

Many complicated problems can be more easily understood by the use of diagrams. The use of a map in a geography lesson gives a much clearer picture of relative positions than could possibly be given by words. The use of an organization chart to describe the functions of a retail establishment and the responsibilities of its personnel greatly simplifies the understanding of the position of each individual in the establishment. Naturally, since the chart is brief and concise, it must be backed up by descriptions, duties, and responsibilities of each job or job classification. All employees, by glancing at the organization chart, can understand the relationship of their jobs to the overall picture and to the lines of authority above and below their positions.

Unfortunately, organization charts do not take into account the personal relationships that exist between employees as a result of the teamwork and cooperation that are the keynote of a successful retailing operation. While the organization chart gives a brief sketch of how an institution operates, it is doubtful that any retailer follows to the letter the minor details of the chart.

Another disadvantage of organization charts is that they always seem to be out of date. No two retailers are apt to have exactly the same organization chart. Even an individual retailer, considering the speed at which retailing constantly changes, does not tend to use the same organization chart for a long period of time. It has even been said that organization charts are generally obsolete on the very day that they are published. While day-to-day changes are generally of a minor nature, the charts must be constantly revised if they are to be used effectively.

Constructing an Organization Chart

The construction of an organization chart requires the operation of the enterprise to be broken down into functions. A function is a type of activity that can be differentiated from other activities. Buying, selling, and receiving are examples of functions. Not all

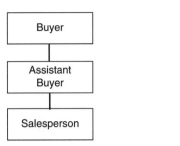

Figure 5–2   Staff relationship

Figure 5–1   Line relationship

stores perform the same functions. Those that maintain charge accounts will have a credit function, which is unnecessary to a cash-and-carry store.

Once the functions have been separated, the next step is to arrange them in lines of authority. In some retail operations sales personnel are responsible to assistant buyers, who are responsible to buyers. On an organization chart this would appear as in Figure 5–1.

The buyer, assistant buyer, and salesperson all are producers or are in decision-making positions for the company. The term producer refers to someone who produces income for the company. They appear in a vertical line on the chart and are called line positions.

In the chart shown in Figure 5–2, the research unit neither produces nor makes decisions. It acts in an advisory capacity to the general manager. This is called a staff position and is indicated by horizontal placement.

SMALL STORE ORGANIZATION

All stores, regardless of size, require organization. The difference between large and small store organization lies chiefly in the numbers of employees involved. In essence, both the large and the small store conduct the same type of operation. The major difference from an organizational point of view is that the small store, with few employees, must require each employee to perform many functions. The large store, with many more employees than functions to be performed, assigns groups of employees to do a single function. The greater the number of employees, the greater the amount of possible specialization. In drawing up an organization chart, it is useless to define a function for which there are no available specialist employees. The organization chart of a small employer is relatively simple. Figure 5–3 shows an organization chart for a store whose personnel consists of an owner and four employees.

Note that the chart gives all employees a clear understanding of their responsibilities (impossible to indicate on extensive organization charts, which merely show lines of authority), and the lines of authority from the salesperson through the manager to the owner. The duties and responsibilities are spelled out in job descriptions, a topic to be discussed in Chapter 6, Human Resources Management. In addition, the owner is able to control all employees by knowing the exact nature of each person's responsibilities. This serves as a basis for tightening up shoddy work or rewarding outstanding effort. Because of lack of understanding or laziness, few small retailers construct such charts, although it would be to their advantage to do so. By clearly defining the responsibility of each employee, the employer would minimize "passing the buck," neglect of duty, and the evasion of responsibility.

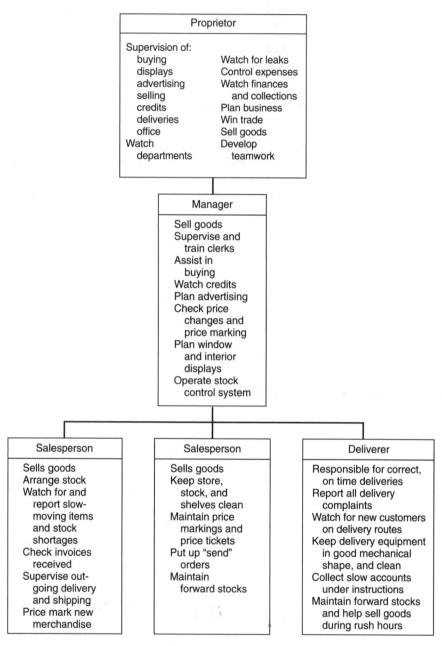

Figure 5–3   Organization chart for a small retail store

It should be understood that the fixing of responsibility by the organization chart should not preclude cooperation among the employees. Thus, while one particular employee is given a certain responsibility, the other workers are expected to help that employee if the situation warrants such cooperation. Giving a person the responsibility for seeing that a task is done is not meant to indicate that that individual is the only one who should perform that task.

EXPANSION OF A SMALL STORE

As the size of a retailing operation grows, the number of employees increases. This permits the store to operate more efficiently by providing for specialists in the workforce. For example, when the volume of receiving, maintenance work, and stockroom activities becomes heavy enough to be done by full-time employees, new functions may be identified and staffed. The work will then be done by properly trained experts devoting full time to the job rather than by salespeople to whom the job is a burdensome chore. The growth of the small store typifies this. As the store's sales volume increases, new personnel must be employed.

An example of this change in operations may be seen by looking again at Figure 5–3. If the store's sales volume required the hiring of a fifth person, the new employee's responsibilities would be taken from the work previously delegated to the original four. This would result in a lessening of each worker's duties. If the new person, for example, were a part-time bookkeeper, that employee would take over all of the clerical tasks that previously were performed by the other workers. The result would be a specialist doing all of the clerical tasks. Since the original workers would no longer be required to perform clerical duties, in which they are probably poorly trained and disinterested, the performance of their other tasks would be improved. The organizational chart pictured in Figure 5–3 would be amended to indicate a new box to the right of the box labeled "proprietor" (connected by a horizontal line, since clerical work is a staff function). The new box would be headed by the title "bookkeeper" and would list all of the clerical functions, which would be deleted from the boxes indicating the responsibilities of the other employees.

The point is that the basic functions of a large retailer are not very different from those of a small store. Therefore, as the number of personnel increases, the functions for which each person is responsible can be decreased until the point is reached in which specialists or teams of specialists can be employed for each function. This is called *specialization* and is one of the principal reasons for the success of American big business.

Departmentalization

As a retail store increases in sales volume and in the number of persons it employs, there is a constant increase in the amount of specialization possible.

In all but the smallest stores, related functions are grouped into departments. There are several advantages to departmentalization, among which are specialization and managerial control.

Specialization

By limiting the responsibility of an employee to one specific function, the employee's knowledge of and, therefore, ability to perform that function is increased. A person who is responsible for major appliances soon becomes expert in the buying and selling of such articles. In a small store the major appliance and furniture functions may be grouped together. This arrangement is preferable to no departmentalization at all.

Managerial Control

As a store grows in size, it becomes more difficult to control. The owner of a small store knows precisely the profitability of each type of merchandise the store handles. In a medium-sized or large-volume store, it is impossible for management to have this information without referring to accounting reports. Income statements (reports prepared by accountants that show profits and losses) can be made for the entire store, or for the various types of merchandise within the store. If the selling functions are divided into departments, the profitability of each department can be determined. In this way weaknesses can be identified and improved, while strong points can be rewarded. Where departmentalization occurs, separate records of sales, inventory, and, frequently, operating expenses are maintained. This permits managerial control over all of these items. A store that does not departmentalize finds itself in a situation similar to that of a person owning three stores in separate locations who does not keep individualized records for each unit. Although unlikely, it is possible under such conditions to find that one store is losing money.

When to Departmentalize

The number of departments in a store ranges from three to four in a small store to more than 150 separate departments in a large organization. The problem of deciding whether to set up a special department is a difficult one that can be solved only by a thorough understanding of the purposes of departmentalization. The principal advantages of departmentalization are specialization and control. When the volume of a specific class of merchandise is so great that managerial control requires exact information, and when the quantity of personnel available permits specialization, a separate department should be set up. Since the quantity of personnel and the amount of control required generally depend upon sales volume, the total sales of a particular item is the primary factor to be taken into account in making the decision of whether or not to departmentalize.

SMALL DEPARTMENT STORE ORGANIZATION

The principal difference between the operational plan of a small retailer and a small department store is that the increased sales volume and the necessary additional personnel of the small department store permits more specialization of workers. The organization chart of the typical small department store is pictured in Figure 5–4.

A comparison of this chart and Figure 5–3 shows several striking changes. The most important difference is that the organization chart of the small department store recognizes two functions—that is, two vertical lines of responsibility of equal authority; neither the director of merchandising nor the director of store operations has authority over the other. Dividing the store into two major functions has the effect of freeing all the merchandise personnel from the chores listed under the operations functions. In other words, although the small department store has too few employees for full specialization, there has been a grouping of functions into two major classifications.

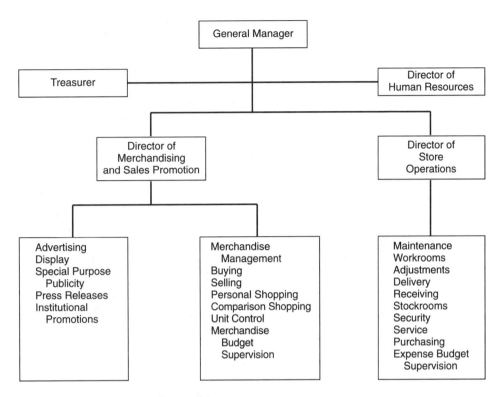

Figure 5–4   Organization chart for a small department store

It must be borne in mind that an organization chart is a graphic representation of a store's operation. As such, it is the result of a great deal of study and debate. For example, many stores include the personnel function under the responsibilities of the director of store operations. This would have the effect of giving that director a great deal of power in the area of hiring the personnel required by the merchandising function. Note also that the manager of publicity is as important an individual as the merchandising manager. By this arrangement, neither person has the final say on publicity. They must cooperate on decisions or appeal to the director of merchandising for decisions that they cannot work out between themselves. Note that the treasurer is a staff function reporting directly to the general manager. Since the financial control of both major functions is the responsibility of the treasurer, to place this position under either of the other two departments might put the treasurer in the impossible position of complaining to the boss of the boss's incompetence.

As a store grows in size and increases in the amount of possible specialization, a third function may be added to the two-function plan pictured in Figure 5–4. A store in which credit sales are an important consideration may be operated under the three-function organization plan pictured in Figure 5–5.

In this typical medium-sized department store, the office of the treasurer has been elevated to an equal standing with the merchandising and operations departments. Many stores of this size that are heavily involved in publicity might break the publicity department away from the director of merchandising and set it up as a separate function.

In comparing the two-function organization chart of the small department store with the three-function chart of a medium-sized department store, note the increase in the number of management and middle-management positions that become necessary

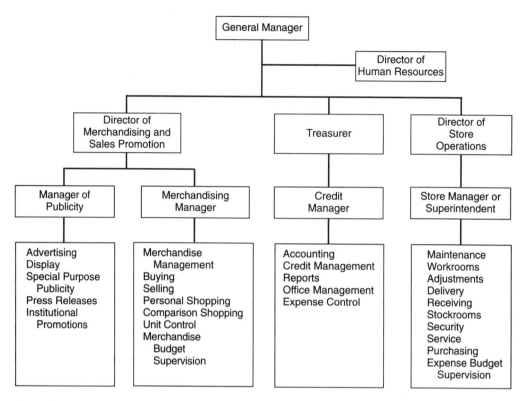

Figure 5–5   Organization chart for a medium-sized department store

as a store grows in size. The director of merchandising and sales promotion of the small store cannot solely fulfill that responsibility in the larger store. The medium-sized store requires a manager of publicity and a merchandising manager to work with the director of merchandising and sales promotion to get the job done.

LARGE DEPARTMENT STORE ORGANIZATION

The large department store with its great number of employees has no trouble in achieving a high degree of specialization. The very size of a large department store complicates its operation and makes operational planning extremely important.

Following the business recession of 1921 to 1923, the National Retail Dry Goods Association (now known as the National Retail Federation) formed a committee to study the operational plans of a group of successful stores and determine a sound plan for effective department store organization. Paul M. Mazur, an authority on the subject, was commissioned to work with the committee. After 18 months, in which 13 stores of varying sizes were studied, the Mazur Plan was evolved. The Mazur Plan had a considerable effect on department store organization from the time of its first publication. Although there have been many variations of the plan since its inception, it still forms the basis of most large department store operations. The organization chart for a large department store based on the Mazur Plan is depicted in Figure 5–6.

As is indicated in the organization chart, the Mazur Plan proposes a four-function operation, with the lines of authority grouped under the controller, merchandise

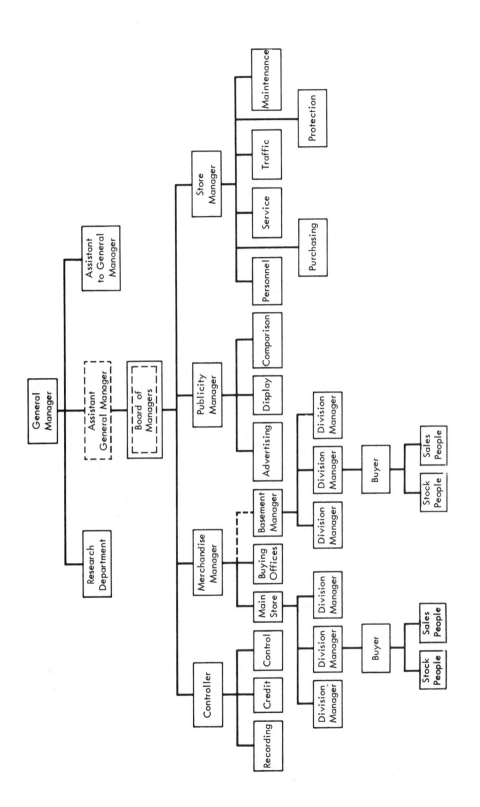

Figure 5-6 Mazur's four-function organization plan

manager, publicity manager, and store manager. The Mazur Plan offered several advantages that were unique at the time of the proposal and have since been gradually accepted as basic to the field of retailing operations.

1. It divided the store into four highly specialized divisions of store operation—control, merchandising, publicity, and store management.
2. The plan indicates the position of each employee group in relation to every other employee group in the store. All employees know their responsibilities and the lines of authority through which they must operate.
3. The board of managers, consisting of the heads of each of the four function groups, provides a meeting place in which the heads of each specialty area can get a perspective of the store as a total unit. This promotes cooperation between the various functions.

It is doubtful if any stores can be found that operate exactly as Mazur suggested. On the other hand, it would be difficult to find a store whose organizational set up is not based upon Mazur's original idea.

Whatever the organizational plan, there are certain features that are universally found. Following is a brief discussion of the characteristics of the four functions suggested by Mazur.

The Merchandising Function

The function of the merchandising manager and his or her department is to maintain the inventory offered for sale in accordance with the requirements of the consumer. The people responsible for the merchandise function can be evaluated by comparing the stock of goods offered for sale with consumer demand. In many stores the sale of goods is also included among the responsibilities of the merchandise function.

Unquestionably, merchandising is the most important function of a retail store. A three-function organizational plan has even been suggested in which the merchandising function is responsible for sales promotion, publicity, and personnel, as well as for the normal merchandising responsibility. Under this plan the retail organization is focused on buying and selling with all other functions serving in a staff or advisory position. Figure 5–7 shows a "staff" person carrying out the testing of a product.

The merchandise manager is probably the most important executive in the store. That person's duties and the duties of the various departments under his or her control, as suggested by Mazur, are as follows:

1. Ensure that the major policy decisions affecting the store's image, price range, and quality, which are set up by top management, are properly carried out.
2. Control all buying and selling so that a cooperative effort is made to consistently give the store the image that is required by top management. For maximum effectiveness, their decisions must be uniformly met throughout all of the divisions and departments in the store.
3. Assist buyers to understand up-to-date market conditions and business trends.
4. Set up and administer a system for merchandise budgeting and control, which will accurately indicate the inventory position of the store at all times. This will aid buyers in their purchase planning and provide reports from which departmental effectiveness can be determined.
5. Give whatever assistance is necessary to individual buyers to help them in carrying out their individual duties.

Figure 5–7   Member of testing bureau testing a product. *Courtesy:* Williams-Sonoma

6. Cooperate fully with the sales promotion and publicity departments in carrying out sales promotion schemes, and ensure that the various merchandising departments cooperate as well.

7. Supervise the buying and selling activities of each department to ensure compliance with the policies that have been established.

8. Provide help to buyers in finding new resources.

It should be noted, that in most of today's department stores, the sales and stock positions have been moved to the store management division. This allows for the department managers in the branches to oversee the sales staff because the buyers rarely visit the branches let alone have time for sales management.

One of the characteristics of sound management is that the number of people reporting to a supervisor should never be so great that the supervisor is unable to give adequate personal attention to each one. As a department store grows in size and the number of departments in the store increases, it becomes impossible for the merchandise manager to give adequate attention to each area. It is customary in large stores to group similar departments into divisions under the authority of a divisional manager. For example, the womenswear division of a large department store would include all departments carrying women's clothing.

To carry out these responsibilities, the merchandise function uses staff positions. Figure 5–8 indicates the manner in which this may be done.

Some of the workers in specialized areas such as budgeting, merchandise statistics, fashion, comparison shopping, and testing serve the merchandise manager as advisors.

The Store Management Function

All of the functions related to the physical operation of the store are grouped together under the supervision of the store manager, superintendent, or director of store operations. Today, many retailers use "operations" as the heading for the store management

Figure 5–8   Organization of the staff positions in merchandising

function. The organization chart pictured in Figure 5–9 is not typical of the responsibilities of all store managers in that it limits the duty of the function to purely operating jobs. In many stores, such areas as customer claims and personnel fall under the supervision of the store manager. In stores that separate buying and selling, the sales responsibility generally is placed under the store management function.

The responsibilities of the various departments that fall under the supervision of the store manager are as follows:

Security Department

1. Detectives
2. Service shopping
3. Outside security agencies
4. Insurance

Workrooms

1. Clothing alterations
2. Merchandise repairs
3. Restaurants
4. Soda fountains
5. Beauty parlors

Service

1. Adjustments
2. Floor services
3. Cashiers
4. Wrapping

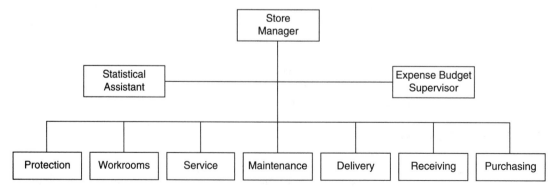

Figure 5–9   Organization of the store management function

Maintenance

1. Repairs
2. Maintenance of mechanical equipment
3. Ventilation
4. Heating
5. Housekeeping
6. Construction and alteration

Delivery

1. Delivery room
2. Central wrapping
3. Garages
4. Warehouses

Receiving

1. Receiving room
2. Marking
3. Checking
4. Stockrooms
5. Invoice and order

Purchasing

1. Equipment
2. Supplies

The Control Function

The control function, under the supervision of the controller or treasurer, is charged with the responsibility of safeguarding the company's assets. To ensure unbiased reporting, the control function should never be subordinate to any of the other functions. Instead, it should operate as a function in its own right or as a staff function reporting directly to the general manager. As is the case with other functions, the controller's duties are performed by a separate department. Figure 5–10 indicates the various departments that make up the control function of a typical department store.

The responsibilities of the control department are as follows:

Accounting Office

1. General accounting
2. Accounts payable

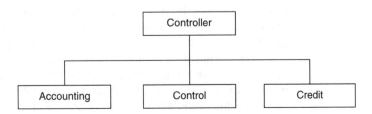

Figure 5–10   Organization of the control function

3. Insurance and taxes
4. Incoming mail
5. Payroll
6. Inventory planning and supervision
7. Reports

Control

1. Expense control
2. Budget control
3. Sales audit
4. Merchandise statistics and reports

Credit

1. Invoicing customers
2. Cashiers in credit office
3. Charge accounts
4. Credit authorization
5. Credit interviews
6. Deferred payments

The Publicity Function

Publicity, a function that is often referred to as sales promotion in some retail organizations, has as its chief a publicity (sales promotion) manager. The responsibilities of this function are sometimes divided into the three areas of advertising, visual merchandising, and special events.

The importance of this division is underscored and significantly discussed in Chapter 13, *Advertising and Promotion.*

BRANCH STORE ORGANIZATION

After World War II, great masses of urban population moved to the suburbs of the large metropolitan areas. These people were generally of the economic class that provided the downtown department store giants with an important segment of their customers. To offset the resulting sales loss, many large stores followed their customers to the suburbs by locating branch stores in prime suburban areas.

The branch store is one of several such units operating under a parent or flagship store, in many cases accounting for more than 50 percent of the total sales volume. In addition to increasing the sales volume, the typical branch operates more inexpensively than the main store. This savings is due in part to the branch store's use of many of the facilities of the parent, such as the computer department. Similarly, many of the branch store's office functions and much of its advertising can be taken over by the parent with a relatively small increase in overall expenses.

The organization of branch stores depends in large part on the size of the branch, the distance between the branch and the parent store, and the policy of top management concerning the splitting up of the responsibility for buying and selling between two individuals. It is likely that every branch store handles its own physical operations under an independent store manager. The personnel function of the branch is also generally under the independent control of the branch unless the distance from the parent is so small that the parent can take over the personnel responsibilities efficiently. The control function of the branch is generally split between the branch and the parent, with the branch performing the operating details and the parent doing the analyses and report making. Merchandising is managed and directed by the parent store.*

SPINOFF STORE ORGANIZATION

These specialty units that belong to department stores, operate in a manner similar to the chains. All of the decision-making is accomplished centrally, with each unit primarily serving as a sales center.

CHAIN STORE ORGANIZATION

Chain store organizations are among the most economical methods of retail distribution; the enormous volume that they do in similar types of merchandise permits the use of scientifically determined economical methods of performing many retailing functions. We have already discussed the independent store, in which each function is performed individually, and the branch store, in which some of the functions of groups of stores can be economically grouped at one location. The chain store is a further extension of the movement toward retailing centralization. Some of the characteristics of chain store organization are:

1. Centralization and control of most of the operating functions are administered in central or regional offices.
2. The operation is generally broken down into a greater number of functions than are generally found in department stores. Chain store operation requires such additional functions as real estate, warehousing, traffic, and transportation.
3. Carefully constructed reports must be filed frequently with the home office to permit adequate control of the various chain units.

The most important decision that must be made in the area of chain store organization is the amount of independence that should be granted to the managers of the individual chain outlets.

Centralization

The argument favoring a highly centralized operation, in which most of the decisions are made at the home office, is that the home office provides highly trained specialists for decision making who are likely to be more competent than the individual managers. For this reason, having a weak store manager need not result in a poorly run store. The most serious disadvantage of centralization is that the home office, often a great distance from a specific outlet, cannot understand the local problems involved. Conditions vary considerably from store to store, particularly when fashion merchandise is involved, and only the store manager is able to make decisions concerning the unique requirements of the store's particular clientele. Those favoring centralization

---

*This discussion of department store branches should not be confused with ownership groups of stores. These are groups of stores whose ownership is the same but whose operations are almost completely individualized.

argue that the home office experts are available for advice and that the close control of the home office tends to minimize errors.

Decentralization

As more responsibility and authority are delegated to the store managers, each store becomes more attuned to the requirements of its specific clientele. Moreover, managers, as their degree of control increases, have more incentive to improve their stores' profitability. True, a weak manager cannot be carried by a decentralized system, but the detailed system of control used by most chain store organizations permits the rapid identification of weak stores and quick corrective action.

The degree of decentralization depends in large part upon the type of product handled. The buying function of a food chain, for example, is apt to be more highly centralized than the buying function of a fashion merchandise chain. Some fashion oriented chains involve the store managers in merchandising decisions. While the buyer still purchases for all of the chain's units, each store manager may alter his or her merchandise mix.

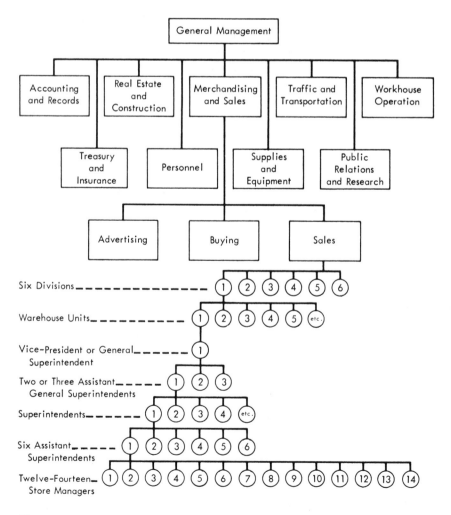

Figure 5–11 Organization of a grocery chain

Regional decentralization is found in almost all nationally organized chains. Under a regional plan, the units in the chain are organized into semi-independent groups according to geographical location. The organization chart of a nationally organized grocery chain which operates thousands of stores throughout the United States is pictured in Figure 5–11.

The annual gross sales volume of the chain is in excess of $5 billion. As may be seen on the chart, the company is divided into six geographical areas, each of which operates as a distinct entity, carrying out all the functions within its territory, including buying. Within each geographic district, the required number of warehouse units are operated. Each warehouse is supervised by a vice-president or general superintendent, who is aided by two or three assistant general superintendents. These assistant general superintendents supervise the activities of assistant superintendents, who operate with the help of six assistants, each of whom is responsible for 12 to 14 store managers.

TRENDS

Separation of Buying and Selling

The vast majority of merchants no longer group buying and selling activities under the merchandising function. The reason for this growing trend is that buyers and merchandisers are often too far removed from the stores to manage the sales staff effectively. In most major companies, selling functions have been moved to the management division.

Centralization Flourishes

Most chains make the vast majority of their decisions at a home office because it is efficient, guarantees uniformity of the operation, and is a cost saver. The individual stores are basically sales arenas and must take their orders from those in central management.

Demise of Some Staff Functions

Titles such as comparison shopper, fashion coordinator, and director of testing are no longer seen in department store organization charts. There is a trend toward using outside companies and consultants to provide these services as needed.

ACTION FOR THE INDEPENDENT RETAILER

Lack of proper organization can be costly to both small and large retailers. However, because an institution increases in complexity as it grows in size, the problem of proper organization is less compelling for the small operator. But considering the competitive disadvantages faced by independent retailers, this is one area in which they cannot afford to be lax. Any time two or more people cooperate toward the same goal, efficiency can be improved if their efforts are carefully organized. Each individual must be assigned and have a clear understanding of his or her duties and responsibilities, or some functions will be unnecessarily duplicated while other chores are not done at all. Naturally, in a small store, some functions must be shared, specialization is minimized, and clear lines of responsibility are difficult to establish. Certainly organization charts and job descriptions are not necessary in a small store, but no matter how informally the organization is run, its efficiency will be improved if the employees know exactly what is required of them.

IMPORTANT POINTS IN THE CHAPTER

1. No organization of two or more people can operate effectively without a clearly understood organization of the duties and responsibilities of each person. The larger the workforce, the more important clear lines of authority and duty become.
2. An organization chart is a device that indicates at a glance the duties and responsibilities of each person in the organization.
3. Large stores with many employees are able to limit the responsibilities of each employee to a specific area. This is called specialization and results in increased worker efficiency.
4. Small stores have too few workers to afford specialization. Consequently, each worker is responsible for more than one function. As a store grows in size, the opportunity for specialization increases.
5. Departmentalization is a form of specialization that includes all similar merchandise and services in separate categories or departments.
6. The first serious effort to organize department stores scientifically was done by Mazur, who divided the store into the four functions under the control of the merchandise manager, the controller, the publicity manager, and the store manager.
7. Variations of the Mazur Plan are found in all large stores. No two stores are organized in exactly the same way since organizational plans are constantly changing.
8. The physical operation of the store is the responsibility of the store management or operations function.
9. The control function includes all record keeping and the safeguarding of the company's assets by means of various bookkeeping devices.
10. Advertising, special events, and visual merchandising are the responsibility of the publicity function.
11. Branch stores may be operated independently, under their own department managers, or dependently, under the jurisdiction of the main store's department managers.
12. In chain store operation the functions are usually divided between the home office and the chain unit, with the merchandise, control, and part of the publicity function in the hands of the home office. There is a trend toward decentralizing chain operations with more responsibilities in the hands of the individual managers.

REVIEW QUESTIONS

1. What are the first steps in organizing a retail operation?
2. Define a line position on an organization chart. Give an example of a line position.
3. What is specialization? How does it affect operating efficiency?

4. List several advantages that may result from setting up departments according to similarity of merchandise. Give examples.

5. Explain the principal differences between the operational organization of a small department store and a small nondepartmentalized retailer.

6. What are the four major line functions of the Mazur Plan?

7. Describe the responsibilities of the merchandising manager.

8. What are the principal responsibilities of the store manager?

9. Explain the disadvantages of placing the control function under the responsibility of the merchandise manager.

10. Discuss the reasons for the increase in chain store operations.

11. What is the effect of central buying offices servicing both branch and parent on the division of buying and selling responsibilities?

12. Describe the characteristics of chain store organizations.

CASE PROBLEMS

Case Problem 1

Cee-Jay's is a small men's shop that has been operating successfully for several years in a suburban shopping center. The store's clientele has grown to a point at which the proprietor has decided to hire a high school student as a part-time stock clerk and another employee as a part-time bookkeeper. The organization chart of the present operation is pictured in Figure 5–3.

Question

1. Prepare a new organization chart that indicates the responsibilities of both the old and the new personnel.

Case Problem 2

Clifford's Inc. is a large, successful downtown department store that is constructing its first branch store at a suburban location 50 miles from the parent store. Top management has been meeting to determine the place of the new unit in the store's organization. The main store is organized under the four-function system pictured in Figure 5–6.

Question

1. Explain how you would reorganize the organization chart to include the branch. In your solution treat each of the following four functions separately, describing the work to be performed by branch personnel and the work to be performed by parent store personnel.
   1. Control function
   2. Publicity function
   3. Store managing function
   4. Merchandising function

Chapter 6
Human Resources Management

Photograph by Ellen Diamond

LEARNING OBJECTIVES

Upon completion of this chapter, the student should be able to:

1. List five functions of the human resources department.
2. Differentiate between in-store and outside sources of human resources supply, giving three examples of the latter.
3. Give five steps in a typical selection procedure.
4. List four areas of testing.
5. Discuss five advantages of a training program.
6. Write a short essay on human resources evaluations, indicating four reasons for this procedure.

THE INTERVIEW CALL-IN . . .

Pic'n Pay Stores is an organization of almost one thousand units that sells shoes. Based in Charlotte, North Carolina, each unit employs approximately five to fifteen employees. Although the store was extremely successful in terms of its merchandising strategy, significant improvement was needed to reduce the rate of employee turnover. Using the traditional recruitment methods, the company was realizing a worker turnover rate of 247 percent. New employees were constantly being hired, but the company found their tenure was extremely short. Without continuity of people in their labor force, Pic'n Pay wasn't able to staff its organization with capable individuals and wasn't able to find a sufficient number of people to promote to higher positions.

The new system that was introduced to the store vastly decreased the turnover figures. The rare was reduced to 124 percent! The process still begins with a potential candidate for employment visiting a shoe center, meeting with the manager, and filling out an application. In order to quickly assess the applicant, the manager conducts a preliminary interview, which lasts no more than a minute, during which he or she can evaluate the individual's appearance and ability to communicate, both so essential for success in retailing. Then the new procedure, known as HR Easy, takes over. It involves the use of a telephone interview. The applicant who passes the brief interview is given an 800 telephone number to call. Instead of a personnel manager speaking to the applicant, an automated process is used in which a computer asks questions and records responses. The one hundred-question interview may be taken at any time of the day or night, making it a convenient task for the interviewee. Yes or no responses are made by pushing "1" for yes, and "2" for no. One of the measurements used for assessment is the time in which it takes an applicant to respond. Five seconds are allowed for each answer, and if a pause is detected, a "red flag" is sent up requiring further analysis by a seasoned personnel officer. Each person who completes the automated portion is then interviewed, by telephone, by one of six interviewers at corporate headquarters. The purpose of the "live" interview is to dig deeper into those areas that presented potential problems as indicated by the automated portion of the interview. Each applicant's responses are then interpreted, and references are checked before a final decision is made.

A key to the success of the program is the training of the interviewers. They must be thoroughly knowledgeable in terms of the legal aspects of hiring and be attuned to the role played by psychology in the workplace. Those with the best interviewing skills and analytical abilities have regularly been able to identify those applicants with drug problems and other potential problems such as a history of theft.

In addition to making the recruitment system less costly and lowering the turnover rate, HR Easy has also reduced the amount of internal theft by 39 percent.

The organization chart provides the skeleton of an enterprise. Covering the bare skeleton with flesh and blood to give it life is the responsibility of the personnel department or human resources department, a name generally used in today's business community. It is up to the human resources department to provide the people who will make the organization chart work effectively. The bare chart, no matter how brilliantly conceived, can be effective only if capable people are employed to carry out the responsibilities set forth in the plan.

POSITION OF THE HUMAN RESOURCES DEPARTMENT IN THE ORGANIZATION

The importance of human resources management to the retail operation does not depend upon the size of the store. No store, regardless of its size, can operate effectively without capable people. In a small store the human resources function can easily be handled by the proprietor. However, the personnel problems of a major retailer become so massive that specialists are required to do the job efficiently.

Theoretically, the human resources department performs a staff, or advisory, function. For example, the salespersons it hires are sent to the selling departments for final approval. In practice, however, thanks to the human resources department's excellent record, the selling departments rarely dispute its judgment. In effect, with lower level employees, the final hiring decision is made by the human resources department. Consequently, while shown on most organization charts as staff (advisory), the human resources department sometimes actually performs a line (decision-making) function.

THE LAW AND HUMAN RESOURCES PRACTICES

In recent years, understanding of the law and how employees are protected has become necessary for human resources managers. On the federal level, government has concerned itself with such areas as salaries, hiring practices, and minority discrimination. Prior to the current legislation, retailers were guided by their own selection procedures and instincts without concern for penalties. Although such practices as race discrimination and lower pay for women were often standard practice, violations of the individual's rights were socially unacceptable as well as legally prohibited.

At the federal level of government, significant legislation has been enacted to protect citizens. The Fair Labor Standards Act addresses minimum salaries and hours per work week for employees in stores grossing more than $250,000 per year. The Equal Pay Act of 1963 requires equal pay for equal work. Title VII of the Civil Rights Act prohibits discrimination on the basis of race, color, and religion. The Age Discrimination in Employment Act protects individuals from bias in hiring because of age. In addition to this legislation many states and municipalities have enacted legislation for the further protection of their inhabitants.

With the passage of these laws and others, retailers have been required to keep records concerning their hiring practices, which could be legally scrutinized by governmental agencies. Unfair practices are frowned upon by these agencies and carry a variety of penalties.

FUNCTIONS OF THE HUMAN RESOURCES DEPARTMENT

The overall function of the human resources department is to provide the store with capable workers. This is done by performing duties in the following area:

1. Recruitment
2. Training
3. Evaluation
4. Compensation
5. Employee services and benefits
6. Labor relations

Recruitment

Before any steps can be taken to hire people, the human resources department must have a clear and exact understanding of the job to be filled. An analysis of every job in the store must be made to ensure that the characteristics of the person hired to do the job match the requirements of the job. Recruitment and training, to be effective, must be tailored to a specific set of requirements for each job. Those duties required for the job are called job specifications. The requirements of the individual are called people specifications.

Job Analyses

Scientific analysis of each job in the store must be cooperatively accomplished by the human resources department and the supervisors of each department. Then, a job description should be formally printed and should be available to the recruiting staff of the human resources department. (See Figure 6–1.) Jobs are usually analyzed by observation, questionnaire, and personal interviews with top and middle management. The analysis should include:

1. Description and title of job
2. The exact duties required by the job
3. Compensation range
4. Working conditions
5. Necessary training
6. Possibilities for advancement
7. Physical characteristics required of the workers
8. Mental ability required by the job, including desired educational level and experience
9. Personal characteristics required, such as appearance, maturity, initiative, and ability to get on with others

From the job analysis, the human resources department is able to formulate training programs and develop interview techniques and recruiting practices for each job. Furthermore, the job analysis focuses management's attention on working conditions and gives the prospective employee a clear picture of the job's responsibilities and of his or her chances for job improvement.

Sources of Human Resources Supply

One of the most important human resources problems of a large retail operation is the high rate of employee turnover. This is due, in large part, to relatively low wages, many young employees, a large number of part-timers, and the effect of the seasonal

```
                        MACY'S NEW YORK
                        JOB DESCRIPTION

        DIVISION  Operations — Selling Service

        TITLE  Return Control Clerical

        DEPARTMENT 51-354-41  Handbags


        TITLE OF IMMEDIATE SUPERVISOR  Department Manager


        BRIEF DESCRIPTION OF DUTIES:

        Sorts merchandise designated for return to vendor
        according to vendors classification, etc., and writes
        return-to-vendor forms indicating vendor's name and
        address, description and quantity of merchandise being
        returned, retail price and terms. Aforementioned
        information is copied from price tickets and vendor's
        terms book. As directed, may inspect merchandise in order
        to extract damaged items to be returned to vendor.

        As assigned may perform miscellaneous stockkeeping duties
        such as sorting merchandise by classification and price
        and placing such merchandise in reserve, assisting in
        arranging merchandise on selling floor, etc. Performs
        minor repairs on handbags such as connecting bag's handle
        to its body, tightening clasps, catches, etc.

        Maintains work area in a neat and orderly condition.

        Guides new employees in the performance of their work.

        Performs other related duties as assigned.
```

Figure 6–1 Job description—return control clerical. *Courtesy:* Macy's Herald Square, New York, NY

nature of retailing on personnel needs. Whatever the causes of turnover, it is a constant problem that can be solved only by establishing sources of supply that will provide workers when they are needed.

In-store Sources.   The high rate of retail employee turnover is not restricted to sales personnel. Top and mid-management jobs are constantly becoming available through turnover and expansion. Most stores still prefer to fill such jobs by promotion. Moving people up to a higher job builds morale by indicating that a person who has been in the store for a while will not be passed over for promotion by an outsider. Since managerial training programs are expensive, it is important that a store select managers who are not likely to leave.

The in-service promotion of one person opens a chain of promotions to the workforce. For example, the promotion of a buyer to the position of assistant merchandising manager may be followed by the promotion of an assistant buyer to buyer, a department manager to assistant buyer, and a salesperson to department manager. In each case the new job holder is a person whose personality, skill, and ability are well known to management. The most sophisticated human resources department cannot learn as much about a new job applicant as the information available from the employment records of an in-service applicant. The chance for a happy marriage between worker and job improves as the information about the worker improves.

Stores depending upon promotions from within to fill vacancies have relatively simple recruitment problems, since they need only worry about hiring for the lowest-level jobs. Although the requirements of low-level jobs are modest, care must be taken that some entry jobs are filled by people of high qualification who will become the raw material for later in-service promotions.

Another advantage of in-service promotions is the ability of a store to attract highly qualified people for lower-level jobs. A store with a reputation for having a good promotion policy will get more high-quality applicants than an organization in which promotions are rarely given. Such stores as the Edison Brothers chains mention in-service promotions in the brochures printed to attract job applicants.

Although it is generally agreed that in-store promotions merit a great deal of attention, it should be understood that a policy that is strictly based 100 percent on promotion from within can actually act as a deterrent for new ideas. Very often this policy of inbreeding results in a reaffirming of "old hat" ideas. It is desirable for the growth and vitality of the organization to recruit managerial talent from the other retail orientations; these people can often bring needed fresh ideas into the company. A blending of applicants from within the organization and from outside sources is most beneficial.

Outside Sources.   Among the outside sources for personnel are advertisements, employment agencies (both private and governmental), schools, and colleges, and transient applicants (persons coming directly to the store for work). Since retailing is highly seasonal, it is necessary for the human resources departments to know exactly which outside sources to use for the type of personnel required.

1. *Want ads.* Advertising for help in the local newspapers is probably the most effective method of attracting large numbers of job applicants. The disadvantage of using this source is that there is no preliminary screening for qualifications. Applicants supplied by any of the other sources mentioned have had some of their qualifications checked before coming to the store. In answer to an ad there is frequently a deluge of applicants, many of whom lack necessary qualifications. The want ads are most useful when large numbers of relatively unqualified workers are needed. Two types of ads are used, blind ads in which only the job is listed and the store's identity is concealed by using a post office box number, and open ads that indicate both the position and the company name. Some retailers employ both techniques or choose the one that is believed to be most appropriate for the particular company.

2. *Employment agencies.* Private and government-sponsored employment agencies are available to supply needed personnel. Employment agencies do not produce as great a number of applicants as advertising. However, the agency matches the applicant's qualifications with the job's requirements and thus saves a considerable amount of the human resources department's time in interviewing.

   Many employment agencies specialize in specific types of employees, such as office workers or managerial executives. Human resources departments should keep records of the various employment agencies in their areas, so they can fill sudden vacancies in a minimum amount of time.

3. *Schools and colleges.* Student recruiting generally begins at the high school level. Most high schools and colleges maintain a job placement office to help find part-time employment for interested students. It is important for the human resources department to keep close contact with the neighboring educational institutions even in times of slow recruitment. The seasonal nature of retail recruitment makes it imperative that large numbers of part-time people be available when they are needed.

Many schools and colleges include cooperative work experience programs among their course offerings. Under this plan, retailing students are given the opportunity to spend part of their school days at the work for which they are being trained. This affords the students an opportunity to learn under actual business conditions, while helping the store fill needed positions. Perhaps the most important feature of the cooperative work experience program is that it gives the store the opportunity to work with the student before an actual hiring decision must be made. Upon their graduation, the store is able to employ those students who have been found to be satisfactory under actual working conditions.

Many of the larger stores compete for college graduates. It is felt that these people will eventually fill the top and mid-management positions. Personnel managers regularly attend college career days specifically for this purpose.

Miscellaneous Sources.   There are additional means of recruiting qualified personnel in addition to the foregoing.

1. *Recommendations.* The use of current employees to help find new people is common. Posting job vacancies on the bulletin board or circulating the information by word of mouth generally results in job applications from friends and relatives of the working staff. One of the causes of job turnover, particularly during the first week, is that the job is not what the newly hired worker expected. Hiring by recommendation may reduce turnover, since applicants come to the store fully informed by their friends or relatives about what to expect from the job.

2. *Transient applicants.* Certainly the cheapest and probably the most widely used means by which jobs are filled are casual (transient) applicants. These are people who show up at the employment department, fill out an application, and either go through the employment procedure if there is work available, or have the information placed on file for later use in the event that no job is presently available.

Selection Procedures

A series of procedures must be undertaken by the human resources department to screen individuals and ensure a proper match of applicant and job requirements. Not only must this process provide the right worker for the job to be performed, but it must also make certain that attention is paid to the prospect's integrity. With the continuing increase in internal pilferage, management must concern itself with careful screening procedures. Management has any number of devices available to determine honesty. One is the checking of references, which will be discussed later. Some companies employ the use of drug testing in their selection procedure. Whatever the process used for screening applicants, care must be exercised to avoid costly errors in employment. Only careful attention, without the pitfalls of hasty decisions, can provide satisfactory employees.

It should be understood that not all stores follow the same procedures. Moreover, the procedures followed within a store may vary from job to job. Thus an applicant for a low-level job might not require reference checking, whereas a person interested in a managerial position would undergo a careful system of reference checking. In addition, the order in which the selection procedures are performed may vary, with supply and demand often the determining factor in how carefully a prospective worker is screened.

The typical steps in the selection procedures of most retail stores are (1) resume review, (2) application form, (3) preliminary interview, (4) checking references, (5) testing, and (6) final interview.

Resume Review.   Especially for mid-management positions or higher, the resume is an important screening device. It enables the company to examine the applicant's credentials and determine whether or not an interview is appropriate.

Application Form.   Most stores require that an application form be filled in. The purposes it serves include:

1. It obtains necessary information from the applicant.
2. It provides a basis upon which the interview can be conducted.
3. If the applicant is hired, it becomes part of his or her permanent file for future reference when necessary.
4. If the applicant is not hired, it may be kept for future use when a worker is needed.

The information found on an application consists of identification data (name, address, personal history), education (schools attended, degrees achieved), prior employment record (jobs held since graduation, reasons for termination), and references (persons to be contacted for further information). In recent years, to eliminate bias, anti-discrimination laws have forbidden the use of photographs and questions relating to race, age, marital status, and religion. The Macy's application pictured in Figure 6–2 is an example of one that was used at one time, and asked for information such as date of birth, age, and marital status, all of which is no longer permitted on job applications. Although Macy's no longer uses this particular application, it is included for use as a comparison to a more recent type, pictured in Figure 6–3.

The prime function of the application is to match applicants with job requirements. Consequently, it must be carefully constructed.

Preliminary Interview.   The preliminary interview, sometimes referred to as a "rail interview" (it is a short, stand-up interview that may be done over the railing of the human resources department), has the function of correcting the application and weeding out those applicants in whom the store is not interested. It is usually used for those applying for lower-level positions. The preliminary interview should be conducted by an experienced person who is thoroughly acquainted with available positions and the requirements for such positions. Although the preliminary interview must be short, time should not be saved at the cost of efficiency. This may result in qualified people being turned away and jobs given to those of mediocre abilities. Weeding out undesirable applicants requires a great deal of tact. Disappointing people without proper regard for their feelings may cause a loss of goodwill to the store. Some stores give the rail interview before requiring the application to be filled out. This is undoubtedly an economy measure, but most progressive stores give every job applicant the right to an interview and an application, to ensure customer goodwill.

A successful preliminary interview should give important information on the applicant's communication skills and appearance.

Checking References.   Checking the background information given on the application is time-consuming and expensive. Therefore, it is often ignored in cases of applicants for low-level jobs. The references given are from friends of the prospective employee who have no experience with the applicant's work habits. It is unusual to get a bad response from a reference supplied by an applicant. Thus, retailers must exercise caution when checking references.

An applicant's background can be more accurately checked by contacting previous employers. Although this can be done by mail, a telephone call can be more informative. The information supplied from former employers on work habits, attitudes, and quantity and quality of a prospect's work can be much more important in the hiring decision than the knowledge gathered by the application form or interview. With all of the expense incurred as the result of internal theft, managers who ignore careful

F. 240A-4-67

APPLICATION FOR EMPLOYMENT

MACY'S
HERALD SQUARE

DO NOT WRITE IN THIS SPACE
P 1 2 3 4
E 1 2 3 4
R 1 2 3 4

IN THE EVENT THAT YOU ARE EMPLOYED THIS BECOMES PART OF YOUR PERSONNEL RECORD, THEREFORE IT IS IMPORTANT THAT YOU ENTER ALL INFORMATION NEATLY, ACCURATELY AND COMPLETELY.

Last Name (Print Clearly)		First Name	Middle Name	Maiden Name	Husband's or Wife's First Name
Number and Street		City, Postal Zone and State		Tel. No.	Social Security No.

| Date of Birth | Age* | Single ☐   Divorced ☐   Separated ☐ | No. of Dependents | Height | Weight | American   Yes ☐ |
| | | Married ☐   Widowed ☐ | | Ft.   in. | | Citizen   No ☐ |

* APPLICABLE LAW PROHIBITS DISCRIMINATION IN EMPLOYMENT BECAUSE OF RACE, COLOR, RELIGION, SEX, NATIONAL ORIGIN OR AGE.

Schedule Full Time ☐ Evenings Other:	Position Sales ☐ Other:	State Salary Desired (Optional)
Preferred: Mid-Day ☐ and Saturdays ☐	Desired: Office ☐	

Relative in Yes ☐	If so, in which	Name of	Read ad in which	Referred to us by Macy Employee
our employ? No ☐	store or dept.	Relative	paper	Name of Employee

Have you ever been employed by Macy's before?	Yes ☐ No ☐	If yes, under what name were you employed?	Position and Dept.	Dates Employed

EDUCATION

SCHOOL	NUMBER OF YEARS	GRADUATED YES	NO	NAME AND LOCATION OF SCHOOL	MAJOR SUBJECT OR SPECIALIZATION	DATES ATTENDED
Grammar						
High School						
College						
Other						

PREVIOUS EMPLOYMENT

PLEASE ACCOUNT FOR ALL TIME SINCE LEAVING SCHOOL, INCLUDING CURRENT EMPLOYMENT AND PERIODS OF UNEMPLOYMENT. STATE IF ANY OF THESE EMPLOYERS ARE RELATED TO YOU.

DATES EMPLOYED	BUSINESS NAME AND ADDRESS	JOB TITLE AND DUTIES	REASON FOR LEAVING	SALARY
From: To:	Last or Present Employer Address			
From: To:	Previous Employer Address			
From: To:	Previous Employer Address			
From: To:	Previous Employer Address			
From: To:	Previous Employer Address			
From: To:	Previous Employer Address			

PLEASE ANSWER ALL QUESTIONS ON REVERSE SIDE

Referred by	Test Scores	Second Interview

Figure 6-2 Application for employment (no longer in use). *Courtesy:* Macy's, Herald Square, New York, NY

GENERAL INFORMATION

No of children,
if any, and ages_____

Date and purpose of
last physical exam._____

Names of personal aquaintances who work for Macy's

_____

_____

_____

Husband's (or Wife's)
Occupation_____

Business
Address_____

Father's
Occupation_____

Business
Address_____

Were you ever arrested (other than Traffic Violations)?

    Yes ☐   No ☐

if yes, indicate date_____

place_____

offense_____

    Were you acquitted ☐   convicted ☐

In case of accident notify:

Name_____Relationship_____

Home
Address_____ Tel.
        Street and City No._____

Business
Address_____ Tel.
        Street and City No._____

Please list any hobbies, training or work experience you have not indicated on the other side of application.

U. S. MILITARY RECORD

Branch of Service	Rank or Rate	Duties or Assignment	Date Inducted	Date of Separation or Discharge

Are you a member of a U. S. Service Reserve Corps?   Yes ☐   No ☐   Army ☐   Navy ☐

Inactive?_____Active?_____   Marine ☐   Air Force ☐

DO NOT WRITE BELOW THIS LINE

Test for:	FT ☐	PT ☐	SO ☐	H.B ☐	R	(	)
☐ SALES		☐ M.C./CHECKER		OTHER:			
☐ CLERICAL		☐ M.C. CASHIER			C	(	)
☐ TEL. ORD. BD.		☐ STOCK/PACKER			P	(	)

AGREEMENT

I hereby certify that to the best of my knowledge all statements I have made on this application are true and correct. I understand that any misrepresentation of facts on this application is sufficient cause for dismissal.

I understand that certain departments have union shop agreements and that if I am assigned to one of these departments I must abide by the terms and conditions set forth in the collective bargaining agreement applicable to that department.

I agree to observe all rules of the store and faithfully perform whatever duties may be assigned to me.

Signature_____   Witness_____

Figure 6–2   *(continued)*

A&S

APPLICATION FOR EMPLOYMENT

ABRAHAM & STRAUS IS AN EQUAL OPPORTUNITY EMPLOYER M/F

PLEASE PRINT ALL INFORMATION

Store	Date
Position Desired	

Last Name	First	Initial	Soc. Sec. No.	

Indicate If You Are
☐ Under 18
☐ Over 70

Home Phone Number	Business Phone Number
( )	( )

LIST CURRENT ADDRESS (IF LESS THAN THREE YEARS GIVE TWO PREVIOUS ADDRESSES)

Present Address	City/State/Zip	Years There Month/Year
		From ....
Address	City/State/Zip	Years There Month/Year
		From ... . To ....
Address	City/State/Zip	Years There Month/Year
		From .... To ....

Have You Ever Worked At Abraham & Straus Before ☐ Yes ☐ No	If Yes, Give Dates: From: .... To	Have You Ever Applied Here Before? ☐ Yes ☐ No If So, When ....
Store Location	Department	Position

Have You Changed Your Name Since Last Working At A&S? ☐ Yes ☐ No	If Yes, What Was Your Previous Name

Do You Have Relatives Working At A&S? ☐ Yes ☐ No	If Yes, Give Name, Relationship, And Store

Have You Ever Been Convicted Of A Crime? ☐ Yes* ☐ No	*If Yes, Please Ask For And Complete Form No. X100

EMPLOYMENT DATA

I Am Seeking (Check One)	I Am Seeking (Check One)
☐ FULL TIME	☐ REGULAR ☐ TEMPORARY
☐ PART TIME	FROM (DAY/MONTH) ..../.................... TO (DAY/MONTH) ..../....................

Approximate Store Open Hours For Each Day Are Shown. Mark Days You Are Available. If Not Available For Store Open Hours, Indicate Your Availability.	S 12–6	M 9:45–9:30	T 9:45–9:30	W 9:45–9:30	T 9:45–9:30	F 9:45–9:30	S 9:45–9:30

EDUCATION

NAME OF SCHOOL AND ADDRESS	MAJOR AREA OF STUDY	FROM (Month/Year)	TO (Month/Year)	GRADUATED (Yes/No)	DEGREE
High School					
College or University					
Trade School					

Are You Attending School Now ☐ Yes ☐ No	If Yes, Name Of School & Address	Major Area Of Study	Year Of Graduation

S0555 (11/83)

(OVER)

Figure 6–3   Application for employment. *Courtesy:* A&S

WORK HISTORY: LIST LAST SEVEN YEARS OF EMPLOYMENT, STARTING WITH LAST EMPLOYER FIRST (If More Space Needed Paper is Available)

DATE	EMPLOYER		JOB CLASSIFICATION & SUPERVISOR	BRIEF OUTLINE OF DUTIES
From (Mo/Yr.)	Name		Position	
	Address		Reason For Leaving	
To (Mo/Yr.)	Salary Start (Wk/Mo)	Salary End	Phone Number	
From (Mo/Yr.)	Name		Position	
	Address		Reason For Leaving	
To (Mo/Yr.)	Salary Start (Wk/Mo)	Salary End	Phone Number	
From (Mo/Yr.)	Name		Position	
	Address		Reason For Leaving	
To (Mo/Yr.)	Salary Start (Wk/Mo)	Salary End	Phone Number	
From (Mo/Yr.)	Name		Position	
	Address		Reason For Leaving	
To (Mo/Yr.)	Salary Start (Wk/Mo)	Salary End	Phone Number	

Are You A United States Citizen ☐ Yes ☐ No   **If Not Do You Have The Right To Work In The United States** ☐ Yes ☐ No

If Not Do You Have The Right To Remain Permanently In The United States ☐ Yes ☐ No   **Alien Registration Number** ....

HOW DID YOU HAPPEN TO APPLY AT ABRAHAM & STRAUS? PLEASE CHECK AND FILL IN WHERE APPLICABLE.

☐ NEWSPAPER ....   ☐ EMPLOYEE REFERRAL (NAME) ....

☐ OWN INITIATIVE ....   ☐ OTHER ....

☐ EMPLOYMENT AGENCY (NAME) ....

PLEASE READ CAREFULLY BEFORE SIGNING

THE INFORMATION GIVEN BY ME ON THIS APPLICATION IS COMPLETE AND ACCURATE. I UNDERSTAND THAT ANY FALSE STATEMENT IS SUFFICIENT GROUNDS FOR IMMEDIATE TERMINATION.
A&S MAY REQUEST A CONSUMER REPORT IN CONNECTION WITH THIS APPLICATION AND FOR THE PURPOSE OF AN UPDATE, RENEWAL OR OTHER EXTENSION OF EMPLOYMENT. UPON MY REQUEST, A&S WILL FURNISH ME WITH THE NAME AND ADDRESS OF THE CONSUMER REPORTING AGENCY THAT FURNISHED THE REPORT, IF ANY.
I UNDERSTAND THAT ON MY LEAVING A&S ANY MONIES OWED BY ME TO A&S MAY BE WITHHELD FROM MY FINAL PAY CHECK.
I UNDERSTAND THAT I AM ON A SIX MONTH PROBATIONARY PERIOD. I ALSO UNDERSTAND THAT MY FAILURE TO COMPLY WITH A&S POLICIES AND PROCEDURES IS GROUNDS FOR MY IMMEDIATE TERMINATION.

THIS APPLICATION WILL REMAIN FOR THREE MONTHS.

_____   _____
SIGNATURE   DATE

PLEASE DO NOT WRITE BELOW THIS LINE

Comments:

Interviewers Name .... Date ....

Comments:

Supervisor Name .... Date ....

JOB GRADE	WORKED FOR A&S BEFORE		ACTUAL WKLY Starting Salary	BASED ON	FTE RATE	PAY CODE	WKCTR & DEPT.	REPORTING DATE	CLASS TYPE
	YES	NO							☐ SALES
									☐ S/SUPP
									☐ DIRECT

Figure 6–3   *(continued)*

reference checking could pay dearly in the long run. A discussion on internal pilferage in Chapter 9, *Loss Prevention,* underscores the need for checking references.

Testing.   At best, the questionnaire gives raw facts that cannot always be verified, and the results of the interview are little more than the personal attitudes of the interviewer. In an effort to get more objective information about prospective workers, many large retailers are turning to various types of testing. Among those used are tests of ability, aptitude, intelligence, and personality.

1. *Ability testing.* For many jobs, ability testing has always been used to rate performance. For example, a secretary is rarely hired without some sort of a typing or stenography test. Aside from some nervousness on the part of the applicant, for which allowances may be made, such tests give an accurate indication of secretarial skills. Wrapping, filing, and machine operation are other areas in which skills may be effectively tested. The major disadvantage of such testing is a lack of standardization. Different applicants may be given different tests under a variety of testing conditions. For best effect, ability testing should be scientifically administered, with all applicants given the same test under the same conditions.

2. *Aptitude testing.* Aptitude tests are generally written and are used to determine an applicant's capacity for a certain type of work. While most aptitude tests are designed for testing mechanical ability, work has been done on the design of aptitude tests for salespeople.

3. *Intelligence testing.* Some large department stores feel that intelligence testing is important to successful employment and require all applicants to take a written intelligence test. They believe that every job classification should be filled by a person having an I.Q. falling within a certain range. All people falling below the minimum I.Q. are ruled out as not having enough intelligence. Those whose scores fall above the maximum are ruled out, since it is believed that they would become bored with the job and quit or perform ineffectively. Intelligence testing is not widespread among retailers. Probably fewer than 25 percent of the stores require such tests.

4. *Personality testing.* There is little doubt that such personality characteristics as friendliness and sociability are advantageous to a salesperson. There are few who would argue the premise that knowledge of personality is important in personnel placing. However, there are excellent arguments to the effect that personality tests have little or no validity. The fact is that none of the tests, with the possible exception of skill tests such as typing, are as yet anywhere near perfection. Although testing has a very promising future in personnel work, the tests available are far from being foolproof instruments. The greatest disadvantage of personnel testing is that too much reliance may be placed on the results. An applicant's test scores are valuable, but should only be used as one of many factors in making a decision.

5. *Drug testing.* Many companies now use drug testing prior to employment or during employment. The tests are generally administered, during employment, at random and at unannounced times. Its usage has helped weed out undesirable employees. Stores like Home Depot make drug testing mandatory for all applicants.

Final Interview.   After all of the preliminary interviewing, application completing, reference checking, and testing have been completed, the final interview is held. This interview may be conducted by a senior interviewer or the head of the department for which the applicant is slated to work. It has the dual purpose of informing the applicant of the duties and responsibilities that will be required by the job and of permitting the interviewer to judge the applicant's knowledge and personality in relation to the specific job opening.

Some stores require that a physical examination be taken by all new employees. It would be wise for all stores to adopt this requirement. Retail work is difficult and can only be performed by persons who are physically fit. Screening out those who do not have the physical stamina for the work reduces personnel turnover. To offset the high cost of physical examinations, many stores require their new employees to have their own doctors fill out a medical form. Many insurance carriers require physical examinations for prospective employees.

Training Employees

A new worker in a small store requires very little time in which to fit into the organization. Soon after an employee is hired, the proprietor introduces the worker to existing personnel. After a few days the worker learns the details of the job's responsibilities and working conditions. In a large store, the orientation of new employees is done in a more formal manner. New employees may be given guided tours of the store, lectures on store regulations, and literature on the history of the store. (See Figure 6–4.) Learning about the store helps the new employee "feel at home" and is a part of the training program.

The training program itself can be informal, as in the case of a small store where a new employee is broken in by an experienced worker. It can be short, as it would be for a new unloader in the receiving department of a large store, who might merely have to be told where to put the cartons taken from the truck. In short, every new job requires a training period that is adapted to the specific job.

The training of employees in a large store is generally the responsibility of the human resources department. (See Figure 6–5.) It is an expensive procedure, both in terms of the time spent by personnel people and the nonproductive time spent by the employee during the training period. Since employees are fully paid during this nonproductive period, the expense of training employees is considerable. A great deal of pressure is put on the human resources department, since management insists upon demonstrable results in return for the expense involved. The following are some of the advantages of a training program:

Figure 6–4 New employee orientation literature.
Courtesy: Macy's, Herald Square, New York, NY

Figure 6–5   A kit complete with training aids for new employees. *Courtesy:* Macy's, Herald Square, New York, NY

1. As a worker becomes more skilled at the job, both the quantity and quality of the work increase. A training program, by shortening the learning process, brings a worker to a high competence level much more quickly than could be done by informal learning.

2. As the productivity of individual workers increases, fewer employees are needed to handle any given volume of work. The training program lessens the time during which a new worker doesn't carry his or her weight, and by increasing worker skills, the total workforce may be decreased.

3. There is a best way to perform every task. Employees cannot be expected to learn this way by themselves. An organization that has set up standardized procedures must be sure that all of its employees are trained to follow these procedures. Work that is not done in conformity with standardized procedures is apt to lead to errors and customer dissatisfaction.

4. A well-trained worker needs less supervision than a poorly trained person. The worker's knowledge and skill reduce dependence on supervisors. This permits a reduction in the amount of supervisory help needed and frees supervisors for other tasks.

5. The well-trained employee is confident and capable, feels secure at the job, and has good chances for advancement. A poorly trained employee, on the other hand, is nervous, lacks confidence, and, as a result, frequently hates the work and is likely to quit.

6. Employees who have benefited from an expensive training program are made to feel that the store has a high regard for their potential. In addition, during the training period, the training personnel always show the store in its best light and attempt to improve morale.

Persons to Be Trained

Since the training program must be given to employees with a wide range of prior experience, the programs given must vary with the needs of the individual workers. Generally speaking, training groups may be broken down as follows:

Sales Personnel.   The training of sales personnel is usually done in two or three full days or spread over a few hours a day for several weeks. The work includes a full explanation of store policies concerning employees, such as dress regulations, employee discounts, and absence from work. In addition, such store procedures as policy on returned merchandise, credit handling, use of point-of-sale cash register terminals, and C.O.D. sales are explained at length. Product information on the goods to be sold is given by the buyer or department manager.

Many retail organizations believe that the training of salespeople is the most important of all the training programs and provide handbooks that can be studied by the new employees at their leisure. The actual course work usually includes such up-to-date teaching procedures as role-playing, slides and movies, and programmed instruction.

Large stores frequently call in outside experts to assist in their training programs. Since this can be an expensive procedure, particularly for smaller stores, it is not unusual for small and medium-sized stores to band together in setting up a training center. By doing this, they minimize the cost of expensive training to the individual store.

The sponsor system is commonly used for breaking in new personnel for both the selling and nonselling departments. Under this system an experienced employee is given the responsibility of greeting new workers and introducing them to the existing staff, explaining departmental procedures, giving product information and the location of stock, and improving the new person's selling techniques. It is the sponsor's further task to periodically evaluate his or her charges and try to keep the new employees' morale at a high level. In most stores the sponsor receives an increase in salary for these efforts.

Nonselling Personnel.   Inexperienced nonselling or support personnel such as stock clerks and office workers have somewhat different training needs from salespeople. In the area of store policy concerning employees (employee benefits, discounts, and so on) the educational needs are the same for all employees and they can be taught together, either by lecture, handbook, or some combination of the two. Training in the duties of the specific nonselling jobs is usually done in the department by the sponsor system. Generally, there are too few nonselling people hired at any one time for formalized class training. Care should be taken that support personnel are being properly trained; much customer dissatisfaction is caused by errors made by nonselling personnel.

Follow-up Training.   Progressive retailers are becoming increasingly aware of the fact that job capability depends upon constant educational growth. Brief introductory training rarely results in maximum job capability. New methods and questions are always coming up, and there must be an occasional meeting for discussion.

The training of regular personnel generally takes the form of individual conferences or small discussion seminars. At such small group meetings the teacher does little more than guide discussion. The workers discuss their problems, suggest new approaches, and arrive at conclusions. When new methods or procedures are to be initiated, the instructor must take a more central position.

Follow-up training is eagerly sought by workers anxious for promotion. It provides them with an opportunity to improve the job skills upon which their promotion will be based.

Executive Training.   Since most large retailers fill many executive vacancies by promoting people from within the store, it is vital that they have well-trained persons available. This can be achieved by means of an executive training program. (See Figure 6–6.)

Macy*s Executive Development Program

"RETAILING'S MOST COVETED SHEEPSKIN IS STILL AWARDED ON HERALD SQUARE
*Alma Mater of what is probably the most distinguished alumni in American
business generally, and in retailing specifically, is no duly accredited college
or university. It's a store. It's Macy*s"*

—From Women's Wear Daily,
—the trade paper with the country's largest circulation

ON THE JOB TRAINING

While there is some "classroom" work, Macy*s training is primarily learning
by doing. Theory is translated into action, as it always is at Macy*s.

If you are selected for Macy*s Development Program, you will be placed on
the company's payroll as an executive as soon as you report for work. During
the first 5 weeks, you will be in the company's special Sales Supervision program
that includes:

Executive orientation and store tour	*Introduction to sales supervision*
Conference on executive leadership	*Meeting on budgeting and scheduling*
Preparation for sales training	*Conference on safety*
Introduction to assigned selling area	*Practice supervision*
Sales training	*Discussion of job reviews*
Conference on employment practices	*Merchandising procedures*
Seminar on shortages	*Conference on adjustment policy*
Role of the sales manager	*You and your job*
Conference on labor relations	

Figure 6–6   Macy's executive development program. *Courtesy:* Macy's, Herald Square, New York, NY

EXECUTIVE CONFERENCE PROGRAM

A series of conferences with top executives of the company will be scheduled during your first 3 months. The subjects and the speakers might be as follows:

"The Store Division": President of the Division
"Function of Divisional Personnel": Vice President for Personnel
"Function of Divisional Control": Vice President for Control
"Merchandising Policies": Vice President for Merchandising
"Merchandising for Volume and Profit": Vice President and Store Manager
"Function of Divisional Sales Promotion": Vice President for Sales Promotion and Public Relations
"Function of Divisional Operations": Vice President for Operations
"Development of the Division to a Multi-Store Group": Vice President for Stores

COUNSELLING

Throughout the Sales Supervision program, you will be assigned to an experienced supervisor who will provide direction and answer your questions about the work and your progress. During your early development, the Executive Personnel Department provides continuous counselling on your career.

PERFORMANCE REVIEWS

After completing each training assignment, your supervisor will appraise your over-all performance. The supervisor's recommendation as to the kind of responsibility that most suits you will be discussed with you, and areas of work where you may need strengthening. At all times, you will know how you are doing.

POSITION ROTATION

During your early days at Macy's, every effort will be made to make your work practical rather than theoretical or academic. Your assignments will be varied, and selected on the basis of your progress. We are anxious to find out as soon as possible whether your future with us lies in the world of fashion, basic merchandise, hard or soft goods, or in store management. Naturally, you will have a say in this, too, because you will soon discover for yourself which area you find most interesting.

Figure 6–6   *(continued)*

The training of executives generally includes conferences, sponsors, work-study arrangements with colleges, evening courses at colleges, rotation of trainees in various departments, correspondence courses, and lectures. The training period for executives may take several years to accomplish. The individuals to be given executive training may be found among present employees or, more often, recruited from among college graduating classes. The earning of a college degree either prior to or during executive training is often mandatory.

Employee Evaluation

If an organization is to be assured of maintaining a high standard of employee performance, it must evaluate its employees periodically. Some of the reasons for employee evaluation are as follows:

1. Nothing encourages workers more than rewards for good performance. Only by an evaluation of an employee's performance can management make a fair decision on the rate of pay to which a person is entitled. Evaluation that is used to set fair salaries becomes an important source of employee good will.

2. Constant employee evaluation identifies those employees who are deserving of promotion and who would do well in an advanced job. Without proper evaluation, promotion tends to be haphazard. This can result in poor supervisory performance.

3. If employees are to improve their effectiveness, they must be informed of their areas of weakness. Such knowledge enables them to seek out means of improvement by training courses, self-help, or conferences with knowledgeable people.

4. All stores have on their payrolls people who have the necessary qualifications for the job, but lack the interest or capacity to meet the required standards of proficiency. Job evaluations are an aid in the process of weeding out such individuals.

Small Store Employees

Probably the most effective job evaluation is done by the proprietory of a small store. Through constant contact with all of the store's employees, the proprietor has thorough knowledge of their merits and shortcomings. The basic disadvantage of evaluations of this kind is the likelihood that the boss's prejudices will make the evaluation personal rather than scientific. As a result, bosses might promote the persons they like rather than the ones best fitted for the jobs.

Large Store Employees

Large retail organizations evaluate their employees by using printed forms at periodic intervals. Figure 6–7 shows an example of an evaluation report. It is usually filled out by the buyer or department head, and at a meeting of the employee, the supervisor, and a human resources department representative, before being forwarded to the human resources department.

Outside shopping service organizations are used by many stores to evaluate salespeople. These people, posing as ordinary customers, prepare a "shopping report," which evaluates such characteristics as a salesperson's courtesy, ability, grooming, and compliance with the store's procedures.

Employee evaluation, if poorly handled, can be destructive to morale. Employees must be clearly made to understand that the purpose of their evaluation is not to hurt them but to improve their effectiveness and, by so doing, to improve their jobs and their pay.

Compensation

Probably the most important consideration of a person looking for a job is the amount of salary being offered. For persons on the job, a fair compensation plan is one of the important keys to high morale. It is likely that the principal cause of employee turnover is the worker's ability to find a better-paying job elsewhere. In short, the maintenance of a sound compensation policy is a vital responsibility of the human resources department. Unlike the areas of recruitment and training, where that department serves in a line or decision-making function, its responsibility in setting compensation policy is strictly staff or advisory. However, top management who make compensation decisions rely heavily on the human resources department for advice and planning in this area.

Requirements of a Compensation System

To be effective, the compensation plan must be drawn up with the following factors in mind:

1. The level of earnings should be such that the employees can maintain a decent standard of living. Salaries must be equal or slightly better than the salaries offered by competitors if a high-quality workforce is to be maintained.

2. An effective earnings plan must be so easily understood by the employees that they can predict their weekly earnings with accuracy. A simple earnings plan has the additional benefit of reducing the office help required to make up the payroll.

3. Earnings must be keyed to productivity. The worker must be made to feel that increased effort will result in increased compensation.

4. Similar jobs should receive similar compensation, and the level of compensation should be fair. Of equal importance, employees must be made to believe that they are being fairly paid.

5. Since employee living expenses are stable from week to week, their salary requirements should be paid regularly. When salary rewards are offered as an incentive to better work, they must be paid promptly if they are to maintain their effectiveness. Salaries should be paid on a specific day of the week, and there should be absolutely no deviation from this date.

Salaries of Salespeople

There are four principal methods of compensating salespeople: straight salary, straight commission, salary plus commission, and salary plus quota bonus.

Straight Salary. The payment of salespeople by a straight salary is still the most widely used of all compensation methods, even though many retailers have turned to the use of commission sales. A person being paid a straight salary receives a specified, unvarying amount each pay period. It can be paid on a weekly or hourly basis.

Advantages

1. It is easily understandable to the employee.
2. Salary payments are definite, permitting the employees to budget their expenses.
3. Workers do not lose income for time spent at nonselling or training tasks.
4. Bookkeeping is simplified.

Disadvantages

1. There is no direct incentive to better productivity. An increase in straight salary as a reward for better production frequently lags far behind increased productivity. This can be the cause of employee resentment.

MACY'S

Salesclerk Performance Rating

DIVISIONAL PERSONNEL

Store No. _____ Dept. No. _____ Job No. _____ Employee Ident. No. _____ Name _____

RATING FACTORS	EXCELLENT	GOOD	MEETS ACC. STANDARD	BELOW STANDARD	UNSATISFACTORY
1. MANNER AND INTEREST IN CUSTOMER	Most pleasing and interested manner to all	Shows sincere interest in customer's needs	Businesslike, courteous, attentive	Indifferent, shows little interest; sometimes brushes off customer	Rude; abrupt; antagonizes customer
2. ALERTNESS TO SERVICE	Immediately approaches waiting customers and acknowledges other waiting customers	Quick to approach waiting customers	Usually prompt in approaching customers	Frequently slow to approach waiting customers	Frequently waits for customer to approach him or ignores customers
3. MERCHANDISE KNOWLEDGE (INC. MATERIALS, CONSTRUCTION, USES AND AVAILABILITY)	Expert knowledge for salesclerk	Knows merchandise well	Has basic knowledge	Has only limited knowledge	Lacks fundamental knowledge needed to sell in department
4. SKILL IN USING MERCHANDISE KNOWLEDGE	Outstanding skill in determining customer's needs, selecting selling points, and presenting merchandise convincingly	Capable in determining customer's needs and arousing interest by methods of presenting merchandise	Generally determines what customer wants and gives adequate information about merchandise	Just an order taker; unconvincing; has some difficulty closing sales	Does not show proper merchandise or present merchandise to advantage; gives incorrect information; has great difficulty closing sales
5. GROOMING		SATISFACTORY ☐		UNSATISFACTORY ☐	
6. COOPERATION	Goes out of way to be congenial and helpful; gets along unusually well with others	Willingly does what he is told to do and does fair share of work; gets along well with others	Does what he is told; assumes his share of work without question	Avoids his share of work in department; reluctantly does what he is told; sometimes causes minor friction	Resents direction; causes serious friction
7. SYSTEM	Thoroughly knows system and makes almost no errors	Knows system well; makes very few errors	Working knowledge of system; makes only normal amount of errors	Has difficulty with system; makes more errors than he should	Makes unusually large number of errors; careless
8. STOCK WORK	Excellent housekeeper; takes initiative in stock work	Keeps stock in very good condition with little supervision	Neat and orderly; performs expected stock duties with normal supervision	Requires more than normal supervision to complete stock duties	Does not perform assigned stock work; careless and untidy in stock work
9. RELIABILITY (inc. adherence to rules and regulations in promptness in returning from lunch, absences due to illness)	Can always be relied upon; does what is expected with minimum supervision	Can be relied on with few exceptions to do what is expected; needs little supervision	Usually can be relied on to do what is expected; requires only normal supervision	Requires more than normal supervision; frequently interferes with department operation by failing to do what is expected	Seriously hampers operation of department by unreliability on any phase of job; needs constant supervision

10. ATTENDANCE

NO. OF ILLNESS ABSENCES _____ ON _____ (number) _____ OCCASIONS.
NO. OF WEEKS COVERED, Exclusive of Vac.& L.of A. _____

NO. OF PERSONAL ABSENCES _____ NO. OF LATE ARRIVALS _____ NO. OF LUNCH LATES _____ NO. OF FAILURES TO CLOCK _____

NO. OF WEEKS COVERED _____ (From _____ to _____) RATING _____

EXCLUSIVE OF _____ WKS. VAC.; _____ WKS. L. of A.; _____ WKS. ILLNESS ABSENCES

ENTER COMMENTS, DISPOSITION AND SIGNATURES ON REVERSE SIDE

F.2278R 1-65

Figure 6–7 Sales clerk performance rating—an evaluation report form used at Macy's, New York. *Courtesy:* Macy's, Herald Square, New York, NY

PERTINENT COMMENTS

Below Standard or Unsatisfactory ratings on any factor
should be explained by a statement of specific criticisms.

DISPOSITION

1. O.K. FOR INCREASE ☐

2. WARN FOR WITHHOLDING
   OF AUTOMATIC INCREASE ☐

3. WARN FOR WITHHOLDING OF
   AUTOMATIC INCREASE AND/OR
   DISCHARGE ☐

4. DISCHARGE ☐

OTHER (SPECIFY) _____

Signature
of Rater _____ Date _____

Telephone
Extension _____

Dept. or
Group Mgr's
Signature _____ Date _____

Approved by
Job Review _____ Date _____

Interviewed By _____

FOR USE OF RECORD OFFICE

RECORD CARD POSTED ☐

WARN FOR WITHHOLDING NOTED ☐

Figure 6-7 *(continued)*

2. To ensure the fairness of individual salaries, employee evaluation must be undertaken frequently.

3. Salaries are not keyed to sales levels. This results in the retailer paying higher salaries than he or she can afford in slow periods and lower salaries than he or she can afford in peak periods.

Straight salary, because of its simplicity, is probably the best payroll system for a retail store. However, it can be used effectively only if constant worker evaluation keys salaries to individual worth.

Straight Commission.   Under this system, which is limited in retailing sales, people are paid only on the basis of the amount of merchandise they sell. At the end of a pay period, each employee's total sales are added and multiplied by a commission percentage to determine the worker's earnings for that period.

Advantages

1. It is easily understood by the employee.
2. A straight commission system can be converted to a regular weekly plan by permitting a drawing account.
3. Since income is calculated on the basis of production, this system is an incentive to increased production.
4. Customer service is speeded and sales help may be eliminated since a salesperson's earnings increase with the number of customers that employee handles. Therefore, each salesperson will handle more customers.
5. Salary expense increases when the store can afford high expenses (peak periods) and decreases during a lull in sales activity.

Disadvantages

1. Competition among sales personnel for high-ticket customers can lead to hard feelings among salespeople.
2. Customer service suffers, since the salesperson is in a hurry to finish and "grab" another customer. The result is high-pressure selling, avoiding low-price buyers, and ignoring browsers.
3. Employees resent nonselling chores since it keeps them from selling and reduces their earnings.
4. Employee morale suffers during slow periods, when their earnings are less than their drawings.

Straight commission systems are not typically used in retail stores. The incentive provided by such a plan is so strong that it becomes destructive to customer servicing and employee morale. Stores like Neiman Marcus and Nordstrom use this method of payment.

Salary Plus Commission.   The use of a straight salary plus a small commission on all sales is an attempt to combine the best features of the straight salary and straight commission plan. Under this system, each salesperson is paid a salary that is slightly less than would be received under the straight salary plan. In addition, a commission is paid on *all* sales. Commission rates used under this system are low, usually running between 1 percent and 2 percent.

Advantages

1. It provides some incentive toward greater productivity.
2. The workers can expect fairly stable regular earnings.

Disadvantages

1. Salary plus commission is somewhat more complicated to calculate. It is often impossible for employees to keep track of their sales, and they occasionally feel that they were cheated.

2. The commission is frequently too small to act as an incentive to some people. To others, it is a great incentive despite its size. This may result in customer dissatisfaction and employee rivalries.

By and large, the salary plus commission wage plan seems a satisfactory compromise between the advantages and disadvantages of the straight salary and straight commission systems. As a result, this form of compensation is widely used by retailers.

Salary Plus Quota Bonus.   Another compromise between the straight salary and straight commission plans is the salary plus quota bonus system. Under this method employees are paid a fixed weekly amount. In addition, a weekly or monthly sales quota is determined. At the end of the quota period, they are paid a commission on the amount by which their sales exceeded their quotas.

The advantages and disadvantages of the salary plus quota bonus system of compensation are similar to those of the salary plus commission compensation method. The salary plus quota bonus system is widely used, and the trend seems to be toward greater acceptance of the plan.

Quota bonus systems are fairly common. Among those using this system are J. C. Penney and Dayton Hudson. Under the Penney plan the store's employees are divided up into teams. During each selling month, sales volume is measured against the same period last year. The team is paid a bonus depending upon the amount that this year's sales exceeded last year's. If the sales change is 40 percent or better, the bonus is $1.05 for each hour worked during the period. As the sales change decreases, the hourly bonuses decrease as well. Thus a 20 percent sales increase earned $.35 per hour and a 10 percent increase yields $.15.

Salaries of Nonselling Personnel

It is rare in retailing to find nonselling personnel who are paid on other than a straight hourly or weekly basis. This is due to the difficulty involved in finding a yardstick with which to measure their productivity. An occasional store may pay bonuses to people whose work is repetitive, such as markers, stenographers, or wrappers, based on their production. Most stores shy away from this because each piece marked, typed, or wrapped offers special problems. As a result, although most retailers recognize the importance of incentive payments, no sound basis for such remuneration has been found.

Other Compensation

To improve employee morale and loyalty, many larger stores offer their selling and nonselling employees a wide variety of monetary benefits.

P.M.s.   Prize money is sometimes offered to sales personnel for selling particular types of merchandise. While such prizes usually take the form of extra commissions, they may also be in the form of vacation trips, appliances, or other merchandise. Such rewards may also be given for the winning of contests or the performance of certain tasks.

Employee Discounts.   Employees are generally given discounts of 10 percent to 20 percent on purchases of the store's merchandise. It is estimated that as much as 4 percent of the total sales of a department store are made to employees. An employee discount policy is an effective way to sell merchandise as well as a method of improving employee morale. Macy's allows employee discounts of 20 percent on merchandise an employee can wear to work, and 10 percent on all other purchases.

Profit Sharing.   Many larger retailers such as Montgomery Ward, J. C. Penney, and Sears maintain profit-sharing plans for all of their personnel. It is felt that such compensation involves the workers in the success of the store by making employees partners in its profits and losses. The management of Sears has indicated that it considers profit sharing to be an important part of its success.

Managerial Compensation

The most frequently used method of compensating managerial personnel is the straight salary plan. To increase the incentive of managers, most stores rely upon bonuses, which may be based on any of the following methods:

Based on the Total Operation.   Under this plan, bonuses are paid in relation to the profit of the entire store. When the store has a successful year, bonuses are high. Low total store profits for the year will result in reduced bonuses. This method attempts to interest department executives in the overall success of the store rather than just of their own specific department.

Based on Department Sales.   Bonuses may be based on departmental sales. This plan can work in several ways: the bonus percentage may be taken on total department sales, in which case a small percentage (1 percent) of the sales is paid as a bonus. Frequently this type of bonus is calculated on the amount by which the department's sales exceed a predetermined quota. In such cases, the percent used would be higher.

Based on Net Income.   Bonuses of 1 percent to 10 percent are sometimes given on total departmental net profit, or on the amount by which the department's net profit exceeds a set quota. Basing managerial bonuses on net profit rather than sales has the advantage of focusing the manager's interest on high profits instead of high sales.

Chain Store Management.   Discount and variety chains generally pay their managers a straight salary plus 10 percent to 15 percent of their store's profits as a bonus. Other firms, believing that the manager is entitled to as much as 20 percent of the profits, deduct the manager's salary from 20 percent of the profits and give that manager the difference as a bonus.

Whatever managerial bonus plan is used, it should be sufficient to attract outstanding people and reward them for out-of-the-ordinary achievement.

Employee Services and Benefits

Both governmental statutes and union contracts provide other employee benefits than those that appear in a worker's pay envelope. Employer payments for social security and unemployment insurance are required by law. Many union contracts require employer contributions to union welfare and hospitalization plans. Most retail stores, to build employee goodwill, offer many other services and activities. These include profit sharing, clubs, athletic facilities, savings and loan arrangements, life insurance, tuition reimbursement, and many other features.

While many of the benefits and services to be discussed come as the result of government legislation or from the expertise of the union negotiator at times of contract renewal, these additional earnings are often the basis for the prospective employee to accept the job. It is certainly true that salary is the greatest motivational factor for employees, but all too often, the salaries from one company to another are similar for particular job titles. This is particularly true at the lower levels, where wages may be set by unions whose involvement may transcend many retail organizations.

For these reasons, jobs are often refused or accepted because of the available benefit or service package. Very often it is the benefit plan that entices an employee who has served a company well to move to another operation. A salary cannot be the only consideration for employment. The extras are often as valuable as the actual take-home pay and are a significant part of the reasons for joining a particular retail organization.

Medical and Health Services

It is not unusual to find a doctor or nurse in continuous attendance at a large store for the benefit of the employees. In addition, visiting nurses are made freely available for the assistance of employees confined to their homes. Retailers that are not large enough to afford full-time medical staffs may offer them on a part-time basis.

Hospitalization, dental, and life insurance are often arranged by the store in order to offer its employees a low group rate. The cost of such plans may be borne by the store, the employee, or both.

Social, Educational, and Athletic Activities

Many larger retail establishments provide facilities for employee clubs and equipment for a wide variety of employee activities from baseball teams to dance bands. Generally, these activities are conceived and sponsored by groups of employees, who find management more than willing to encourage any activity that might promote loyalty and enhance employee morale.

Savings Plans

Typical of an employee savings plan is one operated by Montgomery Ward. That retailing giant contributes some $2 million per year to a plan in which it deposits 25 percent to 50 percent of the amount its employees deposit in a savings account (the employees may deposit up to 3 percent of their annual earnings).

Many such savings plans permit low-cost employee loans, which may be paid back by payroll deduction.

Other Employee Services

The employee services discussed above are far from the complete range of benefits offered by retailers. Typical of other benefits are:

1. The F. W. Woolworth Stock Purchase Plan, which permits employees to purchase company stock at a savings of 15 percent.
2. Sick leave, life insurance, pensions, profit sharing, and other benefits that are available to employees of most large retailers.

Figure 6–8 provides a summary of employee benefits for The May Company employees.

Labor Relations

The growth of the labor movement has added a new dimension to the responsibility of the human resources department. Retail workers have generally lagged behind the rest of the labor force in the increase in union membership, but the growth has been real, if slow, and union contract negotiation has become an area of considerable importance.

Summary of Employee Benefits
May offers its associates an attractive benefits package and highlights are presented here. This should not, however, be considered as a total description of the plans as some benefits and plans vary from division to division.

. . . .

Merchandise Discounts
As a unique and important benefit, particularly to new associates just beginning professional careers, associates are entitled to a discount on merchandise purchased from their respective store company. The percentage of discount varies depending on the merchandise or service being purchased.

. . . .

Relocation Assistance
For the recent college graduate joining the company, most divisions provide assistance for expenses incurred to relocate. One-way transportation to the job location plus an allowance for miscellaneous moving or temporary living expenses are provided.

. . . .

Vacations and Holidays
Vacations generally range from one to four weeks, depending on the length of service with the company. In addition, major holidays and personal holidays are observed by most store companies.

. . . .

Medical Care
All divisions of May offer associates comprehensive medical care programs. All plans are at group rates and feature individual and family coverage options.

Life Insurance
Life insurance is offered under a group term insurance policy. Coverage is adjusted annually for compensation changes.

. . . .

Disability Coverage
In most divisions, short-term disability for minor illnesses or accidents provides full pay for a period of time, after which long-term disability protection becomes effective. The long-term disability insurance plans provide additional benefits if you are disabled for extended periods.

. . . .

Travel Insurance
Travel accident insurance is provided for all associates while traveling on company business.

. . . .

Retirement Plan
Most associates are eligible for retirement plan participation after reaching age 21 and completing one year of service. The cost is fully paid by the company. Retirement credits are based on years of service and average career earnings. Members are fully vested after seven years of service.

. . . .

Profit Sharing Plan
Most associates are eligible for participation in the profit sharing plan after reaching age 21 and completing one year of service. Members make voluntary contributions on a before-tax or after-tax basis with several investment options. Company contributions are credited to each participant's account based on company performance. Members are vested in the company's contributions after a specific period of service.

Figure 6–8 Summary of employee benefits for The May Company employees. *Courtesy:* Lord & Taylor

The human resources department continues to play a growing role in dealing with the labor unions. Perhaps more than any other part of management, its specialists are employed to make certain that the employees deliver services for which they were hired.

While there frequently seem to be management–employee problems, a company can only be successful if the needs of its customers are served. Unhappy workers lead to a decrease in productivity, with profits often being affected. Although human resources directors are a part of management, their roles are seen as buffers between management and labor. How to satisfy employee demands without giving the store away perhaps best sums up their most difficult function.

Prior to contract negotiations, the human resources department's team is often charged with the responsibility of examining employee demands and recommending avenues that would provide the best productivity for the store. In areas such as employee compensation methods and benefits, human resources provides insights on which top management can base negotiations.

Once a contract has been settled, the human resources department is usually called upon to participate in contractual disputes with employees and their unions. Although a contract is in evidence, the translation of legally worded passages is almost always an ongoing practice. Compromises between management and labor must be reached in the contract.

The work of human resources management is delicate. Only through tact and diplomacy can both sides of a labor dispute be satisfied. Personnel managers who appear to be too management oriented can lower employee morale, while too much employee appeasement can hurt the company's role in managing the organization. A delicate balance must be struck.

TRENDS

Hiring of Senior Citizens

Many companies, such as McDonald's, actively seek senior citizens and retired persons to work for their companies. They have found that, as a group, older workers are extremely reliable and perform better than workers in most other age groups.

Employment of Disabled People

Retailers are beginning to move in the direction of hiring qualified persons with developmental disabilities for a variety of jobs. Among the companies that have moved in this direction is the F. W. Woolworth Corporation, which has been awarded the Humanitarian Award from The Arc of New Jersey, an organization that fosters advancement for the retarded, and The Home Depot.

Drug Testing

With the enormous problems that come about as a result of drug use, such as internal theft, a large number of retailers make the drug test the first step in the recruitment procedure. The practice has significantly cut down on the expense associated with hiring, since many of the potential job candidates are disqualified earlier rather than later in the procedure.

Use of Video Programs For Orientation and Training

Instead of using the traditional approach of an instructor teaching new employees the "rules" of the company, many companies are now using a variety of video presentations instead. Not only do these types of programs save the company money, but they also may be viewed again and again as the need arises. It is especially beneficial for chain store units in which a store manager is the only trainer.

ACTION FOR THE INDEPENDENT RETAILER

No matter what the size of the organization, its success is directly dependent on its employees. Small stores cannot afford the services of human resources specialists but must be aware of the appropriate practices necessary to manage even one or two employees.

The selection of employees in the smaller organization often requires even more attention than in the larger retail companies. Not only might individual employees in smaller stores be required to perform a greater variety of duties than the specialists in large stores, but they are also more personally involved with the customers. Where the big retailer has an extensive clientele, and less-than-diligent workers might get lost in the shuffle, the small store employee must often relate to everyone who happens to pass through the doors.

Keeping these factors in mind, care must be directed to screening prospective employees. Although ads and agencies might be used to find people, small retailers often find their best candidates to be the transient applicants who seek employment because of a "help wanted" sign at the store's entrance. This method is simple and inexpensive and can be used at a moment's notice. A complete interview will provide much of the information necessary to find the right individual. It will provide such pertinent information as experience, personal qualities, and required salaries. Training for the small store is best done on the job under the watchful eye of the owner or manager. This training is a plus when compared with large companies where owners and management are usually far removed from lower employee levels. Periodic evaluation, best if informal, provides motivation for improvement. Although the smaller independent store cannot offer the typical benefits of larger companies, it can provide great incentive in larger employee discounts, something the giants simply cannot afford to do.

Careful involvement of the store owner can easily prompt better employee performance. Correction can be made quickly before costly errors result in customer loss. Small stores usually have little employee turnover if workers are carefully selected.

IMPORTANT POINTS IN THE CHAPTER

1. As a store grows in size, the problems involved with employees become so great that specialists are required to handle them.

2. In recent years, the federal government has enacted a significant amount of legislation that has necessitated human resources managers' re-evaluating their stores' employment practices.

3. The human resources department is responsible for the organization's recruitment training, evaluation, compensation, special services, and labor relations.

4. Recruitment, based upon a careful job analysis, requires a knowledge of the sources of labor supply in the area.

5. Interviews serve the double purpose of informing the applicant about the job and the employer about the applicant.

6. After an applicant has been selected, it is the responsibility of the human resources department to provide the training necessary for effective job performance.

7. To ensure the maintenance of a high standard of employee performance, employees must be periodically evaluated. This evaluation is the basis for promotion, additional training, salary adjustment, and discharge.

8. Employee earnings is one of the most important factors in the establishment of good worker–management relations. Retail workers are generally compensated on one of the following bases: straight salary, straight commission, salary plus commission, salary plus quota bonus.

9. The most frequently used method of compensating managerial employees is the straight salary plan. To increase the incentive of managers, most stores offer bonuses.

10. Employee morale may be increased by offering a wide variety of special services, which may include profit sharing, clubs, life and health insurance, and tuition reimbursement.

11. The human resources department is responsible for the negotiations and interpretation of labor–management employment contracts.

REVIEW QUESTIONS

1. Discuss the function of recruitment that is performed by the human resources department. Is it a line or a staff function?

2. Why must the recruitment function begin with a careful analysis of the job to be filled?

3. List nine items that should be included in a job analysis.

4. What are the advantages to the store cooperating with schools in cooperative work experience programs?

5. Discuss the kinds of recruitment in terms of cost to the store. Which is most expensive? Least?

6. What is the purpose of the application form? What sort of information should it require of an applicant?

7. Discuss reference checking. Describe another method of checking on a prospective candidate.

8. Why are personality tests rarely used in personnel work?

9. Differentiate between the training necessary for new inexperienced employees and the training necessary for new experienced employees.

10. Describe the methods by which training of regular employees is accomplished.

11. What are the problems involved in the training of part-time workers? Why is this area of training important?

12. List and discuss the reasons for employee evaluation.

13. Discuss the advantages and disadvantages of paying salespeople on the basis of straight salary. Give an example of the straight salary plan.

14. Discuss the advantages and disadvantages of paying salespeople a straight salary plus commission.

15. What are the problems involved in giving incentive pay to nonselling employees? Give examples.

16. Explain the manner in which a store benefits from the payment of P.M.s to its employees.

17. Explain and discuss several methods of paying buyers incentive money based on sales.

18. Discuss the paying of buyers' incentive bonuses based on profits rather than on sales.

19. Why do department stores provide expensive employee services that they are not required to do by law or contract?

20. Explain the function of the human resources department in the area of labor relations. Is it a line or a staff function?

CASE PROBLEMS

Case Problem 1

Dale's Department Store is a medium-sized establishment located in the downtown section of an urban center. The store is progressively run and has grown in the past ten years from a small appliance store to a department store with 12 departments and 80 employees. As yet there are no furniture or hardware departments, but negotiations are currently underway for additional space in which to house these departments. The profit picture is excellent, and all signs indicate a continued period of growth and expansion.

The human resources department consists of three people, one of them a secretary. Their only function is to bring in job applicants by placing want ads, contacting employment agencies, and so on. The actual interviewing and hiring are done by the selling departments, who are also responsible for employee training. All salespeople are paid on a straight commission basis.

The top management of the store is aware of the advantages of having a full-scale human resources department but feels that the store's profits are inadequate to support such a nonproducing staff organization. Preliminary estimates indicate that a full human resources department would reduce annual profits by 20 percent. Much of this cost would be wasted, since a store the size of Dale's never hires enough employees at one time to form an economically worthwhile training class.

A group of small and medium-sized retailers in the area have banded together to set up a school for all of the members of the group. By using a single school for all of the cooperating stores, classes would be large enough to handle employee training at a fairly low rate per student.

Dale's is considering an invitation to join the group.

Questions

1. What are the advantages and disadvantages of joining the group from the point of view of effective store operations?
2. What are the advantages and disadvantages from the point of view of the mid-management in the selling departments?
3. What are the advantages and disadvantages from the point of view of the veteran salespersons in the departments?
4. The sales school will teach only areas of interest to all of its students. For example, it will teach how to sell, but not how to handle returns, since each cooperating store might have a different system. Outline those areas that should be taught by the sales school and those that should be taught by the store.

Case Problem 2

The Plainview Paint Store is a large individually owned retailer. The store is located in a suburb of a large city that over the past 15 years has grown from a farming area to a heavily populated area. The store has grown with the surrounding area and has reached a size at which it makes a comfortable living for the owner and pays good salaries to its 12 salespeople.

The store serves a population made up of middle- and lower-middle-class homeowners, and most of the sales are to do-it-yourself workers. As a result, the individual sales are small, but the markup on each sale is excellent.

Salespeople are paid well on a straight salary basis. The owner, who has always worked on a ten-hour day, six-day week, no-vacation basis, has decided to reduce his business activities. He was on vacation during the whole month of January, leaving responsibility for the store's operation in the hands of one of the salespeople, whom he appointed as manager with a $150 per week raise.

When he returned from vacation he found that January sales were 20 percent below the sales of the previous January. The year's sales up to January had been running slightly ahead of previous figures; the weather was good and the competition was unchanged. A spot check of the inventory indicated that no merchandise was missing. He rightly attributed the decline in business to the fact that he was not on hand to motivate the salespeople.

Questions

1. Indicate two compensation plans under which the salespeople might be motivated while the proprietor is away.
2. Indicate two plans under which the manager might be motivated while the proprietor is away.
3. Which plan or combination of the above plans would you use? Support your reasons for this choice.
4. Can you think of a noncash type of remuneration that might improve the salespeople's incentive?

Case Problem 3

Soon after her promotion at Barnard's Department Store, Jane Wagner began to encounter a serious problem as manager of the men's department. Competition among salespeople has become so fierce that frequent arguments take place on the selling floor. Wagner is certain the root of the problem is that salespeople are paid on a straight commission basis and are out to make as much money for themselves as possible.

Coupled with this problem, the manager finds it extremely difficult motivating her sales force to perform nonselling tasks such as stockwork, floor moves, and handling returns.

"I just don't know what to do about it anymore," Wagner explains to her divisional manager, "I'm seriously considering asking management to take them all off commission and start using a straight salary plan."

Questions

1. Do you agree with Wagner's suggestion?
2. If you were the divisional manager, what other recommendations might you offer?

Chapter 7
Store Location and Layout

Courtesy: Melvin Simon

LEARNING OBJECTIVES

Upon completion of this chapter, the student should be able to:

1. Discuss the importance of population analysis to site selection.
2. Identify eight nonpopulation characteristics involved in site selection.
3. List five reasons for the growth of suburban shopping malls.
4. List five principles regarding the location of selling departments.

BIGGER IS BETTER . . .

Following the success of Canada's West Edmonton Mall, the largest in the world with 5 million square feet of retail space, and entertainment (pleasures such as a boat ride, performing dolphins, and other entertainment attractions), the United States followed suit with its giant entry, the Mall of America in Bloomington, Minnesota.

With a unique mix of entertainment and shopping, in 4.2 million square feet of space, it is larger and grander than anything ever before witnessed in American retailing. Its vastness is equivalent to four typical regional malls joined together! Since its opening in 1992, the Mall of America has lived up to the expectations of its developer and retail occupants. In its first nine months of operation it attracted an astounding 20 million shoppers from all over the country and some from foreign shores. Traffic, which usually falters right after the Christmas rush, doesn't seem to decrease at the Mall of America. One of the reasons for this phenomenon is the emphasis the Mall places on entertainment. Not only may shoppers avail themselves of the vast number of retail outlets, anchored by such industry giants as Bloomingdale's, Macy's, Sears, and Nordstrom, and scores of specialty shops, but at its core is a seven-acre entertainment park called Knott's Camp Snoopy. Consisting of a roller coaster, various exciting rides, a miniature golf course, and other fun-filled arenas, it attracts local shoppers as well as tourists for unique outings.

Attendance is far above anything expected at even the largest of the regional shopping malls. Typically, from 50,000 to 90,000 shoppers enter the mall on weekdays, with the crowds swelling to as many as 200,000 on weekends. Unlike traditional malls, which draw shoppers from their immediate surroundings, the Mall of America draws 70 percent of its patrons from distances up to 150 miles and the remainder from even farther away. Another remarkable statistic is that 90 percent of the visitors make a purchase!

It is truly a mega-mall that might be the prototype for shopping malls of the future.

Retailers are constantly seeking new locations to expand their organizations. Downtown areas have always been the locations of preference for major department stores for their flagship stores, and enclosed malls have certainly been the favorites for branches of these department stores and specialty chains. Recent years have seen the creation of many new types of retail environments. Some of them, such as the landmark centers, were explored in the introductory chapter. Others, such as the vertical malls and the power centers, will be discussed in this chapter along with the other places retailers use to locate their operations.

With the enormous competition in the field, retailers are concentrating more than ever before on their store layouts. Fixturing, traffic configuration, lighting, and materials are just some of the areas to which they are paying attention. No longer can retailers simply furnish their shops with "cookie cutter" interiors. Instead, professionals in store design and layout are busy creating new store personalities and are differentiating them with exciting interiors. There is so much sameness in the types of merchandise carried by many retailers that the store's environment very often becomes the reason for customer traffic.

In this chapter, attention will focus on the traditional concepts associated with store location and layout, and the latest innovations in both.

STORE LOCATION

One of the most common causes of failure of new retail stores is management error in the location of the store. In recent years there has been more research done in this field than ever before. Despite this, the numbers of retailers who actually subject proposed sites to a scientific survey is still below what it should be. It is generally the small independent retailer who is neglected. It is not the purpose of this section to go into the complicated mathematics of scientific site evaluation. Instead, the discussion will be limited to the important factors that must be weighed before a decision can be made, first on the general trading area for a new retail operation, next on the shopping district, and then on a specific site within that area.

Selecting the General Trading Area

A logical approach to store location is to begin by selecting the general trading area in which the store is to be established. In making this decision, one should carefully analyze the following factors.

Geography of the Area

The size and shape of the proposed area must be analyzed to determine the boundaries within which the customer population will fall. The population within this area can then be studied.

Population

Any analysis of future customer demand must begin with an understanding of the nature of the typical customer. Population size and density are generally agreed upon to be major factors affecting retailing success. A detailed study of an area's population should include the following considerations.

1. It is important to know the predominant age of the population. Since young people's needs and wants differ from those of older people, the success of many types of retail operations depends upon the careful analysis of age data.

2. Differences in sex and marital status have much the same effect on retail sales as age differences, and care must be taken to determine any unusual facts concerning the population's sex and marital status.

3. The size of the population may be subject to seasonal variations. This is true of summer or winter resorts. If the area in question is likely to be affected by such seasonal changes, the information is vital to the location selection.

4. The various religious affiliations, education levels, and national origins of the population must be determined. These differences frequently indicate variations in prejudices, needs, and preferences.

5. The income level of the population can be estimated in many ways. Data on per capita and family earnings are obtainable from the census bureau. Information about the number of telephones and auto registrations per house, and on the value of the dwellings themselves, is available. Since retail volume depends upon income level, the investigation of the earning power of the area must be extensive. Such information as the source, stability, and seasonal nature of the income must be determined and weighed before the decision to locate can be made.

6. The buying needs of homeowners are considerably different from those of apartment renters. Although these differences may not be obvious in the buying of food and clothing, they certainly would be important to the sales of major appliances and gardening tools. Moreover, the buying needs of the new homeowner are considerably different from those of the established homeowner.

Characteristics of the Area

In addition to the study of the characteristics of the population, certain information about the trading area itself is required.

1. An alert, progressive community whose members are willing to tax themselves for a quality school system and other local improvements will probably attract new families for years to come. Such a community is frequently the home of an active chamber of commerce and other clubs. A test of progressiveness is the rate of new development, both of commercial enterprises and of new homes. Active growth is generally a by-product of progressiveness.

2. Of great interest in the location of new retailing outlets is the competition in the area to be selected. Both the quality and quantity of the competition should be judged.

3. The area should have features that attract out-of-the-area customers. Such attractions as parks, theaters, zoos, and athletic events frequently bring transient retail business into an area.

4. Judgment should be made about the accessibility of the area. The roads should be good, the traffic bearable, and after a fairly fast trip the customer should have no trouble finding a parking space. In these times of serious road congestion, this factor has become one of prime importance. In addition to being easily accessible to automobiles, a good shopping area should be fed by public transportation.

5. Proper banking help is important to the retailer. Sound audit control requires the daily deposit of cash sales. In addition, banks are needed to make temporary working capital as well as long-term improvement loans. With the recent wide expansion of commercial banks, lack of banking facilities is rarely a problem.

6. Those retailers that depend upon advertising to promote their merchandise must be certain that the required advertising media are available in the area in which they decide to locate.

7. Many retail customers demand that their purchases be delivered. Facilities for delivery must be available if the store is to offer this service.

8. There must be an adequate labor force in the area to staff the store at a salary level within the store's budget. If the prospective labor force is unionized, the union's requirements must be studied.

9. Local laws must be studied to determine sales taxes, necessary licenses, days in the week the store may remain open, and so on. In addition, such possible problems as difficulty in obtaining insurance and local crime rate should be determined.

10. The history of the area should be analyzed to determine current trends. Is the area the same as it was ten years ago? Five years ago? If it has deteriorated, is it likely to continue to do so? Is any improvement likely to continue? Are the characteristics of the population changing? In what way?

It should be understood that a trading area does not have to score perfectly in all of the areas listed. Few successful stores would have that ideal a report. However, each of the areas indicated should be *considered* before a decision to locate is made.

Selecting the Shopping District

After the general trading area has been selected, the specific shopping district within the area must be decided upon. Like the decision on the general trading area, this decision must be based on a considerable body of facts. There are many types of retail locations, and the relative merits of each type must be carefully weighed.

Central Shopping Districts

The central shopping district located in the hub of a large city has always been the focal point for the strongest retail establishments. It is at this point, where the area's population is at its densest, that the highest volume of sales per square foot of selling space is made. This attracts the retailing giants and the largest department stores. High-promotion stores are characteristic of such areas; the great potential of available customers almost guarantees the success of any worthwhile promotion. Central business district locations are usually at a premium, and the rentals are very high.

Shopping Malls

Although downtown central shopping districts are still of great retailing importance, suburban malls have become the locations considered best by the retailer for expansion of the company. The downtown stores are being subjected to more and more competition from these large regional shopping malls. Many metropolitan department stores have been both adding to and taking advantage of this trend by locating branch stores in suburban malls. The success of the suburban shopping mall has been due chiefly to the following factors:

1. Since 1945, there has been a massive population exodus from the cities. Since the shift in population has been among the upper- and middle-class families, the disposable income loss from the city to the suburbs has been great. As a result, the per capita income of the city families has declined, while the purchasing power available in the suburbs has skyrocketed. Retailers, anxious to tap this mine of purchasing power, have moved to suburban locations.

2. As a result of the increased use of the automobile, downtown shopping areas are marked by traffic congestion and unavailability of inexpensive parking facilities. These transportation difficulties greatly favor suburban stores, where traveling and parking are relatively effortless.

3. As the trend toward suburban living continues, nearby suburbia becomes crowded and homeowners are forced even further away from the city. As a result, many homeowners are simply too far from the city for convenient shopping.

4. The availability of space in the suburbs has played a part in the increase in retailing activity in the outlying districts. Downtown locations are generally poorly planned, overpriced, and difficult to find. In contrast, suburbia offers building to order, cheaper rents, and a choice of locations.

From the 1950s through the early 1970s many regional shopping centers were developed. They were the prototypes of the malls as we know them. Most enjoyed enormous sales volume and went on to become the leading shopping areas for their cities. Recent years have seen the mall grow from its original concept to newer, exciting retail locations. With each new mall development, the original centers have become less satisfying for the shoppers and less productive in terms of profitability.

The last few years have seen the refurbishment and rebuilding of the older shopping centers. Places like Crossroads Plaza in Salt Lake City, Utah; Greenbriar in Atlanta, Georgia; Crossroads in San Antonio, Texas; and Tysons Corner Center in McLean, Virginia have all been redeveloped and expanded to compete with the newer breed of shopping centers.

Many of the older malls have added second and third stories, expanded their restaurant facilities, and included office spaces to make the centers more profitable. Some have even added movie theaters to make the mall a place where people can come to be entertained before and after they have made their purchases.

Figure 7–1 features checkpoints to study before selecting a shopping mall location.

A RETAILING FOCUS   *Tysons Corner Center*

Strategically located west of Washington, D.C. in McLean, Virginia, Tysons Corner Center made its debut in 1968. It was the region's largest single-level mall. It received such overwhelming interest from merchants and shoppers alike that in two years of its opening it surpassed its five year sales goal.

The Center serves the prominent Northern Virginia marketplace where the mean household income is more than $62,000, the mean age of shoppers is 34 years, and the mean expenditure for shoppers is about $80 per visit. These enviable statistics make Tysons Corner Center one of the most profitable shopping malls in the country.

In 1985, the Center was acquired by the Dallas-based Lehndorff Group for $167 million. The Group undertook a $160 million renovation and expansion program that would make Tysons Corner Center the most modern facility in that part of the country. The former delivery and storage areas were transformed into another level of shops and restaurants. Skylights were added throughout and four parking terraces were added for customer convenience. The new facility now houses more than 200 specialty shops on two levels.

In addition to the host of specialty stores, the facility boasts as its anchors Bloomingdale's, Woodward & Lothrop, Hecht's, Nordstrom's East Coast flagship store, and its newest anchor, Lord & Taylor.

Figure 7–1   Checkpoints for Evaluating Shopping Mall Locations

1. Who is the shopping mall developer?
2. How long has he been in the business of developing real estate?
3. What are his financial resources?
4. With whom has he arranged for the financing of the mall?
5. What is his reputation for integrity?
6. Who performed the economic analysis? Does the report cover both favorable and unfavorable factors?
7. What experience has the economic consultant had?
8. Has an architectural firm been retained to plan the mall?
9. Has the architect designed other malls? Have they been successful from a retailing standpoint?
10. Who will build the mall? The developer? An experienced contractor? An inexperienced contractor?
11. Has the developer had experience with other malls?
12. What is, or will be, the quality of management for the mall?
13. Will the management have merchandising and promotion experience? (Some developers are large retailers rather than real estate operators.)
14. What percentage of the leases have been signed? Are they on a contingent basis?
15. Has every facet of the lease been carefully studied?
16. Is the ratio of parking area to selling area 3-to-1 or more?
17. Has sufficient space been assigned to each car?
18. Is the parking space designed so that the shopper does not walk more than 300 to 350 feet from the farthest spot to the store?
19. What is the angle of parking space? (Ninety degrees provides the best capacity and circulation.)
20. What is the planned or actual car turnover? (3.3 cars per parking space per day is the average.)
21. Is the number of total spaces adequate for the planned business volume? (Too many spaces make the center look dead; too few openly invite competition around the center.)
22. Does the parking scheme distribute the cars so as to favor no one area?
23. Is there an adequate number of ingress/egress roads in proper relationship with the arrangement of parking spaces?
24. For the larger malls, a ring road is preferable. Is this the case?
25. Is the site large enough for the type of mall?
26. Is the size sufficiently dominant to forestall the construction of similar shopping malls nearby?
27. Is the mall of regular shape? If not, does the location of the buildings minimize the disadvantage of the site's shape?
28. Is the site sufficiently deep? (A depth of at least 400 feet is preferred; if less, the mall may look like a strip development.)
29. Is the site level? Is it on well-drained land?
30. Does the mall face north and/or east?
31. Can the mall be seen from a distance?
32. Are any structures, such as a service station, located in the parking area? (If so, do they impede the site's visibility?)
33. Is the site a complete unit? (A road should not pass through the site.)
34. Are the buildings set far enough back on the site that the entire area may be seen?
35. Are all the stores readily accessible to each other, with none having an advantage?

Source: J. E. Mertes, "Site Opportunities for the Small Retailer," *Journal of Retailing,* Vol. XXXIX, No. 3, p. 44.

Figure 7–2   Tysons Corner Center, single level mall, before renovation. *Courtesy:* The Lehndorff Group, Dallas

The "New" Tysons Corner Center was the winner of the *Monitor Magazine's* Ninth Annual Center and Stores of Excellence Design competition. Its gleaming brass and steel structure was praised by the judges for "simplicity and excellence." Before and after photographs of the renovation of Tysons Corner Center are shown in Figures 7–2 and 7–3.

Mega Malls

The huge environments, such as the prototype developed in West Edmonton, Canada and followed by the Mall of America, are combination retail shopping and entertainment centers. The concept is to attract local shoppers as well as tourists, and to keep them in the arena as long as possible by offering a wide variety of restaurants, amusement facilities, and theaters that will augment their shopping ventures.

Power Centers

A power center is a shopping environment that features at least two or three high-profile, promotional type stores that bring the crowds. Stores like Price Club, Filene's Basement, Marshalls and T. J. Maxx are typical of the anchors. The key to the success of this type of center is to provide an image of bargain shopping so that vast throngs of consumers will be motivated to shop there. The centers generally range in size from 225,000 to over 500,000 square feet. The locations are easy to reach and are often found on major arteries or highways.

Flea Markets

A carnival-like atmosphere usually pervades the flea market arena. They are found either in parking fields that are primarily used by other businesses such as drive-in theaters, or in enclosed facilities that were once home to defunct department stores. The sizes range from the smaller ones with about 50 vendors to the giants such as the

Figure 7–3 The "new" Tysons Corner Center in McLean, Virginia. *Courtesy:* The Lehndorff Group, Dallas

Figure 7–4   The Mills is an outlet mall. *Courtesy:* Western Development Corporation

one in San Jose, California, the nation's largest with more than 2,000 dealers. Business is generally conducted during a few days of the week in flea markets, except in some cases in which the activity is a seven-day per week venture.

Outlet Centers

All across the United States, there are outlet centers that feature either closeout operations of retailers or stores operated by manufacturers and designers who wish to dispose of their unwanted overruns or out-of-season goods. Some of the major entries are in Freeport and Kittery, Maine; Secaucus, New Jersey, North Conway, New Hampshire; and Harriman, New York where merchandise produced by manufacturers and designers such as Calvin Klein, Liz Claiborne, Ralph Lauren, and Gucci are available at a fraction of what they would normally be sold for. A major entry in the outlet classification is the one known as the Mills, a focus of which appears in the chapter.

Strip Centers

These are the typical, small, outdoor shopping centers that dot towns all across the United States. They usually are limited to about twenty stores, at which apparel, hardware, food, and other merchandise are featured. The mix is often of independent

Figure 7–5   Baltimore's Inner Harbor is a festival market. Photograph by Ellen Diamond

retailers and units of chains such as Hit or Miss, Mandy's, Dress Barn, Record World, and so forth.

Mixed-use Centers

A combination of stores, hotels, office buildings, and residences make up the mixed-use facility. They are found in suburban areas or in major cities. One of the most successful is Copley Place in Boston, Massachusetts, where two hotels, four office buildings, a nine-screen movie theater, one hundred shops, private residences, and restaurants co-exist. With stores like Neiman-Marcus, Tiffany & Company, Charles Jourdan, Jaeger, and St. Laurent–Rive Gauche, the flavor is upscale.

Festival Marketplace

When the Rouse Company redeveloped historical Faneuil Hall and its surrounding area in Boston, it was the birth of festival marketplaces. Such arenas are composites of shops and eateries in festive settings that make shopping a pleasurable and entertaining event. Typically, these centers are converted from facilities that once housed other types of businesses. Some of the more popular are South Street Seaport in New York, once home to the Fulton Fish Market, Union Station in St. Louis, the premises that housed the original train depot before it moved to other quarters, and Inner Harbor in Baltimore, Maryland, a once downtrodden waterfront environment.

A RETAILING FOCUS   *The Mills, A Shopping Experience*

When one enters The Mills, he or she is found inside of an enclosure that typically features two miles of stores under one roof. Located in such places as Ft. Lauderdale, Florida; midway between Chicago, Illinois and Milwaukee, Wisconsin; northern Virginia; and in the outskirts of Philadelphia, Pennsylvania, shopping areas like Sawgrass Mills, Gurnee Mills, Potomac Mills, and Franklin Mills have taken the areas by storm.

The success of these enormous caverns of bargain stores is due in part to the fact that they are located sufficiently far from the typical retail malls and other shopping centers so as not to cause distress to the traditional retail operations. Since both types of arena carry similar or sometimes the exact merchandise simultaneously, closer proximity would interfere with traditional retailing.

The Mills are filled with outlets of retail giant department stores like Saks Fifth Avenue, Nordstrom, J. C. Penney, Macy's, and Speigel, as well as specialty chains such as AnnTaylor, Nine West, and Eddie Bauer. Rounding out the store mix are designer and manufacturer's outlets with names like Tahari, Colours by Alexander Julian, Geoffrey Beene, and DKNY. The common ingredient among all of the stores is bargain merchandise.

The crowds attracted to these shopping environs are comparable to those found at tourist attractions. Vast parking fields, similar to those found at Disney World, abound with private automobiles as well as scores of buses, which take tourists on shopping sprees. The reputations of The Mills are so renowned that many tour operators from foreign countries plan shopping excursions that are led by tour guides much the same as those that are found taking people to cultural attractions.

Free-Standing Stores

Generally, free-standing retail outlets are discount stores, chain specialty shops, or department store branches. They are generally found along major automobile arteries where they may attract clientele from considerable distances. They are easily reached and offer adequate parking. Since single free-standing stores cannot attract as much traffic as a shopping mall can, they rely on heavy advertising and promotions for their customers.

Neighborhood Clusters

In most towns, a number of small stores ranging from those carrying food items to units dealing in ready-to-wear can be found grouped together on a main street. Generally these are family-owned stores that appeal to the local population.

The Specific Site

Once the general trading area for store location and the particular type of shopping district within that area have been decided upon, the remaining step is the selection of a specific site. The decision on specific site is a sensitive one, since 100 feet can mark the difference between an excellent and a poor site. Similarly, a successful high-priced men's shop can fail in an area perfectly suited to a low-price operation. Several factors must be considered.

Neighboring Stores

The nearby stores must be compatible if the site is to be a successful one. Many stores do well by locating near department stores and attracting customers whose prime purpose is to shop at the department store. Similarly, ladies' clothing, accessory, and shoe stores tend to complement on another, particularly if they appeal to customers of the same economic level. A high-priced shop in an area catering to low-income customers is unlikely to be successful. The wrong sort of neighbor may be damaging. A fine restaurant should not be located next to a garage, or a children's shop next to a bar.

Traveling Convenience

If the site selected is in an urban center and if success depends upon nonlocal customers, convenient mass transit systems must be available. In the case of suburban retailing locations, the same logic requires good roads and sufficient parking for a successful location.

STORE LAYOUT

Once the final selection of a site has been made, attention must center upon how to use its interior and exterior most efficiently. The enormous amount of competition in soft goods, hard goods, and foodstuffs, for example, necessitates careful store layout planning. Even in the smallest retail organizations, the store layout is not left to chance. Suppliers to these smaller organizations are only too happy to lend their assistance. Remember, the more efficient the retail store, the more successful are the vendors. Large retail organizations, including the franchisers, go to great lengths to plan store layouts scientifically. Some aspects of layout (the overall plan) are the work of top management and often outside consultants. Middle managers are involved in their respective departments' physical arrangements.

The term *layout* signifies not only physical arrangement; it also involves the selection of merchandise displays, lighting fixtures, and the location of selling, service, administrative, and staff areas.

A RETAILING FOCUS   Schafer Associates, Inc.

Schafer Associates, Inc. was incorporated in 1947, and has since been involved in the planning, design, and documentation of retail operations throughout the United States. Since its inception, the company has been responsible for the planning and design of over 33 million feet of retail space for over three hundred clients. The companies it represents include Belk Stores, Carson Pirie Scott, A & P, Kinney Shoe Corporation, Marshall Fields, Montgomery Ward, Rich's, and Sears, Roebuck & Company.

The company developed its reputation in the retail industry by responding to clients through a team approach for each project. Unlike other design organizations, which have individual designers on specific projects. Schafer Associates uses the combined experience of a project team to attain the highest possible standards.

Each project undertaken begins with a customized set of objectives based on research and the clients' goals for implementing strategies of customer dominance, profitability, and customer targeting. Through constant communication with the clients, the company is able to make certain that all of their needs are met. Many design organizations fail to customize their proposals to specific needs, with the ultimate results producing store designs that are in the "cookie-cutter" mold.

The quality of its design has resulted in long-term relationships with its clients. Many have returned to Schafer Associates each time a new unit is planned or refurbishing is appropriate for an existing outlet.

Customer loyalty is not the only factor that has made Schafer's enviable reputation. A significant amount of recognition has been bestowed upon it by the retail industry,

Figure 7–6 Exciting store layout for Parisian, Cincinnati, Ohio. *Courtesy:* Schafer Associates, Inc.; *Photography:* Milroy/McAleer Photography

including awards from the National Retail Merchants Association, the largest retail trade organization in the United States, and the National Association of Store Fixture Manufacturers. Among them are the Grant Award—Store of the Year by the NMRA in 1985, for Parisian, a specialty chain; Honorable Mention by the NMRA in 1986, for Carson Pirie Scott, the Chicago-based department store organization; The Silver Trophy–Supermarkets given by the Inspiration Press Store of the World in 1988, for the Omni Superstore; and First Place by the NMRA in 1989, for Bockwinkel's, an upscale grocery chain in Illinois.

Schafer Associates' pledge of producing stores that are appropriate to the locale and to their client's mission, superior to the client's competition, efficient in operation and geared to produce the highest sales per square foot possible, profitable in project cost control and in long-term return on investment, has made the company one of the industry's leaders.

Photographs featuring some of Schafer Associates' award-winning, diverse styles are featured in this section of the chapter. Figure 7–6 features an exciting store layout for Parisian, Cincinnati, Ohio.

Exterior Layout and Design

The store's exterior structure and its surrounding parts must be carefully designed to attract the consumers' attention. However, not only must these facilities be appealing to the eye, they must also be functional. The convenience of the customer cannot in any way be sacrificed to the aesthetic quality of the structure. In some types of retail operations the building itself is extremely important as an attention-getting device. However, as is the case in advertising, merely attracting attention is insufficient— holding the attention is important. The store that attracts the consumer passing by in an automobile but doesn't provide the necessary parking facilities will not bring that consumer in to shop.

Today's retail structures are as individualistic as the interiors of our homes. Effort is made to incorporate the image of the operation into its exterior structure. For example, the "preppie" shop featuring tweeds and bulky sweaters often chooses an exterior of roughhewn wood for its building material. The franchisers develop definite personalities for their units and incorporate them into the structure. Pizza Hut, a fast-food franchise, is quickly recognized by the passing consumer merely because of its façade.

An extremely important aspect of exterior planning is the provision for parking facilities. Typically, the large department stores and supermarkets, and often small stores, provide parking in large fields surrounding the store. With the need for more auto space, some stores have two-level parking with access to the store on both levels. Other retail organizations have installed underground and rooftop parking. In an effort to bring the customer right to the selling floor, Macy's, at one of its branches, has introduced an innovation in parking facilities that has become a prototype for many retailers. The main parking area is located around the selling floors of the store. Through the use of ramps, a customer can drive to a particular floor, park the car, and enter the selling area without leaving the building. This arrangement attempts to combine artistic design and function.

Outdoor selling areas have served to expand the selling facilities of retail stores. Outdoor furniture and garden supplies are just two examples of merchandise sold outside the store. Many stores hold special sales on section of their parking fields.

Windows and entrances vary in retailing, where the gamut runs from the windowless store to one with many windows. Image, store policy, and location are just some factors that will determine the types and number of windows and entrances. A more in-depth discussion of windows will be found in Chapter 14, *Visual Merchandising*.

Interior Layout and Design

The appearance of a store naturally affects one's first impression of it. Years ago, the retailer was satisfied with selecting "nice" colors and materials; today's entrepreneur relies upon expertise. Seldom does one find a colorless decor and wooden or other standard floors and lighting in today's retail stores. These have been replaced by newer materials and color arrangements conducive to shopping.

Wall, Floor, and Ceiling Materials

Paint still seems to dominate a store's walls and ceiling. Even the supermarkets compete via store attractiveness. Bold colors, with different departments using different color schemes, separate the store into clearly defined areas. It is not unusual to see food stores painted in bright reds, yellows, and oranges. Some food markets even have wood-panel areas for both a change of pace and function—wood being just about maintenance-free. In the department and specialty stores walls are adorned with paint, paper, fabric, wood, mirrors, and textures such as cork. Of course, image is a tremendous factor in the selection of these materials.

Floors have taken on a new look, and they have also become more functional. There has been extensive use of high quality, easily maintained carpeting in many retail stores. By using such materials, stores are improving their appearance and soothing tired feet. This carpet conceals soil (because of its color combination and construction) and releases it with easy laundering. It is so durable that it is being used in hospitals, theaters, restaurants, and other heavy-traffic areas. Textured vinyl tiles, pretreated wooden planks that resist scratching, poured seamless vinyl floors, and conventional carpeting have replaced the ordinary store flooring.

Lighting and Selection of Lighting Fixtures

Because fluorescent light is the most economical to use, a large number of retailers choose to light their stores in that fashion. The stores seeking to project atmosphere, such as those selling high-fashion merchandise, do not use fluorescent fixtures. Most stores employ experts to help them select the proper lighting fixtures and their locations.

Lighting, if used intelligently, can show the store's offerings to their best advantage. This includes merchandise hanging on a rack, folded on a counter, displayed inside the store or in a window, being tried on by a customer, or being checked out by the wrapping clerk. Proper lighting will also ensure that departments and merchandise can be easily seen and that employees and customers can read merchandise tags.

Today's modern retail establishment makes use of the halogen/quartz bulbs and high-intensity discharge lighting in addition to incandescent lights and houses them in a wide variety of fixtures. The bulbs may be recessed into the walls and ceilings (either in stationary or swivel fixtures) or used as illumination in the most contemporary or elaborate holders. Many retailers are using track lighting systems. They provide the retailer with flexibility in movement as well as beauty. Whatever the choice, it must be appropriate for the particular retail establishment. A more complete discussion on lighting is covered in Chapter 14, *Visual Merchandising*.

Merchandise Fixtures

Fixtures can help to project a store's image; but, more important, they must help to properly stock, display, and finally sell merchandise.

Perhaps the most important factor to be considered in the selection of fixtures is whether the store is a service or a self-service operation. Needless to say, the self-service store employs fixtures that facilitate browsing by the customer. Counters accessible on all sides, racks not separated from the customer by the narrow counters behind which sales clerks stand in service stores, and merchandise cases free of glass doors are examples of fixtures found in self-service units. The service-oriented retail shop, which requires the assistance of a salesperson, will make use of enclosed cases, hanging racks behind counters, and enclosed compartments. Each type of operation and product has its own special requirements. For example, precious jewelry, by its very nature, requires separation from the shopper, while containers of coffee belong on open shelves.

Fixtures come in many materials. Wood, plastic laminate, brass, steel, wrought iron, plastic, glass, and combinations of these are just a few of the materials that are used. The styles have as wide a range as do furnishings for the home. Particular types again depend upon image, cost, taste, and the merchandise. Upscale food store counters are shown in Figure 7–7. Figures 7–8 and 7–9 display other merchandise fixtures.

Specialized equipment used in many nonselling areas of the store will be discussed in the appropriate chapters.

Locating the Departments

Of all the departments, the selling departments are the most important to a store's success. Where to locate them, particularly when a store has many, is a problem that management must concern itself with. Not as important, but also necessary to the store's

Figure 7–7   Upscale food store counters. *Courtesy:* Schafer Associates, Inc.; *Photography:* Les Boschke Photography

Figure 7–8   Enclosed fixtures protect valuable merchandise and require salesperson's assistance. *Courtesy:* Toys "Я" Us

Figure 7–9   Open counters and racks designed for self-service. *Courtesy:* Kids "Я" Us

success, is the location of the supporting departments. The receiving department, stockrooms, administrative offices, visual merchandising department, and advertising offices are just a few to be assigned space.

Some of the factors that must be considered in locating the departments are total space available, assortment of merchandise to be carried, type of merchandise, the number of floor levels, the number of entrances, elevator and escalator locations, and type of operation (service or self-service).

The small retail store should plan the location of its merchandise as carefully as its large counterparts do. While it is true that the small store will not have the same amount of merchandise to display, there is a more limited amount of space available. Many small retailers stock their goods haphazardly. This ultimately leads to a less efficient operation; poor layout planning reduces the amount of merchandise that can be displayed.

Selling Departments.   The principles regarding the locating of departments should be understood by anyone entering the retailing field. Some general rules are:

1. Convenience goods (merchandise that requires little effort in purchasing, such as cigarettes), impulse goods (goods that are bought without much contemplation, such as umbrellas in a rainstorm), and inexpensive merchandise in general should be located in high-traffic areas. These include locations at store entrances, next to elevators and escalators, or next to the refund department. A large New York specialty store opened a ladies' hosiery department next to the refund area and quickly doubled its hosiery sales.

2. Shopping goods (those that require more careful consideration, such as clothing and furniture) should be located at the rear of single-level stores and upstairs in multilevel stores. Generally the more expensive and less-frequented departments, such as furniture, are located at the furthest points to reach in a store.

3. If the store has many levels, it is often wise for a department to display a representation or a portion of its offerings on the main floor. These are called split or satellite departments. For example, men's clothing might be located on the second floor but might have a small area selling just shirts and ties on the main floor. This part of its merchandise offering is usually less expensive than the rest and therefore might be purchased

impulsively. It also may make the potential customer aware of the type of menswear available in the store, encouraging a trip to the main department in another location.

4. Storage areas used to stock additional goods may have a central location in a store (the basement, for example) or may be located within each department. The trend today is for showing as much as possible without great reserve space. In any case, reserve merchandise is best located close to the selling floor, where it can be secured for the customer quickly. Bulky merchandise, such as furniture and appliances, generally necessitates large storage areas away from the selling floor.

5. Department space allocation should be keyed to the percentage of the store's total sales expected for each department.

6. Those departments with related merchandise should be next to each other. For example, the handbag department should be near the shoe department. This allows for the customer to easily purchase a pair of shoes and coordinating handbag and thus leads to increased total sales for the store.

The above list is one which typifies how selling departments are generally arranged, and it is the basis for most retailers' layouts. It should be noted, however that over the past several years, many retailers, at least for a portion of their selling space, have initiated a new concept in the merchandising and location of some departments. Where the concept of location by "classification" is the major concept, some retailers are locating departments by "collection." *Classification* refers to selling department organization according to merchandise type without regard to a specific manufacturer or designer. For example, men's sportswear is a classification, as is ladies' shoes. The departure from this to the newer concept of *collection* areas has proved to be extremely successful and is finding a place for itself in retail operations all across the country. Each collection, or group, of a particular manufacturer is located in an area that is named for that line. The department features merchandise bearing one label, regardless of the different number of classifications it cuts across. This concept provides the shopper with total look. All of the merchandise has a connecting theme and is compatible through color, fabric, styling, image, and so on. Once the customer is satisfied with a collection, he or she is likely to buy more than just one item, an improvement over buying habits in departments that are conventionally arranged.

Such collections as Liz Claiborne, Perry Ellis, Calvin Klein, and Ralph Lauren are being shown this way, which indicates a successful concept.

NonSelling areas.   The prime space in a retail establishment is designated as the selling floor, but without the sales-supporting and administrative departments, retailers could not be successful. These departments are usually located in the rear of single-level units and on the upper floor of a multilevel shop. The further away from the entrance, the less desirable the space for selling.

Department Layout

After a department is assigned space and the appropriate fixtures have been selected, the physical organization of the department takes place. Each department must consider any factors peculiar to its merchandise before deciding upon an arrangement. For example, a precious jewelry department might assemble four counters at right angles to each other, forming an island in the center that may house another, taller floor case. This arrangement permits maximum security and yet enables the customer to see the merchandise. In a budget department, open racks and aisle tables may be placed so that the merchandise receives maximum exposure. Supermarkets generally arrange their shelves back to back in long aisles that permit a continuous flow of traffic. This arrangement allows for mass stocking of merchandise that can be easily selected by the customer without the necessity of frequent replenishment.

Whatever the retail establishment might be, care must be exercised to allow for a smooth flow of customer traffic while at the same time leading individuals throughout the store. Aisles should be easily accessible. Narrow lanes tie up traffic and add to confusion in peak selling periods.

Traffic Movement

Seasoned retailers know that few customers will use the staircase as a means of going to upper and lower floors. Escalators are the main customer-moving devices. They quickly and without interruption move customers from floor to floor. Open-sided escalators also permit shoppers to see the store's merchandise as they pass by. (See Figure 7–10.) Figure 7–11 features island and wall units. As a general rule, the smaller store is best off using an elevator; it requires less space than the escalator and can be installed less expensively. Further, elevators are a necessity for carriages and people in wheelchairs. The retailer not wishing to make an investment in any of these automatic devices might be wiser to confine the selling area to one floor or stock a second story with desirable merchandise that is unavailable elsewhere.

TRENDS

The locations and layouts of retailing continue to change to better address the needs of the shoppers. Some of these trends are discussed here.

Refurbishment and Expansion of Malls

Having entered retailing in the mid 1950s and 1960s, many shopping malls are beginning to revitalize their facilities. Some have added second and third levels and others have tacked on new wings to enlarge their premises. Roosevelt Field, in suburban New York City, for example, has added a second story to house 70 additional shops and a food court and a new wing to house 60 additional stores and another anchor store, Nordstrom. Its expansion will make it the largest traditional mall in the United States. Roosevelt Field is not alone in making this type of improvement. Other malls that are being updated include the Naples Shopping Center in Naples, Florida, the Broward Mall, in Plantation, Florida, and the Great Lakes Mall in Mentor, Ohio.

Power Center Expansion

As more and more warehouse outlets like Price Club and discounters like Kmart plan to open up units, their target locations are the power centers. By grouping these high-volume stores together, greater numbers of people are attracted than if each unit was built as a free-standing store.

Atypical Environments

Rather than continue to build the traditional types of stores in which fixturing and materials merely enhance the merchandise, a trend toward providing stores with thematic approaches has developed. When a customer enters the Disney Store, which is

Figure 7–10 Open-sided escalators at A & S Plaza, New York. *Courtesy:* A&S

Figure 7–11 Island and wall units used for maximum merchandise exposure. *Courtesy:* Radio Shack

replete with animated displays and entertaining videos, he or she is put into a mood that usually motivates purchasing. Another store that uses this environmental or thematic approach is Hanna Barbera.

Other concepts include the minimalistic approach, in which sparse fixturing is dominant; residential concepts, in which the shopper is served in facilities that are reminiscent of homes such as the one Ralph Lauren established in his flagship store on Madison Avenue in New York City; and the warehouse concept where shoppers make selections in surroundings that are typically found in wholesaler's premises, this concept is used by the Price Club.

ACTION FOR THE INDEPENDENT RETAILER

Site selection typifies the advantages of size. Large successful stores not only have a financial advantage; they also have the know-how and the willingness to scientifically survey a prospective location. Although it is true that most small businesses cannot afford the expense of a truly scientific survey, few make any attempt to evaluate all of the information available to them. All too often, a location is picked by hunch. In addition, many sites are selected with more attention paid to the ease of commuting to the proprietor's home than to the needs of the neighborhood in which the store is to be located. As a result, an important cause of small retail failure is poor site selection. The pity is that much of the necessary information is available, free of charge, to anyone willing to spend a little time at the library studying census reports and the like.

The interior and the exterior layout of the small store are important. Since lack of sufficient space and financial strength results in a relatively small inventory, it is important that the available inventory should be shown to its best advantage. We have all seen inviting, beautifully set up small stores that have been designed with a minimum of expense. All it takes is the proprietor's understanding of the importance of proper layout, taste, and effort.

IMPORTANT POINTS IN THE CHAPTER

1. One of the principal reasons for the failure of new retail stores is poor site selection. Despite this, some retailers select locations in an unscientific manner.
2. Site selection should begin with an appraisal of the general trading area, with particular attention paid to the size and characteristics of the area's population.
3. After the general trading area has been decided upon, the shopping district within that area must be determined. Choices between the relative merits of central districts, malls, flea markets, outlet centers, and other areas must be made.
4. During recent years shopping malls have undergone dramatic growth. Some of the reasons for this expansion are one-stop shopping, adequate parking, controlled competition, and unified promotional activities.
5. To ensure maximal use of facilities, store layout should be scientifically determined.
6. Competition for the customer's attention begins with imaginative exterior layout and design. Exterior design should be tasteful, eye-catching, and functional.

7. Interior design begins with wall, floor, and ceiling materials. These should be attractive to the eye, useful in separating areas, and in keeping with the store's image.

8. Lighting fixtures should be attractive, be adequate for good overall visibility, and have the additional function of setting off the store's merchandise to its best advantage.

9. The store's image may be emphasized by the selection of the merchandise fixtures. Self-service stores must display merchandise in a manner that encourages customer browsing. Service-oriented stores usually feature enclosed cases and inaccessible racks.

10. The location of the various departments depends, to a large extent, on store traffic. Convenience goods and inexpensive merchandise should be located in high-traffic areas. Goods that require careful consideration are usually placed in less highly used areas. Such departments frequently display samples of their stock in high-traffic areas.

11. Service departments such as stockrooms are located in areas of light traffic as close as possible to the departments they serve.

REVIEW QUESTIONS

1. Most retailers do not select sites for their store effectively. Why?

2. Indicate six characteristics that should be studied in a location analysis. For each of the factors mentioned, suggest a type of store for which this information would be important.

3. What is meant by the term "festival marketplace"?

4. Why are downtown shopping areas generally of the vertical mall variety?

5. What are the advantages of an enclosed mall?

6. Indicate four pairs of stores that would make poor neighbors.

7. From whom can small retailers get assistance in planning their store's layout?

8. Which classification of department in a store requires the most consideration in the physical layout?

9. Besides visual appeal, what must a retailer consider in planning the store's exterior space?

10. How have some stores converted limited exterior shape into more adequate parking facilities?

11. Discuss those factors that contribute to the number and type of windows a store has.

12. Besides paint, which materials do modern retailers use for their walls and ceilings?

13. In addition to beauty, for what reasons have retailers covered their selling floors with carpeting instead of wood and vinyl tile?

14. What are some advantages of fluorescent lighting?

15. Why do self-service and service departments require different merchandise fixtures?

16. Define convenience goods. Where should they be located?

17. What are shopping goods? Is there anything to consider in determining which of these should be located nearest and furthest from the entrance?

18. Discuss how a store allocates the amount of space for each department.

CASE PROBLEMS

Case Problem 1

Jill Watson has just sold a highly successful supermarket in a suburban location. She opened the store ten years ago as a neighborhood grocery, and because of her ability and the growth of the area, she was able to expand the store to a medium-sized supermarket, for which she received in excess of $500,000.

She is seriously considering opening a small supermarket in a midtown high-density location in which, in addition to the regular supermarket activities, she will make sandwiches and coffee (not to be eaten on the premises).

Question

1. Discuss the following
   a. Traffic count
   b. Prices she can get
   c. Probable rental
   d. Working days and hours
   e. Competition
   f. Breakfast and lunch business
   g. Local competition
   h. Effect of suburban competition
   i. Difficulty of obtaining personnel
   j. Employee salaries

Case Problem 2

All the department managers of Belldocks Specialty Shop were called to a meeting requested by top management. The purpose of the meeting was to discuss the establishment of a special department in a separate location to handle customers' returns and refunds. At the present time, each department is handling its own adjustments. The main reasons for the proposed change are:

1. Customers returning merchandise often take up a salesperson's time, which might be better spent in selling other merchandise.
2. At peak periods, departments often become overcrowded with adjustments.
3. Dissatisfied customers making returns sometimes disrupt order in the departments.
4. The number of people working in each department could be cut down and the money used to hire a few experts on returns and adjustments.

Belldocks is a four-level retail store (including a basement selling floor) selling men's, women's, and children's clothing. Last year they grossed $14 million in their 12 selling departments.

Questions

1. Are there any advantages in having each department handle its own returns? Discuss them.
2. If the decision was reached to centralize returns, where would you locate this new department? Carefully outline and discuss the factors to be considered in the selection of the location.

Chapter 8
Merchandise Handling

Photograph by Ellen Diamond

DELIVERIES MADE EASY . . .

One of the major problems confronting many retailers is getting the merchandise exactly as it was ordered and to the stores in time to maximize sales. In small operations, where the proprietor or manager has a handle on incoming orders and is knowledgeable about what was ordered, the problem is minimized. These individuals check the package's contents to make certain that the quantities are the same as were ordered, the size allocations are correct, and that the quality is the same as it was in the samples from which the orders were placed. This is possible in smaller operations, because the aforementioned owners and managers are often the buyers or have a complete comprehension of merchandise requirements.

In large organizations, particularly chains with significant numbers that use the "drop ship" method of delivery, that is, packages are sent from the manufacturers directly to each unit, problems can arise. Those in receipt of the goods are often careless in checking the contents and are sometimes unaware if the merchandise received is the same that was ordered. Not only might the quality be different, but some manufacturers are notorious for "substitution shipping," a term that describes the substitution of an item ordered with another one.

To ease this problem, some chains such as Mothercare, a 200-store maternity organization based in Secaucus, N.J., has gone the route of using outside distribution centers for deliveries. They were regularly plagued with late shipments, receipt of unordered merchandise, and assortments of wrong sizes and colors. Although the organization considered opening their own centralized warehouse and distribution center, it solved the problem with outside sourcing. They contracted with DMSI, a Charlotte, N.C., distribution center, to handle their problems.

DMSI receives orders, checks them for accuracy, and delivers them to the individual stores in the chain via their own carriers. Not only has the problem been resolved, but DMSI's clout in the industry enables Mothercare to pay lower shipping costs to manufacturers than they did before when they handled distribution on their own.

With lower costs for merchandise distribution and better results from the outside handling, the company is able to turn a better profit and use their resources to expand the company.

In a small retailing operation, the problem of getting the merchandise that has been ordered into stock or onto the selling floor is relatively simple. The person who ordered the goods is generally on hand when the merchandise is unpacked. This enables that individual to supervise the checking of merchandise, mark it with the selling price, and see to its placement in stock or on the selling shelves. Since the receipt of merchandise generally takes place directly on the selling floor, the handling of incoming merchandise is rapid and efficient.

The large retail establishment, where buyers cannot personally check the merchandise received, and where selling floors may be far from the receiving area, faces special problems. Effectively solving these problems results in both financial savings and rapid movement of goods from the receiving department to the selling floor. In periods of high activity, such as the Christmas season, making goods quickly available to the customer is important.

THE CENTRALIZED RECEIVING DEPARTMENT

In small stores, buyers often have receiving as part of their area of responsibility. However, as the size of the operation increases, individualized departmental receiving becomes impractical, and a centralized receiving department (an independent department responsible for all receiving) is necessary. Some of the advantages of the centralized receiving department are as follows:

1. *Better physical control of merchandise.* There is always the possibility of goods disappearing between the time the merchandise arrives in the store and the time it appears on the selling shelves. When the receiving operation is the chore of sales personnel, the procedures tend to be haphazard. Since receiving is not the prime job of salespeople, they are disinterested and careless. In addition, the frequent interruptions that occur on the sales floor practically guarantee errors. In contrast, a properly set up receiving department with standardized routines requires paperwork and signatures for both the receipt of goods into the store and the transfer of goods to warehouses and selling departments. The responsibility of specific individuals is clearly defined. Under such conditions, goods are unlikely to disappear.

2. *Better financial control of merchandise.* By standardizing procedures and fixing responsibilities, which can only be done with thoroughly trained personnel, the receiving department can be closely tied in with the accounting department. In this way, proper credits for damaged goods, shortages, and discounts can be achieved.

3. *More efficient use of equipment and supplies.* The centralized receiving department, thanks to its large volume of activity, can effectively use labor-saving machinery, which the relatively small, departmentalized receiving activities would not have sufficient volume for. For example, an expensive ticketing machine capable of great labor and cost savings would not be practical for the small amount of receiving done by an individual selling department. Similarly, if receiving and marking supplies are to be spread throughout all of the selling departments in a store, there is apt to be considerable waste and an unnecessary investment in the inventory of supplies.

4. *Relieving selling departments of receiving responsibilities.* Since the prime responsibility of sales personnel is selling, any job that distracts them from customers or possible customers is apt to reduce their selling effectiveness, and the receiving operation will suffer as well since it will be treated with boredom and disinterest.

5. *General advantages of specialization.* The advantage of mass production is that when the volume is large enough for a task to be broken down into its various parts and performed by separate individuals, the task can be done more effectively. In a large receiving department, where each worker does a specific job repetitively, that employee becomes proficient at it. This enables standardized procedures, individual responsibility, and the use of specialized machinery. As a result of this specialization, the centralized receiving department is capable of more effectively performing the receiving operation than the individual selling departments.

EQUIPMENT AND LAYOUT

In small and medium-sized stores, receiving functions can be efficiently handled with no special equipment or strictly followed procedures. Incoming packages may be delivered to the selling floor or the back of the store. When time permits, the goods are unpacked, checked, marked, and put on the selling shelves and racks or in the storeroom. As the store increases in size, the volume of receiving becomes so great that more scientific methods are needed to prevent costly errors or serious time loss in getting the merchandise to the selling floors. It is impossible to completely standardize receiving operations in a large store; the receiving department must be prepared at any time to handle a shipment of pianos or spools of thread and, obviously, they must be handled differently. However, there are certain broad principles which, if carefully followed, will improve receiving effectiveness. The Dennison Manufacturing Company suggests that the following ten ideas will improve the effectiveness of any receiving department.

1. *Straight-line movement of all materials with as little backtracking as possible.* Goods should be unloaded from the trucks and the receiving operations performed in such a manner that the first operation to be performed should be done closest to the unloading platform and the last operation to be performed should be done closest to the selling floor or storeroom. In other words, the unpacking operation should be done nearest to the truck, then the goods should be checked at a point closer to the selling floor. Finally, the price-marking operation should be located nearest the selling floor. Such an operation would require a minimum of merchandise handling. (See Figure 8–1.)

2. *Movement of all material through the shortest possible distance and with the fewest possible motions.* While the layout of an individual store depends upon the amount and

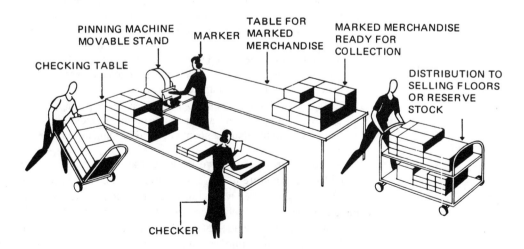

Figure 8–1   Checking and marking operation with stationary tables. *Courtesy:* Dennison Manufacturing Company

shape of the available space, careful study must be made of the use of the space to ensure maximum effectiveness.

3. *Maximum machine operation, minimum hand operation.* By mechanizing operations wherever possible, the receiving department may be assured of considerable time savings. Moreover, in these times of high labor costs, machines can generally do a job more inexpensively, as well as more effectively. An example of this is the use of conveyor belts that bring the goods to workers rather than having the workers do their own carrying of goods.

4. *Determination of the most efficient methods of performing specific repetitive operations, and standardization of these methods.* Most receiving operations consist of simple repetitive tasks. If these tasks are done in any but the most efficient way, time will be lost. It is necessary to determine the best way to do the job, and to do it that way every time.

5. *Careful attention to working conditions.* Improper working conditions can contribute to deficiencies and result in lost time. Such factors as proper table and chair heights, adequate lighting, and good machine layout are very important. Not only must equipment be scientifically laid out, but attention must be given to human production as well. Care must be taken to ensure that working conditions, worker comfort, and worker efficiency be maintained at as high a level as possible.

6. *Careful selection and training of personnel.* Wherever possible, the same operation should be performed by the same people. Receiving department workers require specific talents and must be selected with this in mind. That is to say, a person responsible for unpacking must have the physical qualifications necessary for the job. In stores with a large volume of receiving and many receiving department employees, it is possible to specialize the working force. Rather than training a person to be a jack-of-all-trades, workers should be taught to do specific jobs. Doing the same operations repetitively increases a worker's efficiency.

7. *Adequate supervision.* To ensure that standard methods and standard quality are maintained, careful supervision is required. If procedures are not carefully supervised, there is always the likelihood that the most perfect planning will not be followed. Receiving departments must be set up in such a way that all of the supervisor's responsibilities, both for workers and for machines, are always in plain sight and easily supervised and controlled.

8. *Sufficient equipment.* The efficiency of a large receiving department depends upon the efficiency of its equipment. There must be enough equipment to take full advantage of machine operation even in times of peak production. It is particularly vital that carefully set up procedures be used during rush periods. If the amount of equipment on hand does not have the capacity to handle peak production quantities, procedures are apt to break down, and the errors and inefficiencies that they were designed to overcome will occur.

9. *Standby equipment.* The fullest possible use of equipment, taking into consideration the importance of standby equipment for emergencies, must be insisted upon. The major problem in the receiving operation is errors. The best defense against errors is strict adherence to carefully designed procedures. Machine breakdowns can be very serious, not only in terms of lost production, but more important, because the carefully set up procedures must be altered. Since the personnel have been carefully trained in specific procedures, any change in procedures is apt to cause serious errors. It is vital that, wherever possible, standby equipment is available.

10. *Enough records for adequate control.* Paperwork is perhaps the most annoying function of the receiving department and it should, wherever possible, be eliminated. On the other hand, a certain minimum amount of record-keeping must be performed for proper control.

Although all of the above principles are obvious, they are not simple. It is not unusual for a large store to use engineers to set up their receiving departments.

Frequently, separate receiving areas are used for specific types of goods. Where the volume of receiving of appliances or ready-to-wear is great enough, the use of special receiving areas permits the adaptation of procedures specifically designed for those goods.

Stores rely upon one or several types of equipment in their handling of merchandise.

Stationary Tables

The most commonly used piece of equipment in a receiving room is the stationary table. This type of table is well suited to a small store because it is compact and requires little space. Incoming packages are first brought to the table. The merchandise is unpacked and sorted as it is placed on the table. Then the goods are checked, marked, and taken to the selling floor.

Portable Tables

Where the volume of incoming goods is so great that the operations of unpacking and checking are separated from marking, portable tables are used. The merchandise is placed on tables on wheels, where it is unpacked and checked. Then each table is wheeled to the marking area. After being marked, the goods, still on the same table, may be moved to the selling floor. The use of the portable table minimizes the handling of the goods. The design of the portable table depends on the merchandise to be handled. Racks may be substituted for tables if ready-to-wear merchandise is involved. The portable equipment eliminates the handling necessitated by the use of stationary tables.

Conveyor Systems

Large-volume stores can realize considerable savings in receiving costs by use of conveyor systems. Under such systems, the goods are unpacked onto a large conveyor belt. The belt moves the goods to a line of checkers, who place the goods on stationary tables alongside the conveyor. After being checked, the goods are replaced on the belt and move to the markers. The goods are once more transferred to small tables, marked, and replaced on the conveyor for removal to the sales floors and stockroom. (See Figures 8–2 and 8–3.) In stores that feature hanging soft goods, a different type of conveyor system is used. The merchandise is placed on hangers and put on a rack-like conveyor system. The merchandise automatically moves along, on hangers, to the checking and marking areas and finally to the designated selling areas. Stores using this system have "spurs" that terminate in certain areas of the selling departments so that little physical handling of merchandise is required between the receiving and selling areas.

Receivings in a department store are of a wide variety, and none of the four types of equipment just described is best for every type of goods. As a result, most large stores use a combination of methods.

RECEIVING OPERATIONS

The receiving operation begins with the delivery of merchandise from the carrier to the unloading or receiving platform. Ideally, this should be done indoors to protect against damage by weather, unnecessary handling of cartons, and interference with outside traffic. But because any use of indoor space is likely to reduce the space available for selling, mid-city stores, in which space is at a premium, frequently provide for outdoor unloading of deliveries.

Receiving operations include inspecting, recording, checking, and marking of merchandise.

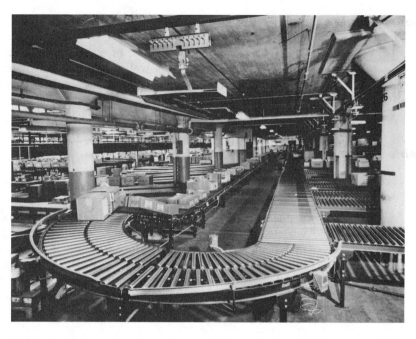

Figure 8–2   A roller conveyor system in combination with live roller lines and belt conveyors. This system is particularly suited for rapid and efficient transport from and to store areas and dispatch points

Figure 8–3   Handler removes needed stock from this 125-foot conveyor; the remainder accumulates on the conveyor

Inspecting

The first phase of the receiving operations is the inspection of the delivered packages or cartons. The newly delivered packages should be inspected (not unpacked) immediately upon unloading from the truck. This should be done in the presence of the driver. The number and condition of the cartons should be checked. Any open or damaged cartons or shortage of cartons should be noted on the trucker's receipt. This information should also be noted on the store's copy of the freight bill, which the trucker must sign as confirmation. The trucker's signature attesting to the discrepancy is necessary if damage claims are to be filed.

Since freight costs are generally paid by the store, it is necessary to check the amount charged for the delivery. Checking freight costs frequently requires weighing the delivered goods. If this is not always possible, spot checks should be made from time to time.

The still-unopened cartons are then marked with department numbers so they can be taken to the particular area of the receiving department designated for the unpacking of that particular type of merchandise.

The Receiving Record

Before the cartons are sent on for unpacking, a receiving record is made out. The form of the receiving record varies from store to store, but it generally contains the following information:

Date and hour of arrival	Condition of packages
Weight	Delivery charges
Form of transportation	Name of deliverer
Number of pieces	Amount of invoice
Receiving number	Department ordering goods
Invoice number	Remarks

A small store, in which the proprietor has complete knowledge and control of the operation, can frequently do without a formal receiving record. In a large store the receiving record is an important document, for the following reasons:

1. In the event of a disagreement between the vendor and the store over a particular shipment, the receiving record provides necessary information. In a small store the proprietor can either trust his or her memory in such cases, or make an informal note on each shipment.
2. The vendor's invoice number on the receiving record ensures that no invoice is paid unless the merchandise has been received. This is done by matching up invoices and receiving records prior to payment. The person paying the invoices in a small store need not worry about whether the merchandise was received. That individual was there when the delivery was made. In a large store, the person signing the check depends upon the receiving record for proof of delivery.

Checking

The next step in the receiving process involves checking the incoming goods. This includes determining if the goods are in agreement with the purchase order, removing the merchandise from the shipping container and sorting it, and checking the quantity and quality of the merchandise.

Unpacking and Sorting

Many stores have the policy of not opening a container until the invoice arrives. Unpacking and sorting without an invoice results in faulty operations because shortages and incorrect shipments become difficult to ascertain. Even when lists of the merchandise received are made out, discrepancies with the invoice are difficult to recheck, since goods delivered to the shipping floor cannot be recounted.

Quantity Checking

There are several methods of checking the quantity of incoming merchandise. Most stores use either the blind check method or the direct check method. There are also combinations of these methods and variations of them. Occasionally a store uses the spot-check method in which a few random items are checked. Since many errors slip through a spot-checking system, this method is not recommended.

The Direct Check.   This system provides for the checking of the quantity of incoming merchandise directly against the vendor's invoice. Shipments for which no invoice has arrived from the vendor are held unopened until the invoice is available. Frequently, the pile-up of unopened packages becomes so great that they must be quantity-checked without an invoice. In such cases, "dummy" invoices are prepared and used as though they were real.

The following are the advantages of the direct check method:

1. With no paperwork to do other than checkmarks against an invoice, the checker can work speedily and economically.
2. In the event of a discrepancy between the invoice and the checker's count, a recheck can be made quickly and efficiently.
3. The description of the merchandise is stated on the invoice and not left up to the imagination of the checker.

Direct checking is the most widely used method of quantity verification in small stores and probably in large stores as well. The problem of not always having the invoice on hand can be overcome by insisting that vendors include duplicate invoices in their packing containers.

The most serious disadvantage of the direct checking method is that it may lead to careless checking. Checking is a boring task, which is subject to carelessness. When the checker is told the quantity in advance (from the invoice) it is possible to check too quickly or, in a rush period, not to check at all.

The Blind Check.   The blind check method is designed to minimize the checking errors that occur with direct checking. The system provides for the checker to prepare a list of the items being received, without benefit of the invoice. Standardized forms are provided to ease the paperwork, but much paperwork remains to be done. This has the effect of slowing down the checking process. The blind check requires the checker to describe the merchandise. When the checker's description does not match the invoice description, costly delays may develop. This method does reduce the handling (and sometimes loss) of invoices.

The Semiblind Check.   The semiblind check method combines the best features of the direct check and the blind check methods. By providing the checker with a copy of the buying order, in which all of the paperwork is already included with the exception of the quantity, the unnecessary paperwork of the blind check method is eliminated. Because they are not told the quantity, the checkers are forced to determine the quantity by carefully counting the merchandise.

Whichever quantity checking method is used, discrepancies must be noted so that claims may be made for short shipments and returns made for overshipments.

Quality Checking

Generally speaking, checkers cannot be held responsible for any quality checking other than obvious errors. Close quality checking is the responsibility of the buyer, the buyer's assistants, or department manager. In practice, branded merchandise that is frequently reordered is rarely subject to quality checking. Merchandise that is to be stored in its original containers (men's shirts in plastic bags) is rarely quality checked. The decision is made by the buyer, who must decide whether the time saved by not checking is offset by customer dissatisfaction with an occasional poor quality item that slipped through unchecked.

Marking

With the exception of single-price stores, or merchandise that has been premarked by the vendor, all merchandise must be marked with its selling price before being offered for sale. This can be done with a variety of labels, by hand, or by a machine process.

Typical of the automated marking machines are microprocessors, which enable retailers to more quickly and precisely mark their merchandise. Figure 8–4 shows the Kimball LIS 1520 laser computer printer that facilitates bar code printing. Figure 8–5 features a system which enables the operator to run several microprocessor imprinters at one time, the ultimate in cost efficiency.

The Price Tag

The information to be found on the tag varies with the needs of the individual store and the type of merchandise involved. (See Figure 8–6.) In a small store, the person who makes the decision on the selling price is generally available when the goods are being marked. Larger stores face the problem of channeling price and other data to the markers.

One way of getting the sales price to the marker is by having the buyer mark the selling price on the invoice after it has been checked. Although this is a common method, it has the disadvantage of the invoice potentially being lost because of the excessive handling.

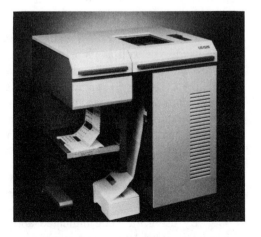

Figure 8–4   Kimball LIS 1520 laser computer printer.
Courtesy: Litton/Kimball Systems

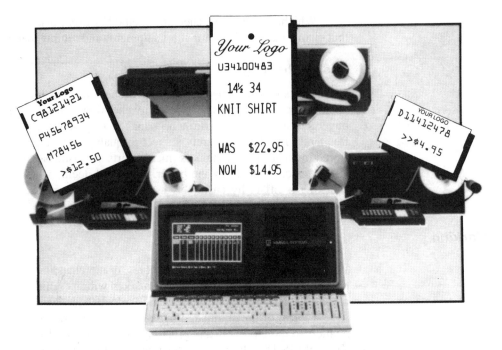

Figure 8–5   Computerized marking system. *Courtesy:* Litton/Kimball Systems

Frequently the buyer may mark one piece of the incoming goods and have someone else duplicate the tag on the balance of the shipment. This has the advantage of having the buyer see the merchandise just before it gets to the selling floor. Unfortunately, this method requires the buyer to be in the receiving department every time a shipment arrives.

Staple merchandise that is rarely subject to price change can be marked from lists supplied to the marker in advance.

The central offices of chain stores prepare lists of retail prices and send them to the individual stores. (Store managers may change these prices in a few cases to meet local competition.)

In some stores the price and other information to be marked are placed on a duplicate copy of the buyer's order, which is sent to the receiving department. In such cases, the information is available to the marker when the merchandise comes into the store.

Coding the Cost.   In many small stores, it is desirable to mark the cost of the merchandise as well as its selling price. Some stores, such as jewelry and appliance stores, whose merchandise does not have a fixed selling price, tag their merchandise with the cost and do not indicate the selling price. Naturally, if the cost is to be marked, it must be done in such a way that it can be easily read by the salesperson and not understood by the customer. A common coding system is the use of a word or phrase containing ten letters, each letter representing a number. The numbers are substituted for the letters to determine the cost.

$$1 \quad 2 \quad 3 \quad 4 \quad 5 \quad 6 \quad 7 \quad 8 \quad 9 \quad 0$$
$$C \quad O \quad S \quad T \quad M \quad A \quad R \quad K \quad E \quad D$$

By using the code indicated above, an item marked C S R M has a cost of $13.75. Any ten-letter word or phrase in which no letter appears more than once can be used for a costing code.

Figure 8–6 Merchandise price tags feature bar codes and other important information. *Courtesy:*Litton/Kimball Systems

Other Information. The balance of the information placed on the price tag depends upon the type of merchandise and the merchandise control systems used by the store. A large department store using up-to-date data processing processing procedures may put extensive information on the tag. Tags may be designed in such fashion that sales informational reports on color, style, and size may be available to the buyer. This can have an important effect on future buying decisions.

Bulk Marking

Low-price items that are subject to frequent price variations need not be marked until they are placed on the selling floor. This procedure is frequently followed by supermarkets. Goods are received in large cartons and the price is marked on the outside of the carton and stored. Not until the goods are brought to the selling floor are the individual items marked. In this way, price changes during the storage period do not require the merchandise to be marked. This procedure is sometimes called delayed marking.

Nonmarking

Certain types of goods need not be marked at all. In all cases of nonmarking, the checkout counters must be provided with lists of selling prices.

1. Merchandise that can be effectively displayed on shelves, counters, or tables can be priced by a sign. This shortcut in the marking function saves time and money.
2. In the case of very inexpensive merchandise, the cost of marking in relation to the profit may make marking illogical.
3. Certain products such as fruits and vegetables may be damaged by marking.
4. Promotional goods or other merchandise subject to constant price change are not usually marked because constant remarking is too time-consuming.

Premarking

As a means of saving space, time, and money, many large retailers have the manufacturers do the marking for them. This is most commonly found in staple goods such as men's shirts or hosiery, where price fluctuation is relatively uncommon.

Outside Marking

Many large stores, such as Marshall Field and Montgomery Ward, have their marking performed by their freight carriers. As in the case of premarking, the retailer must supply all the marking information and specifications to the outside marking firm. In the case of high-fashion merchandise, where every day is important, some retailers feel that outside marking permits a time saving of several days between the day of receipt and the day the goods appear on the selling floor.

Remarking

Many factors may require the remarking of merchandise: markdowns; additional markups; soiled, torn, or lost tags; merchandise returned by customers, and so on. Large retailers who keep track of the retail value of the inventory require special forms to be made out to enable the accounting department to make necessary changes on their inventory control records. This is frequently unnecessary in smaller stores.

There is a difference of opinion on the manner in which remarking is to be done. Many stores draw a line through the old price and write in the new price above it. This may give some customers the impression that they are getting a bargain. On the other hand, there are customers who believe the merchandise was overpriced to begin with. Such customers tend to look with suspicion on other goods in the store that have not been marked down. As a result, many stores handle markdowns by removing the old ticket and replacing it with a new ticket containing a new selling price. In this way, the customer may not be aware of the markdown. (See Figure 8–7.)

Figure 8–7 Reprice markers. *Courtesy:* Monarch Marking Machines

BRANCH AND CHAIN STORE RECEIVING

A large portion of the merchandise received by chain store operations is processed by the receiving departments of centrally located warehouses. Since the centralized location handles much more volume than would be required of any individual unit, centralization permits savings and efficiency not available to the small units. The vast volume enables the maximum use of expensive merchandise handling and marking equipment, and the large workforce permits specialization and standardization of procedures in the most scientific manner. In addition, centralized receiving saves duplication of expensive machinery, supplies, and labor. By minimizing the receiving function of the individual units, more chain selling space becomes available. (In effect, inexpensive warehouse space is being traded for prime selling space.)

The disadvantages of centralized receiving are:

1. *Extra shipping costs.* Goods must go from the vendor to the central warehouse to the store, rather than directly to the store.
2. *Duplication of checking.* Goods are checked at the warehouse (from the vendor) and at the selling outlet (from the warehouse).

TRENDS

In order to speed up the merchandise handling procedure and correct the problems associated with it, several trends are developing.

Outside Sourcing

More and more companies are using outside sources to handle their deliveries. That is, the merchandise is shipped to a company which checks it for quantity and quality, tickets the items according to the store's needs, and forwards it in a timely fashion to the units in the company.

Computerized Merchandise Control

Retailers such as Saks are using a sophisticated computer system that integrates all the aspects of receiving. It keeps track of where the merchandise is in the system, and when each store receives it. When the goods arrive at the distribution centers, the computer directs the clerk as to how the order should be sent to the store, such as in cartons or on hangers. Each shipment is then keyed with a store identification code and shipped to the appropriate destination. The computer keeps all of the records, eliminating any shipping errors.

ACTION FOR THE INDEPENDENT RETAILER

Merchandise handling is another area in which the small retailer has an advantage over the high-volume competitor. Inspecting, checking, and marking of goods can be closely supervised, and the merchandise can be stored or placed on the selling floor with a minimum of errors. In addition, because of the relatively small space involved, there is little time lost in getting goods from storage to the selling floor.

The only time the small store gets into trouble with merchandise handling is in periods of peak selling activity, when the inventory is at its highest level and customer activity demands instant access to goods. At such times, the independent retailer must plan the allocation of storeroom space carefully. Stored merchandise must be organized so that all goods are easily accessible and readily found. Naturally, the fastest moving merchandise must be stored in the most accessible locations.

IMPORTANT POINTS IN THE CHAPTER

1. Active stores that receive a large volume of goods find it advisable to set up centralized receiving departments. This frees the sales personnel of a burdensome nonselling duty and improves the receiving function by providing specialists who use specialized equipment in that area.
2. The effectiveness of the receiving department can be measured by the amount of time that is required to move goods from the incoming trucks to the selling floor. The location, layout, and equipment used by the receiving department are crucial to effective receiving.
3. The receiving department is responsible for the receipt and inspection of incoming goods, sorting and checking, and marking the goods for sale.
4. Many large retailers have their incoming goods premarked by the supplier or freight forwarder. This procedure saves space, time, and money.
5. A large portion of the merchandise received by chain stores is processed by the receiving departments of centrally located warehouses. Although this procedure increases shipping and handling costs, the amount of selling space at the retail outlets is increased.

REVIEW QUESTIONS

1. Differentiate between receiving functions at a large retail operation and at a small one.
2. Centralized receiving departments use equipment and supplies more efficiently than individual departments. Why is this so?
3. List several disadvantages of using salespeople for receiving.
4. Why do downtown receiving departments frequently perform the bulk of their activities at a location some distance from the store?
5. Explain and discuss the importance of a straight-line operation in the layout of a receiving department.
6. Discuss the effect on standardized receiving procedures of inadequate equipment to handle pre-Christmas volume.
7. What are the advantages of a portable receiving table over a stationary table?
8. Discuss the advantages of a conveyor belt in a receiving department.
9. Why is there not one best method of receiving all goods?
10. Discuss the importance of having the trucker sign the freight invoice on which a damaged carton was noted.
11. What are the advantages and disadvantages of checking the freight charges on incoming goods?
12. Explain the importance of a receiving record to a large retailer.
13. Discuss the advantages and disadvantages of the direct checking method of quantity checking.

14. Describe the blind check method of quantity checking. *buyer or direct has knowledge*
15. Why are checkers not responsible for quality checking?
16. A jewelry store that uses the word *blacksmith* to code its cost has an item marked "CSLH." What did the item cost?

CASE PROBLEMS

Case Problem 1

The Roffis Store began operations 20 years ago in the quiet suburb of a large city. Since its opening, there has been a tremendous amount of suburban growth. This expansion, coupled with capable, aggressive management, has resulted in phenomenal growth. At present, the store consists of 20 departments whose annual volume exceeds $25 million.

When the store first opened, deliveries were made through the front and immediately unpacked, checked, marked, and placed on the selling shelves. As the store expanded and responsibilities were divided among departments, receiving and storeroom space was provided in the rear of the store. At present, packages are received in the rear of the store. They are then delivered, unopened, to the various departments, where the balance of the receiving functions is performed.

The proprietor's son, recently employed by the store, argues for the setting up of a centralized receiving room. Mr. Roffis objects to this, pointing out that selling space, already in short supply, will be wasted, that centralized receiving operations would require new personnel (the work is presently being done by salespersons), and that checking and marking can best be done by the departments since only they know the specific merchandise.

Questions

1. Support the son's argument.
2. How would you go about setting up a centralized receiving department?

Case Problem 2

The buyers of a large suburban department store, P. W. Brennan's, are extremely unhappy about the receiving department's procedures. A petition of grievances, signed by every buyer in the store, has been presented to management. The following are some of their grievances:

1. Two full days are required for goods that have been delivered to the store to reach the selling floors.
2. A recent receiving department policy no longer allows buyers to take goods from the receiving department to satisfy specific customers. This loses sales and frequently results in loss of customer goodwill.
3. The success or failure of the store depends on sales. It is a serious mistake to allow receiving functions to take precedence over sales or customer goodwill. Top priority should be given to the sales departments rather than the receiving department.
4. Some of the goods coming through have not been properly checked for quality. For example, a large shipment of ladies' sweaters was sent to the selling floor with loose buttons.

Questions

1. As the manager of the receiving department, how would you respond to the above arguments?
2. As the merchandise manager, how would you handle this serious problem?

Chapter 9
Loss Prevention

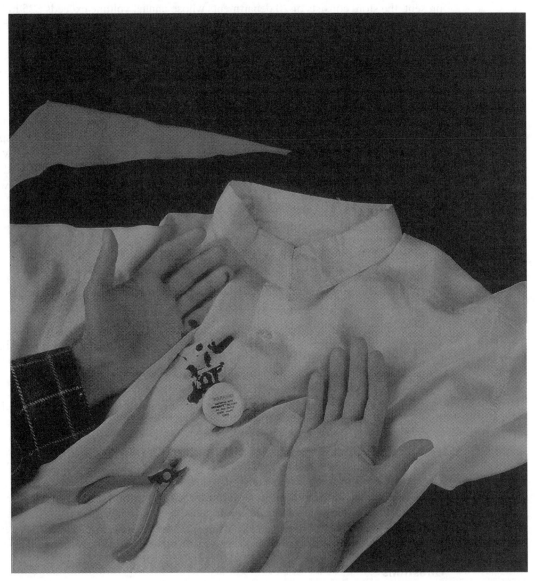

Photograph by Ellen Diamond

LEARNING OBJECTIVES

Upon completion of this chapter, the student should be able to:

1. List six techniques for deterring shoplifting.
2. Discuss five deterrents and controls of internal theft.
3. Explain the system of inktags for loss prevention.

THE THREAT OF DAMAGING MERCHANDISE REDUCES THEFT . . .

Many retailers today are the regular victims of theft by their employees as well as by shoplifters. No matter which systems have been put in place, few merchants have been able to totally stop the theft of merchandise. Surveillance systems, two-way mirrors, armed security guards, plain-clothes store detectives, patrol of changing rooms, locking merchandise devices, and other deterrents have been declared virtually ineffective.

The problem was somewhat lessened with the invention of devices called NOGOS and Sensormatics. They are plastic discs that are attached to garments and are designed to be removed with the use of a special tool. Although they initially deterred some theft, the knack of removing them without benefit of the tool was soon learned by the shoplifters. A pair of pliers or the use of teeth was a quick way to remove them!

The problem has suddenly been considerably alleviated with the creation of a device manufactured by Security Tag Systems, Inc. in St. Petersburg, Florida. It involves the use of a special hard-shell tag similar to the ones previously introduced, but with a difference. The new ones are designed with reservoirs that are filled with ink. Removal of the tag from a garment without benefit of the proper piece of equipment causes the tag to break and spill ink on the garment, rendering it unusable. In order to make the security system known to would-be shoplifters, signs are placed in departments and tags are usually attached to the garments warning of the impending problem with illegal removal. With knowledge that the items are quickly destroyed and left valueless, shoplifters are usually reluctant to tamper with the new inktags and move on to conventionally protected items.

Many stores such as Lord & Taylor and Macy's are using the new device and report that the rate of shoplifting has significantly declined.

Merchants throughout the world are constantly in search of new merchandise as well as techniques to ensure themselves a competitive position in their quest for the customer's dollar. In this, the age of sophisticated retailing, there is one severe problem that continues to plague the retailer at an alarming rate. Simply stated, business executives have not yet been able to prevent merchandise from "walking out of their shops." Reports from all corners of the globe indicate that the pilferage rate is on the rise. Not only does this inventory shrinkage irritate the merchant and significantly cut profits, but it also has an enormous impact on consumer prices. Who must bear the burden of merchandise loss? Certainly, in the long run it must be the everyday, honest consumer!

The National Coalition to Prevent Shoplifting estimates that approximately $20 billion is lost to shoplifters annually. Since these, like all other costs, are passed along to the consumer, the annual cost of shoplifting is more than $200 per American family.

In an attempt to curtail these illegal activities, merchants have resorted to a number of precautionary measures while still searching for more appropriate techniques. Since different retailers have different security problems, there are numerous methods that might be employed to reduce their losses. In this chapter emphasis will be placed upon the problems associated with inventory shortages, techniques by which employees as well as customers steal merchandise, and the security systems that merchants use to curtail shoplifting and internal theft.

INVENTORY SHORTAGES

The problem of inventory shortages is not strictly limited to shoplifting. Shoplifting, the theft of merchandise by "amateurs," as well as professionals who "steal to order," is just one cause of shrinking inventories. In fact, many reliable sources agree that the bulk of store theft is attributable to dishonest employees.

A major retailer, A&S, has initiated the "Red Alert Reward Program" in an effort to combat the ever-increasing problem of inventory shortages. Through employee motivation, the company hopes to reduce the losses which are attributed to both customer and employee theft.

The plan attempts to appeal to employees on two levels. One is through an education process that alerts the employee to the dangers of continuous shortages, and the other provides monetary incentive for providing information that leads to the apprehension of a thief or recovery of stolen merchandise. The rewards are as follows:

- For information that leads to the apprehension of a customer, the employee receives 10 percent of the retail value of the merchandise or money recovered, with a minimum reward of $25 and a maximum of $1,000.
- For information that leads to the apprehension of an employee involved in theft, the employee receives 100 percent of the retail value of the merchandise or money recovered with a minimum reward of $100 and a maximum of $1,000.

The program is under the direction of the company's security director, and it is just one of many devices the company uses to combat shortages.

Both shoplifting and internal theft will be explored in terms of the scope of the problem and the methods used to deter it.

SHOPLIFTING

Who are the culprits involved in stealing from retailers? Are they drug addicts, people from disadvantaged backgrounds, schoolchildren out for kicks, or people who are forced to thievery because of economic pressures? The answer certainly includes all of these. However, stealing is by no means limited to the aforementioned groups. The police chief of a large metropolitan city reported that within a few months his police force had arrested a mayor, the wife of an army general, and two clergymen, all of whom had been caught in the act of illegally removing merchandise from stores. Thus, it is not a simple matter for merchants to be on the lookout for the stereotypical shoplifter.

In addition to understanding that shoplifters come from all walks of life, it should also be understood that the merchandise stolen is not restricted to a particular type of retail operation or a few geographic locations but is evident in all retail organizations as well as every conceivable location. Department stores, specialty shops, discount operations, supermarkets, and chain stores alike, located in downtown areas, shopping malls, and neighborhood clusters on free-standing areas from coast to coast have to cope with this serious problem.

The modern shopping mall with its completely "open fronts" is generally regarded as the shoplifter's paradise. How conducive it is to stealing! Crowds of people milling around in virtually unprotected store entrances make the shopping mall a haven for shoplifters. As the success of this type of retailing center has increased, so have the numbers of reported merchandise thefts. And what about those who are not caught?

An informative study was undertaken by Management Safeguards, Inc. concerning shoplifting in New York, Boston, and Philadelphia department stores. Emphasis centered upon the frequency of shoplifting in downtown areas, the profile of the average shoplifter, frequency of shoplifting, and the methods employed in the stealing of goods. Analysis of the survey shows that all age groups, with minor exceptions, steal with equal frequency, that there is virtually no difference in shoplifting rates between whites and nonwhites, and that one out of every 15 shoppers actually steals rather than buys.

Once having realized that shoplifting is a serious problem that eats into company profits and ultimately drives consumer prices upward, retailers must develop a program to deter theft or minimize the amount of merchandise that is stolen. Different stores are faced with different control problems because of the nature of the goods handled, the method of operation (service or self-service), and the layouts and geographic locations. Whatever the circumstances, however, retailers must begin initially with a program of employee involvement. This does not mean that an abundance of security guards must be hired to safeguard the goods. This could prove to be too costly and might also create an atmosphere not psychologically conducive for shopping. The regular employees—such as department managers, sales personnel, stock people, and cashiers—should be informed about the severity of the shoplifting problem, the store's policy in this regard, and how they can be effectively involved in the security program. This employee awareness is generally accomplished at sessions directed by the store's chief security officer. Typically, the training is twofold. First, employees are generally instructed to make customers feel that they are not alone but are very much in view. This is accomplished by greeting the customer and making oneself thoroughly conspicuous. Second, if the customer's action arouses suspicion, a procedure to follow is outlined. Some stores use a procedure in which a number is dialed on the telephone to alert the security department of the location of the "lurking shoplifter." Other stores use a "code" announcement over the loudspeaker system to indicate a possible shoplifting episode. There are many systems. What is most important is for the store employee to be aware of the shoplifting possibilities, and the proper handling of these situations. The latter is important because improper detention of a suspect could cause the retailer problems of greater severity than that of stolen goods.

Deterrent Techniques

In addition to properly informing and training employees about shoplifting, there are a number of techniques and devices that assist in either the apprehension of a shoplifter or the psychological prevention of the crime.

Surveillance Systems

Many stores have attributed their successful decreases in shoplifting to closed-circuit television and camera systems. Not only have they actually recorded the criminal's actions but they have also proved to be excellent psychological deterrents. The very prominent display of a surveillance camera can almost ensure that many planned thefts will not be tried. In fact, most security specialists agree that the electronic surveillance systems are the best fighters of shoplifting.

The systems available are many. They range from the simple to the sophisticated. In addition to their use as spotters of shoplifters, they are frequently used to "record" issuers of checks. This often prevents the passing of bad checks and facilitates the apprehension of individuals who actually have written them. Figure 9–1 shows the Diebold CL-16 surveillance camera system which, in addition to providing internal surveillance, detects holdups and bad checks. Its sophistication and versatility permit automatic camera filming at specific hours, specific days, or all the time. The system can also be connected to an alarm system.

An innovative surveillance system that some large retail organizations are using involves the use of camera lenses in the eyes of display mannequins to watch the customers.

Two-Way Mirrors

Much merchandise that is stolen from department and specialty stores is hidden under the clothing of shoplifters. What place provides more convenience and privacy than the store's fitting room? This area is one that provides many soft-goods retailers with a severe problem. In order to curtail merchandise concealment in fitting rooms, some retailers have resorted to the "watchful eye." The installation of two-way mirrors, one side for the customer to use as an ordinary mirror and the other side monitored by a store employee without customer awareness, has assisted retailers in apprehending many would-be shoplifters. There are many problems created by these devices, however, and they are considered to be one of the most controversial shoplifting prevention devices on the market. Opponents of the two-way mirrors believe that they are an infringement on people's privacy. Proponents believe that retailers have every right to safeguard their own merchandise. In many states, retailers who use these mirrors in fitting rooms are required to post signs telling of their use.

Merchandise Price Labels

A problem that plagues retailers in just about every type of store is the switching of price tags—the customer changes the price on the merchandise by substituting new

Figure 9–1 Diebold CL-16 surveillance system. *Courtesy:* Diebold, Incorporated

tags with lower prices. Instead of actually stealing the article, the individual makes the purchase, but at a significantly lower price. Stores that are hardest hit are those with large sales volume, a wide variety of merchandise in varied price ranges, and centralized checkout locations. These are easy prey for criminals since the cash register operator is generally not familiar with the merchandise.

Merchants have tried many different types of merchandise tags to thwart the offenders. For "hanging" goods, where all else has failed, tickets with heavy nylon filament string that must be attached by special machines are being used effectively. Although the string may be cut with a pair of scissors, it is impossible to replace it unless the machine, which is cumbersome, is used.

For merchandise that must be labeled directly with a "sticker" tag, would-be label-switchers have found the latest switch-proof label virtually impossible to tamper with. Pictured in Figure 9–2 is the "Switch-Gard™" label created by the Dennison Manufacturing Company. It employs a tough, broad-range adhesive that can only be removed through total destruction. It has been a boon to security-minded retailers who require labels that are capable of sticking to any surface.

Pilferage Detection Systems

If you walk through any modern enclosed shopping mall, you are immediately aware of the open storefronts and their accessibility to shoplifters. Merchants who believe

Switch-Gard™ Labels by Dennison

Tamper with them and you "total" them.

No matter what you label—clothes, cosmetics, tools, toys, you name it—you can stop the slickest label switchers forever with new Switch-Gard labels. It's the latest breakthrough in switch-proof labeling from Dennison, the world's most "security-conscious" retail marking systems supplier.

Here's why we call them "Switch-Gard."

A tough, broad-range adhesive. Specially developed for switch-proof labeling, grabs hold the second you apply the label. Our Switch-Gard adhesive provides a secure bond instantly. You can pull at it, roll it, peel it, but before this adhesive ever lets go, the label will be totally destroyed.

A tender label stock. We wed our tough, tenacious adhesive to a paper stock that's a real weak sister. Strong enough to imprint and apply, but once in place it will tear apart at the slightest tug. Try to peel it and it goes completely to pieces. Roll it and it's in ruins at once.

Unique, die cut design. To make doubly certain that the label tears when removed, Dennison designed a special die cut with omni-directional effectiveness. This extra-added touch is sure to thwart the cleverest label switchers.

Thoroughly tested. Exhaustive tests prove that Switch-Gard labels will stick securely to practically all types of surfaces and conform to any contour. There's no way to tamper with them without totally destroying them.

Test them today. Prove to yourself that Switch-Gard labels are 100% switch-proof. Try the attached samples on the toughest-to-label surfaces you've got. You'll see what we mean by our slogan, "Tamper with them and you total them."

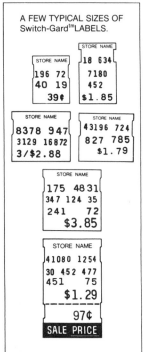

A FEW TYPICAL SIZES OF Switch-Gard™ LABELS.

Made in America.
Products of American ingenuity and labor.

Dennison
Marking & Attaching Systems
Dennison Manufacturing Company
Framingham, Mass. 01701

No. 291   Printed in U.S.A.   8/73 HCG15M

Figure 9–2   Security labels. *Courtesy:* Dennison Manufacturing Company

that the open front is motivation for the shopper to enter the premises are not about to return to conventional store entrances. In order to maintain the open feeling, many retailers have installed systems that are similar to the security installations at most major air terminals.

The system requires that merchandise be "tagged" with special rectangular-shaped solid plastic discs. Removal of the disc is accomplished by means of a special machine. Once the merchandise has been paid for and the disc removed by the cashier, the customer can freely leave the store. Exit from the premises is by way of an installation that resembles a door frame (without the door). But if someone steals an item, the disc has not been removed; passage through the security door frame sets of a very loud alarm that alerts store personnel. The system does require continuous additional expense to the retailer, since each piece of merchandise must be tagged twice, once for the price ticket and again for the security tag. The thwarting of shoplifting by the use of this alarm system has been so successful that it is now being used in more traditionally built stores. Although the system significantly cuts down on shoplifting, some retailers report that people are removing the discs with their teeth. Many retailers are finding success with the Inktag. It is a device, which when improperly removed, releases ink from a well and damages the item. Often shoplifters move on to items not protected with these tags.

3M has recently introduced new anti-shoplifting systems that provide improved retail security protection. The new Echotag ET 3000 Electronic Article Surveillance detection systems from 3M represent the most sophisticated and effective antishoplifting technology for the soft goods market.

The new ET 3000 systems are 3M's third generation of radio frequency technology to protect a wide variety of merchandise. The Echotag ET 3000 systems are designed for retail markets such as apparel, leather, luggage, and sporting goods.

Not only are the new systems more attractive and unobtrusive, they now have a variety of design and color options to choose from. And all the new generation ET 3000 systems are fully compatible with the full line of Echotag merchandise markers and accessories.

All ET 3000 systems feature Multi-Scan Plus, which virtually eliminates false alarms. When the panel detects a marker, it checks and then rechecks the marker before sounding the alarm. The result: a high degree of reliability and better customer relations. Pictured in Figure 9–3, 3M's Horizon antishoplifting system protects double sets of doors and wider store entrances. Fabric cover-ups in a variety of colors will complement any decor.

The Silhouette antishoplifting system from 3M is a very affordable stand-alone system that can be placed in the middle of an entryway or to protect a single-door entrance, as shown in Figure 9–4.

Echotag radio frequency markers from 3M are available in a variety of styles: hard markers that can be tacked or fastened to a garment with a strong steel lanyard: ultralight soft clear plastic markers designed to look like a store or merchandise hung tag; pressure-sensitive stick-on markers with an imprintable label. They are featured in Figure 9–5.

3M's Whispertape™ electronic article surveillance (EAS) system has new discreet security markers designed for college bookstore applications. The Whispertape system replaces bulky security devices with thin, easily concealed three-inch magnetic strips to detect shoplifters attempting to remove unpaid merchandise from stores. 3M EAS customers report reducing loss reductions by at least 75 percent, and recouping their investment in the system within one year. The Whispertape markers

Figure 9–3   3M Horizon antishoplifting system. *Courtesy:* 3M

offer a special advantage to bookstore managers, who prefer their discreet nature and rapid application because the thin strips are difficult to detect. The new markers are available in several forms.

Tuck-in Whispertape merchandise markers from 3M are easily slipped into books, merchandise, or packaging. Self-adhesive Whispertape bar code markers protect records, tapes, videocassettes, and computer software. These magnetic markers offer the highest degree of security protection because they can be detected through clothing, purses, briefcases, and backpacks. Figures 9–6 and 9–7 feature the Whispertape markers.

Fitting-Room Control

As mentioned earlier, the shoplifter's favorite place is often the fitting room. Here a great deal of merchandise can be concealed and lost to the store. Many security-conscious stores use a system that involves placing guards at fitting-room entrances. Typically, individuals are restricted to a limited number of articles in the dressing rooms at any one time. They are given a color-coded plastic device that indicates the number of items brought into the try-on cubicle. (For example, green might represent two items.) When they have finished trying the article on, the customers must return to the "checker" with the number of garments designated by the color-coded device. Some stores have found that even with this system, resourceful shoplifters sometimes substituted their own garments for the merchandise they wished to steal.

Figure 9–4   3M Silhouette antishoplifting system. *Courtesy:* 3M

Figure 9–5   Radio frequency marker labels. *Courtesy:* 3M

Figure 9–6   Whispertape markers. *Courtesy:* 3M

Figure 9–7   Bar–coded tape. *Courtesy:* 3M

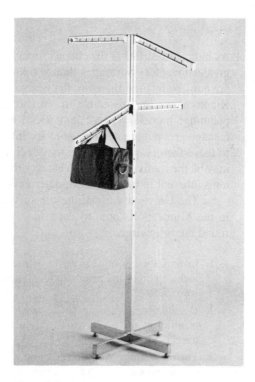

Figure 9–8   Securax locking display system

Magnifying Mirrors

Stores that wish to spend minimal amounts on security but also want to minimize shoplifting install circular magnifying mirrors at out-of-the-way areas on the selling floor. By strategic positioning, store personnel can watch potential shoplifters in these otherwise concealed areas. In addition to providing some view of these areas, the mirrors act as psychological deterrents.

Locking Display Systems

Illustrated in Figure 9–8 is an antitheft locking display system manufactured by Securax, Inc. of Santa Ana, California. These systems are used for high-value merchandise, such as jewelry and leather jackets, in self-service areas. While they all require a salesperson to free the goods for really careful scrutiny, they do permit customer handling and even the preliminary trying on of clothing on a self-service basis without fear of theft. By the time the salesperson's presence is needed, the customer is pretty well sold. These are high-priced items, and even self-service stores prefer salesperson involvement in the final stages of the sale of such goods.

The number of devices employed by stores varies from company to company. With the enormity of the shoplifting problem, even those considered to be as secure as possible are always seeking new devices to use on their selling floors. Evidence of the continuous need for safeguard devices is the continuous growth of producers of loss-prevention devices throughout the country.

INTERNAL THEFT

As indicated earlier in the chapter, many retailers report that internal theft accounts for greater inventory shortages than shoplifting. The factors attributable to internal theft are numerous. First there are the general motivational factors associated with stealing. Kleptomania, an irresistible urge to steal; impulsiveness, the act of stealing without planning; monetary need; and social acceptance (strange, but true, particularly in teenage groups) are some reasons for internal (as well as shopper) stealing. In addition to these factors, an employee may feel underpaid; or simple hatred for the employer may be the motive for theft. Whatever the reasons, retailers must be aware of the problems inherent in internal theft, deterrents, and internal control.

The University of Minnesota surveyed 35 companies employing 5,000 workers in the Minneapolis area to determine which workers are most likely to steal. They found the following:

1. Internal theft is most likely to be found among those who have the least to lose. These include unmarried people in low positions with little seniority to lose or dependents to worry about.
2. Dissatisfied workers are prime candidates for theft. The anger brought about by layoffs, insufficient raises, increased productivity demands, and reduced overtime frequently triggers theft.
3. The most ambitious workers, those who set the highest achievement goals and are most concerned with self-improvement, are also the most likely to steal.
4. Where employees congregate after working hours, the likelihood of cheating increases.
5. Organizations that allow their employees to get away with extended coffee breaks and abuse of sick day privileges, and that show other signs of laxity, suffer more from internal theft than companies that insist on rigid compliance to the rules.
6. Internal security personnel are so involved with external sources of theft that employee theft frequently goes unnoticed.

Another recent study underscored the magnitude of the problem of internal theft and indicated the areas of concern. Among those areas that the study found accounted for theft by employees were misuse of the discount privilege, taking merchandise that was not paid for, claiming more hours worked than were actually performed, underringing of purchases, taking money from registers, padding business expenses, and intentionally damaging merchandise for a bigger discount.

Deterrents and Controls

In order to avoid stealing by employees as much as possible, retailers must carefully charge those in positions of hiring with the responsibility of sound screening procedures. If prospective employees are scrupulously screened before beginning their employment, the company will almost certainly run less risk for internal theft. This by no means should make the reader believe that prescreening completely eliminates thieves, but that it could substantially reduce the number of illegal incidents.

Application Forms

One of the most important screening devices used in hiring employees is the application form. Its careful use can be helpful in determining the possible shortcomings of the prospective employee in terms of honesty. The application form in Figure 6–2 (p. 106) requires the applicant to give information on any arrests, convictions, and previous employment. These sections should not be lightly passed over but studied for possible deficiencies. Employers with special security problems could design an even better application to collect more pertinent information. Whichever form is used, it is important to follow up the information so that appropriate action may be taken.

References

Some retail organizations require the listing of references on the application form or at the time of interview. They include both personal and business references. From these, management can make certain decisions regarding the honesty of the prospective employee. Often, instability and dishonesty are discovered through reference checking.

Shopping Services

Many years ago, retailers engaged outside shopping services expressly for the purpose of evaluating employees on the basis of customer courtesy. In recent years, with the ever-increasing problem of internal theft, shopping service emphasis has shifted to the area of employee honesty.

Shopping services are generally secured on a contract basis. The service regularly checks employees by sending "shoppers" into the store. Employees are checked several times by these investigators to determine their honesty, among other things. For example, there might be an indication that some sales are not rung up on the register.

It is important for the shopping service to have many shoppers and rotate them so that store employees are unable to detect them and differentiate them from real customers.

Smuggling Control

A very serious problem involves employees smuggling merchandise off the premises. Although it is difficult to completely prevent this, cautious retailers have made inroads into this problem.

Stockpersons, in particular, have caused serious stock shortages for retailers. For example, merchandise can be hidden in trash containers for later retrieval outside. In order to correct this situation, some retailers have installed "through-the-wall" security systems. These systems, as pictured in Figures 9–9 and 9–10, require that employees dispose of empty cartons, refuse, and so on through the wall that connects with a compactor on the outside of the building. In this way, if an employee tries to pass merchandise outside, it will be destroyed by the compactor.

This system, or ones similar to it, is widely used today in all classifications of retail organizations. Reports from users indicate significantly fewer losses in merchandise.

Another preventive measure taken by numerous retailers to prevent the illegal removal of merchandise is the institution of a policy that requires employees to check coats, handbags, briefcases, lunch boxes, and so on in lockers before they proceed onto the selling floors. Women requiring personal items such as combs, handkerchiefs, and so forth are permitted to carry them in small, transparent vinyl purses provided by the store. To ensure that the procedure is carried out, a guard is usually stationed at the employee entrance to the selling floor. Any violations or suspicious acts are reported by the guard to security.

Figure 9–9   Through-the-wall security system—outside.

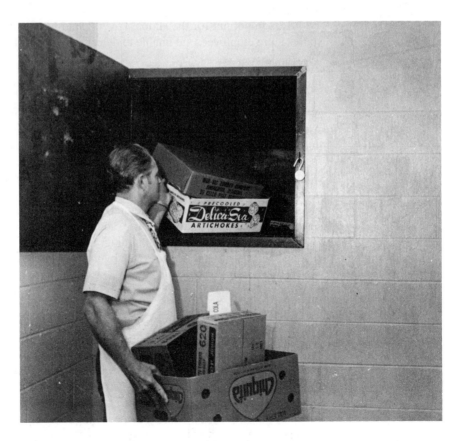

Figure 9–10   Through-the-wall security system—inside.

TRENDS

Year after year, retailers have tried a variety of techniques to control shoplifting and internal theft. The recent trends in prevention are discussed here.

Pre-employment Testing

One of the tests used to reduce employee theft is known as the pen and pencil honesty examination. Many employers are using these integrity tests since the polygraph examination was declared illegal. These tests involve a series of questions in true–false or multiple choice formats and cost from $7.00 to $14.00 to administer to each prospective employee. By getting applicants to admit, in writing, previous theft of items valued at as little as 50 cents, any would-be thieves are eliminated from consideration. Many individuals believe that such minor admissions make them seem even more trustworthy.

Source Tagging

Many manufacturers are tagging merchandise for their retail accounts. The tags are often of a variety that dovetails with the retailer's surveillance systems, but that is unfamiliar to the store's employees. By doing this at the manufacturer's premises, it reduces the need for employees to participate in the tagging and learning how to beat the system when they are ready to steal. Stores such as Kmart, Wal-Mart and Home Depot are among those using source tagging.

Computerized Video Terminals

Some major department stores like A & S are using video devices to record entire customer transactions. In this way, the employee may be watched to determine if he or she is switching labels for friends, neglecting to ring up the proper amounts, or doing anything that is irregular in recording the sale.

ACTION FOR THE INDEPENDENT RETAILER

Shoplifting is not confined to large retailers. Small businesses, which can least afford it, suffer from this evil as well. However, this is one area in which the small business has a decided advantage. Generally, shoplifting thrives in an atmosphere of self-service, and this is much more likely to be found in large stores. Moreover, because of the limited space available to the small retailer, constant surveillance is possible. There are no unpopulated corners in which the shoplifter can operate. In addition, the personnel in a small store can be trained and supervised in the area of theft prevention, at least more effectively than their large store counterparts.

Internal theft occurs in small stores as well as large. It can be minimized by checking the cash register tapes against the sales slips daily to determine that all sales have been rung up and by spot-checking inventory constantly. For example, the owner of a small liquor store goes to lunch, leaving the clerk in charge. Before going, she glances at a shelf of a popular brand and sees eight bottles. After returning, there are six bottles left. The sales slips should indicate that two bottles have been sold. If not, the clerk has some explaining to do. Different goods should be checked during each absence. The clerk should never know which goods are being checked. Where there are items kept in a storeroom, these should be included in the count.

IMPORTANT POINTS IN THE CHAPTER

1. Most inventory shortages result from shoplifting and internal theft.
2. Most studies indicate that shoplifters come from all walks of life. The group includes teenagers, parents, economically disadvantaged people, and kleptomaniacs.
3. Surveillance systems, two-way mirrors, tamper-proof merchandise tags, pilferage detection systems, fitting-room control, and magnifying mirrors are used to deter shoplifting.
4. Prescreening of prospective employees is essential in the control of internal theft.
5. Pen and pencil honesty tests are being used to screen dishonest job applicants.

REVIEW QUESTIONS

1. Do merchandise shortages affect the customer? Explain your answer.
2. Define shoplifting. *Stealing while shopping*
3. To whom are most merchandise thefts attributable?
4. Describe the typical shoplifter. *no typical / variety of shoplifters, homeless*
5. Why do customers steal merchandise?
6. At what time of the year do shoplifters cause the most trouble? Why?
7. What is a surveillance system? How does one operate? *whites / men equal December*
8. Discuss the use of two-way mirrors. Do you believe that they are being used appropriately in retailing? *Dressing rooms/ catch them*
9. Customers, as well as employees, have often resorted to switching price tags. How can this now be avoided?
10. Describe the widely used store entrance pilferage detection system. *Door frames no goes*
11. Why are fitting rooms so conducive to shoplifting?
12. In what way have merchants reduced fitting-room thefts? *limit items colored cards*
13. Define *kleptomania*.
14. It has been said that the employee application form is an excellent device to control internal theft. Do you agree? Defend your answer. *Yes good screening of employee/ outlook*
15. Briefly describe pen and pencil honesty tests.
16. Are employee references aids in controlling internal theft? Defend your position.
17. What is a shopping service? How does it assist the store's security program? *yes because you can call*
18. Discuss compactors and their role in the prevention of employee merchandise smuggling. *hooked up threw wall (destroys it)*

CASE PROBLEMS

Case Problem 1

Some people believe that the cost of store security is too expensive to be practical for the smaller independent retailer. Such a retailer, the Just Jeans Company, is located on the main street of a midwestern suburban community. Just Jeans has been in business for five years and has experienced shoplifting problems that seem to be out of proportion to the amount of business transacted. As business has increased and the crowds in the store have increased, shoplifting has gotten out of hand. One problem confronting the store is its self-service method of operation. People on the selling floor are at a minimum. The store has a manager, an assistant manager, and a cashier. The owner, Mr. Davis, has considered hiring salespeople who would keep a watchful eye on the customers as well as sell. The manager, Eric Shafler, insists that the store's clientele, mainly teenagers, would adversely react to salespeople and that the store would be risking a decrease in sales. The assistant manager, Richard Pearl, suggests a full-time security guard; Mr. Davis has vetoed this idea as too costly.

At the present time, security is limited to circular magnifying mirrors at strategic positions. The operation must now decide which route to take before the shoplifting problem leads to the store's failure.

Questions

1. Do you agree with any of the suggestions made thus far by the store principals?
2. Suggest a security plan to help reduce shoplifting in Just Jeans. Keep in mind the costs involved and whether they can be afforded by the company.

Case Problem 2

For the past twenty years, the Shelby Company, a full-line department store, has equipped its premises with the most sophisticated systems to deter shoplifting. After considerable research, the company has discovered that although shoplifting has declined, inventory shrinkage is still plaguing the company. The problem seems to indicate a significant amount of internal theft. Particular difficulty centers around the soft-goods departments. Not only is merchandise taken by the employees, but much price-tag switching is taking place so that lower prices are actually being paid for merchandise that should sell for more.

Many suggestions have been made by the management. One suggestion is to have a manager at each register who is familiar with merchandise prices and can prevent selling at lower prices. Another point suggested is to gradually replace all personnel with new people who could be better screened before employment.

Questions

1. Do you agree with either of the suggestions? Evaluate each and defend your answers with sound reasoning.
2. Suggest your own plan to assist the company in fighting internal theft.

Chapter 10
The Buying Function

Photograph by Ellen Diamond

LEARNING OBJECTIVES

Upon completion of this chapter, the student should be able to:

1. List five responsibilities of the buyer.

2. Explain the duties of an assistant buyer, indicating five areas of responsibility.

3. Write an essay on "What to Buy." This should include at least six sources of buyer information.

4. Differentiate, giving advantages and disadvantages, between buying from wholesalers and buying from manufacturers.

5. List six reasons for buying from foreign sources.

THE GLOBAL MARKETPLACE . . .

The buyer's task was once simpler than it is today. Traditional store buyers are regularly troubled by competition from their counterparts at off-price stores; private label merchandise is often priced better than the items available from national manufacturers. Many buyers have increased responsibilities because of the expansion of their companies. One of the major changes that has affected the buyer's job is the availability of merchandise from sources all over the world.

At one time in retailing, those responsible for purchasing visited their wholesale markets a few times a year when new lines were introduced, or whenever the need arose to spruce up their inventories. Those concerned with apparel and who were located on the eastern seaboard, would head for New York City's Garment Center to satisfy their needs; those in Chicago would head for that city's Apparel Center, and so forth.

Today, merchandise is available in just about every part of the world. Third world nations are producing items at a fraction of the cost to produce them in the United States, and other countries are providing items that are not domestically available. The store buyer must regularly scan these different markets to make certain that nothing has been overlooked. One month a buyer may make a trip to the Far East to uncover a line of items available at prices that would permit a larger markup; another month might find the buyer in a nation of the Caribbean basin, where prices are even more attractive.

The various trade shows buyers must attend are held worldwide. Menswear buyers often trek to Paris for SEHM, a trade exposition of international renown, or to Pitti Uomo and Uomo Italia in Florence; women's wear buyers go to France for the Paris Designer Collections show, and shoe buyers go to Bologna for MICAM, yet another trade show. A look at the calendar of events for each industry reveals that extensive travel is a must.

With the new trade pacts such as NAFTA, which makes purchasing from Mexico and Canada more attractive, and the passage of GATT with even broader implications for buyers, purchasing has become an international venture.

Whenever retailing students are asked about their future aspirations, invariably a great number respond that they would like to be buyers. The buying function seems to be the most glamorous aspect of the retail operation. Perhaps to the inexperienced it represents a chance to spend a great deal of money in sums that one would never spend for one's own needs. While the buying job does often present glamorous and exciting moments, few jobs in retailing require more ability and disciplined training. In this chapter, emphasis will be placed upon the *store* buyers and how they select merchandise. The next chapter will deal with the role of *resident office* buyers and their relationships to store buyers.

The responsibility for buying does not always belong to an individual called the *buyer*. In most small stores, the purchasing of merchandise is usually a responsibility of the proprietor. Since sales volume is low and employees, if any, are few in number, the store owner is a jack-of-all-trades who buys merchandise in addition to performing many other tasks. Buying for this type of operation is generally less carefully planned than is the purchasing for a larger organization.

As the store organization grows, the responsibility for purchasing becomes greater. The chain organization and the department store with branches buy such great quantities of merchandise for distribution that the buyer's job becomes one of the most important in the operation. Only those individuals with skill and competence can become successful buyers. In order to make students aware of the dimensions of this job, an overview of some of the buyer's duties as well as the qualifications necessary to carry out these responsibilities are discussed.

DUTIES AND RESPONSIBILITIES

Buyer

The responsibilities of the buyer generally include the following:

1. Most important, actual purchasing of the goods. The buyer is faced with the perennial problems of what merchandise to choose from which vendors, in what quantity, and the correct timing of delivery to meet with customers' demands. Included in these tasks are negotiating the price, shipping terms, and extra dating (additional time in which to pay for merchandise). Since these are areas of great significance, an in-depth study of each will be made later in the chapter.

2. After buying arrangements have been worked out, the buyer must price the merchandise to conform with the policies of the store and the markup to be achieved by the particular department. Included in this area are the pricing of the individual items and the repricing of goods that have moved slowly, in the hope that the lower price will move them faster. New merchandise can then be put on the selling floor in place of the slow-moving goods.

3. The buyer selects merchandise for promotion, merchandise that should be displayed, and merchandise that should be advertised; the buyer also plans fashion shows, when relevant, and any special events that might promote goods.

Assistant Buyer

Most buyers have assistants to help with the many chores of buying for a store or a department. Some of the more typical duties and responsibilities an assistant will perform are the following:

1. Reorders of merchandise; most reorders are placed by assistant buyers. This is merely a replenishment of fast-selling merchandise that has sold in the department.

2. Assistants often follow up on orders that have not as yet been delivered. Often, these are orders that were especially placed for individual customers and if not delivered on time will be canceled.

3. The purchase of some new merchandise is done by assistants. Occasionally when a department is large, the buyer will allow an assistant to purchase some lines. Generally the purchase is limited to staple goods.

4. When the buyer plans to purchase goods for a new season the assistant is included in the decision-making group. This arrangement allows for another opinion plus excellent on-the-job training in preparation for a full buyer's job.

BUYER QUALIFICATIONS

In order to aspire to managerial positions in retailing, particularly buying careers, individuals must possess certain qualifications and characteristics. Following are some of those deemed most important by many of the leading retailers who were interviewed:

1. A college degree, preferably in the area of retail business management, is necessary. It is rare today for a high school student to climb the ladder of success from stock clerk to buyer. The sophistication of retailing today demands a knowledgeable individual to step into positions of authority. The success stories often told by oldtime self-educated retailers are part of the history of retailing and not of its future.

2. An enthusiastic attitude is a must for buyers. Buyers (unless the responsibility is not theirs, as in central purchasing for chain stores) are sometimes responsible for the sale of merchandise in their departments. Enthusiasm is one of the most effective methods for motivating employees to sell goods. The buyers' enthusiasm seems to transfer to their subordinates. *Many stores will overlook some of an individual's shortcomings, but few, if asked, will choose an unenthusiastic individual for a buying position.*

3. Product knowledge is extremely important in buying efficiently. It is almost impossible for one to have complete knowledge of every item stocked by department stores. An understanding of style and textiles for the fashion buyer and a knowledge of grades of fruits and vegetables for the produce buyer in a supermarket is almost mandatory for success. Too many people deemphasize the importance of product knowledge, but the individual with the ability to knowledgeably examine goods and make discerning decisions will certainly be ahead in the buying game.

4. A simple working knowledge of retailing mathematics is a must for every buyer. Although computers and hand-held calculators provide ease in accomplishing mathematical solutions, the buyer must be able to understand the principles of markup, markdown, open to buy, and other often-used computations.

5. The ability to get along with people is an important quality a buyer must have. In addition to dealing with the people in the department, buyers continually meet with merchandise managers, vendors, and buying office representatives. Ability to get along with these different parties helps to guarantee a more efficient operation.

6. While students agree that such characteristics as ability, knowledge, and leadership are important qualities that a buyer should possess, they often underestimate the importance of appearance. The buyer's appearance sets an example for the staff, makes a lasting impression on customers the buyer comes into contact with, and often sets the tone in relationships with the vendors from whom the buyer purchases. Rarely does an individual successfully complete an interview and receive an offer for a managerial position in retailing without a professional appearance.

ORGANIZATION FOR BUYING

Not every individual buyer has the same overall responsibilities. The duties required will depend on the policy, size, and scope of the operation and geographic separation of the units for which the buyer is responsible.

In department stores with branches, buyers usually have headquarters in the flagship store and do the purchasing for that store plus the branches. The number of lines each buyer is responsible for varies according to the volume for each line. For example, a smaller department store might have one buyer responsible for all purchases of children's clothing, whereas a very large store would probably have a separate buyer for children's shoes. Some department stores might have separate buyers for departments in branches when the branch operation is dissimilar to that of the main store.

In most chain organizations, buyers do not operate from a main store but from central headquarters located some distance from the individual units. For example, The Limited, Inc., with more than 700 units, houses its buyers in Columbus, Ohio along with other divisions' executives (advertising and display, for example). In this type of situation the buyer is responsible only for purchasing and not for sales within the units. The central buyers rely chiefly on reports from the various units to plan purchases. Since they are far removed from the selling floor, direct customer contact is impossible. The manner in which quantities and styles are determined varies. Some central buyers make all purchases, determine each store's needs, and distribute these goods to the various units. In other chains the buyers select the merchandise for the units, and the store managers or department managers determine the quantities needed. Still another arrangement has the central buyer select styles and negotiate price arrangements and terms with vendors. Then a catalog or list of goods available to the stores is published, and the store's managers pick the goods they desire. Stores using the latter system usually require that all units carry certain specified lines, with the balance to be selected by individual managers. A recent innovation is the system used by J. C. Penney, which involves the use of videocassettes featuring merchandise available from which each store makes its selections.

Whichever system is used, to a certain degree each buyer is faced with all the elements of the buying procedure. In the systems where store managers determine quantities and sometimes the items to carry, they too may be considered buyers since they are involved in the selection of merchandise.

MODEL STOCK DEVELOPMENT

The particular assortment a department has to offer is most important to its success. The buyer must carefully plan the proper merchandise assortment in terms of both depth and breadth. The inventory that contains an appropriate assortment at the time customers are ready to purchase is known as a *model stock*. Development of the model stock varies significantly from department to department, with those that are fashion oriented presenting the most involvement and planning by the buyer. Fashion departments are concerned not only with assortment in terms of price and variety of products, but also with color and style, all of which comprise a model stock.

A model stock is accomplished through the buyer's ability to evaluate both the customer's needs and the demands dictated by store management. By paying close attention to these forces, the buyer may plan the most perfect assortment possible. Large stores, and even some smaller operations, provide their buyers with pertinent information in the form of computerized reports.

Figure 10–1   Buyers and merchandiser developing a model
stock. *Courtesy:* Williams-Sonoma

Before such planning can take place, the buyer must be knowledgeable in the essentials or elements of buying. Armed with this pertinent information, the buyer will have a better insight into model stock development. Buyers and merchandiser are busy developing a model stock in Figure 10–1.

A RETAILING FOCUS   *Williams-Sonoma*

Starting as a modest hardware store in the town of Sonoma, California, Williams-Sonoma has become what many writers refer to as the Tiffany of cookware stores. Just two years after founding the company, Chuck Williams moved his store to San Francisco in 1958 to cater to the needs of those people who had big country homes in Sonoma as well as residences in the city. His superb taste and uncanny ability to spot unique merchandise has given Williams-Sonoma an enviable reputation as the arbiter of good taste for little money.

In 1972 the mail order catalog was developed under the direction of Edward Marcus, a Neiman-Marcus executive who had significant mail order experience. Each catalog surpassed its predecessor in terms of sales. The catalog features only a small portion of the products available in the stores but is designed as a way to motivate people to come to the stores and do their purchasing.

In 1978 the company was sold, and in 1983 it went public. By the end of 1989 the company had 77 stores under the Williams-Sonoma name, 12 Hold Everything stores that feature storage and organization items for the home, a very successful catalog operation known as Gardener's Eden that features goods for the home gardener, and 29-store Pottery Barn chain that was purchased in 1987. Currently the company owns and operates more than 200 stores under the Williams-Sonoma umbrella with plans for significant expansion of the divisions by the year 2000.

Figure 10–2   A Williams-Sonoma store in Tulsa, Oklahoma. *Courtesy:* Williams-Sonoma

Most educated observers of the industry credit the success of the organization to excellent buying and merchandising policies. The buyers are charged with the responsibility to buy well designed and well made products that can be sold at reasonable prices. When one enters a company store or examines the offerings of the many catalogs, it is immediately obvious that the buyers approach their duties with care and expertise. They travel all over the world to identify and develop home-centered items for each of their concepts. Where other companies in the field resort to the typical merchandise resources, Williams-Sonoma merchants make the international market their resource center. The buyers are trained to select merchandise much as they would if they were buying for a special friend or for an important occasion. This personalized approach results in the acquisition of unique and unusual merchandise.

At each of the company's divisions, each item undergoes rigorous in-house testing to make certain that it will hold up under normal home use. The Product Information staff tests products and provides technical feedback to the buyers. This approach also provides pertinent information for copywriters for use in the catalogs, and for salespeople and consumers who eventually purchase the goods. Only after a product has passed the careful scrutiny of the testers does it become a potential product for the company. An inventory management team then assesses sales plans and profit goals to determine how much inventory to carry. At this time orders are placed with the vendors, details of packaging are discussed, and the products are then received at the distribution center which moves the merchandise to the stores and catalog shipping centers.

At a time when many retailers take shortcuts in the running of their operations, a company like Williams-Sonoma takes pains to run a first-class, efficient operation. Their enormous growth indicates that such attention ultimately pays off. Figure 10–2 features one of the many Williams-Sonoma stores.

ELEMENTS OF BUYING

Whether one buys for a small store, a department store with branches, a large specialty store, or a chain organization, four major areas are of concern to all buyers. Sometimes called the elements of buying, they are *what to buy, how much to buy, from whom to buy,* and *when to buy.*

What to Buy

The decision of which merchandise to select from all that is available from vendors is not made by guessing. While some misinformed or uninformed individuals feel that buyers are lucky when they choose the right merchandise, those who are knowledgeable understand the amount of care that is exercised in the planning of purchases.

A buyer tries to determine the customers' wants and needs, and attempts to satisfy these desires by purchasing the right merchandise. Sound marketing tells us that products should be designed and produced with the customer in mind. Good buyers, too, purchase with the customer in mind. In order to determine what the customer wants, the buyer gathers information from a number of sources.

While not all buyers use every source available to them, all of them do study past sales records. An investigation of past sales reveals the best-selling price lines, the most popular sizes, the peak selling periods, the vendors with the fastest-moving merchandise, and any other information that has been recorded by the store.

The method used to record the pertinent information varies from store to store. The smaller the operation, the less sophisticated the system used. Even though computers enormously simplify information gathering, some small stores hand-record all goods received in an inventory book and include whatever information might be meaningful for future purchasing. (See Figure 10–3.) For example, included might be the vendor's name, style number of item, cost price and selling price (to show markup), colors, sizes, number of pieces, and when goods were received. At the end of each day, the sales receipts or merchandise tags (either of which should record any information kept in the inventory book) are used to check off the items sold. (See Figure 10–4.) Whenever the buyer desires, she or he can immediately check the records to see how the merchandise is selling. In addition, this book serves as an inventory and shows what merchandise is still available for sale.

			58
○	DAVID NEIL SPORTSWEAR 3780 MAIN STREET NEW YORK, N.Y. 874-8200		

STYLE	PRICE	COLORS	SIZE BREAKDOWN												
5835	10.75	RED	8	10	12	12	14	14	16	18					
	17.98	GREEN	10	12	14	16	18	20							
		YELLOW	10	12	14	16	18	20							
	JUNE 1														
2564	14.75	BLACK	8	8	10	10	12	12	12	14	14	14	16	16	16
	24.98		18	18	20										
○	JUNE 23														

Figure 10–3 Inventory page (small store)

Figure 10–4 Merchandise tag (small store)

In the larger retail organizations a more sophisticated system of recording sales is kept. The computer keeps the same records as those kept by hand, but does it more quickly and more efficiently. Buyers are given all sorts of past sales data by the computer daily, weekly, monthly, or at any interval necessary for the efficiency of the operation. Food store buyers, for example, often require daily sales information because their merchandise turns over so rapidly. Furniture store buyers, on the other hand, require less frequent information because of the slower nature of the goods. With the introduction of the point-of-purchase register, which is tied into the computer in many stores, the past sales information is always available.

Surveys of different varieties are used by buyers to determine customers' wants. Stores often interview people to determine tastes and buying habits, send out questionnaires to charge customers to inquire about merchandise that might interest them, hold consumer panels to discover likes and dislikes, and conduct fashion counts to discover what people are wearing. Through these techniques, buyers find out firsthand what their customers or potential customers desire. Chapter 19 explores the use of research in the retail store.

Buyers constantly scan trade periodicals to keep up with what's current in their field. Most buyers generally read *Chain Store Age* and *Stores Magazine;* fashion buyers faithfully scan *Women's Wear Daily* for women's fashions and *The Daily News Record* or DNR as it is referred to in the industry, for men's clothing. Each segment of the retail store industry subscribes to the papers and magazines of its trade. These periodicals offer important information to buyers, such as new merchandise available for sale, information about consumers (from surveys taken), best-seller reports, trends in the market, and merchandise forecasting. Figure 10–5 shows the activity of a specific vendor's "hot" item with various retail stores.

Market research is undertaken by some of the trade papers, as well as by newspapers and consumer magazines, and is reported on a weekly or monthly basis, or in special editions.

Fashion reports by such companies as the Fairchild organization offer significant statistics to buyers. Fairchild, publisher of *Women's Wear Daily,* has a worldwide

HOT ITEMS

LOS ANGELES

SPORTWEAR

WARM WEATHER BRINGS OUT A YEN FOR CASUAL COTTONS AND BLENDS. PANTS AND SKIMMERS ARE SELLING AT A FAST PACE IN COOL FABRICS.

FOR THE PATIO AND AROUND THE POOL. The scramble is on for the printed skimmer, pantdress and built-in bra skimmer in brown, bright blue and gray print on white background. Easy care cotton makes them ideal for summer wear. Comes in sizes 8-16 at I. Magnin. Retail for $36-38. From: Tori Richard, Honolulu.

CRISP PANTSUITS LOOK NEAT AT MAY CO. Made of Celanese - Fortrel polyester, they come in lilac, blue, navy and oyster. One style has v-neck tunic with collar and matching belt. The other has wrap top with collar and matching belt. Pants are straight-legged, with elasticized waist. Retail at $30-33. From: Internationale Set, Los Angeles.

AT CONTEMPO CASUALS. BLOUSES ARE GOOD SELL-ERS. A short-sleeved acrylic knit with turtleneck is on reorder. Comes in multitude of colors. Retails at $13. From:

Leroy, Los Angeles. Also soaring is a Victorian-looking, long sleeve voile floral print blouse. Comes in beige and retails for $13. From: Tootique, Los Angeles.

BIRMINGHAM

SCRAMBLE FOR SPORTS-WEAR IN WARM SUN-SHINE. PANT, VEST AND LONGUETTE COAT NEW-EST MOVE IN THE FASH-ION GAME. T-SHIRT DRESSES REORDERING ALL OVER THE PLACE. JEANS GYRATING. PANT DRESSES, PANT SKIRTS SCURRYING. SWIM SUITS SIZZLE IN COIN DOT MIDIS.

TRIPLE TREAT IN PANT, VEST AND LONGUETTE COAT at the 6-store Pizitz chain. An ad on this wowed its viewers. Pants and vest in muted tones of gray, cream, brown. Coat, belted back, is in rich cream. The whole "she-bang" only $76 retail. Customers galore, according to sportswear buyer, Ruth Alford. From: Carnival, New York.

T-SHIRT DRESSES A SMASH at Loveman's, in the Junior department. Buyer Barbara Porter kept busy reordering these. Cotton knit stripers. Primarily navy and red. $10 each, retail. From: Bobbie Brooks, Cleveland.

LEVI'S FOR GALS a knockout at Loveman's these days too. Checks, stripes, solids. Denims. Flare or straight legs. $7 to $12 retail. Levi's for Gals, San Francisco.

PANTS DRESSES PERKING UP THE SALES SCENE at Parisian. Assorted prints. Assorted colors. $11 retail. From: Byer out of California, these are all cottons.

PANT SKIRTS SELLING AT PARISIAN TOO. Flap-panel fronts, back zipped, modified A-lines. Assorted stripes, solids, prints. Cottons, and cotton blends. $5 and $6 retail. From: Byer, out of California.

SWIM SUITS IN THE BIG SALES SWIM at Burger-Phillips. Cheerily checking, according to sportswear buyer, Jane Tabor, are the coin dot midi, at $27 retail, and the twin dot panel midi at $28 retail. Both are in red and white, black and white, red and black. But the red and black flew out first. From: Elizabeth Stewart out of California.

SNAPPY SHORT SLEEVED TOPPER charming all comers at Burger's. BanLon, V-neck, in red, white, navy, yellow, and black. $14 retail. From: Vera, New York.

Figure 10–5 "Hot items." Reprinted by permission from *Women's Wear Daily,* Fairchild Publications, Inc.

staff to cover the latest news on fashion changes and trends. Its reporters attend showings of fabric and garment manufacturers and of Parisian, Italian, British, and other internationally known designers.

Among other widely read trade publications are *Drug Topics, Home-Furnishings Daily,* which covers the home furnishings field, and *Footwear News.*

Consumer newspapers and magazines provide buyers with much information. By merely reading the daily newspapers, food buyers can learn what goods their competitors are promoting and at what prices. Fashion buyers could learn about the styles that have been selected by the consumer magazines to be shown to its readers. Because many readers are influenced by magazines, the store certainly should know the merchandise to which their customers are being exposed.

Salespeople sometimes provide buyers with information. Since salespersons are actually the ones who speak to customers, they know the customers' demands. Such items as price information, styles desired, and qualities wanted are examples of the information salespeople can give their buyers.

Want slips are sometimes used by some large retail stores. (See Figure 10–6.) These are slips of paper that are completed by either the customer or salesperson for merchandise requested but not available. The want slips can be analyzed by the buyer,

SALES CLERKS	If you could not supply an item exactly as the Customer wanted it,—record the item the customer described immediately after the customer leaves—even though you sold a substitute.					
ITEM CUSTOMER DESCRIBED (Style—Fabric—Etc.)		Color	Size	Price	No. Calls	Buyer's Disposition
ITEMS LOW IN STOCK						
CUSTOMER WANT SLIP		Sales Clerk No._____ Date_____				
		Name_____				

Figure 10–6   Want slip. *Courtesy:* A & S

and a determination can be made to add new merchandise or increase particular assortments. This information must be used wisely, since action on each slip can lead to such merchandise diversification that the department can become filled with too much merchandise that is not really widely desired.

Resident buying offices are extremely important aids to store buyers. Because their role is so great in some aspects of retailing, the next chapter will be completely devoted to them and how they help retail store organizations.

How Much to Buy

While the ability to select items from all those available is important in purchasing, the wrong quantities in stock may mean a loss for the department. Many students are aware of the dangers inherent in overbuying, but few realize the dangers in not buying enough. There is nothing quite as aggravating to the buyer as having requests for certain merchandise but not enough pieces to suit the customers' demands.

Generally, the initial step in determining how much to buy is to estimate the retail sales for the period of purchase. This is usually a job encompassing the entire organization and is the responsibility of top management. The buyer is interested in the sales estimate for his or her department and has important input in the planning stages. The estimate or forecast is for a designated period of time, varying according to the merchandise. For example, buyers of perishables might be concerned with daily requirements, whereas purchasers of staple goods might just need a semiannual picture. Although the purchase periods differ, the key items analyzed in forecasting retail sales are about the same for all retailers. Such factors as disposable income (that which is available to be spent after taxes), unemployment, and shifts in population are of great importance to top management. At the buyer level, estimating future sales is usually based on a comparison of how much is being sold this year with last year's sales. By determining the percentage of increase (or decrease), a buyer can add (or subtract) that percentage to (or from) last year's purchases for the same upcoming period. In many retail stores, these figures are readily available through the proper programming of the computer. The buyer is also concerned with those factors that have a local effect. For example, a purchaser of men's workclothes, whose customers work principally for a large plant, must carefully watch that plant's progress. If it is apparent that the factory will lose certain contracts, layoffs will be inevitable. The small retailer is generally more concerned with local conditions than those of national importance.

Other factors that must be considered at the department level are expansion plans for the store (new branches or units), enlargement of the department's selling space, change in selling practices (service to self-service or the reverse), the size of the department's promotion budget (for display, advertising, special events), the possibility of a more diversified offering, and more specialization.

Although it would be easier for buyers to purchase only at the beginning of a new season, they must constantly add merchandise to their initial purchases throughout the period. Goods that were sold must be replaced and inventories kept at the designated levels.

Open to Buy

In order to effectively control their inventories, buyers must carefully plan the amount of merchandise they are going to add at a given time. Since inventory needs vary from month to month, depending upon the season, sale periods, holidays, and so forth, the buyer must always adjust the amounts of merchandise needed. The amount of merchandise that can be ordered at any time during a period is the difference between the total purchases planned by the buyer and the commitments already made. The amount of this difference is called *open to buy,* or as it is referred to in practice, the O.T.B. The formula used is

$$\text{Merchandise needed for period } - \text{ Merchandise available } = \text{ Open to buy}$$

Illustrative Problem

The retail inventory for girls' dresses in the children's department of Haring's Department Store figured at $42,000 on September 1, with a planned inventory of $36,000 for September 30. Planned sales, based upon last year's figures, were $22,000 with markdowns of $2,000 for the entire month. The commitments for September were $6,000 at retail. What was the open to buy?

Solution

Merchandise needed (Sept. 1–30)		
End-of-month inventory (planned)	$36,000	
Planned sales (Sept. 1–30)	22,000	
Planned markdowns	2,000	
Total merchandise needed		$60,000
Merchandise available (Sept. 1)		
Opening inventory	$42,000	
Commitments	6,000	
Total merchandise available		48,000
Open to buy (Sept. 1)		$12,000

It should be noted that large retail organizations have open to buy information readily available on their computers.

From Whom to Buy

In most types of merchandise classifications, the number of resources available from which to choose merchandise is practically limitless. The store buyers are not only faced with the problem of selecting particular resources, but also must decide whether to purchase directly from the manufacturer (or grower) or a middleperson, or sometimes perhaps even produce their own merchandise (if the retail business is very large).

The specific vendor from whom to buy is determined by investigating the same sources mentioned in the section of this chapter dealing with what to buy. Other sources are the shopping of competing stores, trade directories such as those published by Fairchild, reporting services, and discussions with buyers of noncompeting stores (stores carrying the same type of goods but far enough away not to be a competitor).

The main channels of distribution for consumer goods (those goods that are purchased for personal use) are:

1. Manufacturer (grower) → Consumer
2. Manufacturer → Retailer's own stores → Consumer
3. Manufacturer → Franchisee → Consumer
4. Manufacturer → Retailer → Consumer
5. Manufacturer → Wholesaler → Retailer → Consumer

In the first situation the manufacturer actually skips the most common type of retail selling, in a store, and sells directly to the consumer at the producer's factory (or farm, as the case may be) or at the consumer's home. Examples of this distribution technique are the Fuller Brush Company selling door to door and the suit manufacturer selling to the consumer at the factory. The latter situation is becoming more popular with producers throughout the United States.

The second channel presents a situation in which manufacturers, in addition to producing merchandise, also set up their own retail stores from which they sell it. Examples of this method are in evidence all across the United States. Manufacturers such as Ralph Lauren, Hathaway, Mikasa, Bass, and Totes are selling their own lines of merchandise in their own outlets.

The third channel is one in which producers manufacture merchandise and distribute it exclusively to their franchisees. Benetton is one of the most successful companies employing this method of distribution.

The first three distribution methods do not involve store buyers. It is through the last two channels of distribution that most consumer goods flow. In one, the retailer buys directly from the producer. The other involves purchasing from a middleperson. The decision of whether to buy from the manufacturer or wholesaler is not always up to the buyer's discretion; some manufacturers, no matter how large the retail organization, sell only through middlepersons. Where the manufacturer distributes to both wholesalers and retailers, the decision from which type of resource to purchase is the buyer's.

Buying from Manufacturers

The purchase of merchandise directly from the manufacturer is generally restricted to large retailers, except in the distribution of fashion merchandise, which even the small retailers purchase directly. The very nature of fashion merchandise, with its constant changes due to consumer demand and the seasonability of the goods, necessitates this route. These goods must reach the retailer quickly and the use of the wholesaler would slow down the process. The direct purchase of merchandise usually affords the buyer lower prices (than at the wholesaler) and a chance to make suggestions about changes in the manufacturer's design. A typical manufacturer's purchase order is shown in Figure 10–7.

Buying from Wholesalers

Outside the fashion world, purchasing from wholesalers is standard procedure. Some factors that persuade the buyer to purchase from middlepersons are:

1. *Quick delivery.* One of the main duties the wholesaler performs for the retailer is the storage of merchandise. With the wholesaler's warehouse stocked with goods, the retailer can expect prompt delivery, sometimes even same-day service.
2. *Smaller orders.* Most manufacturers require minimum orders that are too large for the smaller retailer. Wholesalers sell in smaller quantities than do manufacturers.
3. *Wide assortment.* While manufacturers sell only their own products, the wholesaler carries the offerings of many manufacturers. This affords the retailer a comparison of goods and also saves the time it would take to shop many manufacturers' lines.
4. *Easier credit terms.* Generally, wholesalers offer more liberal credit terms than manufacturers.

The wholesaler is really a service organization. It manufactures nothing. When the buyer feels one or a number of the services the wholesaler offers is more important

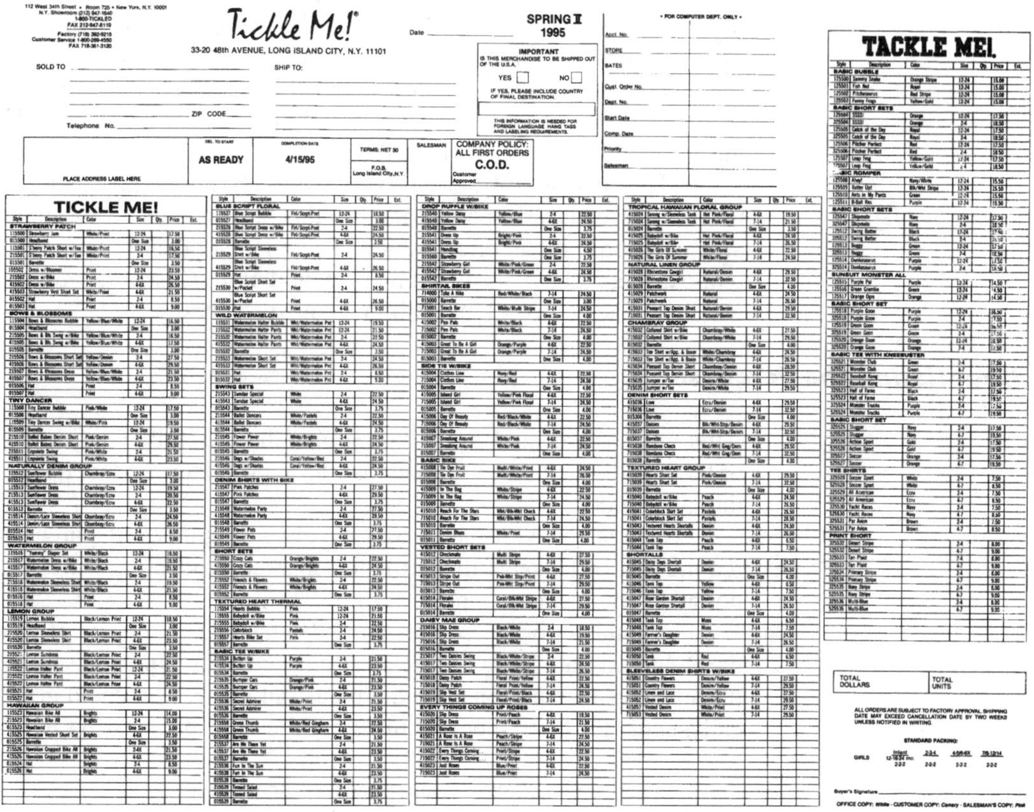
Tickle Me!
33-20 48th AVENUE, LONG ISLAND CITY, N.Y. 11101
SPRING II 1995
SOLD TO
SHIP TO:
ZIP CODE
Telephone No.
IMPORTANT
IS THIS MERCHANDISE TO BE SHIPPED OUT OF THE U.S.A.
YES NO
AS READY
4/15/95
TERMS: NET 30
F.O.B. Long Island City, N.Y.
COMPANY POLICY: ALL FIRST ORDERS C.O.D.
PLACE ADDRESS LABEL HERE
TICKLE ME!
TACKLE ME!
TOTAL DOLLARS
TOTAL UNITS

Figure 10–7 Purchase order. *Courtesy:* Tickle Me!

than price, the buyer will purchase from the wholesaler although it will mean paying more for the goods. Even the largest retailers, which are able to buy direct, use wholesalers when they need immediate delivery and the manufacturer cannot accommodate them. In other cases where, although their overall volume is large, some items are sold infrequently or do not move rapidly, they turn to wholesalers for small quantities.

When to Buy

When to actually purchase goods can vary from every day (small retailers of perishables) to as infrequently as semiannually. In any case, timing is of the utmost importance.

Buyers must buy sufficiently early to allow enough time for the goods to reach the selling floor. Purchasing from wholesalers allows buying merchandise very close to the time the consumer will purchase goods. It is the purchase from manufacturers, coupled with such elements as seasons, weather, and perishability, that poses problems for buyers.

The buyer of seasonal merchandise such as swimsuits, nearly always bought from manufacturers, purchases well in advance of the season. This is necessary because production takes a couple of months and the store wants the goods early enough to whet the customer's appetite. In the case of seasonal merchandise, manufacturers, as an inducement to retailers, often "date" the purchase orders. That is, they extend the period for payment of the invoices. The buyer of seasonal goods who purchases too late might not get delivery. Also, if the customers don't have enough advance exposure to the merchandise, they might be tempted to buy elsewhere.

The weather poses a special problem. Abundant snowfalls will sell snowblowers just as durations of extreme heat will sell air conditioners. While it's difficult to determine weather, it is an important factor to buyers.

Perishability also plays havoc with buyers. Perishable goods must be purchased as frequently as possible and in carefully determined quantities. There is nothing as unsalable as sour milk or wilted roses.

The efficiency of the buyer is extremely important to the store's success. We have discussed how important it is for this person to receive as much help as is available in order to do an effective job. There is, particularly in the fashion field, an aid without whose help many retailers would fail. This is the resident buying office, which will be discussed in detail in the next chapter.

Negotiating the Purchase

After one has prepared a purchasing plan that carefully considers all of the elements of buying, the next step is to seek out the appropriate vendors for the purpose of negotiating an order.

Negotiating with the vendor involves a number of purchasing decisions that require a knowledge of the particular market, product information, discounts, transportation arrangements, and so forth.

Negotiating price requires an understanding of a piece of legislation known as the Robinson-Patman Act, which was enacted to limit price discrimination and protect the small businessperson from the industrial giants who could get lower prices. Basically, under the law, all buyers must pay the same price except in instances where:

- The price reduction is made to meet competition.
- The price is lowered because cost savings result from sales to particular customers.
- The merchandise is obsolete or part of a "job lot."

Once these guidelines are understood, it is the buyer's knowledge of the market and product that enables attainment of a satisfactory price.

A variety of discounts enter into a purchase negotiation. Cash discounts for prompt payment, quantity discounts, seasonal discounts, advertising discounts, and promotional discounts must all be explored to gain the best possible deal.

An important aspect of the negotiation lies with transportation costs. An astute negotiator can often convince the vendor to assume costs of shipping the goods and can thereby actually reduce the cost of the merchandise.

Other negotiating considerations include ventures in cooperative purchasing, where individual orders can be combined for better prices, and consignment buying, which permits payment of goods only when they are sold to the consumer.

Negotiation involves a great deal of expertise and understanding of psychology. Buyers must establish limits for goods they expect to purchase, justify the reasons for the price offered, be willing to split the difference in price when an impasse is reached, and develop relationships that would assure the best possible future deals.

TRENDS

Today's buyers are busily engaged in a variety of activities that are different than those of yesteryears'.

Purchasing By Video

Some manufacturers are using video to bring the buyer's attention to their new merchandise. The buyers, very busy with a variety of time-consuming chores, often use this approach to select items. It is particularly useful when off-price purchases are made and closeouts are considered.

International Travel

Now more than ever before, the availability of foreign-made merchandise has caused the buyer to travel more extensively. It is not uncommon to find the buyer in a domestic market one week and a third world nation the next.

Development of Private Label Merchandise

With so many retailers opting for a portion of their inventories to be in private-label, the buyers are often called upon to become product developers. They are asked to "create" items using the details of many different items and combining them into one salable product.

ACTION FOR THE INDEPENDENT RETAILER

Very often, it is the taste and feel for appealing merchandise that prompt an individual to begin a retail business. Creative buying is an important factor contributing to a store's success, and this is where the independent can compete with even the largest retailer.

The small businessperson who operates a store is generally its buyer. In addition to purchasing, the individual is often on the sales floor within earshot of the customer, if not actually making the sale. Where the buyers for large stores rely heavily upon printouts and other buying tools, the independent is getting firsthand buying information. If it is true that the consumer determines the inventory necessary, who then is better informed than the independent retailer who interfaces with the customer daily? The independents also have the advantage of faster reaction to customer needs. That is, there is no need to clear through management changes in merchandising philosophy that seem worthy. The independent can adjust quickly to the customer's needs.

The creative buyer can motivate customer purchasing. This is one area where store size does not play a significant role.

IMPORTANT POINTS IN THE CHAPTER

1. In most large stores, individual buyers are responsible for purchasing and pricing the goods.
2. The effectiveness of a selling department depends in large part on how successful the buyer is in satisfying customer demand.
3. The basic elements of buying are what to buy, how much to buy, from whom to buy, and when to buy.
4. While some of the buyers' choices are a matter of taste, they have many sources of information available that help them make selections. Among these are past sales records, inventory records, surveys, trade periodicals, and newspapers.
5. Top management sets budgetary restrictions on buying. The buyer must carefully plan purchases to remain within the budget.
6. Open to buy is the difference between the buyer's planned purchases and the buying commitments she or he has already made.
7. In the decision of from whom to buy, the buyer weighs the advantages and disadvantages among various producers and types of sources (wholesaler or manufacturer).

REVIEW QUESTIONS

1. Who purchases goods for small stores unable to afford buyers?
2. What are some responsibilities of the store buyer other than purchasing merchandise?
3. What duties are performed by assistant buyers?
4. What does following up an order entail?
5. Discuss some of those characteristics necessary to a successful buyer.
6. Who generally buys the merchandise for department store branches?
7. Explain central buying.
8. How do the chain store buyer's responsibilities differ from those of the department store buyer?
9. Discuss the variations of central buying practiced in the chain organizations.
10. What should the first thought be when a buyer plans purchases?
11. Which source of information is used by all buyers when planning purchases?
12. How can the large retail store quickly provide its buyers with sales information?
13. Why do buyers scan consumer newspapers and magazines?
14. What factors should be considered in determining how much to buy?

15. Discuss open to buy. Why are buyers constantly determining their O.T.B.?

16. From whom are most fashion goods purchased, manufacturers or wholesalers? Why?

CASE PROBLEMS

Case Problem 1

The Time-Rite Appliance Company is a small retail chain with three units located in New Jersey. It carries a general line of appliances including refrigerators, washing machines, dishwashers, toasters, and electric can openers. It plans the addition of another line of merchandise, air conditioners, because of consumer demand. Most of the items carried are purchased from manufacturers (unless a particular manufacturer distributes exclusively through wholesalers); in an emergency situation some are purchased from wholesalers. All inventory sells throughout the year, with Christmas the peak period. Since the company does not sell any of the newer fashion styles of appliances extensively, you might say its inventory was comprised of "staples." The problem confronting it now is from whom to purchase the air conditioning units—manufacturers or wholesalers. Time-Rite is unsure of the sales volume to anticipate from this line and thus the appropriate quantities to stock.

Questions

1. Compare air conditioners with the company's other lines. What factors must it consider?

2. How advantageous would purchasing be from manufacturers? From wholesalers?

3. How would you suggest Time-Rite proceed with its first year's merchandising of air conditioners?

Case Problem 2

The Men's Shop at Lustig's Department Store is one of the organization's busiest departments. One reason is that, in addition to the great ability of the haberdashery buyer, the store is located in an area occupied by many large firms employing great numbers of male employees. These include advertising firms, sales organizations, insurance companies, and so on.

During the past two months, while the rest of the store has continued to meet and beat their sales figures, the business shirt sales in the Men's Shop have declined considerably. The buyer is uncertain of how to rectify the situation but knows he has to begin with his customer in mind.

Question

1. If you were that department's buyer, what methods would you use to secure customer information that might change the present situation?

Chapter 11
Resident Buying Offices
and Other Market Consultants

Photograph by Ellen Diamond

LEARNING OBJECTIVES

Upon completion of this chapter, the student should be able to:

1. Explain the difference between a privately owned resident buying office and an independent one.
2. Write an essay on the selection of a resident buying office. This should include at least four factors that should be considered.
3. List and discuss ten services performed by a resident buying office.
4. Indicate the importance of foreign resident buying offices, pointing out four services they perform.
5. Discuss the various types of market consultants other than resident buying offices.

COVERING THE MARKET ISN'T THEIR ONLY ROLE . . .

At one point, resident buying offices were primarily concerning with shopping lines for their member stores, making suggestions in terms of buying plans, and following up orders. Young women in attractive outfits regularly combed the wholesale markets, particularly those in New York City, and reported the pulse of the market. Today, the nature of resident buying offices has changed considerably. The offices actually serve as market consultants which provide a host of activities to make the likelihood of profitability more possible for clients.

Like their retail counterparts, their business methods have changed, as has the number of individuals who toil in the wholesale markets. Similarly, as the number of department store organizations has shrunk, so has the number of major resident buying offices. One of the most important of the remaining resident buying offices is Henry Doneger Associates. It began with the most modest of intentions, but it has been catapulted into a giant venture with the acquisition of many of its competitors. Absorbed into the Doneger team are offices such as Hilda Bridals, Steinberg-Kass, The Buying Connection and Independent Retailers Syndicate. Although many of the aforementioned traditional buying activities are still carried out by Doneger, the menu of available services has broadened.

Domestic market coverage has been expanded to include all of the fashion centers of the world. With off-shore production a major aspect of merchandise acquisition, Doneger scouts far off markets to make their customers aware of the best merchandise that can be found.

In a time when the retail department store giants such as Macy's and Bloomingdales are preoccupied with private label merchandise, and chains like The Limited are doing the same, small retailers are finding themselves in the unenviable position of being restricted to the same goods that are found everywhere else. Thus, such circumstances often foster intolerable competition in both assortment and price. Doneger has come to the aid of its member stores with private label merchandise of its own. They design the goods, have them manufactured, and enable their member participants to obtain items that they alone, in specific geographic areas, are able to carry. They eliminate competition.

Fashion forecasting is still another service provided by Doneger. With the addition of a forecasting team headed by the internationally renowned David Wolfe, they provide their stores with advance foresight as to what the market will have to offer well before buying decisions need to be made. In this way, the store buyers are able to plan their future purchases and promotional campaigns in a more appropriate manner. Before this, only the big guns of the industry were able to play the fashion forecasting game.

Addressing the vast increase in off-price retailing, Doneger has established a separate division that scouts the market seeking goods that are well below the regular wholesale price, and passes the information on to the stores they represent.

Henry Doneger Associates continues to thrive in an industry that is wrought with bankruptcies and closings because of its readiness to adapt to the demands of present-day retailers. The company's continuous expansion makes it the envy of the competitors.

In the preceding chapter, an overview of most of the store buyer's sources of information was presented. Perhaps the single most important aid to the buyer's procurement of fashion merchandise is the resident buying office. Unlike retail stores, which for the most part are located away from the wholesale markets, the resident offices are located in these markets. Through affiliation with a resident office, the store personnel can feel the pulse of their market without making many costly and time-consuming trips. By selecting the appropriate office, store buyers can carry out their duties and responsibilities at the store with the security of knowing that someone is constantly scanning the market for new resources and new merchandise for them.

In addition to the resident offices, there are other types of companies that provide retailers with information that may be pertinent to their operations. These companies are collectively known as market consultants and include fashion forecasters and reporting services.

Some companies use both resident offices and the other market consulting firms, while some just rely on one for their merchandising needs. All of these organizations will be discussed in this chapter.

TYPES OF RESIDENT OFFICES

There are two major types of resident buying offices: privately owned offices and independent offices.

Privately Owned Offices

In the strictest sense of the word, the private office is owned by and exclusively aids a single retail organization. Since maintaining a buying office is costly, there are few private offices. Not completely private but certainly more so than the independent offices are those resident offices that are owned by a group of stores. This arrangement allows for expenses to be shared by the members of the group, much like a cooperative. The members of the group are noncompeting stores and can thus safely aid each other in many ways without the fear of jeopardizing their own operations. In the completely private office, this information exchange is unavailable since ownership is exclusive. There are several group offices in New York City. One of the best known is AMC, The Associated Merchandising Corporation.

Figure 11–1   Major Buying Offices

Buying Office	Type
Allied Stores	Corporate*
Associated Merchandising Corp. (AMC)	Cooperative
April-Marcus	Independent
Atlas Buying Corp.	Independent
Belk Stores Service, Inc.	Corporate*
Clothiers Corp.	Independent
Frederick Atkins	Independent
Henry Doneger Associates	Independent
Independent Associated Distributors	Independent
Macy's Corporate Buying	Corporate*
May Merchandising Corp.	Corporate*
Men's Fashion Guild	Independent
Neiman-Marcus	Private
Promotional Buying Exchange, Ltd.	Independent
Retailers Representatives, Inc.	Independent
Sears	Private
Specialty Stores Association	Cooperative

*Division of a retail corporation.

Independent Offices

The independent office has as its members many different, noncompeting retail stores. These offices run the gamut of representing fairly small retail organizations to the large retailers. The fees charged for the many services afforded customers vary according to sales volume, with remuneration generally being a percentage of the sales figures. The fees also vary from office to office, depending upon the services offered. Stores generally enter into contractual agreements with the resident buying offices for periods of one year. Some of the better known independent offices are Frederick Atkins and Henry Doneger Associates, the largest independent office. Figure 11–1 shows a listing of some of the major buying offices and their classification.

SELECTION OF AN OFFICE

Few retailers really have a choice as to the category of office to which they can belong. Only a very small percentage are large enough to warrant a privately owned or semiprivately owned company. The remainder of those retailers needing market representation must choose from the several hundred independent resident buying offices now in existence. Selecting the right office is extremely important. Buying decisions are often based upon an office's recommendation, and poor advice can lead to a store's failure.

One important point to consider in the selection of an office is its size. The office must be sufficiently large to give the store adequate assistance. For example, some offices are so small that their staff members cannot specialize in any one capacity. Perhaps one individual may be responsible for covering both the sportswear and the dress markets in all price ranges. This monumental task surely does not give one individual sufficient time to completely investigate either of these markets. The store cannot then be confident of the office's recommendation.

The other stores that deal through the resident buying office require careful investigation. First, it is important to be certain that competitors are not members. Since the resident buying office is a great place for exchanging information with other store buyers, the inclusion of competition at the same office could be disastrous. Second, the other retail organizations being represented should be similar to one's own. Clientele, merchandising policies, price ranges, and image are just some areas of significance. If the other stores are unlike your own operation, the information exchange will be meaningless. Some resident offices represent a number of different types of retail operations. This is fine, as long as the office is large enough to employ enough people to cater to all the different needs.

The merchandise in which an office specializes is an important factor in its being selected by a store for representation. Only the very large offices run the gamut of hard goods and soft goods. Others specialize in particular merchandise. For an operation that encompasses all types of merchandise (for example, a department store), membership would be most beneficial in an office whose offerings are more diversified. The more specialization in a store, the more specialized the chosen office should be. Both the office and the organization should be interested in the same type of retailing.

The services offered by resident buying offices vary. Naturally, these services are important to consider in selecting the right office.

SERVICES OF AN OFFICE

It is imperative to select the office that offers those services needed to help your operation. Very small stores, unable to afford the fees of full-service resident offices, often join a small office which only advises about new resources and new merchandise available. Most retailers join an office for many additional services. Following are some of these.

Season Overview

Before the store buyers write their orders for the next season they do a great deal of research to determine their actual needs. As we learned in the previous chapter, *The Buying Function,* one of the sources of this information is the resident buying office. To prepare the store buyers for this task, many offices produce books or portfolios spelling out the coming season, which they send to their member stores (Figure 11-2).

Placing Orders

Stores often satisfy their customers by reordering for them out-of-stock merchandise or merchandise not usually carried at all. The resident office will place these special orders and make certain that the vendors deliver the item within the specified time period. Sometimes buyers are in need of new merchandise and are unable to visit the market. Given approximate specifications, resident buyers will actually make purchases for the store.

Most retailers' businesses thrive on reorders of merchandise that has sold successfully. Since the timing of receipt of reordered merchandise is extremely important (it might be needed for an advertisement or a window display), store buyers often depend upon the resident office to place the reorder. With the office located in the market, the resident buyer can carefully check with the vendors to make certain that delivery promises are kept. Only the retailer who has run a newspaper advertisement and not received the merchandise when promised can appreciate this responsibility that is undertaken by the resident offices.

Fashion gets dressed-up again in optimistic colors and high profile fabrics for dressy designs worn with outstanding accessories and maximum grooming.

What the world needs now is some Feel-Good Fashion!

UPBEAT is the new, positive attitude for fashion. It is a violent reaction to the recent seasons of downbeat, dreary, depressing and dressed-down images presented as the height of fashion. That mood may have been a reflection of the times, a reaction to the excesses of the Eighties, but *enough, already!* Now is the time for some feel-good fashion. It's all uphill from here.

Upbeat Colors are optimistically bright and pretty, put together in extrovert combinations.

Upbeat Fabrics are high-profile stand-outs in stunning textures and bold patterns, often combined with 'nary a care.

Upbeat Garment Design is Dressy even though the items themselves may be worn for everyday as well as special occasions. In fact, that is the whole point.

Upbeat Details are definite and decorative.

Upbeat Accessories are attention-getters, sometimes even obviously over-dressed for the fun of it.

This Trend corrects fashion's recent bad attitude problem and provides a style option that is fun and flattering, frivolous and flashy. An upbeat attitude is a welcome change.

Figure 11–2   One of the season's trends. *Uptown* from the Doneger overview. *Courtesy:* The Doneger Group

TREND

UPTOWN

Figure 11–2   (Continued)

Arranging Adjustments

It is not unusual for a store buyer who has carefully ordered merchandise, paying strict attention to style, color, and size selection, to receive goods that were not wanted. A completely different fabric from that which was seen in the sample merchandise is not uncommon in shipments. Handling these adjustments through a resident office is much wiser for the retailer. Vendors are unlikely to ignore the resident buyer's complaints as they might an individual small retailer, since the resident offices are so influential through their recommendations. Sometimes the buying office can convince the vendor to accept a return of merchandise that has been ordered but is not selling satisfactorily. In this case, the retailer handling the situation alone usually doesn't stand a chance. Other adjustment situations include poor fit, inferior workmanship, and poor wearability.

Foreign Market Information

In both hard goods and soft goods, foreign markets are becoming increasingly important. A tremendous amount of merchandise is being imported each year at prices below those found in the United States. The larger resident buying offices have branches in many foreign countries. Because few stores can send their buyers abroad, the information about the merchandise available is becoming an extremely important service.

Locating New Resources

Retailers are always looking for new resources. Since many vendors begin on a small scale with little sales help and advertising, it is difficult for stores away from the market to hear about the newcomers. Retailers are made aware of new resources through the resident office, since every new firm tries desperately to be recommended by them.

Recommending New Items

Buyers purchase sufficient goods prior to each selling season to complete their opening inventories. They generally visit their markets, either alone or assisted by the resident buyer, to select the goods they desire. During the season, when store buyers are involved in duties at the store, they find that they generally need new merchandise to spruce up the inventory. The resident office will scout the market and suggest merchandise that will fit the bill. Often, this recommendation by the resident buyer turns out to be a "hot item." Figures 11–3 and 11–4 show some of the forms used to relate "hot items" to buyers.

Preparing Displays and Promotional Materials

In large stores, the visual merchandising department is charged with the responsibility of creating dramatic, timely windows and interior displays. The smaller shop either periodically engages a free-lance trimmer or trims its own windows. In the latter instances, catchy ideas are always being sought by store buyers. Many resident offices arrange displays in typical window-size settings so that the retailer can copy them. This gives retailers new ideas to bring back to their stores. Similarly, copy for advertisements is prepared. Some offices even provide mats (paper composition printing plates of complete advertisements) to which the store's name is added for newspaper advertisements.

January 31, 1995

ITEM ALERT

THE CHURCH LADY DRESS

Get ready to go back in time. Church Lady dresses made interesting by D.K.N.Y. are a must...layer with the little cardigan for the complete look. Details to look for:

- S   Long, short and that new Mid Length
- S   Lots of Florals and Solids in Dusty to Dark Colors
- S   Antique Lace, Embroidery and Buttons
- S   Skinny Belts
- S   Crepe and Sheer Fabrics
- S   Retro Collars, Necklines & darting details
- S   Contrast Collars and Cuffs

Recommended Resources:

Mfr.:	ROMEO ROMEO c/o VICTORIA WATSON
Address:	214 W. 39th St., 4th floor
Tel. #:	212-575-8858
Contact:	Vicky

Mfr.:	MYSTICAL THREADS c/o STANDING RM ONLY
Address:	1466 Broadway, 5th floor
Tel. #:	212-840-0066
Contact:	Steve

Mfr.:	MICA
Address:	1466 Broadway, 5th floor
Tel. #:	212-354-2664
Contact:	Megan

Figure 11–3 Hot Item Alert. *Courtesy:* The Doneger Group

Preparing Fashion Shows

Resident buying offices typically present fashion shows to their member stores during "market week," a time when most buyers visit the market to begin purchasing for a new season. In addition to these shows, many of the offices prepare complete fashion show "packages" for their retailers to present at their stores. These packages include such important elements as the commentary, suggested musical selections, and background recommendations. Following these prescribed plans makes the presentation of a fashion show a routine job.

Training Salespeople

Some offices aid in the training of salespeople. They provide training materials such as booklets, brochures, and recordings, which describe the art of selling. In addition, some even send counselors to the store. By using this service, the buyer makes certain

Date	12/20/94	
Market	Moderate Misses Dresses	
Buyer	Leslie Shaw - X3658	
M.M.	Roseanne Cumella	

MARKET OVERVIEW:

Pants continue to dominate the reorder activity in the moderate dress area. AM-PM crepes in 1 & 2 piece looks are still a very strong category at retail. Spring merchandise is beginning to be shipped.

HOT CATEGORIES:

- Pant Suits - **R & M Richard, Ronnie Nicole, Virgo, Positive Attitude**

- Palazzo - **Jeffrey & Dara**

- 1 Pc. Crepe Dresses - **Danny Nicole, Virgo**

- Casual Wear - **Calander, Positive Attitude, Renditions**

- Columns - **Renditions**

- Social Occasion - **Karen, Miller, Alex Evenings, Filigree, Nah Nah, Jr. Nites**

- Separates Social - **Michael Marcella, Patra**

REORDERS:

Manufacturer	Style #	Cost	Description/Sizes/Colors	Delivery
Karen Miller	3103	$109.75 8+2	Two piece gold thread knit tunic with chiffon pant. Color: Cinnamon.	AR 2/28
Alex Evening	6217	80.00 +7	Two piece crepe tuxedo pant suit. Colors: Black/White, Taupe, Royal.	AR 1/30
Alex Evening	6863	92.00 +7	Two piece crepe triple gold piped organza collar pant suit. Color: Ivory, Black.	AR 1/30

MARKETFOCUS

Figure 11–4   *Market Focus*. Reorder alert. *Courtesy:* The Doneger Group

that once the purchases arrive at the store, the salespeople will be sufficiently knowledgeable in the dissemination of the proper information concerning the merchandise.

Preparing for the Store Buyer's Visit

The frequency of visits a store buyer makes to the market varies from store to store. Distance from the market, size of the department, and the store's need for the buyer's presence on the selling floor are just some factors that help determine how often the market is visited. Whenever the buyer does decide to come to the market, the resident buying office goes to work to make certain that the trip will be fruitful and that as much as possible can be condensed into that brief period (generally one week). The office's preparation includes:

1. Locating the most desirable merchandise.
2. Publishing the "buyer's arrival" in such papers as *The New York Times* and the appropriate trade papers. This notifies all interested vendors about the buyers who are in town, the length of their stay, and their temporary residence. In this way, advance appointments can be made through the offices.
3. Arranging hotel accommodations.
4. Providing working space at the resident office to study their purchasing plans and to see salespersons and their merchandise.
5. Assigning a resident buyer to accompany the store buyer to market to help with the selection of merchandise.

Market Week

Although the resident offices must have their services available to the retail store members at all times, it is during the regular visits to the market that the resident buyers are busiest serving the store buyer's needs. These periodic visits are generally made during the "market weeks." They are times when the manufacturers of particular industries "open" and show their lines to the store buyers. Because the period is extremely hectic and the store buyer's time away from the store is generally limited to a week, the resident office planning must be perfectly organized. It is during this period that the previously mentioned buyer preparations must be made.

Making Available Private Label Merchandise

A private label is one that bears either the store's label or the resident buying office's name. Private label merchandise permits the store to gain a high markup without the fear of price cutting by competitors, because exact comparison shopping is impossible. Few retailers are large enough to market private labels by themselves. By joining a buying office, small individual orders can be consolidated into large orders. To obtain large orders, manufacturers will gladly produce merchandise to specification and affix private labels. By using private label merchandise, the stores are able to limit price cutting since these goods do not get into competitors' hands as do manufacturer's brands and labels.

Locating Off-price Merchandise

Many offices scout the market in search of goods that are slow sellers and secure them for their clients at rock bottom prices. In this way, the retailers are able to sell items at prices that compete with the off-price stores.

Pooling Orders

On merchandise other than private labels, resident offices often pool orders. This frequently enables a small user to qualify for a quantity discount.

The resident office contract form in Figure 11–5 summarizes the terms of the agreement made between the resident buying office and the retailer.

New York _____

To: Atlas Buying Corp.
       500 - 7th Avenue
       New York, N.Y. 10018

This confirms your agreement to represent us as resident buyer in the New York market and to furnish us information regarding market conditions on the following terms:

Office space in your office will be furnished to our visiting personnel without extra charge. You will charge us at cost for forwarding packages, telephone tolls, and telegrams and other similar items. A flat charge of $ _____ per month will be made for postage. We shall pay you the sum $ _____ per annum at the beginning of each contract year this agreement remains in effect. We shall have the privilege of paying said sum in equal monthly installments of $ _____ each on the _____ day of each month during the term hereof. Should we default in the payment of any such installment, the entire unpaid sum for the whole remaining term of this agreement shall immediately become due and payable without notice or demand. This agreement is binding to heirs and successors.

You will also make available the merchandising facilities of your affiliate ABC Distributing Corp. On any merchandise purchased by said Distributing Corp. three per cent (3%) of the net purchase cost to cover billing, bookkeeping and other similar expenses involved in the handling of such transactions in addition to the net cost of the merchandise. We will pay for all such merchandise within ten (10) days from date of invoice.

The term of this agreement shall be for _____ year beginning _____ 19 ____ .
This agreement shall be automatically renewed from year to year unless, on or before sixty (60) days preceding the end of any contract year, notice in writing is given by either party of the intention not to renew.

                          STORE _____

                          ADDRESS _____

                          CITY _____ STATE _____ ZIP CODE ___

                               BY _____

We accept and agree to the above contract:
       ATLAS BUYING CORP.
By _____

Figure 11–5   Resident buying office contract form

FOREIGN RESIDENT BUYING OFFICES

In addition to the prestige merchandise made available by the leading couturiers, a great deal of other merchandise is finding its way onto the selling floors of American retailers. There are a number of arrangements available to the retailer for the procurement of merchandise for import. Since only the very large retail organizations will invest in trips to foreign lands for purposes of purchasing, other methods are employed by smaller entrepreneurs for the importing of goods.

Similar to those resident offices operating in the United States are the resident buying offices located in foreign countries. Some of the offices, called commissionaires, are completely independent (without American affiliation) and are designed to service buyers from other countries. Other offices are affiliated with the American resident buying offices and their services are available to member stores, as is any other resident buying office service. Whichever type of office represents the American retailer, the services afforded the buyer are the same. Some of the services offered are:

1. The purchase of new merchandise. Purchasing in this manner is somewhat risky for the store because the foreign office must use its judgment and the store must accept what has been purchased. Sometimes, if time is available, photographs or samples of goods are sent to the United States for approval. This eliminates some of the risk.
2. The placement of reorders. Much the same as American resident buying offices, those in foreign countries place orders and follow-up reorders. Even though the office somewhat facilitates purchasing in foreign countries, the reordering of merchandise must be contemplated with caution. Shipping delays, strikes, and so forth can cause merchandise to be delivered too late to be meaningful in terms of sales.
3. The arrangement for shipment of the merchandise.
4. Assistance to those stores wishing to visit the foreign markets. They arrange such things as hotel accommodations and appointments with vendors.

The commissionaires, for their services, are paid a commission on the cost of the purchases they make. The commission charged is approximately 7 percent of the foreign cost.

Although the cost of goods in foreign countries may be considerably less than comparable domestic goods, there are additional costs that must be considered before a purchase is completed. An example of the computation involved in determining the true or landed cost, as it is technically called, follows:

Initial cost 50 sweaters @ 30,000 lire each	1,500,000	lire
100 sweaters @ 60,000 lire each	6,000,000	
Total initial cost	7,500,000	lire
Less 3% discount	225,000	
	7,275,000	lire
Packing charge	227,000	
7% commission on initial cost	525,000	
Shipping charge	552,000	
	8,579,000	lire
Duty 30% (estimated) on goods purchased plus packing charge	2,250,600	
	10,829,600	lire
Other expenses (storage, etc.)	910,000	
Total landed cost	11,739,600	lire

Note: It should be understood that the lire figure is only for an example, since the value of the lire fluctuates daily. This figure is then translated into American dollars.

As has been examined in the preceding chapter, several forces necessitate the purchase of merchandise abroad. Whether the purchase is achieved directly through negotiation between the store buyer and supplier, or arranged through a commissionaire, there are a number of factors to which attention must be paid to ensure that a profit will be possible.

There has always been a fluctuation of foreign currency in relation to the American dollar. Today, the situation is even less stable. Each day the worth of our dollar on foreign markets fluctuates, sometimes to a considerable degree. The buyer must make certain that the terms of purchase include language that provides for protection of price. That is, if the cost due to dollar fluctuation presents a risk to profit once the merchandise is delivered, the buyer should insist upon some protection. Such caution is needed even more where there is a wide time gap between purchase, production, and eventual delivery. The inexperienced buyer could lose a great deal if these price considerations aren't carefully explored.

While the initial price might seem low, the landed cost should always be figured to determine the real cost to the store. Such factors as packing charges and duty charges must be carefully examined to ensure that the product is worth the real cost.

Merchandise from abroad frequently includes selling features not found in domestic goods. Similarly, the merchandise might bring with it quality features that are detrimental to the merchandise. For example, European fit might be narrower than that which is appropriate for Americans. Often, the sample and the delivered goods bear little resemblance to each other. A buyer planning to purchase imported merchandise must be careful to set guidelines for the merchandise that is bought in foreign countries. Returns are difficult and time-consuming, and subquality goods could present problems.

Although it is generally conceded that goods from abroad are necessary to many merchandising plans, care must be exercised in their purchase. The foreign resident representative must be completely instructed as to the requirements of the purchase. Although dollars are important, other factors might prevent successful sale of the goods.

OTHER MARKET CONSULTANTS

Most fashion retailers need as much information as possible prior to and in the midst of a season. They might want to learn, in advance of making their purchasing plans, what trends are being predicted for the next selling season. At other times they might want to learn more about how other stores are doing at a particular time, which merchandise they are reordering, and what is "hot" market news. All of this may be made available by employing the services of fashion forecasters and reporting services.

Fashion Forecasters

These market consultants service the needs of all of the arms of the fashion industry. They help designers select the appropriate materials and colors for their collections, design a manufacturer's complete line, determine with the mills which direction they should take for a particular season, and assist retailers in numerous ways.

We have been reminded throughout the text of the growing use of private label merchandise by retail organizations. Since retailers are not really designers or producers of goods, and since they wish to introduce merchandise styled exclusively for their needs, they often turn to a company equipped to handle fashion design. The fashion forecasters not only predict what trends will develop, but many also have divisions that will crete complete lines of merchandise for retailers. By using the forecasting service, the retailer not only has the advantage of learning about trends far in advance of the selling season, but can also have the forecasters address these trends with their own styling. While merchants who heavily use private label goods often produce their own merchandise that has been styled by in-house product developers, or buy specific styles from manufacturers for the store's exclusive use, many use the services of the fashion forecaster to achieve their private label goals.

Private label production is not the only involvement the retailer has with the forecasting companies. As subscribers of these forecasting services, the stores are able to visit their premises for a number of reasons. One is to learn more about the latest fabric innovations and color preferences expected for the future. The forecasting organizations have complete fabric and color libraries that house all of the important materials for the coming seasons. Instead of having to visit mills all over the world, the retailer can examine the offerings of many suppliers under one roof and compare them. Buyers and fashion coordinators regularly examine these library collections before they visit the vendors to make the next season's purchases.

Many major retailers regularly present fashion promotions to their customers. Since these must be scheduled more than year in advance, and lines of merchandise are unavailable so early, the store's promotion people visit the forecasters to learn about coming trends that they can employ in the future.

Subscribers of these market consulting services gain their information in one of two ways. As already discussed, they can visit the forecasting offices as often as they wish to discuss fashion-oriented problems and review the library's materials, or they can research their needs through the use of information disseminated by the company. Most of these consulting firms produce books, as far as 15 months in advance of a season, that tell all about the company's projections along with vast numbers of illustrations of particular styles. Promostyl, a leading fashion forecaster, produces trend books as far as 12 to 14 months in advance of the seasons on men's, women's and children's clothing, activewear, and accessories. Other fashion forecasters include David Wolfe for the Doneger Group, Nigel French, Tobe Associated, Merchandising Motivation, and Cotton Incorporated.

Reporting Services

In order to keep abreast of the season in progress, retailers often use reporting services. These companies research the varied markets and assemble information that would be of interest to their clients. They regularly send brochures, pamphlets, and newsletters that tell about the hot items in the market, which stores are selling them, and from which vendors they are available. By scouring the market, these services also locate new resources and forward the information to the appropriate retailers. Other information regularly offered to the reporting services' customers are re-order reports, periodic analysis of a season, and anything else that would be of interest to retailers. One of the industry's largest is the Retail Reporting Corporation, which publishes weekly reports for retailers.

Unlike resident buying offices, these market consultants do not make merchandise available, nor do they assist store buyers with their specific merchandising needs.

TRENDS

While much of the business undertaken by the resident buying offices and other market consultants is the same as it was since their inception, different roles have begun to emerge in the industry.

Development of Private Label Merchandise

More and more resident buying offices have divisions that concern themselves with the creation of product lines that are for the exclusive use of their member stores. They design the products and market them to their member stores so that the stores can compete with the retail giants who build their empires based on private label goods.

Off-price Procurement

The larger market consultants are involving themselves more and more in the finding of off-price merchandise. By uncovering these bargains, they enable their member stores to "mix" their regularly purchased items with those that cost less, and produce a generally larger average markup. It also helps the traditional stores to compete more easily with those who deal exclusively with off-price goods by providing "special promotional" goods that attract bargain shoppers.

Communicating With Member Stores Via Video

In addition to the use of flyers and newsletters, many resident buying offices are interacting with their clients by means of videos that feature the hot items of the market. Although the traditional photographs and direct mail pieces serve a purpose, the live-action displayed on video makes the merchandise easier for a store buyer to appreciate.

ACTION FOR THE INDEPENDENT RETAILER

The counterpart of the independent retailer is the independent resident buying office. For a nominal fee, the retailer can receive a wide variety of service assistance as well as a market representative to do some purchasing. Without investing in specialists to participate in the management of the store, the independent retailer can be satisfactorily served through resident office affiliation.

One should join an office that provides only those services that are sought. For example, if market representation is all that is required, a more expensive office that offers other services would be a wasteful cost.

Joining a resident office will not only provide pertinent information, but it can also free the store buyer from making many trips to the market and thus permit more attention to the store. Thus, although membership involves a cost, it can also provide a savings by allowing the buyer to perform other in-store functions sometimes necessitated by hiring part-time personnel. If soundly used, a resident office could provide the professional advice generally out of the independent's reach.

IMPORTANT POINTS IN THE CHAPTER

1. A resident buying office is an organization located in the heart of the wholesale market. It performs many buying services for small stores and stores whose geographic locations make coming to the market difficult.
2. Since there are a wide variety of sizes and types of resident buying offices, a retailer must select an office uniquely fitted to its buying needs.
3. Among the functions of the resident buying office are placing and following up orders, arranging adjustments, locating new resources and items, helping prepare displays and special events, and preparing for the buyer's periodic visits to the market.
4. Foreign resident buying offices serve domestic retailers who are unable to shop foreign markets.
5. Fashion forecasters and reporting services provide retailers with information needed in the merchandising of their stores.

REVIEW QUESTIONS

1. In what ways can it be more advantageous for a large retailer to be part of a group owning a "semiprivate" office than to operate a completely private office?
2. Define the term *independent buying office*.
3. Which type of office is generally associated with the giant retail organizations?
4. On what basis are members charged for the services of an independent office?
5. Why is it emphasized that retailers should not belong to the same office as their competitors?
6. Of what importance is the merchandise specialization of the resident office to the retailer?
7. In which cases do resident buyers actually purchase merchandise?
8. Is it likely that the resident office can more easily arrange adjustments with vendors than can the individual retailer? Give an example.
9. Where are the resident buying offices located? For what reason?
10. Are resident buyers ever located abroad? What purpose would this serve the store?
11. If the resident buyer is able to easily locate new resources, why isn't it as easy for the store buyer?
12. How can the resident office satisfactorily notify a member store of a "hot" fashion item?
13. In addition to brochures and pamphlets, describe two techniques used by the resident offices to help train retail stores' salespeople.
14. Where are notices of "buyers' arrivals" published? What purpose do they serve?
15. Does the resident buyer accompany the store buyer to market? Why or why not?
16. Define *private label* merchandise.
17. What are some advantages of carrying "private label" merchandise?
18. How does a commissionaire serve the American retailer?
19. Describe "landed cost."
20. What services does the fashion forecaster provide for the retailer?

CASE PROBLEMS

Case Problem 1

Clement's Inc. is a large department store chain with 35 full-size department store units. It is located in the middle Atlantic states, with the main store, from which top management operates, located in Philadelphia. The organization has been functioning under the control of its original founders, the Clement family. Its policies over the years have been rather conservative, and sales are beginning to decline. After complete analysis, it was recommended that the organization either affiliate with a few other stores to organize a somewhat private buying office, or form its own completely separate buying office with branches in all the major resource markets. As strange as it might appear, Clement's has until now completely depended upon its store buyers to make purchases and scout the market. The research report suggests that its problem concerns merchandise selection and other merchandising matters.

The board of directors has met for several weeks, convinced that it must use resident buyers, but has reached a stalemate concerning which type of organization to develop.

Questions

Keeping in mind that Clement's is a very large conventional department store carrying the full complement of hard goods and soft goods, in prices that range from budget to high price:

1. What are the advantages of forming a completely private office?
2. Which benefits will Clement's lose if it has its own office?
3. After considering its present position, which type of structure would you recommend? Why?

Case Problem 2

ATC, the American Trading Company, is an independent resident buying office specializing in children's wear. It has been in operation for five years and represents about 200 small children's retail shops throughout the country. It offers many of those services typical of resident buying offices, but the main problem has been an inability to provide enough personal attention for store buyers during market week. The total volume of the member stores combined does not warrant a large number of resident buyers, and during market week it is impossible to assign every member a resident buyer. The rest of the time store buyers are busy at their respective stores and only occasionally come to market.

ATC charges less than the large offices with full staffs, which makes it possible for these small stores to afford membership in the group. An increase in its fees would eliminate most of its clientele.

In an effort to keep the fees low and service at a level necessary to satisfy its members, ATC is looking for a plan to put into operation only during market weeks to ensure customer satisfaction.

Question

1. Present a plan that would allow ATC to maintain its present buying staff but would solve the problem it faces every market week.

Chapter 12
Merchandise Pricing

Photograph by Ellen Diamond

LEARNING OBJECTIVES

Upon completion of this chapter, the student should be able to:

1. Define markup and perform the calculation of markup based on cost and on retailing, inventory turnover, and markdown percent.
2. List eight factors that affect pricing.
3. Explain the advantages and limitations of merchandise inventory turnover.
4. Define price lines, listing four advantages of their use.
5. List and discuss five reasons for markdowns.
6. Discuss the timing of markdowns, including automatic markdowns.

THEY CAN TURN A PROFIT WITHOUT MAKING A SALE . . .

At the close of the 1970s, most retailers were experiencing a great deal of success. Those in the department store game were expanding their operations with branch stores, and chains were opening unit after unit, enlarging their companies. The traditional retailers were enjoying significant markups that were generally known as "keystone," or the doubling of their cost. Some outlets, such as the upscale stores, were realizing even greater markups. The need to work at lower points was not a concern because the off-price and discount outlets weren't posing serious threats at the time.

In 1978, the Price Brothers developed a retail plan that would eventually revolutionize retailing. Using a concept far from the conventional means of doing business, they opened a warehouse-type facility that restricted purchases to specific groups, and the shoppers had to pay a fee for the privilege of shopping there. It was the birth of the Price Club. Who would have thought people would eagerly fork over money to merely enter a store's portals before they could make their selections?

The concept was to limit shoppers to those with some affiliation with a labor union, guild, organization, or business. Those who patronized the facility were never sure to find the same merchandise mix as the time before, but they were assured that what was available was priced lower than at other retail outlets. Food, household products, electronics, clothing, and other items were co-mingled to make up a nontraditional product mix. Little by little, the curious shelled out their membership fees and started to make their purchases. Service was at a minimum, packing was done by the consumers who brought their own bags; the concept took off. Unlike other retailers who offered goods in a variety of quantities, the Price Club featured only large-size packages. Paper towels, generally sold by the roll in supermarkets, were bundled in packs of one or two dozen.

The success of the first operation quickly spread across the country, and overseas operations are now in existence in places as unlikely as Korea. The rock-bottom pricing was foreign to the industry. The merchandise is marked up an average of 7 percent, unheard of in retailing. With attention to cost-saving measures, the profit turned is about 3 percent. While this is a neat profit for so little markup, the company need not make a sale to be profitable. With a membership of 1 million people that doubled in 1994 after its merger with Costco, and membership fees at $35 per family, Price Club/Costco takes in $70 million per year before they even open their doors.

A visit to any of the warehouses and knowledge of their enormous expansion program immediately reveal that merchandise pricing need not follow the traditional path of other stores.

There are as many different policies involving merchandise pricing as there are types of retail operations. Top management usually decides on a general policy to be followed by those responsible for the departmental operations. Although policies are generally set, each buyer may exercise some freedom in pricing his or her merchandise. For example, the misses' coat and suit department might work on an average markup of 50 percent. This does not prevent buyers from putting a 60 percent markup on merchandise they feel has great appeal or a 40 percent markup on something that will attract more customers at that price. Top management is more concerned with the total profit picture for each department than in individual prices and markups.

Whatever the pricing policy is for a retail organization, it rarely changes. Customers expect certain prices at certain stores. Once these are set in the minds of customers, a change is unlikely unless the entire organization is to undergo change.

MARKUP

Markup is the difference between the amount that is paid for goods and the price for which the goods are to be sold. In retailing, where profits are made only through selling, the markup must be high enough to provide for all of the expenses of operating the store plus a profit. For example a department with merchandise on hand that cost $100,000 and operating expenses of $25,000 must sell the goods for $125,000 to break even. The profit would depend upon the amount in excess of $125,000 for which the goods can be sold.

Whatever the selling price, the markup will be the difference between cost of the goods and its selling price, or

$$\text{Selling Price} - \text{Cost} = \text{Markup}$$

Illustrative Problem

A shirt purchased for $25 and offered for sale at $40 would have a markup of $15.

$$\text{Selling Price } \$40 - \text{Cost } \$25 = \text{Markup } \$15$$

Markup Percent Based on Retail

Formerly, markup was always based on cost. However, thanks to the efforts of the National Retail Merchants Association, now the National Retail Federation, retail research bureaus, and many universities, most retailers are currently using a system of markup based on retail. These are the advantages:

1. Since sales information is much more easily determined than cost, a markup based on sales greatly facilitates the calculation of estimated profits.
2. Inventory taking requires the calculation of the cost of merchandise on hand. The "retail inventory method" used by most retailers is based on markup at retail and provides a shortcut for determining inventory at cost.
3. Most retailers calculate markup based on retail. This provides interstore comparisons of such vital information as gross profit and net profit.

4. To the consumer, the smaller the percentage of markup, the more reasonably priced the store. Markup based on retail provides a smaller percentage.

5. Salespersons' commissions, officers' bonuses, rents, and other vital operating data are based on sales. It is reasonable to base markup on sales as well.

To find the markup percent based on retail, the dollar markup (the difference between the cost and the retail price) is divided by the retail price.

Illustrative Problem

A shirt that costs $13 retails for $20. Find the markup percentage based on retail.

Solution

To find the dollar markup:

$$
\begin{aligned}
\text{Markup} &= \text{Retail} - \text{Cost} \\
&= \$20 - \$13 \\
&= \$7
\end{aligned}
$$

To find the markup percent based on retail:

$$
\frac{\text{Markup}}{\text{Retail}} = \text{Markup \% on retail}
$$

$$
\frac{\$7}{\$20} = 35\% \text{ markup on retail}
$$

Illustrative Problem

A retail store buyer purchases a jacket for $35 and sells it for $42. What is the dollar markup? What is the markup percent based on retail?

Solution

To find the dollar markup:

$$
\begin{aligned}
\text{Markup} &= \text{Retail} - \text{Cost} \\
&= \$42 - \$35 \\
&= \$7
\end{aligned}
$$

To find the markup percent based on retail:

$$
\frac{\text{Markup}}{\text{Retail}} = \text{Markup \% on retail}
$$

$$
\frac{\$7}{\$42} = 16\tfrac{2}{3}\% \text{ markup on retail}
$$

If we compare the markups in both illustrative problems, we find they have the same dollar markup. By computing the percent and comparing them, we see the importance of markup percent to the retailer. The first markup percent, 35 percent, was certainly better than the second, $16\tfrac{2}{3}$ percent.

Markup Percent Based on Cost

Although basing markup on retail has become common in recent years, there are still retailers who use a markup system based on cost. While this is frequently the result of inertia and resistance to change, some establishments are better served by calculating markup on cost. Typical of this is a dealer in produce whose costs of fruits and vegetables vary from day to day, according to the supply and demand at the wholesale produce markets. Under such conditions, where the cost of inventories is unimportant (they completely sell out every few days) and the profit-and-loss figures can be easily determined, the use of markup based on cost is preferable.

To find the markup percent based on cost, the dollar markup is divided by the cost.

Illustrative Problem

A camera cost the retailer $33 and sells for $44. Find the markup percent based on the cost.

Solution

To find the dollar markup:

$$\text{Markup} = \text{Retail} - \text{Cost}$$
$$= \$44 - \$33$$
$$= \$11$$

To find the markup percent based on cost:

$$\frac{\text{Markup}}{\text{Retail}} = \text{Markup \% on cost}$$

$$\frac{\$11}{\$33} = 33\tfrac{1}{3}\% \text{ markup on cost}$$

FACTORS AFFECTING PRICING

As we have seen, the selling price of an item consists of its cost plus a markup that will be sufficient to yield a profit after covering the operating expenses. The prime function of management is to maximize profits. The pricing policy is the key to profit determination. This does not mean that the higher the prices, the greater the profit. It does mean, however, that management must choose a pricing policy that will result in the greatest profitability. The alternative pricing schemes range from the discounter who feels that the additional business brought into the store by low pricing will more than offset a smaller profit margin, to the high-fashion store that offers many services and a prestigious label in return for a higher price. Before a pricing policy can be selected, there are many factors that must be considered.

Buyer's Judgment of Appeal of Goods

It is unusual to find a store that uses a uniform percentage of markup for all of its goods. Even within a department, the percentage may vary from style to style. A good merchant should have a feel for pricing. This person should know what customers are willing to pay for an item, and mark up accordingly. In fact, there is frequently little relationship between the cost of an item and its customer appeal. Within certain established minimums and maximums, a buyer should set prices at what he or she thinks the goods should bring in. Bearing in mind what the competition is doing, the retailer can frequently improve the overall markup of a department by pricing certain styles in excess of the average markup. The department's average markup, rather than individual markup, is most important to the store.

If all buying decisions could be automated, it would not be necessary for retail operations to employ buyers. Most professionals, however, agree that buyers and their judgment provide in great part for the success or failure of the store. If buyers' skills were measured, their abilities to judge the appeal of goods would be at the top of the list.

To retail an item at a fraction lower than is feasible is a potential threat to profit, while marking merchandise too high could possibly result not only in lower sales, but also conceivable markdowns. It is the keenly aware buyer whose ability permits the proper price for the greatest sales potential.

Competition

One consideration when setting prices is the pricing policy of competing stores. Decisions must be made as to whether to set prices above, at, or below those of a competitor. If the services, conveniences of location, and other factors are such that consumers will pay a higher price for goods from our store than from a competitor's, perhaps we should use a high pricing policy. On the other hand, a high price policy would certainly drive some business away. How much? Does it pay to set high prices? These are the sort of problems management must face. This is an area for market research specialists.

Whatever the pricing policy selected, it is vital that a store know the prices and quality being offered by its competitors. For this purpose, stores employ comparison shoppers—people who spend their working hours studying the competition and reporting on prices, hot items, services, and other vital information.

To emphasize the importance of competition in pricing, it should be pointed out that some retailers advertise that they will meet all prices of competition. Some go so far as to refund the difference if it can be shown that merchandise purchased at its store could have been purchased more cheaply elsewhere.

To have customers find that they can buy the exact item at a lower price in a competitor's store is damaging to a retailer's image. The customer's impression is that not only were they overcharged on the item in question, but that overpricing may be the general policy of the store. To overcome this situation, retailers are forced to find items on which they can mark up liberally with no fear of being undersold by a competitor, in addition to their regular goods. This merchandise is available as private branded items and exclusively offered goods.

Private Labels

One way to minimize competition is to sell an exclusive item, which cannot be compared with an item available in another store. It is only when a customer can find the same item, exact in every detail and carrying the same label, in two stores that prices can logically be compared. If the items are dissimilar, the higher-priced item can always be claimed to be of better quality and worth more. It is for this reason that the use of private labels is becoming increasingly important. Stores all across the United States do a significant amount of their total sales in brands that are exclusive to their own stores.

Exclusivity

Another method of limiting price competition by the principle of exclusivity is by agreement with the manufacturer. In such a case, a dress shop in a small town gets an agreement from the manufacturer that the manufacturer will not sell to any of the shop's competitors in that town. A customer is then unable to compare prices between stores. Agreements with manufacturers are not limited to small users. In large cities with many competing department stores, one can often find a style only in one store.

Characteristics of Goods

The amount of profit that various classifications of merchandise must bring in depends in large part on the specific characteristics of the goods. For example, staple goods, which are not subject to fashion changes or seasonal losses, may be sold at a smaller markup than seasonal or perishable goods. Similarly, some goods are bulky and require large amounts of floor space, whereas others require expensive selling personnel. In large part, it is the nature of the goods that dictates pricing policy.

High-Risk Merchandise

High-risk merchandise is made up of items that because of their perishability, seasonal nature, or high styling are almost certain to suffer some markdowns before finally being sold. The markup on such goods must be sufficient to cover such eventuality.

Fashion Goods.   When we speak of fashion goods, highly styled ladies' wear comes to mind. The characteristics of this merchandise can be explained by example. The buyer of the ladies' dress department has a hot style. Ten of the initial order of 14 were sold in two days. Since then the buyer has brought 200 pieces into the store, of which 180 have been sold. The number is now beginning to slow down and it appears that the buyer will have to mark down about ten dresses. Although the style has been highly successful, some markdowns must be taken. The markup will have to be high enough to cover both this style and other less successful ones. Contrast this with sales in the hardware department, where staples are sold and markdowns are negligible. It is obvious that high-risk fashion goods are subject to markdowns and that, to be successful, their selling price must be sufficient to cover these losses.

Seasonal Goods.   Another type of high-risk goods for which the selling price must be high enough to cover future losses is seasonal goods such as bathing suits, furs, and toys. Characteristic of such goods is the fact that once the season is over the retailer is faced with the choice of either cutting the price drastically or putting the goods aside until next year. Holding merchandise until the following season ties up capital that should be used for salable merchandise throughout the year. Moreover, held-over merchandise must eventually compete with newer styled goods; further, it has been handled, and customers may remember it from the previous year. Also, the merchandise may no longer be desirable. When retailers of seasonal goods walk around with a worried expression on their faces during an unusually rainy spring, there is good reason for it. Many stores charge high prices at the beginning of the season, under the assumption that customers who shop early are willing to pay more. This provides a cushion for the markdowns that will come later in the season.

Perishable Goods.   Consider florists. They run businesses without markdowns. Once a rose is withered, it's unsaleable. Florists can't sell out to the last piece, since they do not want to lose trade by not having goods available to be sold at any time. Here again we find retailers with built-in inventory losses who must price their goods at a level that will cover such losses.

A produce market where fruits and vegetables are sold faces a similar problem. These retailers, too, cannot be in business without taking inventory losses. Every day a certain percentage of produce must be drastically reduced in price or actually thrown away. This must be taken into account when prices are set.

High-Overhead Merchandise

Certain classifications of goods, by their nature, require an unusual amount of overhead. In pricing such goods, provision must be made for any unusually high overhead costs so that a normal profit will remain after the additional expense is paid. Merchandise of extreme bulk or high value is part of this group.

Bulky Merchandise.   Such merchandise as furniture and carpeting, because of its size, requires an unusually large amount of floor space, and consequently, rent expense. In marking up such goods, the selling price must be high enough to cover the excessive rent charges. As a result, traditional furniture stores usually double their costs to arrive at the selling price (50 percent on retail). Failure to set a high enough selling price would result in losses.

Precious Jewelry.   The additional expenses that are required to carry a line of precious jewelry are considerable. A vault must be built to store the goods overnight. Highly paid salespersons are necessary, since the items are expensive and a knowledge of the subject matter is required. However, some of the additional overhead is counteracted by the fact that less rental area is required for a jewelry store or department than for displaying many other goods.

Merchandise Turnover

Of great importance to the pricing policy of a store is its turnover rate. The turnover rate is the number of times the inventory sells in a year. The higher the turnover rate, the lower the markup needed; the lower the turnover rate, the higher the markup needed for a profit.

In Chapter 17, *Accounting Procedures and Operational Controls,* a more careful look will be taken at merchandise turnover.

Promotional Activities of the Store

Another factor affecting retail pricing policies is the amount of promoting and advertising that a store does. This sort of activity is expensive, and the cost of getting the customer into the store must be included in the selling price of the goods. This is not meant to indicate that the stores with the highest advertising budgets are those with the highest markup. Quite the reverse is true. Frequently, the biggest promoters are those stores that depend upon small markups to increase their turnover and in this way pay for their promotional activities. The point is that whatever the pricing policy of the store, the markup must be sufficient to cover the advertising budget. Should each individual department's pricing policies be sufficient to cover its individual advertising budget? This becomes slightly more difficult since a store might be willing to break even on a department (such departments are called leaders), or even sell below cost (loss leader department), as a promotional means of getting people into the store. It is felt that a customer who is brought into the store by a leader or loss leader is likely to buy other items from more profitable departments.

Leaders and Loss Leaders

Several fundamental requirements of a good leader follow.

1. It must be an item that would interest a large number of customers. Since the purpose of the leader is to bring customers into the store, to be successful the item must appeal to a large segment of the buying public.
2. It must not be an item used as a leader by a competitor, since this would reduce the number of customers brought to the store.
3. The price cut must be important enough to bring the customers to the store in quantity.

There are advantages to the use of leaders and loss leaders. For one thing, the shopper may not buy anything but that merchandise, resulting in a loss. Some stores featuring these items in their promotional schemes advise their salespeople to try to sell the customer regular goods. This frequently leads to customer resentment. Leader and loss leader merchandising is unfair to competitors who charge a legitimate price for the same item. This last aspect is so important that many states have laws making it illegal to sell goods below their cost.

Store Image

It is wrong to assume that all purchasers are price-conscious. Many stores, particularly in the higher price ranges, are able to attract customers despite a higher than normal markup. The store's name or image, for example, is more important to some customers than the prices it charges. Many shoppers willingly pay a premium to have a Nordstrom, Saks Fifth Avenue, or Brooks Brothers label on their garments. Other customers are willing to pay more to these prestige stores for the extra services offered, or because they like the wide assortment of merchandise, the way it is displayed, and so forth.

Prestigious stores, although they benefit from their higher than normal markup, are not necessarily more successful than their opposite, the discounters. The prestige factor often requires a very high cost of operations. Improved sales service means more and higher-priced sales help. The store's furnishings, fixtures, displays, and so on are more expensive, as are many of its other operating expenses. Since massive clearance sales would be detrimental to its image, the store has serious problems in disposing of slow-moving goods. Consequently, although it has to some degree taken itself out of the rat race of price competition, it is only at the cost of a new set of problems.

Alterations

Once the decision on pricing policy has been made, the question of whether the customer is to be charged for alterations has been answered. That is, stores that have decided on an above-normal markup in return for additional services generally consider the cost of alterations as one of the services offered to their customers. On the other hand, a discount store that has curtailed services so that it can employ a less-than-normal markup would be unlikely to offer free alterations. There is room for compromise in this area. For example, a menswear department does not charge for shortening sleeves or cuffing trousers. However, it either refuses to do major alterations or charges extra for this service. In the event that alterations are to be freely given to customers, the selling prices must be adjusted to reflect this additional expense.

Goods Easily Soiled or Damaged

Toys, white gloves, and a host of other merchandise classifications become shopworn in a short period of time. They frequently require special handling on the shelves and special care from the sales personnel. Markup, by definition, must be sufficient to cover the costs of the item and provide a profit. If no provision is made in the markup for possible soilage or damage, the profit on fragile goods will be below the amount expected.

Pilferage

In recent years, losses through pilferage have increased at an alarming rate. This has occurred despite a substantial increase in the cost of security maintenance. It is unfortunate that honest shoppers are forced to pay for the losses incurred through dishonest people. If a store is to be successful, its markup policy must be one that will cover the high cost of security, as well as the merchandise losses that result from shoplifting. A full discussion of pilferage is found in Chapter 9, *Loss Prevention.*

PRICE LINES

Most store are not large enough to carry merchandise at all prices. Very few are able to offer a full assortment of goods that suits the needs of both the low-income and high-income family. In an effort to present a wide range of merchandise to satisfy their specific group of customers, retailers select certain "price lines" of merchandise. For example, ladies' shoes might be limited to $22.95, $24.95, and $27.95; men's gloves at $14.98, $16.98, and $18.98. Only the giant department stores and specialty chains generally offer merchandise in many price ranges.

Some advantages of setting specific price lines follow.

1. A wider assortment of merchandise can be offered than could be if many price lines were carried.
2. Customers are not confronted with merchandise at so many prices. Thus, selecting may be easier.
3. Customers know about how much an item will cost before they enter the store.
4. Planning purchases is easier for the store buyer.

There is no definite trend in price lines today. On the one hand, there are specialty stores being established that sell a very limited price line. On the other side, there are the super department stores with a range from budget department prices to custom-made designer costs, with various price ranges in between.

MARKDOWNS

Markdowns are reductions in selling price. To fully understand the nature of markdowns, one must start with the concept that the original price is nothing more than a temporary estimate of what the customer is willing to spend.

Reasons for Markdowns

Markdowns may be caused by faulty sales price, buying errors, selling and merchandise handling errors, and other reasons not related to human mistakes. When the original selling price is set at too high a level, or at a level above competitors' prices, markdowns inevitably result. Generally, these price reductions are such that the final selling price is lower than the amount that the goods could have been sold for if they were properly marked originally.

Buying Errors

Many markdowns are the result of buying misjudgments. Overbuying is probably the principal cause of markdowns. It may come about through large initial orders instead of small lot ordering to test consumer appeal. Overoptimistic sales planning is another common cause of overbuying.

The inability to forecast perfectly the buying habits of a store's clientele frequently leads to markdowns. Often, goods that would be readily salable in the proper colors and sizes cannot be sold because of these errors. This, of course, results in markdowns.

Markdowns are frequently the result of ordering goods too late in the season. Goods bought too late often cannot be sold because the customer is no longer interested.

Selling Errors

Faulty sales practices result in markdowns. Merchandise that could have been sold with proper display or salesmanship or departmental neatness is sometimes marked down and this decreases profits.

Lazy sales personnel, who take the line of least resistance by selling the fast-moving numbers instead of taking the time to sell the slower movers, cause markdowns. Overeager salespersons whose high-pressure tactics end up in returns late in the season are also a cause of markdowns.

Nonerror Markdowns

Not all markdowns are the result of errors. Some are beyond human ingenuity, others are actually planned. Occasionally, new products reach the market that make the older goods obsolete. In such cases, the entire stock of obsolete merchandise must be marked down drastically and quickly.

No matter how competent the buyer or how talented the salespeople, there will always be odd sizes and styles and shopworn merchandise that cannot be sold without markdowns.

High Opening Prices

Reasoning that a person willing to purchase early in the season will be willing to pay a premium for his or her purchases, some buyers set higher than normal opening prices on their goods. This both helps to make up for future losses and gets a good price from those shoppers who wait for markdowns before making their purchase.

Weather

Seasonal goods depend upon the weather. A store stocks a certain amount of merchandise in anticipation of certain weather conditions. If the weather does not behave as expected, the goods are not sold and customers must be lured in by markdown prices. In New York City, spring is short and uncertain. After a particularly rainy spring, markdowns follow as certainly as summer.

Poor Assortment

It is a bad policy for a store to offer a limited assortment of goods at any time during a season. Future sales depend on a customer's confidence in being able to always find an abundance of goods to choose from. Many merchandisers will protect the store's image by buying goods, to provide a rich assortment, late in the season. They do this knowing full well that many of the goods are destined for eventual markdown.

Timing Markdowns

Markdown or Carry Over

When the markdown required to sell merchandise becomes excessive, a merchant is faced with the decision of whether or not to carry the goods over to the same season of the following year. Frequently, the goods will bring a higher price at the beginning of the season in the following year than at the end of the current season. This fact must be weighed against the following disadvantages of carrying over.

1. The money tied up in the carried-over inventory will not be available for new styles for a full year. This will have the effect of reducing the assortment of new styles until these old goods are sold.
2. It is expensive to carry over in terms of warehousing costs, insurance, warehouse labor, and interest on money borrowed to carry additional inventories.
3. Carried-over goods tend to become shopworn or broken.
4. The store's image will be damaged in the eyes of those shoppers who remember the goods from the previous year.

Generally, well-managed stores limit their carry-overs to those staple goods that are packaged in such a fashion that they will retain their fresh look in the following year. Fashion merchandise should never be carried over.

Early Versus Late Markdowns

Of principal importance in the timing of markdowns is whether to reduce prices early in the season on an individual basis, or to hold the prices firm until late in the season and then have a storewide sale. There is considerable difference of opinion among retailers on the issue of when to mark down. The arguments favoring early markdowns are

1. Goods that are reduced early in the season while the customers are still in a buying mood can generally bring in more money than they would at the end of the season. Thus, the amount of markdown will be less.
2. The money brought in by early markdowns can be used for newer and better styles that may be turned over many times.

3. End-of-season sales frequently require additional sales personnel and therefore raise the cost of operations.

Arguments favoring late markdowns are

1. Customers become aware of a store's early markdown policies and will wait to make their purchase, knowing they can buy reduced merchandise early in the season.
2. Some goods that do not sell well early in the season suddenly take off and do very well. If these goods are marked down early, they will not bring in as much money as they should.
3. Prestige stores prefer not to have bargain hunters in their stores until they need them. A policy of limiting markdowns to season-ending sales accomplishes this.

Many stores compromise between early and late markdowns. When the sales of an item slow down, and the quantity on hand is excessive, it will be reduced for quick sale. At the end of the season, a clearance sale will be used to clean out all of the unsold goods.

Automatic Markdowns

The policy of automatic markdowns involves the reduction of prices at regular intervals. Retailers who use this system indicate several prices on their merchandise tags, each determined by a period of time. The system speeds up the turnover of the inventory and doesn't require new merchandise ticketing every time a price reduction is deemed necessary to help sell the goods. Stores such as Filene's Basement, which originated the concept, and Syms use this markdown method. A Retailing Focus about Filene's Basement, in this chapter, explores the system that the store has used in its famous flagship store since 1909.

How Much to Mark Down

Because the purpose of markdowns is to move goods, the amount of price reduction must be enough to satisfy customers. A $19.75 item marked down to $18.75 will probably not increase its sales appeal; shoppers willing to pay $18.75 would probably pay $19.75 as well. To sell the goods, a reduction to $16.75 would probably be necessary. When markdowns are taken early in the season, there is frequently time for a second markdown before the season ends. Consequently, early markdowns are usually smaller than late-season reductions. Markdowns are usually taken on an individual basis, depending on quantity, original price, and time of markdown.

Calculating Markdown Percent

An important aspect of markdown is the markdown percent based on actual sales. The markdown percent may be calculated when the markdown from the original retail (selling price) is known.

Illustrative Problem

A retail store buyer decides to reduce the price of her entire belt inventory 15%. The inventory is $5,000 at retail. What is the markdown percent based on sales, assuming she sells the entire inventory?

Solution

1. Determine the dollar markdown:

$$\text{Original Retail} \times \text{Reduction Percent} = \text{Markdown}$$
$$\$5,000 \times .15 = \$750$$

2. Determine the actual sales:

$$\text{Original Retail} \times \text{Reduction} = (\text{New Retail})$$
$$\$5,000 \times \$750 = \$4,250$$

3. Determine the markdown percent on sales:

$$\text{Markdown \%} = \frac{\text{Markdown}}{\text{Sales}}$$

$$= \frac{750}{4,250}$$

$$= 17.6\%$$

A RETAILING FOCUS   ***Filene's Basement***

When Edward Filene first announced his intention of creating the Basement Store with its automatic markdown plan in 1909, his colleagues predicted big losses for the company. If one visits the Boston store (the only location where the company's automatic markdown system is in operation), one knows immediately that it works perfectly. A question that is often heard coming from the customers' mouths is, "If the markdown is guaranteed, why not wait for the lowest markdown?" Shoppers who regularly patronize the store know that this is gambling. Since the merchandise moves out so quickly, waiting for even one day might result in the goods being purchased by someone else.

The purpose of the Basement was to serve as a clearinghouse for merchandise that didn't sell on the upper levels of the store, and a place where manufacturers could get rid of their unsold goods. Although the manufacturers had to take a loss when they sold to the Basement operation, it helped them make room for newer goods.

In addition to store inventory that didn't sell and items from manufacturers' overstocks, Filene's Basement became a place where merchants from fashionable stores disposed of their merchandise. Since these stores catered to clienteles that always sought the latest in design, leftovers were unacceptable on the selling floor. A quick way to dispose of items that were no longer in demand in the fashionable shops all across the country was to send them to Filene's Basement. It helped clear the sales floor for these stores, and gave Filene's fashionable merchandise that was acquired at very low cost.

The Boston Basement still functions as it was originally set up by Edward Filene. Every item is tagged with the price and date of its first offering. After 12 selling days, any item still unsold is automatically reduced to 25%. After six more days it is reduced another 25%, and six days later another 25%. If after 30 days the item is unsold, it is given to charity. An examination of the stock indicates that very little is left to be given away.

Expansion of the Basement Store began with movement to the Boston suburbs of Saugus and Framingham, and later to suburban regions in the New York metropolitan

Figure 12–1   Filene's downtown Boston store, birthplace of the automatic markdown. *Courtesy:* Filene's

area. The branches provide bargains, but do not use the automatic markdown plan. Filene's downtown store in Boston, the company's home of the automatic markdown, is featured in Figure 12-1.

TRENDS

With the competition that faces today's retailers, it is obvious that research is necessary to point up the directions that they should take. Research as discussed in the following paragraphs, takes many forms.

Focus Groups

Many large retailers are using focus groups to advise them on matters such as merchandise selection, price points, services desired, extended shopping hours, and other matters.

Store Location

Retailers are paying closer attention in the selection of store locations. Some are using in-house staffs to study trading area potential, transportation facilities, competition, and so forth, whereas others are opting for outside marketing research firms to do the work.

Evaluation of Potential Employees

With a high rate of turnover for employees, some large retailers are researching ways in which to better predict the reliability of their people. Research has turned up some devices, such as pen and pencil honesty tests, which, in most cases, have reduced the amount of turnover and minimized internal theft.

ACTION FOR THE INDEPENDENT RETAILER

Too often, misunderstanding the way in which markup and other factors affect pricing has adverse effects on small retailers in particular. In order to realize a profit, it is imperative to have a working knowledge of pricing principles. Retailers must cover their expenses before they can achieve profits.

Independents often cater to a narrower market than do their chain store counterparts. They have the advantage of direct customer contact and should gear their merchandise purchases accordingly. Knowing firsthand the needs of the customer results in fewer markdowns.

Areas of caution include the timing of the markdown and the amount of the reduction. Smaller retailers too often wait too long and mark down at too low a rate. If a larger, earlier reduction were implemented, it would make room for newer and perhaps faster-moving merchandise. The early, substantial markdown motivates more customers to buy, freeing up "dead capital." Whereas the large chain must wait for a more bureaucratic decision, the independent has the advantage of quick action.

With the enormous expenses of the giants, it is often possible for the independent to compete on price. While services probably cannot be on the same level as those of the giant retailer, the price, if lower, could motivate the customer. Size, often an advantage in retailing, doesn't have to hinder the independent's chances for success. If all aspects of pricing are carefully explored and properly acted upon the independent can successfully compete.

IMPORTANT POINTS IN THE CHAPTER

1. Markup is the difference between the cost and the retail.

2. Although markup may be based on either cost or retail price, retailers generally base their markup calculations on retail. This enables them to estimate gross profit when the sales for a period are known.

3. To make a profit, a retailer must sell goods at a price in excess of the cost of the goods and the expenses required to run the organization.

4. The price for which goods are offered for sale is influenced by competition, the characteristics of the goods, the risk involved in carrying the goods, and the overhead expenses required by the goods.

5. Some stores are able to set prices above competitive levels by offering their customers such services as convenience, a high-prestige name, and alterations.

6. Markdowns are reductions in selling price that may be necessitated by buying errors such as overbuying, wrong color or size selection, or poor timing.

7. Markdowns can also be caused by selling errors such as poor departmental management or a weak sales force.

8. Not all markdowns are the result of errors. Price reductions frequently are needed to move shopworn, obsolete, or oddly sized goods.

9. The problem of whether to mark down goods or to carry them over to the following season and offer them at regular price is a serious one. Most stores limit their carry-overs to staple goods that are packaged in such a fashion that they will retain their fresh look in the following year.

REVIEW QUESTIONS

1. The buyers for a particular department know more about pricing their particular goods than any other person in the store. Why aren't they allowed complete freedom in setting pricing policies?

2. Define *markup*.

3. A bridge table and four chairs cost $95. If the buyer retails it for $150, what markup percent on retail will the store achieve?

4. The swimsuit buyer for Brandt's Specialty Shop buys a dozen swimsuits for $156. If the suits are marked up 48 percent of cost, what would each suit retail for?

5. A supermarket purchasing agent buys a gross of potted plants for $432. At what price should each plant be retailed if the agent wants a markup of 35 percent of cost?

6. Explain the effect of competition on pricing.

7. Explain the effect on retail prices of an "exclusive agreement" between the retailer and the vendor.

8. Why must special pricing consideration be given to seasonal goods?

9. Discuss the pricing of precious jewelry. Why should it be different from the pricing of regular merchandise?

10. Explain the effect of pricing on a store's image.

11. Some very successful retailers set prices above those of their competitors. Why are some consumers willing to pay these higher prices?

12. Give three examples of markdowns that could have been avoided by proper buying decisions.

13. Discuss two instances of markdowns that are the result of inefficient department management.

14. Buyers are frequently faced with the alternative of marking down or carrying over until the next year. Discuss this in relation to high fashion goods and staple goods.

CASE PROBLEMS

Case Problem 1

Liquor stores are a unique type of retail operation in that, with the exception of a few private labels, all stores carry the exact same merchandise. In New York State, liquor stores are privately owned, and the retail prices suggested by wholesalers yield a gross profit rate of about 25 percent.

Carl's Wines and Liquors has operated successfully for 35 years as a small neighborhood store. Retail prices have been set at the levels suggested by wholesalers, and Carl has saved enough money to retire in the next few years.

A recent change in the state laws enabled a competitor with a cut-price policy to open a store within a block of Carl's. This has resulted in a shrinkage of Carl's annual sales by 40 percent. Carl has maintained his pricing policy in the belief that his old customers would stand by him. His competitor has been operating for two years, and Carl has reason to believe that he is losing money. Carl is barely breaking even at his reduced volume, and any cut in prices without increasing volume would put his store into the red and require money he has set aside for his retirement.

Carl would like to sell his store and retire now, but at the present sales level the store is unsaleable.

Question

1. What might Carl do to remedy this situation?

Case Problem 2

Eight years ago the Buy-Rite Sales Corp. opened a large discount store in a rapidly growing suburban area. It sells appliances and housewares at discount prices, and its clientele consists of homeowners who are attracted by the store's low prices. Since most of the new homeowners in the area are price conscious, the store is very successful.

The store's aggressive management is constantly searching for areas in which to expand and is presently considering a suggestion from the houseware buyer that it take in a nationally advertised line of kitchenware that will not be sold at a reduced price. The buyer argues that the line is very successful in other stores and that Buy-Rite's heavy customer traffic would ensure success. Moreover, the customers are changing from price conscious new homeowners to more established homeowners who are more selective in their buying habits.

Questions

1. What effect will carrying these items have on the store's reputation for underselling?
2. The kitchenware is too expensive to be bought on impulse. Would a customer planning to buy the goods be more likely to go to a traditional store?
3. The merchandise is frequently bought as a gift, and the store does not maintain a wrapping department. Will that hurt sales?
4. The store is doing better than ever, indicating that there is no lack of price conscious customers. Are these people interested in that type of goods?

Chapter 13
Advertising and Promotion

Photograph by Ellen Diamond

SWEEPSTAKES OF A DIFFERENT NATURE . . .

Ever since the first retailers opened their doors, they invested in varying degrees in advertising and promotion. A look at the daily newspapers indicates that enormous sums are being spent to lure customers into stores. Consider too the magnitude of Macy's Thanksgiving Day Parade, which takes about a full year to plan and involves enormous numbers of participants, and costs the retailer a hefty sum. The parade and other promotional endeavors, such as the obligatory fashion shows, personal appearances, demonstrations, salutes to foreign countries, and so forth, are used to distinguish one operation from the others. The aforementioned techniques are commonplace in retailing, often causing a strain on promotional budgets.

Although traditional forms of advertising and promotion do seem to work for their users, from time to time, merchants have developed concepts that brought significant success with a minimum of expense. One such endeavor was the Loehmann's Wild Card Sweepstakes.

As an attempt to draw traffic into the store and increase volume, the promotion was put into place. Loehmann's mailed sweepstakes cards to "Insider Members," those who are on their mailing lists and are notified of special sales. With close to one hundred stores across the country, the mailing list is a significant one. In order to maximize the promotion's success, each store also distributed sweepstakes cards to those who entered their premises. Each shopper was guaranteed discounts that ranged from 10 percent to 30 percent off the already low prices charged by the store, and coupled the offer with another that provided an equal discount off a Royal Cruise Line vacation, a $500 shopping spree at the store, a free ten-day cruise for two, and round-trip air fare to any destination in the United States on Continental Airlines.

The advertising mailer assured that "Everyone's A Winner." This helped to motivate people to make their way to the store. By merely scratching off a box on the entry card, the prize was revealed. The success was enormous; lines at counters swelled to numbers that the store had never before realized for such a short period of time. The interest was heightened not only by the impending discount, but by the potential to be a double winner, by receiving one of the aforementioned prizes.

Loehmann's cut its promotional costs by convincing other companies that giving away some prizes would bring attention to them. Most airlines rarely sell all of their seats, and cruise lines generally are unable to fill all of their accommodations, so the cost to them would be insignificant. The plan enabled noncompeting companies to join forces and reap the benefits. Cooperative advertising is standard in the retailing industry, and Loehmann's has set the stage for cooperative promotions that benefit all concerned, even the customer who gets a bargain and the potential for a prize.

Retailers make the consuming public aware of their organizations and merchandise offerings through any number of devices. Most professionals agree that advertising and promotion, in one form or another, is the key to spreading the word. The sums spent for advertising and promotion vary, of course, from company to company, with such factors as size, merchandising philosophy, location, competition, and business conditions begin given consideration before a budget is decided upon. Advertising is the major part of an overall promotion budget that management must apportion. Promotion includes special events, demonstrations, sampling, and in-store video displays.

THE SALES PROMOTION DIVISION

In most large retail organizations there is a separate division responsible for creating the store's advertising and promotional activities. Figure 13–1 illustrates the typical departmental structure within the division. It is headed by an overall expert in promotion, whose task it is to manage all of the division's activities. Although each department is headed by its own manager, the promotion manager has responsibility for ultimate approval of advertising and display, and coordinates events that involve all of the areas of promotion. For example, in cases where a storewide special event is being presented, it is the sales promotion director who must make certain that each aspect of the event complements the others. Only with cooperation among the various departments within the division will a successful campaign be realized. In contemporary retailing, where the multimedia concept is prevalent, a spirit of cooperation is necessary to convey totally the store's desired image.

The chapter is divided into two main sections: Advertising and Promotion.

Figure 13–1   Organization of a sales promotion department

ADVERTISING

As defined by the American Marketing Association, *advertising* is "any paid for form of nonpersonal presentation of the facts about goods, services, or ideas to a group." By comparing advertising with some other promotional techniques, its concept is more easily understood. Publicity is free, whereas advertising is paid for; display actually shows the merchandise, but advertising merely tells about the goods through words and illustration. An example of one of retailing's earliest advertisements is shown in Figure 13–2.

Large stores generally have their own advertising departments. They may be independent departments or a part of a larger sales promotion department. Small retailers, who are either unable to afford their own advertising departments or find it unnecessary because of the limited amount of advertising they do, make other arrangements to satisfy their needs.

Figure 13–2   The first Neiman Marcus newspaper advertisement. *Courtesy:* Neiman Marcus

Store-Operated Advertising Departments

The size of the advertising department varies according to the size of the organization and the type of advertising in which it engages. Figure 13–3 shows a typical advertising department in a large retail organization. Figure 13–4 is a chart showing advertising organization that would be appropriate for a giant in the field, in which advertising is spread over various media.

Whatever the organizational structure of the advertising department (and these examples are by no means the only ones in operation), its function is the same. It is completely responsible for the planning and preparation of advertising. Planning includes all the research necessary to ensure successful results. The preparation of the advertisements includes such areas as the following:

1. *Writing copy.* Copy is the written text that is usually found in the advertisement.
2. *Preparing artwork.* This involves the creation of the illustrations, either by photographers or by artists who prepare sketches.
3. *Producing the advertisement.* After the creative aspects such as the illustration and copy have been arranged and presented in a layout (the overall arrangement of the ad), the next step is to set it up for printing. The people involved in this part of advertising must have complete knowledge of the various printing processes. Since retailing managers rarely become involved in it, the more formal aspects of production will not be discussed.

The smaller advertising department depends upon a limited number of persons to perform all of the advertising responsibilities. Therefore, each person must be proficient at more than one advertising task. For example, one person might create the artwork and the accompanying copy. In the very large department, specialization is prevalent.

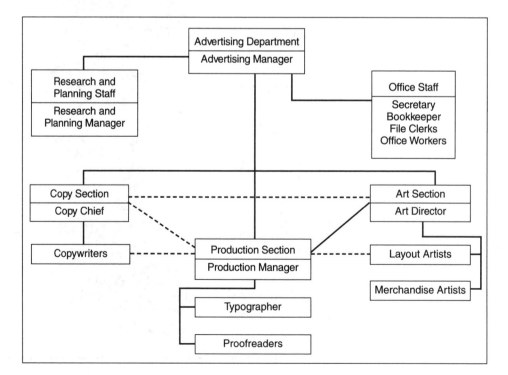

Figure 13–3   Advertising department of a large retail operation

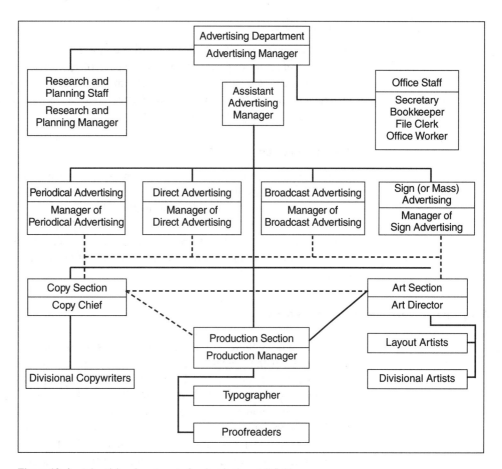

Figure 13–4   Advertising department of a giant in the retail field

Small Store Advertising Arrangements

It would be impossible for a small store to afford its own advertising department. Such a department would be completely unnecessary because of the limited amount of advertising it would be required to generate. There are a number of outside organizations that offer advertising services to the small retailer.

Advertising Agencies

Advertising agencies offer complete service, ranging from the execution of a single advertisement to a complete advertising campaign. Remuneration to the agency can be in the form of an allowance or a discount on the space it purchases for its customer from the various media (that is, it receives the difference between what the store would pay directly to a newspaper and the price it actually pays for the space), or it can be a flat fee.

Wholesalers and Manufacturers

The wholesaler and manufacturer, who are only as successful as the retailers to whom they sell, sometimes offer advertising assistance. Most commonly, manufacturers offer advertising mats (paper composition printing plates) to their customers with complete layouts of artwork and copy and space for the retailer to insert the store's name.

Free-Lancers

A free-lancer is an individual who will prepare a complete advertisement. The free-lancer is generally experienced in one aspect of advertisement preparation, such as layout, and engages others to execute the artwork and copy, which the free-lancer then arranges in the ad. Free-lancers usually specialize in one type of merchandise, such as children's clothing or groceries.

Media Services

Generally the media, in addition to selling space or time, offer complete advertising services to their retail customers. Their services range from the planning stages to the actual preparation of the advertisements. The media are continuously involved in research so as to better serve the needs of their clients. For example, their research will offer such information to retailers as characteristics of a newspaper's subscribers. This is invaluable information when selecting the proper newspaper in which to advertise.

Preparation of the Advertisement

In stores where there are advertising departments, the advertising specialists are responsible for the preparation of the advertisement. The buyer, however, determines which merchandise is to be advertised. In some large operations, the buyer works in conjunction with the merchandise manager in making the decision. Since advertising cannot sell merchandise that people don't want but *can* improve the sale of desirable goods, only the buyer, with more knowledge about the goods than anyone else in the store, should select the items to be promoted. Small, inexperienced retailers often waste promotional funds by advertising slow-moving merchandise in the hope that these goods will sell.

In the small store, the proprietor usually provides all the pertinent information concerning the merchandise to the outside agency. This information includes merchandise specifications such as price, color, fabric, sizes, and anything else peculiar to the specific item. The remainder of the advertising tasks are performed by the company charged with the creation of the ad; final approval rests with the proprietor.

In large retail organizations, a procedure along these general lines is followed:

1. The buyer fills out a request form similar to the one pictured in Figure 13–5.

    The buyer only completes the form after carefully checking to see that there are sufficient funds available in the budget for the advertisement. In the appropriate areas on the form, the buyer fills in the information about the item and lists other features of the goods that are important enough to be mentioned in the ad. For example, noting that a dress is "wash and wear" might make it more appealing for travel. Similarly, if a suit was designed by a famous European couturier, it probably would be attractive to high-fashion clientele.

    Before becoming committed to the advertisement of a particular item, it is extremely important that the buyer make certain there will be sufficient quantities available in the department when the advertisement is printed. Many times buyers have found themselves in the embarrassing and aggravating position of having a successful advertisement only to find that the goods are out of stock. Besides being inconvenienced, customers often become disillusioned and do not respond to the future advertising of the store. Generally a loan slip accompanies the item to be advertised, and the completed form is nothing more than a receipt to be completed by the advertising department and

ADVERTISING REQUEST

CIRCLE ONE | Z | DI | X

THIS FORM WILL NOT BE ACCEPTED UNLESS INFORMATION IS COMPLETE

DEPT. NO.

	DATE	SIZE		DATE	SIZE
☐ TIMES			☐ COLONIE		
☐ NEWS			☐ AMSTERDAM NEWS		
☐ POST			☐ SUFFOLK SUN		
☐ L.I.P.			☐ OTHER (LIST)		
☐ NEWSDAY			☐		
☐ WEST. GRP			☐		
☐ N. H. REG.			☐		

MERCHANDISE FOR NEW ART WORK IS DUE IN 15th FL. LOAN ROOM WHEN PINK SHEET IS DUE

EXCEPTION: Ready-to-wear merchandise is due directly after weekly Merchandise Review Meeting. Bulk merchandise should be available on the floor for movement to studio, or for sketching, when called for. Merchandise in LOAN ROOM? Yes | No

Do not request New Art Work BEFORE checking file FOR OLD ART.

No. of Illus.	Illustrations to be featured. Points to be emphasized
No. of New	
No. of Old	Date and medium in which old art ran last (attach proof)

OTHER MEDIA. ☐ MAGAZINE NAME____ ISSUE____ ☐ SALE BOOKLET ☐ OTHER DIRECT MAIL ☐ RADIO ☐ TV

MAIL ORDERS Yes ☐ ☐ No PHONE ORDERS Yes ☐ ☐ No COUPON Yes ☐ ☐ No

TOTAL AMT. OF MDSE. AT RETAIL $____ NO. OF UNITS____ DAY SELLING IS TO BEGIN____ NUMBER OF DAYS ON SALE____

ON SALE AT: (CIRCLE) ALL STORES - H. S. - R. F. - HUNT. - B. S. - JAM. - W. P. - PARK. - FLAT. - NEW HAV. - QUEENS - COLONIE - NEW ROCHELLE - SM. HAV.

ABOUT THE MERCHANDISE: (NOTE: Please complete the following IN DETAIL.)

ITEM	STYLE NO.	CURR. RETAIL	ADV. PRICE	QUOTE PHRASE & PRICE*	SIZES	COLORS
1.						
2.						
3.						
4.						
5.						
6.						

MOST IMPORTANT SELLING POINTS (from customer's view) AND SUPERIORITY TO COMPETITIVE ITEMS. (Use other side if necessary.)

IMPORTANT: PINK SHEETS WILL NOT BE ACCEPTED UNLESS THE FOLLOWING INFORMATION IS PROVIDED.

1. TEXTILE FIBER PRODUCTS List all information on the product label. If available, a fiber identification tag may be stapled in place.	2. NON TEXTILE PRODUCTS Copy from label or tag all information relative to composition of parts of product including finishes.	3. ELECTRICAL ITEMS Copy all name plate ratings including volts, amps, watts, horsepower, BTU, CFM, etc. Indicate if UL approved.

THIS IS A ☐ SALE LAST PREVIOUS DATE____ LAST PREVIOUS PRICE____

☐ CLEARANCE ☐ SPECIAL PURCHASE ☐ MFG'S CLOSE-OUT ☐ OTHER

INFORMATION ON COMPARATIVE PHRASES: (Note: Complete in detail as applicable.)

1. ☐ "REGULARLY" - means temporary reduction. Refers to price immediately before sale and price to which merchandise will return following sale.
   (a) period during which merchandise was selling on floor at regular price____
   (b) approximate number of units____ Is this the normal selling rate?____
   (c) Is stock to be augmented with merchandise which is not identical?____
2. ☐ "ORIGINALLY" - means first price during the recent course of business. (Recent course of business is current selling season for seasonal merchandise such as apparel and sporting goods, etc. and not more than 12 months for non-seasonal merchandise such as furniture, appliances, etc.).
   (a) period during which merchandise was selling on floor at original price____
   (b) approximate number of units____ Is this the normal selling rate?____
   (c) Is stock to be augmented with merchandise which is not identical?____
3. ☐ "COMPARABLE VALUE" - merchandise of equal grade and quality in all material respects,
   OR
   ☐ "VALUE" - identical merchandise selling in other stores.
   Indicate stores at which merchandise is likely to be found.____
   ____If in Macy's stock, indicate style # and price____

BUYER OR ASST. BUYER | MDSE. ADM. OR V.P. | COMP. OFFICE REPRESENTATIVE

PART 1 ADVERTISING DEPT. COPY

Figure 13–5 Advertising request form. *Courtesy:* Macy's, Herald Square, New York

returned to the buyer. In this way, the buyer has a record of all goods that are temporarily out of the department.

2. The buyer sends the item to be advertised and the accompanying forms to the advertising manager. The advertising manager checks the request form to see that all the pertinent information has been provided. The advertising manager also verifies that the department has sufficient funds to produce and run the ad. Then staff members are notified of their roles in the construction of the impending advertisement. In a small company's advertising department, the advertising manager might be responsible for copy and layout, and only the artwork would be executed by someone else. In the very large departments, different specialists in layout, copy, and art work as teams to complete an advertisement. Whatever the situation, those responsible for advertisement consult the request form for information and often discuss ideas with the buyers when additional assistance is needed.

3. After the layout is completed and approved by the advertising manager and the buyer, it goes to the production department. The production manager is responsible for following the orders indicated on the layout, such as the selection of type that is to be used. It is the production manager who marks instructions on the layout and sends it to the newspaper or magazine.

4. The newspaper prepares a proof (a sample of the printed advertisement) and sends it to the store. All the interested parties examine the proof and make notes on it wherever changes are necessary. Proofreader's marks, which are easily understood by everyone in advertising, are used to note such changes. The corrected proof is then returned to the newspaper.

5. After receiving the returned proof and making the corrections, the newspaper sends a final proof to the store for authorization. At this point, the store gives permission to run the ad. (After the ad has been run, a "tear sheet" [actual copy taken from the publication] is sent to the store.)

6. It is at this time, if the advertisement is to be fruitful, that all the divisions of the store must work as a team. Stockpeople should be notified to replenish the advertised item's inventory, and salespeople should be made aware of the advertised merchandise through a meeting with the buyer or a copy of the ad on the employee bulletin board. Even elevator operators should be notified of the whereabouts of the advertised goods if unusual traffic is expected to be generated. The display departments should be contacted to arrange an interior display of the item to make it more easily located and eye-catching. Any other interested departments should be alerted, to guarantee a successful promotion.

7. Advertisements should be evaluated after they have run. Some stores carefully compare an item's sales before it was advertised and while it was being advertised. This evaluation is important to future advertising and can be checked by employing any number of research techniques. Occasionally it becomes necessary to cancel, add to, or change an advertisement. In such cases, it is necessary for the buyer to use a form like the one in Figure 13–6.

Advertising Terminology

Although it is not necessary for management to be fully knowledgeable about the technical aspects of advertising, an understanding of some of the terminology used in advertising is desirable. Comprehension of these terms will improve a buyer's relationship with the advertising department.

- *Point.* A unit of measurement describing the height of type is the point. One point is equal to 1/72 of an inch. Type that is one inch high is 72 points.

A&S ADVERTISING DEPARTMENT SUPPLEMENTAL MEDIA REQUEST

CANCELLATION ADDITION CHANGE

DMM/DIVISION: ______ BUYER/DEPT. ______ DATE ______

MEDIA: NEWSPAPER	BROADCAST	DIRECT MAIL	INSERT	OTHER
FROM DATE				
AD NUMBER	TV 10 SEC 30 SEC	DATE	DATE	MEDIA
FROM PAPERS LINEAGE	RADIO 30 SEC 60 SEC	TITLE	TITLE	
	EVENT			REQUEST
	AIR DATES ADDITION			
	REVISION	REQUEST	REQUEST	
	SALE DATES ADDITION			
	REVISION			
	NOTES/EXPLANATION			
TO DATE				
AD NUMBER				
TO PAPERS LINEAGE				
		NOTES/EXPLANATION	NOTES/EXPLANATION	NOTES/EXPLANATION
NOTES/EXPLANATION				
VENDOR$	VENDOR$	VENDOR$	VENDOR$	VENDOR$
BUDGET$	BUDGET$	BUDGET$	BUDGET$	BUDGET$

DMM APPROVAL ______ MVP APPROVAL ______ EXECUTIVE VP APPROVAL ______

MEDIA

LESLIE BUSINESS FORMS DIVISION OF LESLIE LITHO CORP.

Figure 13–6 Advertising department supplemental media request. *Courtesy:* A&S

- *Pica.* A unit of measurement describing the width of type is called a pica. One pica is equal to 1/6 of an inch in width, or 12 points. Two picas would be 1/3 of an inch or 24 points.
- *Type Face.* The term *type face* refers to the style or shape of the specific type used. Different type faces convey different moods. For example, *Old English* is very ornate and is similar to the lettering used in old manuscripts, whereas Futura offers a modern impression.

This is Futura Bold, a Sans Serif face.

This is Futura Medium, a Sans Serif face.

This is Old English Text, a serif face.

- Figure 13–7 shows an advertisement with "arrowed" directions to the compositor using such advertising terms as "pica" and type face designations like "A. G. Demi" and "A. G. Book."

Classifications of Retail Advertising

The type of advertising a store uses depends on the clientele served, the merchandise offered, and the image the store wishes to project. Basically there are two types of advertising, institutional and promotional. *Institutional advertising* is used to project

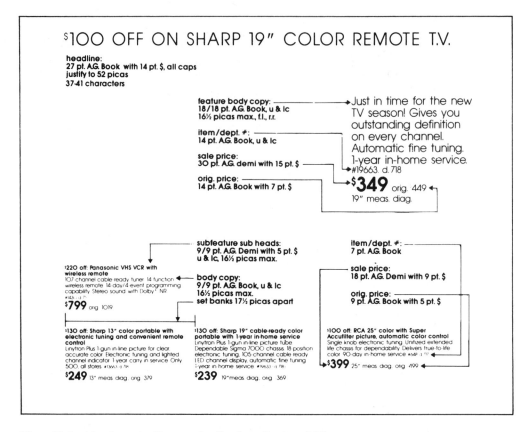

Figure 13–7   Advertisement with compositor directions. *Courtesy:* A&S

an overall image rather than to sell a specific item. A store that advertises something other than merchandise or that promotes its numerous customer services is engaging in institutional advertising. Figures 13–8 and 13–9 display two types of institutional advertisements.

The object of *promotional advertising* is to promote particular items. It is promotional advertising that results in immediate business for the store. The effectiveness of institutional advertising is more difficult to measure. Figure 13–10 shows promotionally oriented types of retail advertising.

Whichever method is used, and many organizations use both, it is important to bear in mind that neither type of advertising, if used very sparingly or irregularly, will be beneficial to the store. Advertising must be used on a continuous basis so that customers can become familiar with a store's ads and learn to recognize them quickly.

Advertising Media

The advertising media available to the retailer include newspapers, magazines, shopping publications, radio, television, direct mail, hand-distributed circulars, signs and billboards, car cards, and even skywriting. Some organizations make use of all those media listed (plus others), while some limit their use to one type.

At break of day on a New South Wales sheepwalk, jackeroo Jim Capell and his trusty Kelpie muster the sheep that supply the wool for the Shetland Sweaters of Lands' End.

The Kelpie is a short-haired dog with pointed ears, with a gift for herding sheep, and a lively, almost fiendish interest in doing so.

All of which makes him, along with the motorbike, invaluable in helping his "jackeroo" (cowboy) Jim tend the gigantic flocks that tread the sheepwalks of Australia. Sheepwalks such as the 330,000-acre set of properties owned by F.S. Falkiner and Sons Proprietary, Ltd., which serves up its rich grasses to an average grazing population of 110,000 sheep.

This is our kind of wool.

The wool of these Merino sheep, descendants of the original Spanish flocks, has the special softness and crimp that makes it ideal for spinning the lightweight, yet soft and warm, yarn that makes our Lands' End Shetlands such quality sweaters.

Once we buy the wool at the fortnightly sales in such centers as Melbourne, Australia, we have it shipped to the British Isles to take full advantage of the spinners and knitters in the U.K. who, for generations, have made Shetland sweaters they believe have a special "sparkle." (After all, if you go to Yorkshire for Yorkshire pudding, why would we go to the Orient for Shetland sweaters?)

And this is your kind of price.

This year, exchange rates could be described as outrageous, but despite them, Lands' End is offering our soft, fluffy, British-made Shetlands at just $29.50. Nothing short of remarkable, considering that we're talking fully-fashioned construction, and top-dyed colors. Eight "sparkling" colors, in fact, ranging from Lapis to Charcoal in heather-soft tones, in a full assortment of regular sizes for men and women, and our long size for men (2 inches longer in the body, 1½ longer in the sleeves).

The $29.50 price tag also reflects our function as direct merchants. No middlemen. No heavy mark-ups to permit later "sales." Just us, our U.K. suppliers, and you are involved.

Our phone number and guarantee.

Ours is a well-answered 800 phone number—1-800-356-4444—in personal service 24 hours a day. And our guarantee is unrivaled anywhere. It's GUARANTEED. PERIOD. We can hardly be more unconditional than that—and it covers everything we make and offer from Shetlands to shoes to shirts, and line after line of soft luggage and accessories.

©1989, Lands' End, Inc.

There's one thing more. When we say we go to the four corners of the earth to bring you quality items at reasonable prices, we really mean it. In this case, we couldn't bring you the Shetlands you deserve without an itinerary that reads "U.S. to Australia to the U.K. to the U.S." We don't believe in shortcuts!

"Hello. This is Eileen. May I help you?"

"Yes, please send me a free catalog."

Save 25¢ with a call, or write us.

Please send free catalog.
Lands' End, Inc. Dept. D-32
Dodgeville, WI 53595

Name _____

Address _____

City _____

State _____ Zip _____

Or call toll-free:
1-800-356-4444

Figure 13–8   Institutional advertisement for company image building. *Courtesy:* Lands' End

Newspapers

The medium that receives the greatest share of retail advertising is the newspaper. Store advertising runs the gamut from such widely distributed papers as *The New York Times* to small local publications. The decision as to which newspapers are best suited to the needs of the store can be determined through independent research or, more commonly, by calling upon advertising agencies or the newspapers themselves for advice. Both have considerable data on newspaper readership.

Some of the advantages of newspaper advertising are the following:

1. The newspaper's offerings are so diversified that they appeal to almost every member of the family. Even a child looking for the funnies can be attracted by an advertisement that is of importance to him or her.

Figure 13–9   Institutional advertising commemorating a holiday. *Courtesy:* Lord & Taylor

Figure 13–10   Promotional advertisement. *Courtesy:* A&S

2. The cost is low when the number of prospects reached is considered. The cost per consumer is lower than any other medium.

3. The newspaper can be examined at one's leisure and therefore its life is greater than broadcast advertising. If the consumer takes a moment away from the television set, the commercial won't be seen.

4. Newspapers enter into almost every home daily and therefore easily reach a large consumer market.

There are also some drawbacks to advertising in a newspaper:

1. Some of the readers are too far from the retail store for the advertisement to be meaningful. This problem has been lessened somewhat with the continued growth of phone order business, and the advent of regional newspapers.

2. The life of the message, while longer than radio or television, is only for a short period of time. Sometimes it lasts for only part of the train ride home from the office.

3. The quality of the stock used often limits the attractiveness of the item being offered for sale. Color is infrequently used because of registration of color and accuracy of reproduction.

Cost and Placement of Newspaper Advertisements

The cost of running an advertisement varies from newspaper to newspaper, depending on the size of the paper's circulation. Space is sold on the basis of the number of lines used for the ad. To determine the true value of the money spent on newspaper space, stores must figure the cost of the ad per reader. The cost per reader is determined on the basis of the "milline rate." The following formula is used to determine the milline rate:

$$\frac{\text{Rate per line} \times 1{,}000{,}000}{\text{Circulation}} = \text{Milline Rate}$$

If the rate per line is $1.80 and a paper's circulation is 900,000, then the milline rate is

$$\frac{1.80 \times 1{,}000{,}000}{900{,}000} = \$2.00$$

By applying this formula to the various newspapers' rates and circulations, a store can determine whether a higher line rate might actually cost less per reader.

In addition to the cost per line in newspapers, the costs vary according to placement or position of the ad. The least expensive method of advertising placement is called "ROP" ("run of press"). This means that the advertisement will be placed at the discretion of the newspaper. "Regular position" guarantees that a store's advertisements will be placed in the same position all the time. It is costlier than ROP, but readers soon know where to find a store's advertisements. "Preferred position," the most costly, locates the advertisement in the most desirable spot in the newspaper for that particular ad. The position may be adjacent to a pertinent newspaper column. For example, men's sporting goods advertisements would be more effective if placed next to a sportswriter's daily column. This positioning guarantees exposure to the appropriate readers.

Taking all of these factors into consideration, a retailer is often wise to run a smaller advertisement in a newspaper with a large circulation positioned in the best location than a larger ad without these important features. After a careful examination of all the variables, the actual rate per line might not be the most important consideration.

Magazines

The magazine is infrequently used by retail stores. Those organizations operating such prestige outlets as Saks Fifth Avenue make much use of this medium. Others like Kmart, which seek a wide market, use newspapers. One of the principal reasons magazine advertising is limited is that the store's trading area is generally much smaller than the market reached by the magazine and thus the store is spending (and magazine advertising is very costly) a considerable amount to reach people who are unable to become customers. Some magazines, however, overcome the disadvantage of reaching past the market. By publishing regional editions, publishers enable retailers to reach a narrower market and, thus, advertise at a lesser cost. Also, most magazines take many weeks to prepare before their publication date. Most retail stores cannot plan to advertise particular items so far in advance. Such stores as Nordstrom, Macy's, and Lord & Taylor, which do participate in long-range magazine advertising, feel that magazine advertisements in such periodicals as *Elle, Harper's Bazaar,* and *Vogue* lend prestige to their operations and do bring a certain return. Figure 13–11 shows an image building magazine advertisement. Also, such stores as Sears, with sufficient outlets and catalog customers available across the country, advertise in magazines. This type of advertising is more institutional than promotional and can therefore be planned well in advance of the publication date.

Independent Shopping Publications

In many cities, periodicals are published primarily for the purpose of retail advertisements. They are almost completely devoted to the advertising of the local retail stores. It is extremely attractive to this segment of retailing in that it is less expensive than regular newspaper or broadcasting advertising and reaches a clearly defined market in which the store's customers live. These publications are either mailed to prospects in a particular area or are hand delivered to the home free of charge. Their success is evidenced by the increasing number of shopping publications now in print.

Radio and Television

By comparison with the other media, broadcast advertising is still sparingly used by retailers; however, the dollar amounts spent by retailers on radio and television have increased.

Radio is showing greater use, particularly with local commercials. It is not unusual to hear local merchants advertise their goods as "spot" commercials on the airwaves. It should be understood that they do not sponsor complete programs but purchase commercial time throughout the day at the most appropriate time slots and on the most suitable programs for their products. For example, retailers of teen-ori-

Figure 13–11   Image-building magazine advertisement. *Courtesy:* Tiffany & Company

ented merchandise would generally choose as sponsors radio stations and programs that feature rock music.

One example of successful radio use is that of Innovation Luggage, a New Jersey-based chain of stores. It couldn't compete with the major stores in newspaper advertising. Its small advertisements were buried by those of the giant retailers in the field. In radio, where there is little competition, it had considerable success.

Television is, in two ways, being used considerably more than before. Retailers are paying for "spots," as in the case of radio. When TV programs pause for station identification or break for a commercial, it is often the retailer who purchases the spot. These spots are local and perfect for the retailer who can present merchandise to a preselected, limited audience. In this way, Bloomingdale's might reach the New York market, while at the same time, Marshal Field could target Chicago. The giant retailers are beginning to sponsor complete television shows; it is not unusual for Sears or J. C. Penney to cosponsor entire television specials.

Direct Mail

One of the most effective methods used to bring a particular advertisement to specific individuals is direct mail advertising. Using the mail, retailers are able to send, to both regular and prospective customers, a variety of direct mail pieces such as merchandise brochures, sales announcements, letters, catalogs, booklets, and circulars. A detailed discussion of direct retailing is presented in Chapter 15.

Hand-Distributed Advertisements

Some of the forms used by the direct mail medium may also be hand-delivered to a store's prospects. The supermarkets in particular make extensive use of this medium. Many supermarkets distribute circulars to announce the store's weekly specials. Since prices fluctuate rapidly in the food industry, it is important to notify the customer at what prices their "key" items are being sold during a particular period. Many shoppers carry these circulars to the supermarket as a guide to purchasing.

It should be noted that some communities have passed legislation that no longer allows hand-delivered advertisements. They consider them to be eyesores. In these areas, merchants must distribute through the mail.

Billboards

Retailers make some use of billboard advertising. Billboards are either permanently painted or are covered with prepared advertisements that can be frequently changed. Billboard space is generally available on a rental basis, the cost depending on size and location of the billboard. While it is an inexpensive medium, as the cost per observer is little, the audiences attracted are usually moving quickly (in an automobile, for example) and are not selected on any scientific basis except for locale. Newspapers, for example, have particular audiences, and a retailer can select the most appropriate one. The billboard medium does not allow for such precise selection. Since the reader is aware of the billboard for such a limited period, the message must also be brief. Thus billboards are used by retailers more in an institutional manner than a promotional one.

Billboard examples are pictured in Figure 13–12.

Cooperative Advertising

The cost of advertising is usually alarming to the newcomer to retailing. In spite of the bite it takes from the promotional budget, advertising is necessary if a company is to be successful. One of the avenues an organization has available for expanding its advertising dollar is cooperative advertising. By definition, cooperative advertising is an arrangement in which the retailer and supplier share the advertising expense. A cooperative advertisement is easy to recognize. Not only does the retailer's name appear in the ad, but the manufacturer's or wholesaler's name is also prominently displayed.

Figure 13–12 Outdoor ads such as billboards are used by retailers to attract passersby. Photographs by Ellen Diamond

Figure 13–12   (Continued).

In practice, two parties generally share the expense for cooperative advertising. The amount usually made available by the manufacturer or wholesaler is a percentage of the retailer's purchases from that company. For example:

Retailer A buys $200,000 from a manufacturer who offers a cooperative advertising allowance in the amount of 5 percent of total purchases. The allowance would be

$$\$200,000 \times .05 = \$10,000$$

Retailer A then would receive $10,000 in advertising allowances toward $20,000 of the store advertising, or 50 percent of the cost of the ad.

Not all suppliers offer advertising allowances, but if they do, under provisions of the Robinson-Patman Act, they must make the same offer to all of their customers.

The Law and Advertising

As are other industries, retailers are under the constant scrutiny of a number of governmental agencies that regulate advertising practices. Although many businesses choose to operate in the vein of *caveat emptor* (let the buyer beware), government at all levels has become the watchdog for the unsuspecting consumer. There are many practices through which retailers can color advertisements by subtly using words, or blatantly deceiving customers with enticing offers. Whatever the reason and however the approach is taken, governmental agencies regulate retail advertisements.

Bait-and-Switch

Probably the oldest ploy for luring customers into stores is to offer attractive merchandise at lower than expected prices. In this practice, a store advertises a particular product at a very low price to bait customers and motivate them to come to the store. Once the customer arrives, high-pressure selling takes over, with the store hoping to switch the customer's original want to a higher-priced product that brings in a larger profit.

Bait-and-switch advertising is illegal and carries penalties in the form of fines. Retailers who understand the legal ramifications of such deception and realize that the frustration of the disgruntled customer can lead to a negative store image are unwise to use bait-and-switch tactics. Not only will the penalty pose an immediate cost to the company; the customer unhappiness it causes could also spread through word of mouth.

Deceptive Terminology

Advertisements often include key words or phrases that tend to mislead readers and listeners. Comparative terminology such as *regularly, originally,* or *comparable value* are extensively used, with customers being misled about their real definitions. Generally, the local governmental agency polices the use of these terms and serves notice on the retailers who abuse their placement in ads. *Regularly* indicates only a temporary reduction in price, *originally* indicates the opening or first price of an item, and *comparable value* is an indicator of a product's value in relation to similar products.

The last term is the one generally responsible for customer confusion, as it is incorrectly interpreted to imply the same meaning as *regularly* and *originally*. As in the case of bait-and-switch, misuse of terms can result in fines and customer decline.

Media Regulation

Many newspapers, magazines, and television and radio networks regulate proposed advertisements before they are accepted for production. They do this not only to comply with government regulations, but also to protect their subscribers from unscrupulous practices and to avoid any customer backlash. Although the advertisement is the responsibility of the store, and the copy is their creation, any customer unhappiness may be attributed to the media in which the ad appeared. Media managers are aware of the problems associated with unethical practices and generally choose to police themselves.

Regardless of the Federal Trade Commission, the local department of consumer affairs, or the local Better Business Bureau (the latter without legal bite), retailers are wise to engage in self-regulation. With the enormous amount of direct competition each retailer faces, unethical practices can only turn customers into angry bad-will ambassadors.

PROMOTION

No matter what the time of year, those responsible for promoting the store's image to the customer are constantly searching for new promotional ideas and techniques. Countless dollars are spent to make certain that the store reaps its fair share of both regular and prospective customer attention. Advertising and visual merchandising command a considerable amount of money and time to reach the consuming market. By coupling these activities with a variety of special events and other promotional tools, the store management hopes that the media will be sufficiently enticed to provide free publicity, extolling the store's virtues. Creativity is the key to planning promotions that will not only increase sales immediately, but also help to cement lasting relationships between the store and its clientele.

Promotions such as fashion shows may be developed at modest cost by using models from educational institutions or members of charitable organizations. Some producers, especially of foods, are often willing to send some representatives to stores to feature and offer samples of their products without cost to the retailer. With a little creative thinking and planning, promotion is easily available with little or no expense to merchants.

The Multimedia Concept

In advertising, professionals generally agree that the exclusive use of one particular medium is insufficient to reach all customers. Just as it is unwise to involve the store solely in newspaper advertising, it is also unwise to limit promotion to one tool. Sophisticated promotional campaigns require blending all worthy and available promotion techniques to reach the desired sales goals. A melding of advertising, through the various media, displays, and special events, will achieve better results. Where advertising informs the customer of the promotion or event, display continues to whet the appetite as the customer enters the store. By rounding the package out with appropriate demonstrations and so forth, the flavor of the campaign will be constantly absorbed by the store's clientele. Most retailers agree that increased sales will be achieved by relying on the multimedia or multipromotional concept.

Special Events

Whatever the type of retail organization, special events are tools that can be used to increase volume. Supermarkets, discount operations, traditional department stores, and specialty shops alike all have avenues available to them for reaching their customers. The breadth and depth of these endeavors depend considerably upon the available promotional dollar commitment as well as the experts employed to achieve the desired results. Larger companies employ sales promotion directors whose responsibility it is to coordinate and manage the various promotional departments. Without proper leadership to ensure a joint effort by all departments, the money set aside for promotion will not bring about the best results. In promotion, as in any other aspect of retailing, cooperation is essential to success. Special events are often major undertakings, with many planning months needed before the presentation. Sometimes outside agencies are called upon to assist with the promotion if its magnitude is too much for the regular staff to handle, or if the staff's capacity is just sufficient to handle regular advertising and visual merchandising.

A RETAILING FOCUS   *Bloomingdale's, Chicago*

That it is one of the most famous stores in the world is no accident. Beginning as a "Hoop Skirt and Ladies' Notion Shop" in 1872, Bloomingdale's has gone on to receive accolades and great prestige. With the arrival of each fashion innovation, Bloomingdale's abandoned the old and welcomed the new. This concept of constant change, considered daring at the time, became the cornerstone of "Bloomingdale's Style."

One of the mainstays of the company's promotional endeavors has been the world famous country promotions, of which "China," remains one of the most successful. Other famous country salutes include "Casa Bella" concentrating on Italian home fashions, "India: The Ultimate Fantasy," and "Fête de France." Although these storewide celebrations have helped Bloomingdale's achieve great publicity, the company also sponsors numerous other special events as part of their promotional program.

Bloomingdale's, Chicago, has also made an enormous entrance into the promotional arena. Situated on the city's fashionable North Michigan Avenue, which is aptly referred to as "the Magnificent Mile," the store has as its neighbors such prestigious retailers as Neiman Marcus, Saks Fifth Avenue, Marshall Field, Lord & Taylor, and I. Magnin. In order to compete successfully with these established stores, Bloomingdale's has taken the promotional route to capture the attention of Chicago shoppers.

Preopening festivities on September 23, 1988 were kicked off with a benefit for the Chicago Symphony Orchestra that featured Karen Akers in concert and an international designer Karl Lagerfeld and a French Haute Couture and a Prêt-a-Porter fashion show. The excitement generated by these special opening events signaled that Chicago would respond favorably to other events that the store would sponsor.

Many of the special events that followed were charitable promotions. In conjunction with other businesses, Bloomingdale's became a store that sponsored events, the proceeds of which were donated to charities and municipal institutions. One such event was the cosponsorship of "The Best For Spring" by the Mount Sinai Hospital Service Club and Bloomingdale's. The collaboration resulted in substantial monies for cancer research. Another theme centered on the celebration of Mickey Mouse's 60th birthday. It was a store-wide event that featured all of the Disney characters in the windows and throughout the store. The "When You Wish Upon A Star" display, which required $2.00 donations from each shopper, resulted in a substantial amount of money for the Children's Memorial Medical Center.

Other promotions that have helped to establish Bloomingdale's in the Chicago market have been "California, The New International Style" and the "SELF Expressions" event. The former reflected upon California as a fashion leader, and featured the outdoor life style of Californians from the beach to snow-capped mountains. Each of the store's departments featured the California look. SELF Expressions was a week-long promotion sponsored in the store by SELF Magazine. It featured fashion shows, seminars, and demonstrations on fashion, beauty, fitness, travel, entertaining, and home. The promotion also addressed the need for businesses to become involved with the arts and benefited the Hubbard Street Dance Company.

While Bloomingdale's is a renowned retail giant, it recognizes that its entry into Chicago posed the problem of attracting the shoppers who had long patronized the city's established stores. Through its promotion expertise, the company hoped to become Chicago's leading department store. Figure 13–13 features the store's Chicago flagship.

Fashion Shows

The display of fashions on live models has been a regular sales promotion device for both large and small retail stores. Although some executives feel that the presentation of a fashion show is primarily for prestigious purposes, stores can achieve immediate business from them. One need only watch customers rise from their chairs to rush over to the racks of clothing right after a showing of European fashions to realize the instant success of the showing in terms of immediate sales. The partly emptied racks surely dispel the theory of prestige value exclusively. Even if a fashion show presentation doesn't result in immediate sales, it is valuable in that it exposes the store's fashion merchandise to potential buyers in a lively and exciting manner that is unobtainable in any other media. If the production is properly conceived and executed.

Figure 13–13   Multilevel Chicago flagship of Bloomingdale's. *Courtesy:* Bloomingdale's, Chicago.

appetites are likely to be whetted for future patronage. Figures 13–14 and 13–15 feature two types of fashion shows.

Types of Shows

Fashion shows are by no means limited to women's fashion. At a rapidly increasing rate, the male model is becoming important in fashion shows. It is not unusual to see menswear take up about one-third of the merchandise shown at what was once "a woman's fashion show." Although it might be considered wasteful to include menswear, since fashion shows are almost exclusively attended by women, stores feel it is practical, because a large proportion of menswear purchases are either directly made or influenced by women.

To be considered a fashion show, the presentation needn't be an extravaganza. Shows run the gamut from informal modeling to elaborate productions staged in imaginative settings.

Runway Shows.   The runway show is perhaps the easiest show to produce, and it is also the least costly. This type of production simply presents a succession of models displaying their outfits on a runway in the store, a restaurant, or in an off-site environment. This type of show doesn't make use of any particular theme but simply presents the store's most timely merchandise. The staging doesn't lend itself to complicated backgrounds or space for the models to do intricate turns. Music is generally limited to a pianist.

Formal Fashion Show Productions.   The major production requires a great deal of preparation. This show is presented in an auditorium or theater and is truly theatrical in nature. Generally the fashion coordinator (the person responsible in most large retail operations for the show's production) selects a theme for the show. It might be travel, back-to-school, or the wedding. After the theme has been established, background sets are constructed, the clothes are selected, a script complete with commentary is written, and appropriate music is selected to be played by a band.

Production Costs

A fashion show can be presented with very little cost to the retailer. Small retailers with limited promotional budgets, and even large retailers who do not wish to make heavy investments on fashion shows, can give successful shows for a nominal amount. The greatest expense incurred is the payment of modeling fees. Students may be used as models in a show directed to the attention of the campus set. This serves a double purpose. First, students participating in such a production, particularly those majoring in retailing, find the involvement an excellent learning experience. For the store, this arrangement eliminates the cost of the professional model while guaranteeing an audience of the model's friends. Involvement with an educational institution provides students who will build sets, write and deliver the commentary, and work out other production problems in addition to modeling. Often the school band will play accompanying music, free of charge. Similarly, large fund-raising organizations are excellent sources for the presentation of fashion shows. As in the case of the student shows, these fund-raising groups use their own members for modeling as well as for the performance of the other necessary tasks. The use of the group's members provides models to whom the audiences can relate. For example, a size-14 model may be more meaningful and realistic to a group of homemakers than the "perfect" size-8 professional models.

If a store decides to have a more professional show, many local modeling agencies can provide a sufficient number of male and female models to fulfill its needs.

Figure 13–14   An in-store runway show. Photograph by Ellen Diamond

Figure 13–15   An off-premises runway show. Photograph by Ellen Diamond

Figure 13–16   Macy's Thanksgiving Day parade. *Courtesy:* Macy's

These agencies also have lists of commentators, bands, and so on, to make the show a success.

Whatever the budget of the store, a little ingenuity can guarantee a successful presentation.

Parades

An institutional device that is used by a number of large retailers is a parade to mark some occasion. For example, an annual event costing hundreds of thousands of dollars is Macy's Thanksgiving Day parade in New York City (Figure 13–16). The occasion is its official opening of the Christmas season. The show provides entertainment for the public while reminding them that it is time to begin shopping for Christmas gifts. Similar parades are presented throughout the United States. Even in small towns, groups of independent retailers often collaborate on similar presentations. This cooperation spreads the cost among the participating businesses.

Storewide Celebrations

A major effort that seems to be capturing the attention of consumers today is the "extravaganza" that has retailers across the country transforming their entire stores into elaborate celebrations. Spending millions of dollars on merchandise to be sold

Figure 13-16   (Continued)

and huge sums to visually merchandise the store as an appropriate setting for the goods has become commonplace for many merchants. Initially the brainchild of Neiman Marcus, with its famous "Fortnights," other stores such as Bloomingdale's followed suit with major productions.

Institutional Events

Macy's annual Flower Shows (Figure 13–17) and Fireworks displays (Figure 13–18) are events that create excitement and bring the store's name before the public. The Flower Show, for example, attracts thousands of shoppers into the store to view the exotic floral arrangements and then stay to shop.

Figure 13–17   Macy's annual Flower Show promotion. *Courtesy:* Macy's

Other Special Events

There are many other types of special events that both large and small stores take advantage of to attract customers and increase goodwill. These range from small store support of Little League and bowling teams to major art exhibits and lecture series offered by large institutions. The variety of these events is almost unlimited. The advertisement in Figure 13–19 announces special events for Valentine's Day. While special events may be tied to the sale of specific merchandise, many such programs are intended solely to attract customers to the store and build goodwill by promoting the idea that the store is a kind of community center that supports cultural and athletic programs. Large stores that have the necessary facilities often reinforce the community center idea by offering their tearooms, dining rooms, and auditoriums to such consumer organizations as women's clubs and parent-teacher associations for meetings and special events.

To beef up its "Stork Club" baby registry, Dayton's ran a four-day program called "The Magic Years." Seminars were held in the auditorium of its Minneapolis store dealing with prenatal to preschool issues. There were 42 seminars in all given by nationally known physicians, educators, and neighborhood hospitals and child care centers. Booths were set up with people from local hospitals and child care centers plus vendors to answer specific questions. In-store day care was provided for parents who brought their children. Attendance for the four-day symposium totaled about 5,000 people, most of whom targeted specific seminars. Many others took days off

Figure 13–18   Macy's Fourth of July fireworks display. *Courtesy:* Macy's

from work to attend all of the events. Needless to say, the pre-event promotion was excellent, including radio, newspapers, handouts, and a direct mail piece to Stork Club registrants.

As a result of the special event, the Stork Club registry boasted a huge increase. The event coincided with one of the store's three annual sales. Sales in the children's departments ran 25 percent above that of a similar sale in the previous year.

Special Demonstrations

From the cooking demonstrations in Fortunoff's and Bloomingdale's, at which chefs show how exquisite menus may be prepared using appliances such as food processors, to the "beauty makeover" at cosmetics counters, special demonstrations are commonplace in retailing.

In the cosmetics field alone, where competition is extremely keen, one of the ways passersby are motivated to stop and purchase are demonstrations, which are essential to the success of the many competing counters in the department. Trained cosmetologists eagerly seek out willing subjects who will agree to a "makeover." The crowds that congregate at these demonstrations often become purchasers of the very products used in the demonstration. Since most cosmetic purchasing is made on impulse, such activities are of great importance to their sales.

Other products that have benefited from the special demonstration are computers, cleansing agents, scarves, and video cameras.

*Fifth Avenue takes
you to heart!*

*M*onday to Wednesday,
Street Floor, Noon to 2:

A Guest To Treasure
She's Iris Lane, talented jewelry
designer, here with her collection.

Valentine Melodies
Presented by our pianist.

Fourth Floor:

Woo her with Luxury and Lace
Our loveliest lingerie,
informally modeled.

*T*uesday and Wednesday,
Street Floor, Noon to 2

**Your Silhouette for
Someone Special**
Sit for our artist. It's a gift
with purchase!

We'll Serenade Your Sweet One!
Our barbershop quartet will
personalize your favorite song on tape!
(Only 5.00 with any purchase.)

Complimentary Calligraphy
Gift cards personalized
with your purchase.
(Also on Fourth Floor.)

**Our Red Rose Service Knows
What Your True Love Wants!**
Valentine suggestions are as
near as your phone:
Fifth Avenue(212) 391-3519
Westchester (914) 723-7700, ext.210
Stamford(203) 327-6600, ext.234
Garden City (516) 742-7000 ext.244
Bridgewater Commons
(201) 707-9000 ext.260
Livingston Mall
(201) 994-0800 ext.259
Ridgewood-Paramus
(201) 447-0400, ext.315

Figure 13–19 Advertisement announcing special events for Valentine's Day. *Courtesy:* Lord & Taylor

Sampling

Supermarkets and the warehouse clubs are arenas where food manufacturers and wholesalers increase the sales of their products by means of sampling. At the head of the important aisles, or locations near the stores' entrances, food of every variety is being prepared for the shoppers to taste. Beverages, frozen foods, microwaveable items, bakery goods, canned products, and others are in ready supply to motivate the passersby to taste and purchase.

The cosmetic and fragrance industry has embraced sampling with equal gusto. Shoppers are invited to try the latest fragrance, which is being dispensed by attractively clad promoters, in the hope that they will purchase a supply of the product. Attractively packaged samples by cosmetics companies such as Estée Lauder, the originator of the concept, Chanel, and Ultima are available throughout the year in department stores, with the purchase of a company item.

It should be understood that the sampling technique is only appropriate when the cost of an item is insignificant and additional purchases are predictable.

In-Store Video

With the success of MTV, young people have become enthralled with this type of video production. Capitalizing on its success, many retailers such as A&S, Bloomingdale's, and Macy's regularly feature these formats in their departments that target younger shoppers. Music reaching high pitches and exciting visuals are featured, helping to attract the younger shoppers to stop.

Other retailers have also adopted in-store video promotion. From the on-screen "how to tie a scarf" demonstration to videos of the runway shows of names like DKNY and Anne Klein, the events provide excitement and often motivate shoppers to purchase.

PUBLICITY

In this chapter, publicity refers to the promotion of the store without cost. Free publicity is the result of a store's advertising, display, special events, or other promotions that are noteworthy enough for a publication or commentator to mention them without cost to the retailer. For example, a store might present a fashion show that is so outstanding that the local newspaper's fashion editor will review it in a column. A store's holiday parade might get attention on a television or news broadcast. The larger stores employ a public relations person, who is charged with the responsibility of preparing releases about the store's activities that might attract media and, therefore, customer interest. The free publicity a store receives is not always kind, and could work adversely. For example, a newspaper exposure of incorrect weights on meat packages in some New York supermarkets certainly hurt sales.

Free publicity can be in the form of favorable comments concerning the store's community activities, merchandise promotional activities, or place in the business community. The purpose of free publicity, like all other sales promotional activity, is to create sales by presenting the firm's name in the most favorable light. An advantage of free publicity over conventional advertising (in addition to the cost savings) is that promotional material found in advertising is presumed to be biased and is not taken as seriously as the same material would be if it were found in the nonadvertising section

APRIL 8/21, 1990 · HERALD SQUARE

FOR IMMEDIATE RELEASE

MACY'S 16TH ANNUAL FLOWER SHOW

On Sunday, April 8th, Macy's Herald Square will unveil its 16th Annual Flower Show. For two weeks (through April 21st), Macy's flagship store will burst into glorious color with elegant flowers, blossoming trees and exotic plants from around the world. Nature's finest showing of horticultural delights will fill over 265,000 square feet of the Main Floor, as well as other newly designed areas, including Men's fragrances, Private Lives on 6, and the Corner Shop Antique Galleries on 9.

No Easter would be complete without a rabbit, and Bugs Bunny™, that "wascally ol' wabbit" himself will join Macy's April extravaganza in his own garden high atop the 151 West 34th Street marquee. Sponsored by Warner Bros. Inc., this 32' tall cold-air inflatable balloon, grasping a 9' long bouquet of colorful tulips and daffodils, will majestically tower over 34th Street throughout the 16th Annual Flower Show. Bugs Bunny excitement will continue in-store with daily character meet and greets. For the young (or the young at heart!), Bugs Bunny and his friends, Daffy Duck™, Tweety™ and Sylvester™, will perform in a mini-musical revue on Thursday, April 12th.

The Flower Show will also treat visitors to exciting daily in-store entertainment that Macy's is known throughout the world for. In the Corner Shop Antique Galleries, noted gardening authors and experts, as well as celebrated interior designers such as the "Prince of Chintz", Mario Buatta, will make personal appearances during the April extravaganza to talk about their areas of expertise. And, the center aisle on the 8th floor will showcase Spring-themed celebrity table settings by Geoffrey Beene, Mario Buatta, Dixie Carter, Oscar de la Renta and Bobby Short, each reflecting the individual style of its creators.

Macy's 16th Annual Flower Show opens on Sunday, April 8th at 10:00 a.m. and will fill the air with color and fragrance through Saturday, April 21st. For more information call the Macy's Flower Show Hotline at (212) 560-4495.

Figure 13–20 Macy's uses the press release to gain publicity for the company. *Courtesy:* Macy's, Herald Square, New York

of the newspaper. Publicity for retailers is sometimes achieved by use of press releases similar to the one shown in Figure 13–20.

The term *free publicity* is somewhat misleading. In fact, large firms spend a considerable amount of money on publicity. Large stores frequently assign the responsibility for publicity to one or more members of their sales promotion department to spend their full time in reporting newsworthy information to the local media. These people establish contacts with local newspapers and radio stations and actually write the articles and comments that, if accepted by the media, appear in the news sections. Smaller stores employ the services of free-lance writers or public relations agencies for this purpose.

The newspapers and other media are well aware of the fact that their audience, particularly women, is interested in news concerning merchandise. Newspaper editors are constantly on the lookout for stories that supplement their advertising pages. Information such as the opening of a new season's fashions or a fashion show is important to readers, and editors are pleased to accept stories and photographs concerning such events. Many newspapers appoint special editors and writers to cover fashion events and report such news as a regular feature.

Studies have shown that there is a direct relationship between the amount of advertising space a company buys and the amount of free publicity it receives. This is probably due, in part, to the newspaper's willingness to please their good customers. It is also likely that a store with a large advertising budget probably engages in many newsworthy promotional activities.

TRENDS

Advertising and promotional endeavors continue to bring business to retailers. Some of the trends in these areas are discussed below.

Cooperative Advertising and Promotion

With the expenses soaring for both advertising and promotion, the trend is for retailers to demand, as part of their purchase orders, a certain amount of money to be contributed by manufacturers and wholesalers. Many retailers are shying away from the companies that do not provide them with these funds.

Minimizing Extravagant Promotions

At one time, stores like Neiman Marcus and Bloomingdale's spent huge sums on the transformation of their stores into environments that mimic particular nations. Neiman Marcus' "Fortnights" and Bloomingdale's foreign promotions have been eliminated from their promotional calendars. Although the publicity achieved from such events was considerable, the costs to mount them didn't justify the sales they produced. Only certain spectacles such as The Thanksgiving Day Parades, initiated by Macy's and followed by other stores, continue to be used.

Decrease in Institutional Advertisements

Although institutional advertisements provide image building for the stores, the results, in terms of sales are hard to measure. With soaring advertising costs, many retailers are opting for promotional or product ads that result in an immediate sales response.

In-house Advertising

Some of the major department stores are returning to in-house production of advertisements because of the advent of numerous computer publishing programs. Ads may be completed with a minimum of expense, because the agency specialists' work may be eliminated.

Television Advertising

Major retailers who once relied primarily on the print media are using television as a means of reaching their markets. Although the expense is considerable, by using spot or local commercials they may target audiences that can buy in the stores or purchase through catalogs.

ACTION FOR THE INDEPENDENT RETAILER

Although aware of the benefits of advertising, few independents pay any attention to it. Most often the reason given is the lack of available funds. Given this, enlightened independent retailers can involve their stores in advertising that requires imagination rather than significant dollar commitment. There are many avenues available to make the appeal to customers meaningful, without spending large sums, such as independent shopping publications. Cooperation from suppliers, sometimes to the extent of sharing 50 percent of the cost, is often available.

Many small retailers transact a good part of their business with private charge accounts. In those cases, adding customer notices to the end-of-month charge statements in order to announce special sales or merchandise features makes use of advertising without adding considerable expense. Since the postage is already required for statement mailing, the extra cost is only attributable to the statement enclosure. In small stores, a handwritten note is often considered a perfect way to personalize this advertisement.

Promotions, such as fashion shows may be developed at modest cost by using models from educational institutions or members of charitable organizations. Some producers, especially of foods, are often willing to send representatives to stores to offer samples of their products.

IMPORTANT POINTS IN THE CHAPTER

1. Retailers engage in advertising programs to make the consuming public aware of the store and the merchandise it offers for sale.
2. Advertising is any paid form of nonpersonal presentation of the facts about goods, services, or ideas to a group.
3. Large stores, which can afford to hire specialists, generally have their own advertising departments. Stores whose advertising budget is too small to support their own departments use advertising agencies for their needs.
4. Frequently suppliers and the advertising media, by supplying materials and services, help reduce advertising costs.

5. Large retailers use carefully prepared procedures to ensure cooperation between the buyer and the advertising department. This includes follow-up to evaluate the advertisement after it has been run.

6. Institutional advertising is used to project the image of the institution. Promotional advertising has the purpose of promoting specific items of merchandise.

7. Of all the media, newspapers receive the greatest share of retail advertising nationally. They are widely read and the advertising is inexpensive when calculated on a cost-per-reader basis.

8. Cooperative advertising is an arrangement in which the supplier and retailer share the cost of the advertisement.

9. Retailers use special events to improve their store's image as well as to sell goods. Typical of this is a fashion show, which brings many customers into the store to buy goods while improving the store's reputation as a style center.

10. Live demonstrations and samples are used to increase customer interest in merchandise by demonstrating its use. When goods are expensive or complicated to use, demonstrations are a better promotional device than samples. For products that require a considerable amount of consumer skills, series of classes are frequently arranged.

11. Publicity refers to the promotion of the store without cost. Noteworthy events such as parades and fashion shows are frequently interesting enough to be reported by media in their regular news stories. This may result in an improvement in goodwill toward the store at no cost to the retailer.

12. The multimedia promotional concept involves the coordination of all promotional tools, such as display and advertising, to promote the store.

REVIEW QUESTIONS

1. Is advertising too costly for the small retailer? Explain.

2. Why do stores advertise?

3. Who is responsible for advertising in a large retail organization? In a small organization?

4. Preparation of an advertisement includes three major areas. Discuss them.

5. In what way can a manufacturer help the retailer with advertising?

6. With whom does the advertising request begin? How does it gain the attention of the advertising manager?

7. Define *pica* and *point*.

8. How does institutional advertising differ from promotional advertising?

9. In which newspaper position must an advertiser spend the most money? Why might the advertiser choose this space?

10. What sort of stores advertise in magazines? Why?

11. Discuss the types of television advertising used by retailers.

12. Describe the method by which retailers can stretch their advertising budget.

13. What is meant by bait-and-switch advertising?

14. Define *multimedia concept*.

15. What is a special event?

16. What purpose is served by a store's Thanksgiving Day parade?

17. Contrast the runway show with the formal fashion show.

18. How valuable is the use of demonstrations in retail stores? Discuss in terms of a particular item.

19. Is free publicity always an asset to the store?

20. How might the small retailer, with a limited budget, carry out a special promotion?

CASE PROBLEMS

Case Problem 1

Carter's Emporium is a newly established retail organization that plans to open its doors to the public in approximately three months. Carter's is a ladies' specialty store, occupying two stores, with a sales expectancy of $8 million for its first year of operation. It is considered to be semipromotional in that the bulk of its merchandise will be regular priced and sold with the aid of salespeople, while it is anticipated that about 30 percent of sales will result from special purchases (merchandise bought at less than the regular cost) and offered at a savings to customers.

Although the policies governing general store management procedures and merchandising have been established, there is great concern regarding the store's advertising practices. Several suggestions have been forthcoming from the general management as well as from the store's own advertising department. At the present time, an impasse has been reached concerning the advertising approach. General store management is of the opinion that promotional advertising would bring immediate results to the store and that the advertising should follow that route. The advertising manager strongly advocates the use of institutional advertising so that the store would be established as somewhat different from the other semipromotional stores, most of which employ only promotional advertising. She feels that at this time, three months prior to opening its doors, institutional advertising would afford a proper response and would continue to do so on a regular basis.

Questions

1. Do you agree with either side completely? Defend your position.

2. Develop the approach that you would employ in publicizing the store through advertising.

Case Problem 2

A large New York City department store has been running a fashion show for many years. Owing to the excellent promotion of the event, the show has become an important fashion event of the city. The free publicity the store receives from the showing is excellent, with all of the important newspapers giving prominent space in their fashion columns to the occasion. In addition to the excellent publicity, the show produces a very important boost in sales volume. The customer attendance at the show is standing room only, with many interested people being turned away because of insufficient space.

The format of the show is ladies', men's, and children's clothing. This year a proposal has been made to have three individual showings, one each for ladies', men's, and children's clothing. It is reasoned that by dividing up the shows, there would be more publicity, more sales, and more seats for interested customers. In addition, each line of goods can have more time for display and show more merchandise.

Questions

1. Can you think of any more arguments favoring the split?
2. List the arguments opposing the split.
3. As merchandise manager, what would you do? Why?

Chapter 14
Visual Merchandising

Courtesy: Macy's

A SIMULATED AIRPLANE HANGAR SETS THE SCENE . . .

When retailers had large windows in which they displayed their merchandise, they would tell shoppers what to expect once inside the store. With predictable regularity, "trimmers" would mount displays that ranged from the simplest to the most extravagant. Except for the major downtown central district department store flagships, and some stores that were built when the window was the "silent seller" that motivated shoppers to enter, the formal window structure has fallen by the wayside. In their place, modern structures have been built that deemphasize the traditional windows and use the majority of the space for selling.

With malls the dominant shopping district of many retailers, the "windowless window" has taken center stage. Viewers are immediately able to see the store through the large panes of glass, or through open fronts that close only after the hours of operation have been concluded. This configuration has prompted some retailers to provide an environment that has extraordinary visual appeal.

One such retailer is Aeropostale, a spinoff of Macy's that carries unisex clothing. The visual merchandisers have used an airplane hangar motif to enhance the merchandise offering. Wings of airplanes, hangars where pilots stored their gear, metal fixturing, and props that recall aviation transform the store into an inviting environment. Not only does it eliminate the necessity to change displays from season to season as was heretofore the pattern followed by retailers, but it eliminates the need to have display teams on staff to change seasonal displays regularly. With each new Aeropostale opening, the props get more and more realistic, providing a setting that is both permanent and eye-appealing.

While this environmental approach doesn't necessarily fit each retailer's needs, it is sure to set the tone for others.

Visual merchandising is the method of presentation that a store uses to attract the potential customer to the store and to its merchandise. In the past, the term *display* was used, but this word really doesn't address all of the aspects of visual presentation. It was used to describe the store's windows and the trimming of such interior fixtures as showcases, counters, pedestals, shadow boxes, and so forth. Although the visual merchandiser still pays considerable attention to these aspects of promotion, visual merchandising is not limited to these areas.

Today, some retailers use their entire selling floor as an exciting visual presentation. Hanna Barbera creates environments that resemble large play areas, whereas Ralph Lauren and Bergdorf Goodman use the residential approach to instill an elegant, at home feeling (Figure 14–1).

Merchandise presentation in every area of the sales floor must be carefully handled. In The Gap, diamond-shaped self-service units are found at the store's entrance and continue to the rear of the shop. The merchandise featured on these units is neatly stacked according to color. The impact on the eye is astounding. This is visual merchandising!

There are many functions that visual merchandising performs for the retailer. Among them are:

- The appearance of the store or specific merchandise should attract customers' attention and motivate them to buy the featured items.
- Windows should catch the attention of passersby and persuade them to come into the store.
- Shoppers' attention should be held so that each displayed item may prompt a purchase.
- Related items, when properly featured, will result in larger individual purchases.
- Visual merchandising presents the store's image to potential customers.

Today many stores no longer concentrate primarily on their windows, but instead approach all of their visual tasks equally. The reason for this approach is that a great number of stores do not have separate traditional windows in which to feature their merchandise. In malls, for example, except for very few stores, the window structures that once flanked the store's entrance are no longer there. Instead, stores employ that space for selling and merely use the storefront as a glass divider between the store and the mall.

It should be noted, however, that most of the giant department store organizations have their flagship or main stores in downtown areas. These stores have traditionally featured many large windows, and still use them to display their goods. Stores like Lord & Taylor, Macy's, Bloomingdale's, Saks Fifth Avenue, Carson Pirie Scott, and Marshall Field still pay considerable attention to their flagships' windows. They plan their presentations for these "silent sellers," as they are often called, many months in advance. They plan schedules for each window space, paying careful attention to their shapes, sizes, and location. Figure 14–2 shows a visual merchandiser finishing a window display. Figure 14–3 features a mid-1800s window display at Tiffany & Company.

This chapter will focus on the various ways different retail operations approach visual merchandising, the stores' windows, the elements visual merchandisers use in creating their presentations, some themes that feature merchandise, and how a visual presentation is executed.

Figure 14–1   Bergdorf Goodman uses a residential design. *Courtesy:* J. T. Nakaoka Associates

DEVELOPING VISUAL PRESENTATIONS

The responsibility for the development of the store's visual program varies from company to company. Basically, there are three approaches that retailers use to accomplish their visual presentations.

The giant department stores use in-house staffs to accomplish their goals. A director of visual merchandising, who very often enjoys the title of vice president, develops plans that are executed by the store's visual team. The team consists of trimmers, who actually install the presentations, and others such as painters, carpenters, signmakers, prop developers, and photographers, who prepare the materials used.

Chains may go the route of having display teams periodically visit each of their stores to make the necessary interior and window changes. However, many of the very large chain organizations are using centralized visual merchandising techniques to accomplish their visual tasks, in which they send photographs of displays, and installation instructions, for the store's manager or assistant manager to reproduce. Williams-Sonoma is one chain that uses the centralized visual merchandising approach. Figures 14–4 through 14–7 (pages 286–289) show one of their plans.

Small stores, and sometimes small chains, often use the services of free-lancers to design and execute their visual displays. For a fee, the free-lancers will supply the necessary display materials and install the presentation. Some free-lancers insist upon annual contracts from the stores for their services.

Figure 14–2   Visual merchandiser putting finishing touch on window display. *Courtesy: The Pottery Barn*

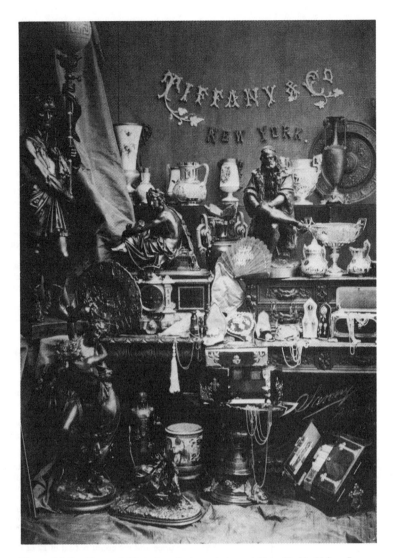

Figure 14–3 Cluttered Victorian display window at New York's Union Square Tiffany store in the mid-1800s. *Courtesy:* Tiffany & Company

WINDOW SCHEDULES

Large stores should develop a schedule for their window presentations. Through careful advance planning, each department of the store will have an opportunity to feature its desired merchandise at the most productive times of the year. The development of such a schedule or calendar is even more important since many buyers compete for the assignment of the available windows.

Window schedules are planned as far as six months in advances, with almost every window assigned at that time. Some stores leave a small percentage of their display space unassigned to take care of last-minute requirements. For example, an extended cold spell might warrant additional window space for outerwear, skis, snow shovels, or other cold weather goods. The remainder or bulk of the windows are assigned as determined by the store's director of visual merchandising.

The forms used vary from store to store but always include the dates of the display, the assigned window number, and the merchandise or department featured in the

---

WILLIAMS-SONOMA   No.: 21

DISPLAY MEMO

To: All Store Managers   c.c.: G. Friedman
                                                        T. O'Higgins
From: Cynde Lanna   RM's
                                                        DM's
Re: "Misc. Notes - Spring I Program   Buyers
                                                        Distributors

---

* The Spring I Program will be in place until May 1st.

* In order to maximize our sales per square foot for this packet will utilize item mass merchandising within select features.

  One to two products per feature have been chosen to be stocked out in quantity; ie. - the sundae glasses and ice cream goblets in Feature #27, or stacks of Botanical dinnerware in Feature #30.

  The item mass merchandising should allow customers to shop the features with greater ease, cut down on trips to the stockroom for store staff and give the store a fuller cleaner and crisper merchandising statement.

* A new "Focus Feature" #33 will be added to all stores as a complete mass merchandising approach of one or two items that will change every 2 - 4 weeks.

  This Feature will focus on items with good margin and quantity ownership that are either basic or seasonal in nature.

  The Feature should be located midway into the store, in an impulse location. Its size should be approximately 3 cubes or 2 cubes and a rolling cart.

* Please note, some items used in the photos are substitutes for new items not yet received in the stores. The display memos will note the correct assortment per Feature.

* Stores unable to relocate the range to an interior cookware Feature location, should use cookware Feature #24 on the range top in similar format. Use an Enclume Rack overhead and suspend 3-5 copper omelet pans.
  Use #23 Basic Breakfast Window in place of Cookware Feature.

* When unboxing items sold in a boxed set (ie. Picardie 8 oz. and 12 oz.) for open stock mass out on plexi - each item must be ticketed with short SKU - set price and set quantity (set of 12 or S/12)

* All stores will receive (via D/C) 3 dozen - <u>very realistic</u> faux display cherries. 18 for Window #22 and 18 for Bakeware Feature #25.

* All stores should take a cash dispursement of $15.00 for Sparkling Water Bottles 4-6 pc #29; 2, 3 Lg. loafs of French bread #30, 6 green pears #31. Managers must sign all receipts and note April Display prop.

* Please note, if your windows are accessible to customer shopping, they should be restocked ASAP to keep them as full and intact as possible.

* The new Cherry Dinnerware should be represented in the Earthenware wall along with the table top window.

* If you have any questions, please contact your DM, RM or myself.

Figure 14–4 Excerpted illustrations from a centralized visual merchandising plan. *Courtesy:* Williams-Sonoma

WILLIAMS-SONOMA
D I S P L A Y   M E M O

No.: 26

To: All Store Managers

From: Cynde Lanna

Re: Electric Feature - "Special Equipment"

c.c.: G. Friedman   Buyers
      T. O'Higgins   Distributors
      RM's
      DM's

SKU	DESCRIPTION	QTY	COLOR	SPECIAL INSTRUCTIONS	SKU	ALTERNATE
391946	Deluxe Electric Fryer & Bonus Fry Cutter	1	Chrome	Position on cube behind rolling cart w/ fry cutter and sign.		
368415	Cucina Utensil Jar	5	Blue - yellow	Fill one w/ Potato Nest fryer and position next to Electric Fryer - Fill 2 w/ kitchen towels (see diagram).	317164	Daisy Utensil Jar
386771	Electric Grill	1		Position on rolling cart w/ top open and sign.		
303743	Potato Nest Basket	6-8		Position in Utensil Jar next to Electric Fryer.		
137729	Electronic Super Slicer (Optional if space allows)	1		Position on front cube and sign.		
357301	Popolska Kitchen Towels Set of 6	2-3 sets	Stripes	Fill 2-3 Utensil Jars (See diagram)		
145003	Scouring Pads S/4	48-60 pcs.	Yellow/ Blue	Fill - very full - an oyster Basket & position by cart		

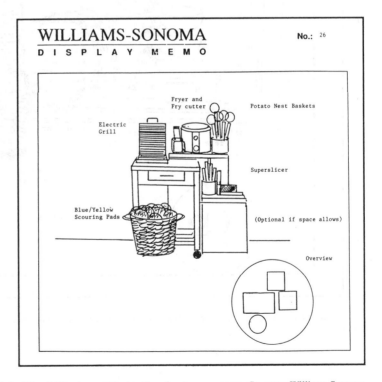

Figure 14–5   "Special Equipment" instructions for store managers. *Courtesy:* Williams-Sonoma

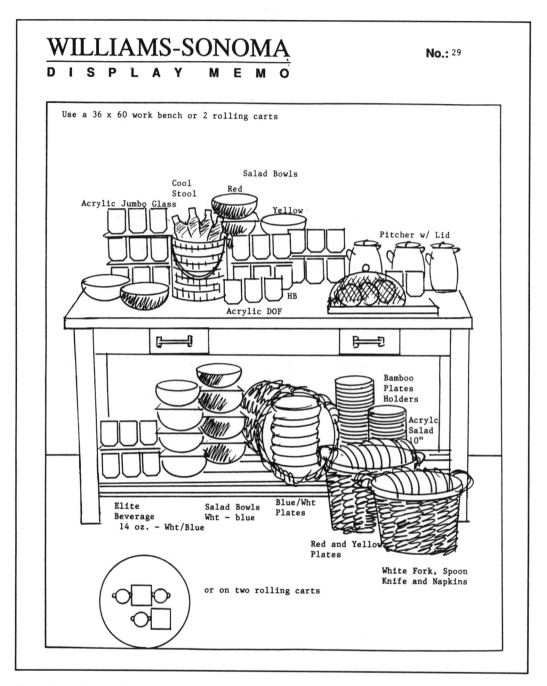

Figure 14–6   Drawing of visual presentation for store managers to duplicate. *Courtesy:* Williams-Sonoma

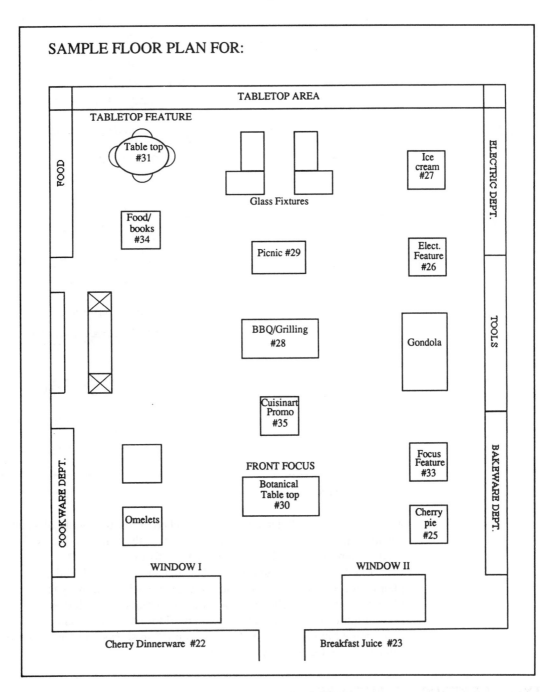

Figure 14–7 Floor layout for visual presentations. *Courtesy:* Williams-Sonoma

```
                        Window Schedule - January

        Date        Window                    Merchandise

        Jan. 5        14        Avalon antron prints, Daytime Dresses.

                      15        Art deco print jersey, Bobbie Brooks,
                                Juniorite, Jr. Sportswear.

                      16        Men's polyester knit slacks, Hagar,
                                knit shirts.  (12/22)

        Jan. 9         1        Furniture & Accessories

                       2               "

                       3               "

                       4        Lamps

        Jan. 12        5        Bridal Lingerie

                       6        Guest at the Wedding: Chiffon costumes,
                                Young Modes, Don Sophisticates, Gold Room.

                       7        Bridal Registry with Lenox.

                       8        Bridal gowns:  Priscilla, Pandora,
                                Bride's Boutique Collection.

                     Stage      Polyester knit dresses, long torso,
                                moving skirts, Moderate Dresses.

        Jan. 26                 What a Bright Idea!

                       1        Crinkle patent suits & sportswear -
                                battle jackets, skirts, Jr. Suits &
                                Sportswear.

                       2        Crinkle patent handbags, gloves, Spring
                                brights.

                       3        Linen coatdresses, melon, brown, Sue
                                Brett, Colette, Jr. Dresses.
```

Figure 14–8   Window schedule—January

window. Figure 14–8 depicts a window schedule for the month of January for a large department store. Some stores also include in the schedule the type of props to be used, requirements for the sign shop, and so forth.

Many retailers, in addition to the calendar type of schedule, also publish a floor plan of the various windows and indicate in each window space what is to be displayed, what is to be changed, and what is to remain as holdovers from previous displays. Figure 14–9 shows such a window floor plan for the same department store as that featured in Figure 14–8. Close examination shows its conformity to the week of January 12 on the window schedule.

TYPES OF WINDOW STRUCTURES

In days gone by, retailers were generally restricted to parallel-to-sidewalk windows that were found in large department storefronts in their downtown flagships, arcade windows in which the entrance was set back and two windows flanked a vestibule, corner windows from which merchandise could be seen from two converging streets, islands or glass cases that were found in entrance vestibules, angled windows that featured a glass panel that started at the store's building line and angled to the entrance, and windowless windows that eliminated the need for formal windows and merely had glass through which shoppers could see the store's interior.

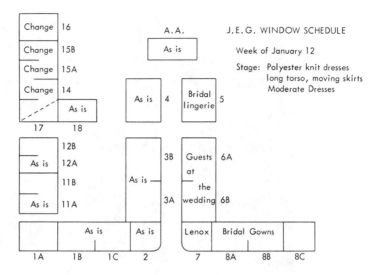

Figure 14–9   Window floor plan—January 12

Today, the windowless format (Figure 14-10) dominates because of the limited space available for the traditional types, leaving the others primarily to older structures and some retailers who still find a need for them.

INTERIOR PRESENTATIONS

Retailers are spending more time and money developing interior presentations than ever before. The giants in the field, such as Neiman Marcus, Macy's, and Bloomingdale's, often use storewide promotions to attract customers to their stores. It is the joint effort of the various divisions to develop each new promotional concept, but it is the departments within the promotional division that carry out the plans. The visual merchandisers are the ones charged with the responsibility of developing the materials and props to be used in these campaigns, and of installing the new "environments." Featured in Figure 14–11 is a prop that was constructed by visual merchandising carpenters at Neiman Marcus for a promotional theme about Great Britain.

Figure 14–10   Windowless windows leave more space for selling. Photograph by Ellen Diamond

Figure 14–11   "Britain: Then & Now" celebration. *Courtesy:* Neiman Marcus

The visual team is regularly called upon to design, construct, and install interior settings for the many promotions undertaken by Bloomingdale's. Such themes as The Year of the Dragon, Hooray for Hollywood, and Fête de France necessitated considerable efforts from the visual presenters.

One of Macy's New York's regular spring promotions involves transforming a significant part of the store into a garden of flowers. The arrangement of the living plants in settings conceived by the visual team makes for one of the most attention-getting promotions in the store.

With the open fronts, rather than just windows, that show the store in its entirety, interior spaces continue to receive a great deal of attention. Counters, shadow boxes, tabletops, aisles, platforms, pedestals, and so forth must regularly be maintained and changed as the need arises. In many of the large stores, trimmers take a regular, daily walk-through to freshen the displays that have been handled and disturbed by the shoppers. Without attention to such details, the selling floors would lose their visual appeal. Figures 14–12 (p. 293) and 14–13 (p. 294) feature two types of interior presentations. The former shows an interior counter display and the latter shows in-store windows.

SIGNAGE AND GRAPHICS

At one time, retailers used signs sparingly. They were usually relegated to the roles of displaying the store's name over the entrance, identifying departments, and carrying an accompanying message for a visual presentation. A glance at a modern retailers' premises shows how important signage and graphics are to its operations.

There are several ways in which retailers avail themselves of these devices. The larger stores usually have in-house staffs that create the signs and graphics that the store needs. Some use outside sources. Signage specialists will create anything for the retailer, and more and more manufacturers are beginning to supply these materials to the store. In the cosmetics industry, the producers offer an abundance of signs for the retailers. One that has made a considerable impact on the cosmetic customer is the "backlit transparency," which is a material that when placed in a light box offers lifelike images.

Types of signage include banners, wall signs, backlit transparencies, valence signs, pennants, and moving message signs. The latter feature an electronic unit that enables the retailer to continually change the messages for the shopper.

Until recently most signs were individually created by graphic artists. They were hand lettered and painted. Today, with the use of a computer, signs are quickly and easily made in any quantity desired. Some stores that use a great deal of signage have their own computers, while others, with fewer needs, place their orders with outside computer sign companies.

Not only are the signs informative, but they often provide visual excitement for the retail environment. Signage and graphics are depicted in Figures 14–14 and 14–15, p. 295.

DISPLAY FIXTURES

Display fixtures are the devices on which merchandise can be shown to its best advantage. The fixtures can either be forms that simulate the human figure or parts of the figure, or various types of stands, platforms, pedestals, and discs, which are used to drape and elevate the merchandise. Other items such as ladders, barrels, and so forth, which were not designed as display fixtures, but come from the visual merchandiser's creativity, are also used. In order to prepare a visual presentation, one must be familiar with these fixtures.

Figure 14–12   Interior counter display. *Courtesy:* The Pottery Barn

Figure 14–13   In-store windows provide formal interior settings for A & S in A & S plaza, New York. *Courtesy:* A & S

Human Form Fixtures

Mannequins are used to show an entire outfit. Men's, women's, and children's forms are available in a variety of materials, such as plastics, plaster of paris, burlap, velvet, raffia, papier maché, rubber, and wood. They range in design from lifelike replicas of humans, complete with imaginative hair stylings, to stylized forms. In selecting the proper mannequins for a retail store, the store's image should be kept in mind. For example, a store catering to teenagers would hardly select conventional lifelike mannequins. Similarly, the typical ladies' shop located in a midwestern shopping center most probably wouldn't pick the stylized variety. Large department stores, some with hundreds of mannequins, often have all the types mentioned. Their wide variety of merchandise necessitates this collection of human forms. The retailer with a visual merchandising budget that only occasionally allows for the purchase of new mannequins, and with a narrower assortment of merchandise than the department store, should select those forms that most typify the store's image. The greatest percentage of human forms purchased today are plastic and lifelike. The plastic is lightweight and chip-resistant, and the lifelike variety is more easily accepted by the majority of consumers.

One proponent of the lifelike concept is Adele Rootstein, the London-based manufacturer of display mannequins. Figure 14–16 (p. 296) shows some of the realistic mannequins available today.

A trend has developed in which alternatives to regular mannequins are being used. Stores are saving money and creating interesting props by having visual merchandisers create their own mannequins (Figure 14–17, p. 298).

In addition to the full figure mannequin, the following human forms are also used extensively in display.

1. *Woman's torso or 3/4 form.* Used for bathing suits, jackets, suits, lingerie, blouses, and skirts.
2. *Man's suit form.* Used for suits and sports jackets. Traditionally, this form is used more than a full man's mannequin. Men's suit forms are shown in Figure 14–18, p. 299.

Figure 14–14   The sign clearly identifies the department. Photograph by Ellen Diamond

Figure 14–15   Graphics add life to displays. Photograph by Ellen Diamond

3. *Woman's shoulder–head form.* Used for millinery, scarves, jewelry, and hair ornaments. (Usually these forms are abstract or stylized.)

4. *Woman's blouse form.* Used to display blouses, sweaters, and lingerie.

5. *Woman's hand.* Used to display gloves, jewelry, scarves, and watches. It is also used extensively to drape merchandise such as blouses, skirts, slacks, and sweaters.

6. *Hosiery legs.* Used to display hosiery and socks.

7. *Shoe form.* Used for shoes and slippers.

Figure 14–16   Realistic mannequins are the mainstay at traditional retailers. Photograph by Ellen Diamond

Adjustable Stands

Adjustable stands are devices that can be adjusted to various heights and to which several attachments can be secured for displaying dresses, blouses, lingerie, hosiery, textiles, table linens, and so on.

To these stands the most frequently used attachment is the "T" rod. When used in combination, it is called a "T" stand. Blouse forms and display hangers are also used for display with these stands.

Figure 14–19 (p. 300) shows examples of interior display units that attractively feature gloves, millinery, and scarf displays. These units permit customers to touch the merchandise, which often contributes to the motivation for buying. One important aspect of these units is the ease with which anyone can dress them. A professional display person is not needed for changing the items as often as necessary.

Pedestals and Platforms

To achieve a variety of heights, pedestals and platforms in various sizes and shapes are used. These devices elevate the merchandise to the desired height to enable the merchandise to be shown to advantage.

The pedestals are generally available in clear plastic, wrought iron, wood, chrome, and brass. Pedestals are shown in Figure 14–20 (p. 301). The majority of platforms (the fixture used atop the pedestal) are made of glass or clear plastic.

A complete understanding of the display fixtures previously discussed and the infinite variety of combinations achieved by assembling and reassembling them is of utmost importance in display. Not only are the stands adaptable to different devices (hangers, "T" rods, and so on), but mannequins' arms also can be interchanged, positions can be adjusted, wigs can be changed to fit the merchandise, and so forth. One need only go to the local department store and watch the display people manipulate the fixtures in preparation for a new display to realize the many ways in which these fixtures can be used.

Most important in the interior display is that the featured merchandise be available for purchase. While windows often cannot be changed to coincide with the sale of all of the displayed items because a display person's services might be required, interiors can be changed more frequently. Department managers, assistants, and sales personnel can easily make the changes as needed. A simple knowledge of the workings of such display properties as mannequins, stands, pedestals, and other props can make almost any store employee adept at interior display. Featuring merchandise that is no longer available is a waste of valuable display space.

LIGHTING

To carefully prepare the most beautiful merchandise, display fixtures, and background materials and then not pay attention to proper lighting is to completely destroy a display. Without lighting effects, the theater could never achieve the desired moods. Similarly, visual presentations cannot be complete without good lighting.

Light Sources

There are several types of light sources, each providing a different look and feel. Fluorescent bulbs are mostly used in places like warehouse clubs, off-price stores, and discount operations to illuminate a large general area. They come in both cool and warm tones, and serve as a low-cost lighting source for stores that are looking to save money.

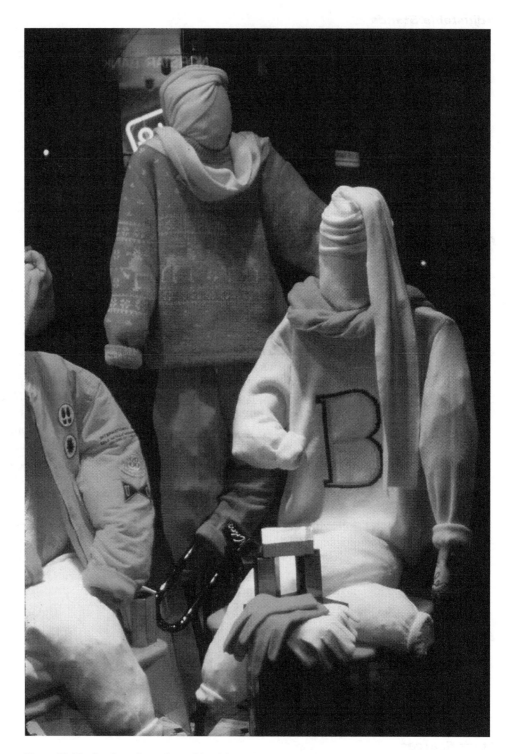

Figure 14–17   An alternative to the traditional form. Photograph by Ellen Diamond

Figure 14–18   Men's suit forms are used by traditional retailers. *Courtesy:* J. T. Nakoaka Associates

Although the fixtures that house the bulbs are moderately expensive, the bulbs are long lasting and inexpensive. Incandescent light has been the mainstay for visual lighting for many years. It is available as spotlights, for highlighting purposes, or floodlights, which provide overall coverage of an area; these are typically found in department and specialty stores. They are available in many wattages, do not distort the merchandise, and can be housed in a variety of fixtures. The only disadvantage is the higher energy cost associated with use of this type of bulb. Neon is a decorative light source that comes in and out of favor from time to time. Currently, many visual merchandisers have chosen neon to create a particular image for a specific display or for a store's environment. It is initially expensive to purchase, but it is long lasting and an energy saver. There is widespread use of one or two types of bulbs more recently introduced to the visual field. The first, halogen/quartz, is providing a good deal of lighting excitement. The beam is much brighter and whiter than the previously mentioned light sources, and the life of the bulb is extremely long. The trimmer is able to get more precise lighting for visual enhancement from a bulb that is ¼ the size of a standard incandescent. The other new choice is high-intensity discharge bulbs, or HIDs as they are referred to in the industry. They are good for bright illumination, achieving of shadows, and concentration on narrow areas. The major drawback of both of these newer bulbs is the high cost, which accounts for their infrequent use by visual merchandisers.

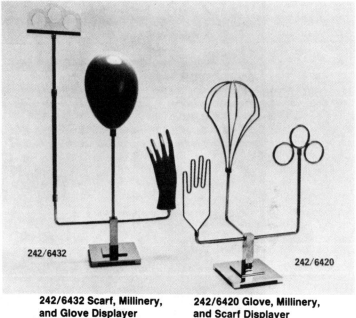

242/6432 Scarf, Millinery, and Glove Displayer   **242/6420 Glove, Millinery, and Scarf Displayer**

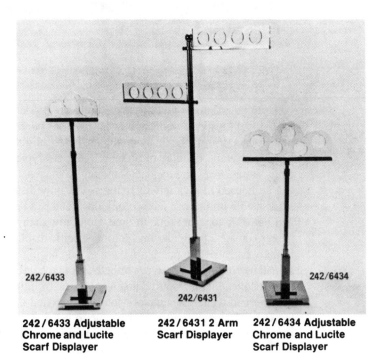

242/6433 Adjustable Chrome and Lucite Scarf Displayer   **242/6431 2 Arm Scarf Displayer**   **242/6434 Adjustable Chrome and Lucite Scarf Displayer**

Figure 14–19   Scarf, millinery, and glove displayers. *Courtesy:* D. G. Williams, Inc.

Figure 14–20   Pedestals used in housewares display at A & S in A & S Plaza, New York. *Courtesy:* A & S

Overall Lighting

To provide general light (overall light) to an area satisfactorily, either incandescent floodlights or fluorescent lighting is appropriate. In both cases, the fixtures should be recessed into the ceiling. These lights should be used in both daylight and evening hours. In addition to providing illumination, overall lighting can overcome any glare. This general lighting should use only white bulbs. Colored lighting effects should be achieved through highlighting with adjustable spotlights, but such special effects must always be used with extreme care to get proper results.

Highlighting

Spotlights, when used in windows, should be mounted behind either a valance or a frame. They may also be placed on the floor to highlight the focal point. This will set the mood and bring attention to an explanatory show card. For the novice, white spotlights are best. They throw a direct, bright, colorless, narrow beam in the direction pointed. Color, while most effective in display, can be disastrous if not employed correctly. Use of the wrong color light will change the color of the merchandise. In the theater you may have seen, purposely staged, the colors of costumes changed many times with lighting. For theatrical showmanship this is useful, but a customer entering a store and asking for the color seen in the window should find that color.

The important rule to remember when using colored light (achieved by using colored bulbs or, more commonly, by attaching colored gels, or colored transparent sheets, over white bulbs) is to use only lights of the same color as the merchandise you wish to highlight. A red light on a red dress will intensify the color; a different light will change the color.

With attention paid to these simple lighting fundamentals, a display can be well lighted and exciting enough to attract customers. With some experience and experimentation, more dramatic effects can be achieved. And drama is an attention-getter.

COLOR

Whether you are preparing to feature merchandise in a showcase, on a counter top, or in a window, the correct color coordination of merchandise is necessary for an eye-catching presentation.

An intensive survey of color is not intended in this book. The discussion will be limited to just enough information to permit the one responsible for merchandise selection to choose the appropriate color combinations for use in the presentation. The visual merchandiser's job is to show it to its best advantage.

Basically there are six colors, plus the neutrals, black, brown, and white. Three are primary colors: yellow, red, and blue. Orange, violet, and green are secondary colors. The easiest way to choose a color scheme is to use a color wheel.

There are unlimited color combinations that can be achieved by using these colors, but the person attempting to create an attractive display, perhaps on a platform in his or her department, should stay with some of the simpler color combinations.

Monochromatic Color

Monochromatic (*mono,* meaning one, and *chroma,* signifying color) arrangements center around the use of one color. Therefore, the merchandise would consist of all yellows or all reds, for example; for interest and variety, different values (lights or darks of the one color, such as light yellow to dark yellow) and different intensities (brightest to dullest tones of the same color) are used. Thus, a manager might select a wide range of blue merchandise, avoiding monotony by choosing light blues, dark blues, dull blues, and bright blues. Blacks, browns, and whites, technically not colors, can also be used, still maintaining a monochromatic scheme. In seasons where there is a particularly, universally accepted "fashion color," the monochromatic arrangement is perfect in a display.

Analogous Color

The incorporation of more than one color in a window can be achieved by selecting colors that are analogous (next to each other on the color wheel). For example, yellow and orange is an analogous color scheme; likewise blue and green, green and yellow, and so on. As was true in the monochromatic arrangements, different values and intensities plus black, brown, and white are added for interest and variety. An entire display might be worked around a two-color printed piece of merchandise (blue and violet, as an example) as a central or focal point in a window, with various other pieces in blues and violets. In this way, prints done in analogous combinations can be attractively displayed in both windows and interior displays. Artists' designs and color sections are often based on the same arrangements taken from the color wheel.

Complementary Color

Again, one must go back to the basic color wheel. By definition, complementary colors are direct opposites on the wheel. Yellow and violet, blue and orange, and red and green are complementary colors.

There are many, many other combinations, both common and unusual; such as split complementaries, double complementaries, and triadic schemes that can be used. Those with special color knowledge will automatically select other creative combinations. Until one gains that skill, staying within the simple guidelines will allow for the creation of safe color combinations of merchandise displays.

MATERIALS AND PROPS

The materials selected and the props used are important in enhancing the merchandise for sale. Window floors and platforms are covered in a variety of fabrics, carpets, paper, stones, plastics, simulated grass, sand, and other materials, while backgrounds employ from the simplest to the most elaborate papers, wood, or fabrics, depending upon the nature or theme of the display. A visit to the local supply house (most cities have them so that trimmers can select their background materials) will show the enormous variety of available materials. Props can vary from simple household articles such as chairs, ladders, and room divider screens to elaborate displays built by the store's visual merchandising department. Figure 14–21 (p. 304) shows an interior display that uses ladders as display props. Displays are also available, either by purchase or lease, from display houses, which one can visit when planning a Christmas presentation to see the wondrous creations for use in windows and interiors. Fully moving Santas, dancing elves, and skating children are just a few of the props available.

The selection of the materials and props without the assistance of a professional is often difficult. Keeping in mind the message you are trying to project plus the merchandise you are planning to sell will help you select the right materials. Aid is always available at the supply houses. The modern retailer who wishes to keep abreast of what is current and available in visuals should faithfully read the monthly publication, *Visual Merchandising & Store Design.*

SELECTING A THEME

As we discussed earlier, some retailers are taking a route that uses the environmental concept, which doesn't require constant changes for seasons, holidays, events, and so forth. The traditional approach, however, is still the one most widely used. Using their windows and interiors, retailers are constantly enhancing their environments with ever-changing visual presentations. The theme might be a holiday such as Christmas, which always uses the major portion of the visual department's budget. Or it might merely be the showing of a totally outfitted mannequin in a display case in the store or in a window. Themes might concentrate on just one product or might be rather general in nature. There are many approaches to use to achieve the store's goal.

Traditionalists still employ a variety of themes to enhance their stores. They include the *seasonal* types in which winter or summer props and colors, for example, depict the arrival of merchandise for a specific period of time, *ensemble* presentations in which an entire outfit is featured, *unit windows* that display an abundance of one item, *themes* that show a setting such as a beach, and *institutional* installations, such as a window that recognizes a charitable organization and is used to enhance the store's image.

A RETAILING FOCUS   Lord & Taylor

Lord & Taylor, a division of The May Department Stores Company, was established in 1826. It began as a small dry goods shop on Catherine Street in the heart of New York's commercial center. From the very beginning, the company provided its customers with the very best merchandise that could be found. Along with quality merchandise, the clientele was offered a high quality of standards and fine service. In 1914 the store established its flagship store on Fifth Avenue in New York City, where it still remains a grand, dignified establishment.

Figure 14–21   Interior display. *Courtesy:* Neiman Marcus

In addition to all of the pleasures of fashion merchandise that it has long provided, Lord & Taylor has gained recognition as one of the trail blazers in unique visual merchandising. While all stores in the organization feature carefully executed visual presentations, it is the New York City flagship that sparkles. Throughout the year, seasons and holidays are welcomed with grand visual displays. The centerpiece is the collection of grand windows on Fifth Avenue, which comes into its glory at Christmas.

The tradition of Lord & Taylor Christmas began in 1914 when the Fifth Avenue store's hydraulic windows were installed. To this day, Lord & Taylor is the only store in the country whose Christmas windows are assembled below street level and through the magic of hydraulic lifts are raised into place at street level. Each year the unveiling of the windows is a special ceremony that marks the official beginning of the Christmas season.

Creating the windows is a year-long process. The theme is discussed in January, when the current window's occupants have become history. Designs are started in February and final drawings of each window are completed by May. At that point, final research is undertaken to create a scene whose details are precise to the period and place depicted. Construction of the sets begins in July, and by the end of October the scenes are shipped to the store where the in-house team of visual merchandisers installs, decorates, and adds finishing touches.

Window themes have chronicled periods from as far back as the 1600s, depicting the historic houses of New York City, all the way up to modern day sites including the Roosevelt Island tramway and the New York City subway system. The 1989 windows depicted Radio City Music Hall, the lobby of the Daily News building, and the Rainbow Room (an elegant New York supper club) as they were in the 1930s. The displays were honored with awards from the Art Deco Society of New York.

Added interest in recent years has been the use of mechanical figures in each display. They move, swirl, and dance to the delight of the many onlookers. So huge are the crowds that assemble to view the spectacular windows that Lord & Taylor puts up brass rails, to keep the crowds in order, and a system to move the people along so that everyone may view the presentations. At Christmas, a trip to New York is not considered complete without attendance at the spectacular Lord & Taylor windows. Figure 14–22 features a Christmas window at the New York flagship store.

Figure 14–22   Christmas window at Lord & Taylor, New York, featuring antique toys in the City of New York Museum, 1932. *Courtesy:* Lord & Taylor

EXECUTION OF A PRESENTATION

An orderly plan should be followed in preparing a window or interior display. Generally, a window display is a more difficult task, but the suggestions previously discussed should be adhered to in the preparation of any visual project.

Selecting Merchandise

Although a great deal of emphasis is placed on background materials and props, the merchandise to be displayed is the most important consideration. Too often, the visual merchandiser overpowers the merchandise to be sold by paying excessive attention to the nonmerchandise factors. The merchandise should be timely, clean, carefully pressed (if this applies), and desirable in every way. A limitation of display often ignored by some retailers is the fact that it alone does not sell unwanted merchandise. But it does help to sell greater quantities of desirable merchandise. So, select those goods that will make the customer come through the door to purchase. Perhaps consumers will buy some unwanted merchandise once they are inside.

Selecting Materials and Props

For floor covering, fabric is easier to handle than paper. In addition, fabrics have a longer useful life. Stores frequently invest in neutral carpeting for window and interior platforms, eliminating the necessity of frequent change. Whatever is used, care should be taken to eliminate wrinkles and creases and to conceal staples.

Walls can be painted or lined with paper, fabric, or other material. The most important consideration in the selection of floor and wall coverings is that they must not overpower the merchandise, but enhance it. With attention paid to careful color selection in background materials as well as the merchandise, there will be color harmony.

The props should be consistent with the theme selected. For example, a back-to-school display might make use of chalkboards, school desks, rulers, erasers, and so on. A beach scene might employ such props as sun umbrellas, lifeguard chairs, beach chairs, and water wings. The props are important in setting the stage on which the merchandise is to be presented, so they should be carefully selected.

Some props are functional in addition to being decorative and permit an interesting display of merchandise. A dress draped over a settee, clothing suspended from a clothesline, and shoes arranged on a ladder are examples of imaginative ideas from a creative visual merchandiser.

Selecting Fixtures

Mannequins, "T" stands, blouse forms, and other fixtures should be selected next. If a wide choice of mannequins (or changeable wigs) is available, select those that best fit the merchandise. The youthful-looking, casual, standing female mannequin with a long, simple hair style is certainly better in a teen swimsuit window than is the sophisticated one with an elegant hair style.

If the props selected provide for the display of merchandise, fewer fixtures will be needed. The reverse is also true.

An overcrowded presentation leads to confusion. Select only those fixtures appropriate to the merchandise. Fight the tendency to include even one more than is absolutely necessary.

Preparations of Components

The preparation of the physical parts of the actual display centers around a program of "cleaning." In a store window, glass should be carefully washed before each display is executed. A film settles after a while on the inside of the glass because of gases, soot from heating devices, and so forth. Anything that distorts the viewer's ability to clearly observe the display must be eliminated. Care should be exercised in avoiding "streaks" from washing; handprints, often left by trimmers on the inside glass, should be removed.

The floors and walls of the window should be cleared of staples, nails, wires, and soil marks. All fixtures, including mannequins, should be cleaned. This not only guarantees a perfect picture for the customer, but also it avoids soiling the fresh merchandise being displayed.

A window is worthless without lighting, so light bulbs should be replaced when burned out. Colored bulbs or "gels" used to change white bulbs to color should be prepared if they are to be used.

Planning the Merchandise Arrangement

Perhaps the most difficult task for a person with no display experience is the problem of where and how to place the merchandise in an interesting and attractive arrangement. Following are some of the most important factors to consider in arranging the merchandise:

Balance

There are basically two types of balance: symmetrical and asymmetrical. The *symmetrical* is frequently referred to as formal balance. This is an arrangement in which, if the window were divided down the center, each side would have equal weight. This balance often tends to be dull, unoriginal, and monotonous to the viewer. An *asymmetrical* or informal balance is achieved by placing merchandise arrangements without a central axis. These displays are more difficult to execute and, while more exciting, should be left for later attempts.

Emphasis

Each presentation should have a point of emphasis, or focal point. This can be achieved through using a spotlight, setting the main item apart from the rest, featuring one item in a contrasting color while the remainder of the display is another color, and many other methods. Experience teaches different ways to achieve emphasis.

Contrast

Contrast can be achieved by use of more than one color, various sizes and shapes of merchandise and fixtures, and so on.

Space

Avoid overcrowding. Separating the various pieces in a window is important. If one piece of merchandise overlaps another, without being part of an ensemble, the eye doesn't know which belongs with which. The eye is incapable of absorbing very large segments. By allowing floor space to be visible between objects, the eye can outline each piece of merchandise separately. Raising merchandise from the floor on pedestals can help achieve separation and add interest to the display.

Trimming the Window

Once the plan is determined, the actual arrangement of merchandise on the floor, stands, platforms, pedestals, and mannequins takes place. The proper planning, with attention paid to all of the points discussed, should result in an attractive, well-coordinated window. An additional basic principle, which can be practiced by the trimmer only while actually "trimming" rather than being indicated on a layout plan, is the placement of various items. Small items should be placed up front. If they are placed in the rear of the window, they will not be seen. Generally, merchandise is arranged with the smallest in the front and the largest in the rear. Naturally, mannequins should not be placed in front of other merchandise that is displayed in the window.

The actual draping, pinning, and folding of window merchandise cannot be mastered by reading about it. This ability comes with the understanding of materials, shapes, and forms. A trip to a large store's visual department to watch how it's done, or instruction in this area will show how simple this operation is.

Preparing Price Tags and Copy Cards

The attractiveness of the merchandise in the proper setting will surely get a customer's attention. In the case of window displays, the store wants to bring the right customer inside to make a purchase. Since few consumers are knowledgeable enough to determine the prices and pertinent facts about the merchandise such as material content, the written part of the display is important. Without the price, at least, departments could become overcrowded with consumers who are not real prospects. In today's world of retailing, only the inexperienced retailer avoids the use of prices and copy cards to accompany his or her displays.

Before the preparation of the written material, the colors to be used for this purpose should be carefully selected. A safe choice is black lettering on white stock. This combination is neutral and easy to read. Other easy-to-read color arrangements are black on yellow, green on white, red on white, blue on white, and white on blue. In using these colors, make certain that they do not clash with the display's color scheme. Today, the computer has replaced the need for hand-lettered signage. With simple programs, a wealth of signs in all shapes and sizes may be constructed.

TRENDS

The methodology of visual merchandising has changed significantly over the years.

Less Use of Formal Windows

The newer retail environments are using the windowless window structure in place of traditional window types. Space is often limited and costly to lease, so this approach dominates the field.

Mannequin Types

Many retailers are opting for alternative mannequins in place of the traditional types. In addition to costing significantly less money, they are able to serve a greater variety of merchandising needs. The headless varieties, stylized "dressmaker forms" and figures that visual merchandisers create themselves are now commonplace in the industry.

Signage

In-store computers are used to create signage at a moment's notice. The day of the handwritten sign is practically nonexistent, and the need to go outside of the store, except for permanent signage, is often unnecessary.

Lighting

More and more use is being made of halogen/quartz bulbs, high-intensity discharge bulbs, and reduced wattage bulbs in both interiors and windows. Little fluorescent lighting is used except for overall illumination in value and discount operations where costs must be minimized.

Decrease in Use of Formal Displays

Instead of making visual changes every week, as was once traditional in retailing, many stores are opting for settings that are long lasting and do not require changes. Ralph Lauren, for example, stays with a residential atmosphere that transcends seasons, and Disney relies upon animation that is appropriate year round.

ACTION FOR THE INDEPENDENT RETAILER

Visual merchandising, to be effective, must be timely. To have appeal and properly motivate purchasing, a presentation need not be overwhelmingly expensive. If the independent retailer keeps in mind both of these points, the displaying of merchandise could bring increased sales.

A waste of valuable space occurs in both the store's window and its interior if the theme has passed. For example, a Valentine's Day display that lingers a few days after the holiday is valueless. Large stores that have separate visual personnel and adhere to window and interior calendars are usually on target. It's the independent who often exhibits a stale display. A little planning could alleviate such a problem without requiring much money.

Since the sums spent by the larger companies cannot be expended by their smaller counterparts, the independent retailer's dollar must be wisely spent, Free-lance trimmers are available. Often, their fees include the use of their own props. If the store is fashion oriented, displays could be professionally executed, once for each season, and for some of the important sales-related holidays. In between, with a little effort, the featured merchandise in the display could be changed by the owner or an employee, without changing the background props. With a completely different color scheme each week, the display could have a fresh look. If this approach is used, it is best to ask the free-lancer to install neutral props that can be easily adapted to a variety of merchandise.

In situations in which hiring a professional person is too costly, even on a periodic basis, the retailer could use permanent background materials that could be slightly accented with seasonal additions. For example, a men's shop might install a permanent wooden wall in the window, carpet the floor, and use sturdy glass, wooden, or chrome display fixtures. A sprinkling of autumn leaves might be sufficient to indicate a change in season.

By constantly scanning the windows and interiors of larger stores, the independent with even the smallest store can become "visually educated" and satisfactorily execute the store's window and interior displays.

IMPORTANT POINTS IN THE CHAPTER

1. The development of the store's visual program is carried out by in-house teams, visual merchandisers who plan displays centrally, or free-lancers.

2. An environmental concept for visual presentation has been adopted by some retailers.

3. One of the functions of visual merchandising is to attract customers' attention and arouse enough interest to make them want to investigate the merchandise more fully.

4. A window schedule should be prepared for large stores to properly apportion space as well as give management the proper amount of time for specific displays.

5. Devices on which merchandise can be shown to its best advantage are called display fixtures. Fixtures may be forms that simulate the human figure or parts of the figure. Various types of stands, platforms, and pedestals are used to drape or elevate the merchandise.

6. Human form figures are available in a variety of materials that range in design from lifelike human replicas to stylized figures. The type of figure used depends in large part on the image of the store and the merchandise to be featured.

7. The imaginative use of color and lighting are vital if a visual presentation is to be a provocative, eye-catching device. Color and lighting provide the dramatic possibilities that make effective visual merchandising an art.

8. In the execution of the installation, selecting the merchandise to be displayed is the most important consideration. The merchandise should be appropriate, clean, carefully pressed, and desirable in every way.

REVIEW QUESTIONS

1. Who develops the retailers' visual merchandising approaches?
2. What are the important functions of visual merchandising?
3. What is meant by environmental visual merchandising?
4. For what purposes are colored lights used?
5. What kind of care must be exercised in selecting the colored lights to be used on merchandise?
6. Define *intensity* and *value* as they relate to color.
7. What is a monochromatic color scheme? How can the display person avoid monotony with this color arrangement?
8. What is an institutional display? Why do stores use them?
9. What is the most important part of any visual presentation?
10. What is the difference between symmetrical and asymmetrical balance?
11. What is a focal point? How can this be achieved?
12. Why must a visual merchandiser plan a window before executing the installation?
13. Are price tags always important in a window display? Defend your position.
14. Why, with all the merchandise attractively shown in windows, is a copy card generally deemed important?

CASE PROBLEMS

Case Problem 1

Frank Rogers and Peter Daniels have decided to open the first of what they hope will be many ladies' specialty stores. The first store is located in the middle of a large shopping center and has overall dimensions of 18 feet by 100 feet. It caters to a clientele generally in the $25,000 to $40,000 income bracket. There are a great number of stores in the center carrying the usual diversification of merchandise. Rogers and Daniels, after much planning, have decided to appeal to women of 20 to 40 years of age. Their merchandise assortment will be fashionable, but not extreme. The price range will be moderate. For example, dresses will retail from $75 to $150, pants and sweaters from $30 to $70, and so on.

The two partners have decided on all policies, assignment of responsibility, store hours, and so on. The decision hasn't been settled thus far as to which type of mannequins should be purchased. Many suggestions have been offered, but the two partners can't come to a final decision.

Questions

1. What factors should be considered in determining the type of mannequin to use?
2. Which type would you select? Why?

Case Problem 2

Each year at Hagelman's Department Store, the buyers and department managers are asked by the store's visual merchandising director to submit those dates that are important to their respective departments for space in the store's windows. Since there isn't enough window space for each department to display its merchandise all the time, the space must be allocated in order of importance. For example, a toy department might be given preference at Christmas. Generally window displays are left intact for one week.

Hagelman's, like most department stores, has many departments, such as misses' coats and suits, junior sportswear, lingerie, bridal clothing, menswear, toys, appliances, shoes, hosiery, and sporting goods. The window space is limited to six windows that are parallel to the sidewalk, three on either side of the main entrance. Traditionally, departments have requested and received all windows at one time. It has been felt that in this way a department could really show the public its wide selection of goods.

At this time, all department's requests are in for window space. There is duplication of the dates needed by various departments. The display manager now has the task of making the window assignment.

Questions

1. List those dates or events that you would submit to the visual department for each department mentioned in the case.
2. What factors would you consider in assigning space if more than one department requested the windows for the same period?
3. Do you believe it sound for one department to occupy all six windows at one time? Choose a position and defend it.
4. Prepare a window calendar, listing the departments (from those given) you would assign space and for which dates they would be assigned.

Chapter 15
Direct Retailing

Courtesy: Neiman Marcus

LEARNING OBJECTIVES

Upon completion of this chapter, the student should be able to:

1. Discuss the reasons for the growth of direct retailing.
2. Explain the advantage of toll-free 800 numbers to the direct retailer and the consumer.
3. Differentiate between internal and external lists.
4. Tell about the importance of cable TV to direct retailing and the expected future of this outlet.
5. Differentiate between the merchandise mixes of store inventories and those of direct retailers.

YOU NEED NOT LEAVE THE HOUSE TO BUY A 56-CARAT DIAMOND . . .

It is no trick today to satisfy one's purchasing needs without going to the store. Shoppers might opt to sit comfortably and make selections on the numerous shopping networks without leaving their seats. Consumers in search of even greater selections may browse through the many catalogs that come with regularity to their homes. The merchandise available through each of these media includes everything from exotic foods to household items and fashion apparel and accessories. Many residences receive an average of three catalogs a day during the peak selling periods such as Christmas, Easter, and back-to-school times, and the choices are practically unlimited. There is, however, a shortage of truly unique items that are available to those who shop at home. Although Hammacher Schlemmer, for example, offers interesting novelty items for the most discriminating of shoppers in its catalogs, and Patagonia does likewise for cold-weather enthusiasts, and Neiman Marcus takes the prize for offering the most outrageous items, items not to be found anywhere else but in its Christmas Book.

The Christmas Book is mailed in October to everyone with a Neiman Marcus credit card. It features a variety of traditional fare, but also offers a selection of products that few ever imagined existed. As a special feature in what is known as the world's most famous catalog, "His" and "Her" gifts have been made available in limited quantities for more than fifty years. Previous catalogs have featured such novelties as airplanes, ermine bathrobes, submarines, camels, mummy cases, windmills, and, of course, his and her diamonds that are not available anywhere else. Featured in the 1985 Christmas Book, his stone was a natural yellow 56-carat diamond, the largest ever certified as "intensely natural yellow" by the Gemological Institute of America; hers was a smaller gem of 21 carats in the same coloration. The startling fact about these offerings is that they actually sell. Neiman Marcus has successfully marketed these products for years and years.

The key to success of any direct mail piece is to have full knowledge of the market one is trying to reach and to be able to satisfy the needs of that market with the right merchandise mix. The success of the Neiman Marcus catalog indicates that this company has regularly been on target.

Throughout this text we have discussed retailing as it involves customers visiting stores to select the merchandise that suits their tastes. In recent years there has been a surge in retail volume that depends upon customers who shop without leaving their homes. The major area of in-home selling has been through catalogs, which have increased their sales volume by 10 to 15 percent per year—twice the growth rate of traditional retailers during the past five years. The amount from home television buyers, though smaller in volume than catalog sales, has also been on an upward spiral.

The fact is that anyone living within the limits or in the suburbs of a large or medium-sized city can find just about any merchandise listed in a retail catalog by simply going to a local department store or a branch of one of the specialty chains. Moreover, the goods can be felt, tried on, and often found at a better price. Not too long ago catalog users were only those people who lived in rural areas and had no other access to the merchandise. Why then the growing appeal of catalogs?

REASONS FOR GROWTH

Among the reasons direct retailing is growing are convenience, toll-free numbers, credit cards, and others that will be discussed.

Convenience

The main attraction of shopping from home is its convenience. Some years ago the traditional role of a housewife was to stay at home and care for the family. Shopping time was fairly easy to arrange, and a trip to the store was often fun. In 7 out of 10 of today's households there is no adult at home during the day to do the shopping. In such homes shopping is anything but fun. It requires a hassle with traffic, crowded stores, and the waste of very limited, precious leisure time. How much easier it is to thumb through a catalog, make a free call to an 800 telephone number (at any time, day or night), use a credit card, and wait for delivery. Not only that, it is also fun to receive the package. Any catalog shopper will tell you that although one knows what to expect, opening the package is a little like Christmas. As the number of two-earner families continues to increase, direct retailing will keep pace.

Another segment of the population that is turning to in-home shopping is the elderly. Here too, convenience is the principal motivation. Compare leafing through a catalog, or even several catalogs for ten minutes, with the hours it would take to complete a shopping trip. For people who tire easily, or do not always feel well, in-home shopping offers great advantages. America is and will continue to be an aging country. The use of in-home shopping services to this segment of the country will continue to grow. Shopping is made easy with the use of catalogs like the one from Horchow in Figure 15–1.

Toll-Free 800 Numbers

Not long ago, catalog buyers placed their orders by filling out an order form that was found in the catalog and mailing it, with a check or money order, to the catalog

Figure 15–1 The Horchow catalog makes shopping easy. *Courtesy:* The Horchow Collection

retailer. The widespread use of the 800 toll-free telephone number has changed all of this. Now placing an order is as simple as making a telephone call at any time, day or night, and speaking to a polite, well-trained operator. The customer order form in Figure 15–2 clearly features the use of the 800 number 24 hours a day, seven days a week.

A new type of telephone number is now being considered by retailers. This is the 700 number. It is exactly the same as the 800 number except that there is a 50 cent charge for the call. In return for this, the caller would get some kind of special treatment. This could include having the call answered on the first ring, or having the order filled first if there is not enough inventory to fill all of the orders.

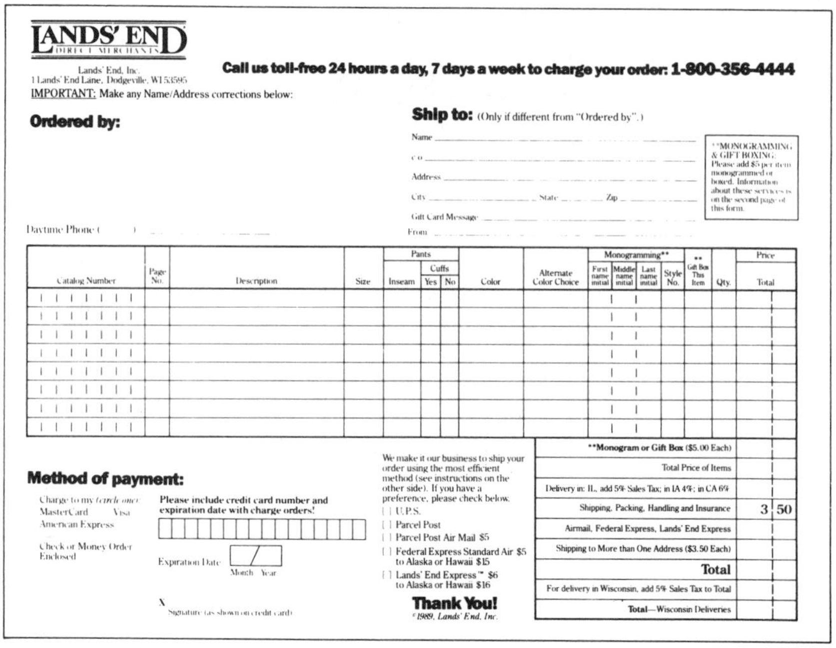

LANDS' END
DIRECT MERCHANTS

Lands' End, Inc.
1 Lands' End Lane, Dodgeville, WI 53595

Call us toll-free 24 hours a day, 7 days a week to charge your order: 1-800-356-4444

IMPORTANT: Make any Name/Address corrections below:

Ordered by:

Daytime Phone ( )

Ship to: (Only if different from "Ordered by".)

Name
c/o
Address
City State Zip
Gift Card Message
From

**MONOGRAMMING & GIFT BOXING: Please add $5 per item monogrammed or boxed. Information about these services is on the second page of this form.

Catalog Number	Page No.	Description	Size	Pants: Inseam	Pants: Cuffs Yes	Pants: Cuffs No	Color	Alternate Color Choice	Monogramming**: First name initial	Monogramming**: Middle name initial	Monogramming**: Last name initial	Monogramming**: Style No.	** Gift Box This Item	Qty.	Price Total

Method of payment:

Charge to my (circle one): MasterCard Visa American Express

Check or Money Order Enclosed

Please include credit card number and expiration date with charge orders!

Expiration Date Month Year

X
Signature (as shown on credit card)

We make it our business to ship your order using the most efficient method (see instructions on the other side). If you have a preference, please check below.
[ ] U.P.S.
[ ] Parcel Post
[ ] Parcel Post Air Mail $5
[ ] Federal Express Standard Air $5 to Alaska or Hawaii $15
[ ] Lands' End Express™ $6 to Alaska or Hawaii $16

Thank You!
© 1989, Lands' End, Inc.

**Monogram or Gift Box ($5.00 Each)	
Total Price of Items	
Delivery in: IL, add 5% Sales Tax; in IA 4%; in CA 6%	
Shipping, Packing, Handling and Insurance	3.50
Airmail, Federal Express, Lands' End Express	
Shipping to More than One Address ($3.50 Each)	
Total	
For delivery in Wisconsin, add 5% Sales Tax to Total	
Total—Wisconsin Deliveries	

Figure 15–2 Customer order form for direct merchandise orders. *Courtesy:* Lands' End, Inc.

Credit Cards

The use of credit cards helps direct retailers in several ways. Of course, without credit cards, telephone ordering would not work. In addition, credit card users are not required to pay their bills until the following month. This extra time is important to many people. Finally, many people want to see the merchandise before the payment is actually made.

Improved Catalog Operations

Another important factor in the success of direct retailing is the improvement in catalog and in-home offerings. Catalog retailers have improved their offerings, targeting, catalog layouts, and service. Where once their offerings were staples offered to rural customers, they now offer highly styled merchandise to sophisticated buyers.

Among the various types of retailers that cater to the in-home buying markets, catalogers are by far the most important. It has been estimated that as many as 12 to 15 billion catalogs are distributed each year. While this seems like a glut on the market, experts point out that the problem is that there are too many *mediocre* catalogs being mailed, rather than just too many catalogs. Dramatic stories of success in this field have led many people to jump into the catalog business as an easy way to become rich. In fact, success requires a great deal of knowledge, skill and specialized ability.

The Target

As in all successful retailing, the more the retailer knows about the target (that is, the customer or prospective customer), the better the chance of satisfying his or her needs.

This knowledge permits the merchandise mix and prices to be focused on the specific requirements of the potential buyers.

Lands' End, a very successful cataloger whose operation is widely accepted as a model of catalog efficiency, knows a great deal about its customers. By comparing customer information with that provided by the U.S. Census Bureau, it has come up with the following information:

- 40 percent of the total United States population has some college education versus 90 percent of Lands' End customers.
- Lands' End customers are five times more likely to have some postgraduate study.
- Professional jobs are held by 70 percent of its customers.
- Of Lands' End's women customers, 75 percent work outside of the home.
- While only 33 percent of United States families have incomes in excess of $35,000 per year, 65 percent of Lands' End customers have such income.

In addition to this census type of information, the company also understands its customers' attitudes and lifestyles. It knows, for example, that its customers are involved in many outdoor sports and do more traveling than the general population.

With this information, and much more that has not been noted here, it becomes relatively easy to provide a merchandise mix, catalog format and text, and price range that make up the company's mailing list.

The Merchandise Mix

The major difference between merchandising for a traditional retail store and merchandising for a catalog is targeting. Anyone can, and indeed does, walk into a retail store. The merchandise mix, therefore, must offer a wide assortment. The customers must go through everything on the racks before finding the item that pleases them. In contrast, the catalog merchandiser knows the customers and has a good idea of what they are looking for. Essentially, the catalog retailer goes through the racks for the customer and helps with the selection procedure. By limiting the merchandise mix to that which the targeted customer has in mind, the same amount of money invested in inventory can offer the in-home buyer a much wider selection of goods.

One of the problems that catalogers have with merchandising is that they cannot be flexible in their offerings. Where a traditional retailer can pick up a trendy new, "hot item" almost overnight, catalog retailers have to live with their catalog for months. For this reason the merchandise selected for the catalog must be classical and traditional. They can be "updated" classics, but they can't be fad-like.

Another difficulty with catalog selling is that some goods simply do not sell well in catalogs. Their appeal lies in being seen or felt. Catalog photography cannot do justice to a beautiful, small print, nor can a picture of an expensive cashmere sweater indicate its silky softness of texture. Figure 15–3 shows how the J.C. Penney catalog helps to sell goods that are otherwise difficult to sell in catalogs.

Service

One very important factor in the success of a catalog operation is service. Naturally, telephone calls must be answered promptly and courteously, but the operator's job goes much further than that. Because of space limitations, catalog descriptions must

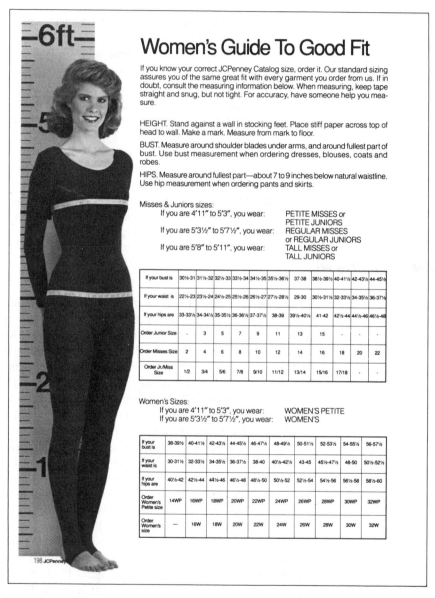

Women's Guide To Good Fit

If you know your correct JCPenney Catalog size, order it. Our standard sizing assures you of the same great fit with every garment you order from us. If in doubt, consult the measuring information below. When measuring, keep tape straight and snug, but not tight. For accuracy, have someone help you measure.

HEIGHT. Stand against a wall in stocking feet. Place stiff paper across top of head to wall. Make a mark. Measure from mark to floor.

BUST. Measure around shoulder blades under arms, and around fullest part of bust. Use bust measurement when ordering dresses, blouses, coats and robes.

HIPS. Measure around fullest part—about 7 to 9 inches below natural waistline. Use hip measurement when ordering pants and skirts.

Misses & Juniors sizes:

If you are 4'11" to 5'3", you wear:	PETITE MISSES or PETITE JUNIORS
If you are 5'3½" to 5'7½", you wear:	REGULAR MISSES or REGULAR JUNIORS
If you are 5'8" to 5'11", you wear:	TALL MISSES or TALL JUNIORS

If your bust is	30½-31	31½-32	32½-33	33½-34	34½-35	35½-36½	37-38	38½-39½	40-41½	42-43½	44-45½
If your waist is	22½-23	23½-24	24½-25	25½-26	26½-27	27½-28½	29-30	30½-31½	32-33½	34-35½	36-37½
If your hips are	33-33½	34-34½	35-35½	36-36½	37-37½	38-39	39½-40½	41-42	42½-44	44½-46	46½-48
Order Junior Size	-	3	5	7	9	11	13	15	-	-	-
Order Misses Size	2	4	6	8	10	12	14	16	18	20	22
Order Jr./Miss Size	1/2	3/4	5/6	7/8	9/10	11/12	13/14	15/16	17/18	-	-

Women's Sizes:

If you are 4'11" to 5'3", you wear:	WOMEN'S PETITE
If you are 5'3½" to 5'7½", you wear:	WOMEN'S

If your bust is	38-39½	40-41½	42-43½	44-45½	46-47½	48-49½	50-51½	52-53½	54-55½	56-57½
If your waist is	30-31½	32-33½	34-35½	36-37½	38-40	40½-42½	43-45	45½-47½	48-50	50½-52½
If your hips are	40½-42	42½-44	44½-46	46½-48	48½-50	50½-52	52½-54	54½-56	56½-58	58½-60
Order Women's Petite size	14WP	16WP	18WP	20WP	22WP	24WP	26WP	28WP	30WP	32WP
Order Women's size	—	16W	18W	20W	22W	24W	26W	28W	30W	32W

198 JCPenney

Figure 15–3 "Proper measuring" eliminates customer returns when ordering by catalog. *Courtesy:* J. C. Penney

be brief, and the operator must be able to fill in details at the customer's request. In addition, the operator should be adept at cross-selling. This is a procedure in which the would-be purchaser is advised of a particular handbag that would go well with shoes that are being offered. Calling attention to this week's specials is another example of cross-selling. Obviously, the operator must be a skillful, highly trained individual. Since no operator can be knowledgeable about all of the merchandise in a large catalog, computer terminals are usually found at each operator's desk. The software involved must provide the operator with product information as well as all of the information necessary for cross-selling. Interestingly, customers seem to build a better relationship with long distance operators than with retail salespeople that they meet face-to-face. Customer feedback, so valuable to merchandisers, is far greater in volume for catalogers than for traditional retailers.

Good service does not end with telephone operators. Orders must be taken from stock and sent with a minimum of delay. Catalogers must bear in mind that they are competing with retail stores where the merchandise is handed over to the customer as soon as the sale is made.

A RETAILING FOCUS   L. L. Bean

When L. L. Bean was 39 years old and a partner in a small dry goods store he had an idea for a hunting boot that would keep the feet dry. He had a local shopmaker sew a light weight leather upper to the bottom of an ordinary pair of galoshes. He tried it, it worked, and he sent circulars to prospects who had Maine hunting licenses. He called it the Maine Hunting Shoe. It was a flop—90 of the first hundred pairs came back because the stitching didn't hold. Bean returned the money ($3.50 each), tried again, and the L.L. Bean organization was off and running.

That 100% Guarantee continues to be the foundation of L. L. Bean's customer philosophy. The company, still located on Main Street in Freeport, Maine, sells more than 16,000 products through 26 catalogs and a downtown retail store. Although L. L. Bean has evolved and grown since those early days, one constant remains—a strong customer commitment, backed by the same satisfaction promised by Leon Leonwood Bean, more than 80 years ago.

In retail stores, a customer can see, feel, and try on the merchandise. An in-home shopper can do none of these things. He or she must depend upon the integrity and quality of service of the merchant. L. L. Bean built a huge retailing empire by offering confidence-building service from day one. Figure 15–4 shows an L. L. Bean Catalog.

Another important service area is returns. Liberal return policies have become a standard for the industry. Lands' End permits returns at any time, for any reason. At Talbot's, a combined retail store and catalog company that mails out 70 million copies of its catalogs per year, catalog returns may be made at any of its retail outlets. The store and catalog operations work very closely together. The stores each have Red Line Telephones. These are connected to catalog operators, and the customer can make an immediate call to place a catalog order for an item that is not available in the store.

Price

Pricing is a very sensitive area for catalogers. Most of their offerings are classically and traditionally styled. Since this is the case, the same merchandise can easily be

Figure 15–4   L. L. Bean catalog. *Courtesy:* L. L. Bean

found in most stores. It can and will be comparison shopped. Therefore, pricing must be at least competitive or slightly lower. After all, if a customer has to wait a week for the delivery of a solid color sweater, he or she should not have to overpay as well.

Integrity

One of the principal difficulties to be overcome in converting a traditional shopper to a catalog user is embodied in the comment, "How can I shop by catalog when I cannot be sure of what I'm getting?" The cataloger can only respond by acting with complete integrity. The merchandise must be delivered absolutely as presented in the catalog. Repeat customers, the lifeblood of any retail operation, cannot be maintained by shipping goods that do not meet promised standards.

Department Store Shortcomings

Department stores are encountering serious problems. Faced with enormously high overhead and strong competition from specialty shops and catalogers, some have been forced to cut back on expenses. One of the few areas available for cost savings is sales floor salaries. As a result, shopping in a department store has become difficult. Salespersons are difficult to find and cashier lines are long and slow moving. How much easier it is to thumb through a catalog and dial a toll-free number.

RETAILER TO CATALOGER

Many large retailers, recognizing the importance of catalogs, have met this competition by joining it. J. C. Penney is a typical example. It uses its catalogs to build volume in its stores, and to sell to those with limited time to shop. Recognizing the fact that no store can stock the tremendous assortment of sizes, colors, and styles that can be shown in a catalog, Penney considers its catalog a huge, 12-million-square-foot back-up store. This vastly expands the merchandise offerings available to the customer. When a shopper is unable to find a particular item in a store, he or she is led to a catalog center and instructed in its use. A number of freestanding catalog centers are located in markets not served by the company's stores.

J. C. Penney takes orders placed by customers 24 hours a day, seven days a week. There are 7,000 order takers at 16 locations, and a sophisticated communications system routes each call in order of priority to the center best able to handle the calls during the busy hours. The operators take the orders or suggest alternate merchandise in out-of-stock situations. The orders can be picked up at the store in two or three days, or delivered directly to the customer's home. Unsatisfied customers can return the merchandise for any reason. Most credit cards are acceptable.

The major portion of Penney's catalog sales volume comes from its two big books:Fall/Winter and Spring/Summer. Each of these is sent to some 10 million customers and contains merchandise for the entire family. They include merchandise not carried in the J. C. Penney department stores such as lawn mowers, golf clubs, cameras, and toys. They run about 1,500 pages each. These catalogs are supplemented by about 50 seasonal promotional and specialty catalogs. Specialty catalogs are much smaller and are targeted at such markets as large-sized women, tall women, big men, brides, maternity, workwear, and uniforms. Many of these catalogs are sent to regular store customers.

Unlike J. C. Penney which considers its catalog business a means of building retail store volume, Talbot's runs its mail and store operations as two separate divisions that work together to serve a single targeted customer: a woman over 25 years old with an above-average education who is likely to hold a professional or managerial job. Talbot's mails a total of 70 million copies of its 24 catalogs in the United States and 16 foreign countries. The product is women's clothing and accessories. The merchandise shown in the catalog is similar to that found in the stores, but the assortment shown in the catalog is much wider. Although run as separate entities, there is some overlap between the catalogs and store divisions. Stores, for example, will accept catalog returns, and catalog customers may have the merchandise ordered delivered to the store or home according to the customer's need. Another area of integration between the two divisions is the Red Line Telephone found in each store. A customer who cannot find a desired size or color in the store can use the Red Line Telephone to place a catalog order.

Many catalogers maintain chains of stores to capitalize on their good names. Brookstone, Banana Republic, and Sharper Image are typical. Lands' End maintains eight outlet stores at which it sells overstocks, end-of-season closeouts, and customer returns. L. L. Bean, on the other hand, has only one store, but it is a winner. The store contains 120 thousand square feet of space and grosses about $70 million a year, making Freeport, Maine a tourist attraction and luring some three and a half million shoppers there each year.

One advantage that catalogers get by opening stores is that the retail outlet provides catalog customers. At Brookstone, for example, 25 percent of its mail order lists are from sales generated at its stores. There are disadvantages as well. For one thing, it is much more expensive to build, equip, and staff a retail store than it is to add pages to a catalog, and the return on investment is much lower. Moreover, the retail store business is quite different from the catalog business. Running a successful catalog operation does not guarantee success in retail stores.

COMPETITION

The Direct Marketing Association, the major trade association for catalog companies, estimates that some ten thousand catalog companies will mail in the neighborhood of 12 billion catalogs each year. That comes to about 50 catalogs for each person living in the United States. The result of this is that while the annual gross sales of the catalog industry as a whole continues to show strong growth, the competition has become very fierce. A problem arises from the fact that the start up costs, the cost of getting into business, are relatively small. This, coupled with the amazing success stories of people who have gone into the business, results in a steady stream of new catalogers. In addition, third-class postal rates and paper and printing costs are steadily rising. All of this has led to an industry-wide decrease in the sales per catalog, an important indicator of success.

Some of the catalog giants are among those having the greatest difficulty. Spiegel Inc., one of the big three, has had trouble. Montgomery Ward's, Esprit De Corp, and Pier I Imports all went out of the catalog business. Even mighty Sears ended its catalog operation in favor of store expansion.

KIOSKS

Perhaps the most important indicator of the importance of catalogs to the American public is the fact that they are being sold in newsstands in direct competition with magazines. There has been a trend in recent years for catalogers to charge for their more lavish publications, so the shock of paying for a catalog is not too great. They are being sold in thousands of locations in freestanding kiosks next to magazine counters and are doing very well. Newsstands love them since the catalogers, anxious to get their message across, are much more liberal in giving the newsstand a share of the profits.

DIRECT MAIL

Another important method that marketers use to attract the retail business of in-home shoppers is direct mail. It is similar to catalog selling in that the postal service is used to solicit customers and to deliver the merchandise. However, rather than send a catalog displaying a wide range of merchandise, direct mailers send a letter (or package), containing information on a single or a few related items. Naturally, with so few offerings, the sales volume that can be achieved by a direct mailer does not approach that of a cataloger. Another negative in the comparison of direct mail and catalog operations is the fact that printing and mailing costs per piece are far lower for catalogers where the total printing and mailing costs are shared among many items of merchandise. But many people, businesses, and even catalogers do very well by sending direct mail pieces to carefully selected customers.

There are advantages as well. Principal among them is the availability of creativity. Direct mail is not limited to the format and brief message required by catalogs. For example, when Porsche Cars North America, Inc. saw dealership inventories accumulating for its 1988 model 944s, it sent a mailing of 200,000 pieces of a three-dimensional package. The mailing was sent to a carefully selected list of males aged 35 to 55 with an average income of $80,000 per year (other characteristics were taken into account as well). The mailing, including a poster of a red Porsche, was sent in a tube-like package. The campaign resulted in the sale of 308 cars at about $45,000 each in a five-month period.

Another advantage of the use of direct mail is flexibility in scheduling. Other advertising media depend upon the availability of time or space. Even catalogs are restricted by dates of mailing. Direct mailers, on the other hand, can send out their packages whenever they wish to.

LISTS

As we have seen, a major portion of the success of the cataloger lies in its ability to target its books to people whose characteristics make them likely prospects. That is, Lands' End looks for well-educated professionals who have family incomes in excess of $35,000 with two working spouses. Its computers keep lists of such families and constantly updates them, dropping those that are no longer active and adding new names when they become available.

Targeting is far more important to direct mail sellers than it is to catalogers. The books offer a wide range of items, and the chance of finding a fit between their merchandise and the customer's needs are fairly good. Consider, on the other hand, the problems of the direct mail sellers who have only one or a few closely related items to sell. Considering the high cost per item of the mailing, it is vital that their lists be extremely sharply focused. If, for example, the item to be sold is an expensive baby car seat, you would have to know the size and make-up of the family, and the type of car (no pick-up trucks), as well as financial status and other demographic information.

Internal Lists

The most important lists are those generated from a company's own files. The people most likely to buy are those who have bought before or those who have made inquiries directly to the company. The lists should contain as much pertinent data as possible; age, family size, economic status, and so forth, in addition to names and addresses. Where specialty catalogs or direct mail pieces are used, information on the products previously purchased is vital. Men who buy work clothes should receive the specialty catalog that features them. J. C. Penny, for example, uses a special designation added to the style number for large-sized women. A woman who orders a size 42 blouse from its general catalog is then automatically added to its list of those who receive the specialty catalog for large-sized women.

Because of the mass of data involved in these lists (called databases), powerful computers are required to keep the information available and up to date. However, even the largest computers become overburdened and care must be taken to limit the information in the database to that which is absolutely necessary.

External Lists

Internal lists rarely satisfy in-home retailers who use the mail to sell their products. They tend to grow stale and do not increase in size quickly enough to satisfy the expansion plans of management. External lists are readily available. These are generally purchased through brokers and are bought by even the largest of catalog sellers. The brokers get the lists from a wide variety of sources including magazine publishers and even competitors. Research has shown that letting competitors have a list of a cataloger's customers has very little, if any, effect on the list-selling company's sales volume. List selling is an important source of income.

There are thousands of lists available for sale. They include such information as annual earnings, automobile preferences, leisure sport activities, vacation preferences, grocery products used, and much more. In fact, it is probably possible to acquire a list or group of lists that will yield any combination of characteristics desired. The problem is that the per name cost will be very high. A more typical list is this one, advertised in a recent issue of the periodical *Direct Marketing:* "1,000,000 nurses that subscribe to *Nurses Magazine* that are book, catalog, and videocassette buyers." This list might be a good bet for a direct mail piece or cataloger offering nurses' clothing.

Direct mailers who face the problem of pinpoint targeting frequently use Zip code numbers for their mass mailings. There are approximately 43,000 Zip codes in the United States, and using the theory that "birds of a feather flock together," they send their offers to all residents in a particular Zip code. Each Zip code contains about 4,000 families who generally have such similar characteristics as ethnic and religious backgrounds, annual income, and so on. As a result, residents of Zip codes 90210 (Beverly Hills, California) and 60022 (Glencoe, Illinois) will receive mail offering gold credit cards and expensive cruises, while those families living in Zip code 10032 (Harlem, New York) will receive offers of inexpensive life insurance. The trouble with Zip codes is that they are really not pure enough. Within each Zip code live families that do not fit the predominant characteristics. This results in the waste of an expensive mail offering. To overcome this, the United States Census

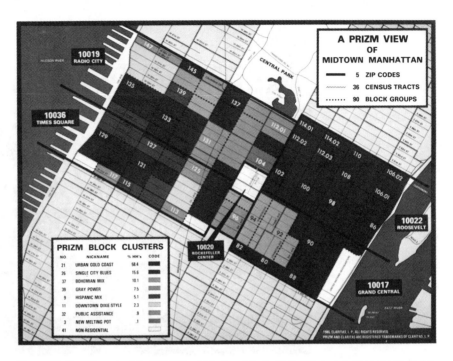

Figure 15–5 "Clustering" the 250,000 neighborhoods in the United States into 40 segments or clusters. *Courtesy:* Claritas Corp., Alexandria, VA

Bureau offers, at cost, what they call census blocks. These are breakdowns of Zip codes into smaller units, with more common characteristics. It is even possible to obtain lists by carrier route, that is, the families covered by the route of a particular mail carrier. Unfortunately, as the targeting becomes finer, the costs of such lists rise dramatically.

Clusters

Perhaps the most sophisticated lists are those provided by the Claritas Corporation of Alexandria, Virginia. They have arranged the United States' 250,000 neighborhoods into some 40 clusters with similar lifestyles. Each cluster is given a name and, although widely scattered geographically, the residents live remarkably similar lifestyles. For example, the cluster called "Young Suburbia" consists of college-educated, white-collar workers, aged 25 to 44, who are mostly white, and conservative voters. In addition, Claritas gives some 60 other characteristics such as television, food, automobile, and investment preferences. Young Suburbia members are likely to live in Pleasantown, California; Egan, Minnesota; Dale City, Virginia; and many similar places throughout the country. Figure 15–5 features a graphic presentation of clustering.

CABLE TELEVISION

When in-home shopping first exploded on the retailing scene in 1982, the idea was to sell closeout merchandise at bargain prices. By 1990 industry-wide sales exceeded $1.5 billion and the closeouts, porcelain figures, stuffed toys, and other knick-knacks

Figure 15–6 Programming schedule for QVC Network, Inc., a cable TV network selling to the in-home market. *Courtesy:* QVC Network, Inc.

Figure 15–7 QVC hostess, Kathy Levine, explains and demonstrates each product for the cable audience. *Courtesy:* QVC Network, Inc.

Figure 15–8   Operators taking orders for merchandise featured on cable television. *Courtesy:* QVC Cable Network, Inc.

were replaced by the regular merchandise of J. C. Penney, Neiman Marcus, Brooks Brothers, and Jordan Marsh.

Industry growth has not been without problems. From 1982 to 1988 everything was great, and everybody, including several of the retailing giants jumped in. In 1988, high costs, competition, and a shortage of cable channels caused a shake-out in the industry, and since then, 30 of the 50 shopping channels have gone off the air. These included Kmart, Dayton Hudson, and Consolidated Stores. At the time of this writing the problems seem to have been solved, and industry-wide sales are booming again. Figure 15–6 features a programming schedule for cable TV and Figure 15–7 shows a cable TV hostess demonstrating the products to the audience.

The television sales industry is dominated by two major organizations that together account for about 90 percent of the total volume. These two, the Home Shopping Network and the QVC Network, are vying for industry leadership. Until 1989 The Home Shopping Network dominated the field with QVC in third place. At the end of 1989, QVC bought out the second place firm CVN, and it and The Home Shopping Network are about equal in size.

QVC (Quality, Value, Convenience) breaks its programs down into segments and sends its customers a program guide that lists a date and time for each segment so that viewers need not spend hours waiting for the product in which they are interested to be shown on the screen. For example, at 1:00 Pacific Time "Ideas to Beautify Your Home" will appear, followed at 2:00 by "Fashion Coordinates." Like all television shopping programs, QVC offers games and prizes. Once an hour a scrambled word game appears on the screen. Viewers who can unscramble the word win merchandise credits. Similar credits can be won in the twice-hourly Lucky Numbers Drawing. Over 1,500 prizes are awarded each week. QVC uses a soft-sell approach. There are no hyped discounts, and, unlike many of its competitors, it clearly indicates handling and shipping charges. The company accepts returns within 30 days for any reason. The QVC program is produced live and broadcast continuously 24 hours a day, seven days a week. Over the 1989 Thanksgiving weekend, QVC received 310,000 phone orders that totaled $25.6 million of sales. The enormity of the operation is shown in Figure 15–8, which features a large number of operators taking orders for cable television merchandise.

The continued success for in-home television shopping seems to be certain. As long as shopping convenience continues to be important and cable television continues to spread, the industry will continue to flourish.

TRENDS

The growth of direct retailing is enormous. Some of the trends that dominate the field are discussed in the following paragraphs.

Increase in Numbers of Catalogs

Each year the numbers of catalogs mailed to consumers' home increases. Companies that are primarily catalog oriented continue to spring up, and those that operate traditional retail ventures make more use of catalogs than ever before.

Catalog Offerings Differ From the Store's Merchandise Assortment

Specialty stores, by definition, restrict their product lines. Some carry only one item, such as the Knot Shop, where ties are the only game in town, whereas others merchandise a slightly larger assortment, such as Victoria's Secret where a diverse line of intimate apparel is available. The limits established by these and other companies are often related to the competition in the places in which they are located. Some stores, such as Victoria's Secret, recognizing the vast, untapped resources of direct mail, offer a catalog that goes far beyond the merchandise it sells in its stores. A host of women's apparel fills Victoria's Secret catalog pages because the company recognizes that the at-home shopper is just as likely to order a sportswear item when she buys a nightgown. The average sale is therefore immediately increased.

Shopping Via Television

While the verdict isn't in yet, many retailers are either considering starting their own shopping programs, or using others to sell their items. Stores like Saks 5th Avenue and Macy's, at this time, are in the development stages of producing their own shows.

Upgrading of Merchandise Available Through Cable Television

No more is the merchandise menu available through TV limited to chintzy jewelry or poor quality, inexpensive apparel. Designer products, at steep prices, are hitting the airwaves, with many new "fashion names" joining the rosters. In 1994, as a test, a channel offered a suit designed by Ivana Trump that retailed for several hundred dollars. It quickly sold out! This certainly gave many producers the notion that the days of selling only lower priced items were over.

ACTION FOR THE INDEPENDENT RETAILER

Small retailers must realize that in-home shopping is a factor they must contend with. It is not only here to stay, but will continue to grow. Like the retail giants, independents must react to this new and rapidly growing competition.

One way of doing this is by joining them. Customer lists containing the necessary customer characteristics should be maintained and even expanded through small purchases from list brokers. When small flyers or direct mail pieces are sent, the offer of delivery should be included.

It is not being suggested that small retailers go into the catalog business, but occasional pieces should be sent. Rather than being invitations to shop in the store, they should be treated as mini-catalogs. Some manufacturers offer direct mail pieces to retailers for their use in achieving direct mail business. These mailers describe specific merchandise and leave room for the store to have its name printed. In this way, with little expense, the smaller independents can become involved in some direct mail business.

IMPORTANT POINTS IN THE CHAPTER

1. In-home shopping has been expanding at twice the rate of traditional shopping and has become an important competitor in the battle for retail volume.

2. The chief advantage of shopping at home is the convenience it offers. This is very important to the growing population of two-worker families and the elderly.

3. The widespread use of credit cards and toll-free numbers is among the principal reasons for the growth of direct mail retailing.

4. Catalogs are the most important media for those who shop at home. One reason for their success is the careful targeting of customers.

5. In order to compete successfully with traditional retailers, catalogers must provide prompt, efficient service and integrity.

6. Many major retailers have gone into the catalog business. Similarly, many catalogers have opened stores.

7. Direct mail selling is similar to catalog selling, but with only one or a few related items offered. The expense per item is much higher.

8. Direct mail selling requires extremely careful targeting. Lists of customers with the required characteristics can be generated internally or purchased.

9. In-home shopping by cable television grew rapidly, leveled off, and is currently resurfacing as the networks become more sophisticated in their programming.

REVIEW QUESTIONS

1. List and discuss four reasons for the growth of in-home shopping.

2. In what way have catalog operations improved?

3. Why is targeting so important to catalogers?
4. List four characteristics of the typical Lands' End customer.
5. Compare the merchandise of a cataloger with that of a retail store.
6. Discuss the cataloger's problem with "hot" new items.
7. What is cross-selling?
8. How does catalog customer feedback compare with in-store customer feedback?
9. How do catalog prices compare with those found at a retail store?
10. What are the department store service shortcomings that have aided the growth of catalog sales?
11. Differentiate between specialty catalogs and "big books."
12. Why do some catalogers open retail stores?
13. Why do some retailers go into catalog operations?
14. Discuss the flood of new catalogs on the market.
15. Differentiate between direct mail and catalog selling.
16. What are internal lists?
17. What are external lists? How are they acquired?
18. Define and discuss the importance of Zip codes, census blocks, carrier routes, and clusters.
19. How has the merchandise mix of cable television merchants changed in recent years?
20. Discuss the future of cable television.

CASE PROBLEMS

Case Problem 1

The American Boat Builders Corporation is a manufacturer of motorized pleasure boats. Its products range from 22 to 36 feet, are powerful, very well fitted out, and expensive, selling from $35,000 to $125,000. The boats are designed for fishing, family outings, and short trips.

The company has been is business for 50 years and has an established reputation for quality. It has a substantial share of the market, selling through selected dealerships nationwide in all of the areas appropriate to its products.

Recently, because of heavy competition and a softening of the pleasure boat market, dealers' inventories of unsold boats have been growing at an alarming rate. The company plans an expensive direct mail piece to all prospective customers within its trading areas.

As director of marketing, you are faced with the task of compiling a list of likely prospects.

Questions

1. What characteristics will you target in compiling this list?
2. How will you compile the list?

Case Problem 2

Boutique, Inc. operates a very successful catalog operation. Although it has only been in business for eight years, its sales have grown to $20,000,000 annually during that period. The company sells upbeat ladies' fashion goods through a specialized catalog sent quarterly to over 2 million households. The target market consists of women aged 25 to 45, holding professional or managerial jobs at which they earn in excess of $40,000 per year. Other characteristics are targeted as well, but these are the most important ones.

In the trade, Boutique is considered a model of how a catalog operation should be run. Each has seen a substantial increase in both sales volume and profits, thanks to excellent service, a carefully selected merchandise mix, and well-managed up to date support systems.

Management is considering opening a small chain of retail stores.

Question

1. Discuss the advantages and disadvantages.

Chapter 16
Personal Selling

Photograph by Ellen Diamond

LEARNING OBJECTIVES

Upon completion of this chapter, the student should be able to:

  1. Discuss the personal characteristics essential to a successful salesperson.
  2. List five areas of merchandise with which a salesperson must be familiar.
  3. Write a brief paragraph on the selling of additional merchandise after a sale has been made. At least three methods should be included.
  4. List six sources of product information that are available to a salesperson.

QUESTIONS ARE ANSWERED THROUGH THE TOUCH OF A SCREEN . . .

If you have ever walked through any number of retail operations in search of a salesperson, or seeking specific product information, you know that frustration is often the result. Merely finding someone to assist you is difficult enough, but expecting answers to questions concerning the merchandise is yet another problem that shoppers must cope with. Many retail operations are reducing the size of their selling staffs in an attempt to cut costs. Although costs may be reduced, the customers are often short-changed in terms of getting prompt attention to their needs.

Detroit-based Frank's Nursery & Crafts has instituted a program that efficiently addresses the problem. It has installed a system in its stores that involves a 15-inch touch monitor enhanced with a wide assortment of color graphics. In a store in which technical information is often needed to answer such questions as the appropriate growing conditions for a particular plant, the amount of care that must be administered to guarantee positive results, the proper timing for planting, and so forth, the system helps to handle these and other questions automatically.

The enormous assortment of plants that fill the stores, each with specific requirements for successful growth, renders it virtually impossible for the company to have a staff of salespersons both available and sufficiently knowledgeable to handle the queries. Without the proper attention to maintenance of the products, returns could easily reduce the company's profitability.

The plan eliminates the need for a traditional sales staff, and uses cashiers to handle questions using the new system. A shopper who wants to know, for example. which type of fertilizer should be purchased to obtain the best results for rose bushes is immediately supplied with the information. The cashier merely keys in the item number assigned to roses and presses a product-inquiry section on the screen. The requested information is quickly supplied and a printed copy is available that the customer may keep for future reference.

Another area is which salespeople are often ill-prepared involves knowledge of merchandise that is on sale. Stores that are promotion-oriented regularly feature specials at reduced prices, which attract large numbers of shoppers to the stores. Often, those on the selling floors or registers are unaware of the price reductions. The system at Franks can immediately reveal copies of the various advertisements so that the right prices are charged.

Although many stores recognize that there is no substitute for excellent personal selling, some companies, such as Frank's Nursery & Crafts, may improve sales by installing technology that can handle problems associated with selling.

Today, most of management's attention is focused upon the scientific determination of merchandise needs with the aid of such sophisticated tools as the computer. The activity that is often the lifeblood of the store, being a good salesperson, is in danger of being neglected. The lack of attention paid to upgrading selling techniques is apparent on entering various selling floors. It is true that to a certain extent retailers are making more extensive use of self-service. While customer selection without the aid of a salesperson is perhaps suitable for particular types of merchandise, such as the items found at the discount operations like Kmart and Wal-Mart and the warehouse clubs such as Price/Costco, self-service is not the answer for all goods. Items such as furs, higher-priced apparel, major appliances, carpets, and furniture generally require trained sales personnel. The demand for personal attention is certainly not as important in the discount operations, where price is deemed more important than service, but in the service-oriented, conventional department and specialty stores personal ability to sell goods is a component necessary to the achievement of satisfactory sales. It should be stressed that, to be meaningful, the personal method of selling used with the customer must be efficient. Efficient personal selling by no means requires a hardsell, "fasting-talking" approach. With today's more sophisticated and better educated consumers, this type of selling can lead to customer dissatisfaction, an increase in merchandise returns, and a poor image for the retail store.

In an effort to counter the void that is created by unenthusiastic salespeople, some stores have taken the lead, instituting programs by which they hope to turn the problem around.

The route that some retailers have used involves the use of videocassettes. One company, Video Learning Resources, has developed a cassette that promises to increase sales by 15 percent. By covering such topics as approaching the customer, determining needs, presenting the merchandise, overcoming objections, closing the sales, and suggesting additional merchandise, the viewer is presented with an organized, concise selling procedure in a manner that doesn't require trainers.

ESSENTIALS FOR THE SALESPERSON

Too much emphasis cannot be placed on the importance of the salesperson's ability. The image of the store is directly affected by the impression that person makes on the prospective customer. It is important to remember that, until the individual shopper makes a purchase, that individual can only be considered a prospect. Personal selling ability, more than any other selling aids such as advertising and display, is the main activity in retailing that builds or destroys the shopper's confidence. Normally, the salesperson is the store's only representative. To the public, the salesperson *is* the store and many times a customer purchases or does not purchase because of him or her.

Often when a shopper states, "I don't like that store," it is the sales force that is being referred to. With the enormous amount of competition facing the retailer, the store's main liaison with the public, the salesperson, must be properly prepared.

Appearance

Before helping shoppers with their purchases, the salesperson must make an impression that is conducive to purchasing. The first impression is the result of the salesperson's appearance. The prospective customer isn't apt to be receptive to the advice of someone who isn't appropriately attired.

In small stores, dress regulations are not as stringent as they are in the larger organizations. Most small storekeepers deal with only a few salespeople and can supervise their dress habits informally. In some larger stores, where management often deals with several hundred salespeople, a uniform dress code is established. For example, such colors as black, brown, navy blue, and gray may be prescribed. The main reason for this regulation, often frowned upon by employees, is that it makes certain the salesperson's attire will not detract from the merchandise, and shocking colors and patterns will be avoided. The simple statement that "employees should dress in good taste" is not adequate. Taste is too personal to be left to chance. The salesperson should avoid wearing any type of outfit that might be offensive and that could discourage a customer from asking for sales help. For example, the younger employee working in a conservative men's shop should avoid wearing extreme styles. If salespersons choose to dress in a manner unlike the atmosphere of the store, the potential customers might not seek their advice.

Salespeople at A&S, a New York-based department store, receive a copy of a booklet called *Your Appearance Counts,* which serves as a guide in the selection of appropriate styles and colors for business use. In the booklet, the following questions are posed, which, when answered affirmatively, contribute to proper appearance.

Women

- Is your hair neatly combed?
- Is your skin clear?
- Are your hands clean and well manicured?
- Is your makeup just right . . . not too heavy . . . not too light?
- No runs in your stockings?
- Are you wearing neat, well-heeled (and comfortable) shoes?
- Is your attire businesslike and fresh looking?

Men

- Is your hair trimmed and clean?
- Do you shave daily?
- Are your hands well scrubbed . . . nails clipped and clean?
- Are your shoes well shined?
- Is your shirt or uniform clean and pressed?
- Are your collar and shirt fresh?

Enthusiasm

The term *enthusiasm* does not imply that a salesperson should be overly aggressive and "come on strong." Being too aggressive may lead to overpowering the customers and convincing them to buy items they might not really want. An enthusiastic salesperson is one who shows a real feeling for the merchandise and stimulates the customer's emotions. If the salesperson discusses the merchandise enthusiastically, the enthusiasm may transfer to the customer. Too often, shoppers are helped by lethargic salespeople who encourage a poor frame of mind.

Voice and Speech

A voice that is sufficiently audible and speech that properly uses diction are important to good selling technique. Salespersons do not, by any means, need theatrical training to make a clear presentation to customers, but they should exercise care in the manner in which they speak and in their choice of words. The salesperson who speaks properly will more easily establish rapport with the shopper.

Tact

Being tactful is essential to selling in the retail store. The salesperson's job is to help satisfy the customer's needs. Should the salesperson allow the customer to purchase something that the salesperson knows is wrong, even though the customer wants to make the purchase? Allowing this purchase to be made might lead to criticism (by the customer's friends) and eventual return of the goods. On the other hand, the salesperson's suggestion that the shopper's choice is a poor one might be an affront. For example, if a stout woman would like to purchase a dress that accentuates her figure in the wrong places, extreme care must be taken not to offend the customer, but to direct her tactfully to something more appropriate. Tactfulness is something that comes only with extreme caution and experience.

Self-Control

It is unlikely that even the most even-tempered salesperson hasn't had the desire to punch a customer in the nose. Prospective customers' personalities and attitudes are not all the same. A salesperson who is to be successful must keep in mind that "the customer is always right" and must control emotions even when this quoted statement seems intolerable. Abusing the customer will only lead to the loss of sales. The individual who is easily excited by the shortcomings of others shouldn't pursue a sales job, or for that matter any career in retailing.

In addition to the previously mentioned essentials for good selling technique, a prospective salesperson should show initiative and sincerity, and be cheerful, knowledgeable, and resourceful. It may be unusual for one person to have all these qualities, but the more that are possessed, the greater are the chances for success in a sales position.

HOW TO SELL

Perhaps the most difficult job to learn from a textbook is how to sell. Salesmanship can be improved by many techniques, such as role-playing, but there are basic steps in the selling process that should be learned before refinement can take place.

Know the Merchandise

Salespeople who say that they can sell anything without knowledge of the product are either naive or do not have any understanding of good selling methods. The ability to sell merchandise in a way that will gain the customers' confidence and satisfy their shopping needs requires an understanding of the merchandise for sale. The inability to answer the shoppers' specific product questions tends to make salespeople bluff, or avoid the queries. Using proper technique may result not only in an immediate sale; it may also lead to future customer purchases. While it is not really possible for a salesperson to be completely knowledgeable in all areas of hard goods and soft goods, it is important to have some fundamental information about the merchandise. Complete unfamiliarity with the goods (in the case of a new employee or a transfer from another department) necessitates getting the necessary product information. (The sources of product information will be discussed later in the chapter.) The following areas should be completely familiar to the salesperson.

Merchandise Location

Not all merchandise is arranged in shelves or on racks that are easily accessible. Some goods are kept in reserve (under counters or in stockrooms, for example) and the knowledge of their exact location is important. The need to search for merchandise detains customers and wastes time. Even for merchandise that is exposed, it is important to know the exact location.

Merchandise Uses

While it is obvious what purpose a dress or a suit serves, some goods have less obvious uses, or numerous uses. For example, a vacuum cleaner, in addition to cleaning rugs, may be adapted for upholstery and drapery cleaning, and perhaps even for spray painting. Even in soft goods, some items might be adapted for various uses. With a different blouse, an outfit can be used for daytime or evening wear.

Styles

Styles that are in fashion vary from season to season. Besides knowing which styles are fashionable or suitable for a particular purpose, salespeople should know the appropriate styles for their customers. For example, the lines of a double-breasted jacket are arranged in such a manner that they somewhat conceal a bulging midsection. Knowledge of styles and their uses can help in closing a sale more quickly. Style is not limited to soft goods. Refrigerators, ranges, dining room tables, and chairs are examples of other types of merchandise that are available in a variety of styles. It is important for a salesperson who sells refrigerators to have sufficient knowledge of that department's various models and their advantages to satisfy the most discriminating customer. For example, a customer might want to know the advantages of a double-door refrigerator–freezer as compared with a conventional model.

Sizes

In addition to clothing and accessories, other merchandise comes in a variety of sizes. Sofas, chairs, dishwashers, television sets, and pool tables, just to mention a few, come in different sizes. Salespersons should have an understanding of the sizes in their departments so they can quickly help customers choose the right items. Some years ago a person selling women's clothing was concerned only with misses' and junior sizes. In an attempt to approximate the female figure more closely and eliminate costly alterations, manufacturers have introduced many new size ranges. In addition to the two already mentioned, sales personnel must know the differences among junior petites, misses' petites, diminutive, half sizes, junior plenty, and women's sizes. (See Figures 16–1 and 16–2.) Sizes for the male figure run an equally wide gamut.

Department	Special Information	Sizes								
Junior	Short waisted, narrow figures	3	5	7	9	11	13	15		
Junior Petite	5'2" and under	3	5	7	9	11	13			
Missy	Average female figure	4	6	8	10	12	14	16	18	20
Missy Petite	5'5" and under	4	6	8	10	12	14	16		
Half Sizes	Full figure, short waisted	$14\frac{1}{2}$	$16\frac{1}{2}$	$18\frac{1}{2}$	$20\frac{1}{2}$	$22\frac{1}{2}$	$24\frac{1}{2}$	$26\frac{1}{2}$		
Women's	Full figure, average height	38	40	42	44	46	48	50		

Figure 16–1 Size Range Chart

Price and Quality

Aside from just remembering the prices, a salesperson must often justify them. Remembering the prices without consulting the price tags gives a customer the impression that the salesperson is familiar with the merchandise. This knowledge, while it might seem insignificant, often establishes confidence. In those areas where prices vary according to changes (the use of one fabric instead of another on a chair), it is less likely that a salesperson will remember all the prices.

Justifying the price requires a knowledge of quality and the recitation of the product's salient features. Quality can be impressed upon the customer with the intelligent discussion of such information as materials ("this is linen, which is one of the costlier fibers"), construction ("this glove is made with an outseam, which eliminates stitches on the inside and allows for maximum comfort"), guarantees ("this refrigerator is unconditionally guaranteed for three years"), and workmanship ("the lapel is handsewn, which provides for a neater look").

Care of Merchandise

The special care or the ease in caring for an item is important to good selling. A statement indicating that a dress is unconditionally washable and dries without wrinkles just about convinces the travel-minded customer to buy. Similarly, the customer purchasing a garment that requires special cleaning attention, such as a suede coat, is apt to receive longer wear if he or she is familiar with the care of the coat. The salesperson should be absolutely certain about how to care for such goods because mistakes can lead to unnecessary returns and customer dissatisfaction.

Approaching the Customer

After becoming familiar with the merchandise to be sold, the salesperson is ready to greet prospective customers. Customers should be greeted with a friendly smile. The greeting used to begin a conversation is most important. One should not begin with a question that might bring a negative response. For example, approaching a customer by asking, "May I help you?" might bring a reply of "no." Although this is typical of retail store selling, it is a poor way to begin a sales presentation. Preferably a salesperson might begin by saying, "Good morning, I'm Mr. Smith. I'd like to help you with your purchasing needs." Another desirable approach is to strike up a conversation regarding an article of merchandise that a shopper is examining—for example. "That chair is as comfortable as it is good-looking. Try sitting in it." When a customer approaches a salesperson for help, the greeting is less difficult because the customer sought assistance. A mere "Good afternoon" is sufficient. Even "May I help you?" is acceptable, since in this situation it will not bring the possibility of a "no" response.

STYLE: 65S078775

CUT #: 6696

COLOR #: 01X

BLACK

55% ACETATE
25% RAYON
20% POLYESTER
MADE IN U.S.A.

PETITE
2

Figure 16–2   Special size tag

At this early point in the sales demonstration, it is time to determine the shopper's needs. Certainly, approaching the customer who is examining an item gives the salesperson an idea of what is desired. In cases where the customer isn't studying the merchandise, a determination of what is needed is a little more difficult. Some brief questions (which become second nature with experience) pertaining to style, color, size (if applicable), and so on will guide the salesperson in the selection of appropriate merchandise. Keeping in mind what the store has available for sale, the salesperson is now ready to show the merchandise to the customer.

Presentation of the Merchandise

Telling the customer about the merchandise, the salesperson should include all of those features that make it distinctive. Such factors as construction, materials, and uses are generally discussed. To make the item more desirable to the customer, an outstanding feature should be stressed. For example, the mention of the name of the designer, if he or she is one of renown, would probably be more meaningful to a fashion-minded customer than any other information. Similarly, to shoppers who are interested in easing their household chores, the mention of completely "wash and wear" should be most meaningful. It is beneficial to invite the customer to try the merchandise. A piece of jewelry becomes more exciting if it is tried on rather than viewed on a counter. The person interested in a lounge chair should be invited to sit in it rather than merely admire it. The comfort achieved (if it is comfortable) will help close the sale. How many suits and coats would a man purchase if he didn't try them on? Whatever the item, the customer's involvement is extremely important for closing the sale.

If an item can be demonstrated, it should be. What could be more convincing than the demonstration of a vacuum cleaner in action? Would stores sell as many color television sets without showing them in operation? Some other examples of the power of demonstration are the purposeful dropping of an unbreakable dish or the crushing of a wrinkle-proof blouse. There are very few types of merchandise that do not lend themselves to customer involvement or demonstration.

Handling Objections

Even after spending time considering a purchase, the shopper might hesitate and raise objections. These objections might be excuses telling the salesperson that the customer isn't going to buy, or they might be sincere objections that need further reassurance. Whatever the reason for the objections, the salesperson must overcome them to close the sale.

Some of the more common objections are those invoking price, the product's features, inadequate guarantees, the delivery time, and poor fit. Even the salesperson's attitude might deter buying. The experienced salesperson is prepared to handle these objections and does so in a number of ways. One technique is to agree with the customer but then to offer another selling point. For example, Mrs. Jones shows interest in the dress she is trying on but declares, "The price is high." The salesperson might reply, "Yes, but the fit is so perfect the cost generally involved in alterations will be eliminated." Aside from the use of "yes, but" to handle objections, these phrases may be used:

- I agree with you, sir, but another factor to consider . . .
- You're right, Mr. Peter, however . . .
- One of my customers felt exactly as you do, but she finally made the purchase because . . .
- It certainly is a long time to wait for the table, Miss Adams, but . . .

The above statements are by no means the only ones to be used but are intended to serve as guides for the new salesperson.

Another technique employed in handling objections is to ask questions of the customer. In this way, a salesperson can separate excuses for not buying from real objections. Examples of some questions to use are:

- What color would you prefer?
- Why do you object to the style of this refrigerator?
- What would you consider an appropriate price for a sofa?

Still another technique to be used, but with caution, is to deny the objection. Salespersons must be absolutely certain of their information when employing this method.

Customer's Objection	Salesperson's Response
I think the fabric will shrink.	Oh no, madam, the shirt has been preshrunk.
The Elite Shoppe sells it for $5 less than your price.	Our store always sells that item at a price lower than the Elite Shoppe.
I don't think the rug will be delivered in time for the party.	I guarantee the delivery date, Mrs. Reihing.

If the salesperson uses this method but doesn't provide truthful information, the customer will be dissatisfied upon learning the truth and probably will never again trust the store's sales personnel.

Closing the Sale

After presenting the information necessary to answer all the customer's questions and any objections have been overcome, the salesperson should try to close the sale. The recognition of the appropriate time to close comes with experience. The seasoned salesperson looks for signals that indicate that the prospect is about to become a customer. Only the naive or inexperienced salesperson expects to hear from the customer something like, "O.K., I'm ready to buy." Some of the closing signals are:

- How long will it take for the alteration to be completed?
- Can I charge this purchase?
- When can I expect the merchandise to be delivered?
- Are these items exchangeable?
- Is the guarantee for one year?

The salesperson who recognizes what he or she believes to be the opportune moment should then proceed to close the sale. Choosing the right words at this time might seem difficult to the student of retailing. Using the question "Are you ready to buy?" is certainly not the correct approach. The use of the questions and statements such as these prove to be effective:

- Shall I gift-wrap it for you?
- Would you like to wear the shoes out of the store?
- Which would you like, the blue one or the brown one?
- Will that be cash or charge?
- Would you like it delivered or will you take it with you?
- After today this item goes back to its original price.
- This is the last one in stock; a special order will take four weeks.

Even the most experienced salespersons sometimes find that they have not chosen the appropriate time to close the sale. It may take several attempts before a sale is finalized. Retailing students should keep in mind that not everyone is really a customer, and also that not every shopper can be satisfied with the store's offerings. The customer's words in refusing to buy should be evaluated. For example, a definite "no" might indicate that the customer can't be satisfied. Reactions such as "I'd like to see another style" or " No, I'm still uncertain about the fit of this garment" are signals that perhaps more selling effort is necessary. Whatever the degree of negativism, a seasoned salesperson should not give up after the first attempt. How many attempts should be made? Too few might let the customer slip away. Too many tries might tend to make shoppers feel they are being high-pressured. The right number of times before one gives up will eventually be perceived through experience.

After making an unsuccessful attempt, a salesperson must be able to proceed again to a point that will result in success. In order to do this, the salesperson must keep some information in reserve that will perhaps whet the customer's appetite. For example:

- If you purchase today, you will be entitled to buy a second pair at a 20 percent reduction.
- This is the last day of our special sale; tomorrow the price will increase by 10 percent.
- Did you know that these shoes are *wear-dated* and are guaranteed, under normal use, for one year?

Some stores provide their new sales employees with printed suggestions on how to sell. The training department of the Personnel Division of A&S provides its employees with a card entitled, *"How to Sell to Close the Most Sales."* (See Figure 16–3.)

HOW TO SELL
TO CLOSE THE MOST SALES

Step No. 1—*KNOW*	Step No. 2—*SHOW*
Know The Merchandise—	*Show Alertness—*
Location, use, type or style, size, price, quality, care.	*Contact* customers promptly. Greet customers positively.
Know How To Stock It—	*Show Courtesy—*
Arrange for ease in selling. Assort and keep neat.	Customers expect a friendly attitude, a pleasant smile, and help in selecting.
Know that *the more customers you approach, the more you will sell.*	*Show Merchandise—*
	Determine customer needs in relation to stock. Show medium price first. Display to best advantage—dramatize, demonstrate use. Be enthusiastic.

KNOW	**SHOW**	**TELL**	**SELL**

HOW TO SELL
TO CLOSE THE MOST SALES

Step No. 3—*TELL*	Step No. 4—*SELL*
TELL:	SELL:
the facts or distinctive features of the merchandise.	benefits—something that the merchandise does for the customer which appeals to pride, pleasure, profit, protection.
Size, type or style, use, construction, manufacturer's name, care.	There is a sell point for every tell point.

CLOSE THE SALE
NARROW THE SELECTION
ASSUME THE CUSTOMER IS BUYING—ASK HER TO BUY.
SUGGEST ADDITIONAL MERCHANDISE.
ASSUME TAKE-WITH.   THANK CUSTOMER.

TRAINING DEPARTMENT	**ABRAHAM & STRAUS**	**PERSONNEL DIVISION**

Figure 16–3   How to sell to close the most sales. *Courtesy:* A&S

SUGGESTING ADDITIONAL MERCHANDISE

Although the salesperson should be pleased with having closed the sale, it is at this point that the experienced employee should try to tempt the customer with additional merchandise. The customer is in a buying frame of mind and with some expert selling effort it might be possible to build on the sale. Suggestion selling should in no way be considered as high pressure, but rather as a way of assisting the customer. There are a number of ways in which this can be accomplished.

1. The suggestion of accessories to be used in conjunction with the purchase. For example, an alert salesperson having sold a customer a suit could suggest such items as shirts and ties with which the suit could be coordinated. Instead of asking whether or not the customer is interested in these other items, the creative salesperson selects the accessories that are most appropriate and demonstrates to the customer how perfectly they blend. Even if the shopper has no intention of purchasing a shirt and tie, their display might be tempting. Accessories need not be limited to soft goods. At the close of a vacuum cleaner sale, attachments and disposable bags might be suggested. Similarly, the sale of a stereo might result in a larger total purchase if records and cassettes are suggested to the customer.

2. The suggestion of more than one of the items sold. For example, a customer having selected a pair of socks might consider buying additional pairs if the salesperson can offer an advantage of the multiple purchase. In practice, you can convince a customer to buy a second pair of sock by saying, "If you buy a single pair and one sock becomes damage, you'll have to dispose of the other. By buying two pairs, you will still be left with one pair even if a sock from the second pair is destroyed." Similarly, upon completing a rug sale, you might suggest additional yardage for stress areas (stairs) that might wear away before the rest of the carpet.

3. The suggestion of a special offer. Very often purchasing one item may entitle the customer to take advantage of another item at a reduced price. In a dollar sale, a customer who purchases one item at the regular price may buy a second item for an additional dollar. Service contracts are offered to customers having just purchased an appliance, at a price less than the customary price.

SUGGESTIONS TO PROMOTE FUTURE BUSINESS

Although completing the sale is extremely important, once having done so, the resourceful salesperson takes the opportunity to guarantee the customer's return for future purchases. Retailers seek to establish a reputation that will encourage other transactions. Spending a few extra moments with the customer at this time will promote good will and encourage that individual to return. Some suggestions for achieving these ends are:

- Here's my card, Mr. Bennett. It has been a pleasure helping you with your purchases. I'd like to do so again in the near future.
- Mrs. Avidon, I'd like your telephone number in case something special comes in that I feel would be appropriate for you.

Rushing to the next customer without the use of these important courtesies is not as important as the few moments spent to solidify a customer relationship. This time might establish a rapport that the customer will recall when ready to shop again.

SOURCES OF PRODUCT INFORMATION

There are a great number of sources salespersons can investigate for information pertaining to the merchandise in their departments. Some of these sources are easily found within the store; others demand that the salesperson look elsewhere.

The Buyer

The most knowledgeable person in the department in regard to the product is the buyer. Buyers generally specialize in a particular type of merchandise, such as junior dresses, sweaters, or produce. In the larger organizations the buyer's range of merchandise is highly specialized. In the smaller store the buyer's purchases may be more diversified. The continuous exposure to merchandise coupled with a sound education in retailing provides the buyer with the needed know-how.

In flagship stores where the buyer comes into direct contact with the sales staff, he or she is the best source of information for salespeople to tap. In organizations such as the larger chain operations, where the buyer is not easily accessible to the sales personnel, salespeople must resort to other sources of merchandise information.

Managers

Store managers and department managers are about the most knowledgeable merchandise experts in the store. They often select the merchandise their stores will feature from lists made available to them by the central buyers, and they have a working knowledge of the merchandise. Salespeople working in large operations will find that their managers can provide the information necessary to make them knowledgeable sales personnel.

Vendors' Salespeople

Most stores are visited by manufacturers' and wholesalers' representatives. These representatives call upon the retailers to show their lines of merchandise. If the retailer cannot conveniently visit the market, these people must visit the retail store. After purchases have been made, it is not uncommon for them to offer selling suggestions to the store's sales force. Particularly in areas in which merchandise fit and care are important factors, this salesperson can be extremely helpful.

Other Vendor Aids

In addition to the informal knowledge a manufacturer's or wholesaler's salesperson can provide, vendors sometimes provide brochures and even recorded lectures about their merchandise's features. Some years ago a swimsuit manufacturer prepared a recording that was mailed to retailers; it discussed fabrics, construction, quality, fitting suggestions, and style information. The use of the record gave salespeople firsthand information about the vendor's products, which made selling them easier.

Formal Study

Colleges and universities offer courses in product information, which can be invaluable for salespeople. Such courses and the highlights covered are:

- *Textiles.* The study of all types of fabrics, their uses, the necessary care, the life expectancy, and the government regulations concerning textiles. This course is valuable for every salesperson selling soft goods.
- *Fashion accessories.* The study of leather gloves, shoes, jewelry, furs, handbags, and neckwear. Styles, methods of construction, and the care of garments are discussed.
- *Home furnishings.* The study of dinnerware, glassware, silverware, furniture, clocks, and other household accessories.

TRENDS

Efficient personal selling has long been a problem at many retail operations. Some of the trends that have helped to improve the problem are discussed.

Commission Sales

With Nordstrom as the leader, other retailers such as Neiman Marcus, Bloomingdale's, and Macy's in some or all of their departments have improved selling by paying people on straight commission. If they don't sell, they don't earn! This has motivated the here-to-fore "uninspired" salesperson to try harder.

Improvement of Training

At too many retail operations, the standard training period for salespeople included nothing more than a few hours to learn the use of the cash register. Today, stores such as Bloomingdale's are using role playing and training films to upgrade their employees' performances in such areas as approaching the customer, answering questions, and closing the sale.

ACTION FOR THE INDEPENDENT RETAILER

If there is one area in which the independent can compete with the large company, it is in personal selling. Being able to recognize and relate to individual customers has been the secret of success for many smaller retailers. While the large stores experience a high rate of salesperson turnover, the independent generally has a much better record. Many customers who patronize the independent retailer do so because of the attention they receive from the salespeople.

Without the need for complicated training in such areas as the various methods for recording sales, the independent retailer has the advantage of being able to train salespeople on the floor and observe their performances. Continuous informal training about greeting customers, assisting customers, building sales, and so forth encourages improved performance. In large stores where management is often preoccupied with other tasks, selling practices are usually given less attention than is necessary. Through efficient selling, the independent can gain customer loyalty.

IMPORTANT POINTS IN THE CHAPTER

1. The trend toward scientific retailing controls and automation must not be permitted to deemphasize the importance that management gives to personal selling.
2. The image of a store is directly affected by its salespeople. To impart the proper image to customers, salespeople should be neat, tactful, enthusiastic, and should possess a good voice and grammatical speech patterns.
3. Capable selling technique requires a thorough knowledge of the merchandise, including its location in the store, uses, sizes and styles, and prices.
4. The effective salesperson is friendly in approaching customers, presents the merchandise in its best light, and points out the outstanding features of the goods. Since customers will always raise objections, the salesperson should be prepared for them.
5. As salespersons gain experience, knowing the method and timing of closing the sale becomes easier. After the sale is safely closed, a good salesperson should suggest additional merchandise for immediate or future sale.
6. The product information that is required by salespeople may be obtained from the buyer, manager, vendors' salespeople, and through formal study.

REVIEW QUESTIONS

1. In which type of operation might the salesperson's job be eliminated? For what reason?

2. What adverse effect can the "hard sell" approach have on customers?

3. When a customer says, "I don't like that store," to whom is the customer often referring?

4. Why is the salesperson's appearance important?

5. If dress regulations merely stress "good taste," might there be some problems?

6. For what reasons do stores forbid their sales personnel to wear loud prints and stripes?

7. How can a salesperson's enthusiasm or lack of it play an important role in selling ability?

8. Define *tact*. Why must a salesperson be tactful?

9. Discuss the various factors the salesperson should know concerning merchandise.

10. Besides remembering the prices of merchandise, for what other purpose may the salesperson be called upon in regard to price?

11. Why, besides making it a selling point, must the salesperson be certain of special care requirements of merchandise?

12. "May I help you," although commonly used by salespeople, is not a preferred approach. Why not?

13. Is it important to demonstrate the merchandise that can be demonstrated? Defend your answer.

14. State some objections a customer may have for not making a purchase.

15. In addition to the "yes, but" technique of overcoming objections, describe another commonly used method.

16. Describe some of the signals that indicate a closing attempt should be made by the salesperson.

17. Should a salesperson try to close again if the first attempt was unsuccessful? Why?

18. Define *suggestion selling* by giving some examples of its use.

19. Why are the few extra moments spent with the customer after the sale has been made important to the retail store?

20. Who in the department store's flagship is the best source of product information?

CASE PROBLEMS

Case Problem 1

Recently, Ellen Frances was watching television and saw a commercial advertising a sale on "fun furs" at Stevan's Department Store. The commercial indicated that the selection, specially priced, included rabbit, muskrat, raccoon, and mink paw. The price range for this special sale was from $500 to $1,500.

Tempted by the advertisement, Mrs. Frances visited Stevan's and was further excited by the store's elegant window displays featuring the fur coats. With her appetite whetted, she rushed to the fur department to make her selection. Because she was unfamiliar with fur, she sought the assistance of a salesperson who could help her choose a coat. No salesperson approached her, so Mrs. Frances made the first overture. The conversation that followed went something like this:

Mrs. Frances:	I'd like some assistance with a fur coat.
Salesperson:	Oh, they're all on sale. Look through the rack.
Mrs. Frances:	I'm not familiar with some of these furs—could you help me?
Salesperson:	I'd like to, but I'm not that knowledgeable about furs, myself.
Mrs. Frances:	(after looking through the rack and choosing one to try on) Do you think it fits right?
Salesperson:	It looks OK.
Mrs. Frances:	Does this coat require any special care?
Salesperson:	I'm not sure.
Mrs. Frances:	I don't think I'm going to purchase a coat today.
Salesperson:	At these prices, we wouldn't really worry.

Mrs. Frances, thoroughly disgusted, left the store without making a purchase.

Questions

1. Do you think the salesperson had those qualities essential for good selling? Which were lacking?
2. Did the salesperson have enough knowledge of furs to sell them effectively? How might this knowledge be gained?
3. What could the store do to improve such a salesperson's ability?

Case Problem 2

Mr. Ben, a small chain organization featuring conservative men's clothing, has ten units located in the suburbs of New York City. Its salespeople do not receive any special training because the company feels that the cost involved to do a meaningful job is prohibitive. Besides that, with the increased trend of self-selection, management rationalizes that even though its salespeople are not specifically trained, their help is better than complete self-selection.

The following is the essence of a conversation between a salesperson and a customer at Mr. Ben's:

Customer:	I'd like to see a gray suit.
Salesperson:	(Selecting the least expensive first) This is a good number.
Customer:	May I try it on?
Salesperson:	Yes.
Customer:	(Returning from the dressing room) It seems to fit right. How much is it?
Salesperson:	$150
Customer:	That's less than I anticipated. I'll take it.
Salesperson:	Cash or charge?
Customer:	Cash.

The suit was packed, and the customer paid for it and left the store.

Questions

1. Do you think the salesperson was effective? More effective than self-selection in this case?
2. Was the customer sold the right-priced suit?
3. How could the salesperson have increased the final amount of the sale?
4. Is management's attitude correct regarding training of salespeople? Defend your answer.
5. What methods could be employed to better prepare salespersons at Mr. Ben's?

Chapter 17
Accounting Procedures
and Operational Controls

Photograph by Ellen Diamond

LEARNING OBJECTIVES

Upon completion of this chapter, the student should be able to:

1. Define accounting and explain the responsibilities of that function.
2. Describe the use of the income statement.
3. List and discuss five advantages and three disadvantages of the retail inventory method.
4. Define and solve simple problems in costing inventory by LIFO, FIFO, and weighted average.
5. Discuss each of five reasons for the importance of merchandise control.
6. Define dollar control and discuss three types of merchandise classification.
7. Define unit control and indicate six advantages it offers over dollar control.
8. Give four advantages of preparing an expense budget.

FOLLOW THE MONEY TO INCREASE GROSS MARGINS . . .

The concern that surrounds shoplifting and internal theft in retailing is ongoing. Shrinkage continues to plague retailers of all sizes all over the world. Newer and more sophisticated surveillance and other detection devices are constantly being put into place to alleviate the problem. Although some of the newer technologies have reduced the criminal actions, retailers are still unable to make significant impact on the incidence of theft.

Typically, management has looked for patterns of fraud among the thousands of transactions that are recorded. Such "red flags" as greater-than-anticipated merchandise returns, or "voids," which are sales transactions that are eliminated owing to some clerical error, are often tell-tale situations that require further investigation.

At Dayton Hudson, a new approach has been instituted to zero in on internal theft. The reason for the greater attention to employee stealing, rather than shoplifting by consumers who pose as customers, is that the former is far more costly to the store. During a trial, five-month period, shoplifting cases totaled slightly more than 1,000 with a retail value of $226,000. The average cost per theft came to about $225. For the same time frame, the company uncovered 19 cases of internal theft that cost them a total of $418,000, or approximately $22,000 per case!

Through a new system at Dayton Hudson, known as Follow The Money, the store focuses its attention on poorly performing departments, rather than looking at overall numbers. The investigators carefully study each department in terms of gross margins, return rates, and expenses. If there is a discrepancy from an established set of expected figures such as lower-than-anticipated gross margins, close attention is paid to that department. Once a particular trouble spot has been identified, the loss prevention department can follow its procedures to weed out the culprits. By looking at the store as the problem, too much time and effort was being wasted on areas that didn't warrant concern.

With store profits being enormously affected by internal theft, Dayton Hudson believes it finally has found a way to minimize the problem.

Among the most important tools available to all retailers are accounting services. Basically, these services consist of setting up systems for recording business transactions, interpreting their results, and giving advice based upon the interpretation. The services are performed either by an in-house staff or by an outside consultant. Through careful analysis, the accountant can help the retailer decide upon such areas as possible expansion, changes in inventory, and expense controls.

ACCOUNTING PROCEDURES

Accounting has often been referred to as the "language of business." As such, some understanding of accounting is necessary for the success of anyone engaged in any area of business. The degree of accounting understanding necessary to a specific job is keyed to the level of the job. Thus, high management requires a considerable knowledge of accounting principles, whereas less know-how is required as the job level decreases. Since an introductory retailing course is pitched at about a middle-management level, this text will limit the retail applications of accounting to that level.

Accounting Terminology

1. *Cash receipts.* Cash that the retailer receives.
2. *Cash payments.* Cash that the retailer pays out.
3. *Sales.* The revenue from sales.
4. *Purchases.* The merchandise bought for resale to customers.
5. *Payroll.* The salaries paid to employees and any deductions made from salaries, such as social security and withholding tax.
6. *Inventory.* The retailer's investment in merchandise that is to be sold to customers.
7. *Accounts receivable.* The information concerning the amount charge customers owe the firm.
8. *Accounts payable.* The amount that the store owes its creditors and suppliers.

Computerized Accounting

There is probably no field of business that has been more widely adapted to the computer than accounting. The massive volume of repetitive clerical accounting chores required of a large business is a perfect match for the capabilities of a computer. As a result, the high cost of computerization is more than offset by the savings in time, accuracy, and clerical salaries. Even smaller establishments that cannot afford to purchase or lease computers of their own are renting time from computer-servicing companies on an hourly basis.

Income Statement

Among the informational statements prepared by the accountant, the income statement is the most important for managerial control. It may be defined as a summary of the results of doing business for a specific period of time (such as one month or one year). It is a formal way of taking the total revenue (sales) and deducting from it the various costs and expenses of doing business. When the total revenue exceeds the total costs and expenses, the results of the operations are profitable. When the total costs and expenses are greater than the revenue, a loss occurs.

The following is an example of an income statement:

Ideal Ladies Shop
Income Statement for the Year Ended June 30, 19—

Net sales	$100,000
Cost of goods sold	60,000
Gross margin	$ 40,000
Operating expenses	30,000
Net profit	$ 10,000

1. The *net sales* of $100,000 were determined by deducting from the total merchandise sold, the amount of goods returned by customers.

$$\text{Total Sales } - \text{ Sales Returns } = \text{ Net Sales}$$

2. The *cost of goods sold* ($60,000) indicates the cost to the store of the goods that were sold for $100,000. It includes the cost of the goods sold that were purchased this year as well as the cost of the goods that were sold out of inventory. A more detailed analysis of the determination of the cost of goods sold will be presented later in the chapter.

3. The *gross margin* (or gross profit) of $40,000 indicates the excess of the selling price over the cost of the goods that were sold. During this period, merchandise that cost $60,000 was sold for $100,000. The term gross profit (margin) is used because the $40,000 is not the final profit; there are still other expenses to be deducted from the $40,000.

$$\text{Net Sales } - \text{ Cost of Goods Sold} = \text{Gross Margin (Profit)}$$

4. The *operating expenses* include all expenditures other than the cost of the merchandise. These consist of such items as rent, salaries, heat, light, advertising, and so on.

5. After the cost of the goods sold and the operating expenses have been deducted from the net sales, the amount left is the *net profit*. In our example, goods that cost $60,000 were sold for $100,000. In addition, there were expenses of $30,000. Therefore, the operations for the period resulted in a profit of $10,000.

$$\text{Net Sales } - \text{ (Cost of Goods Sold } + \text{ Operating Expenses) } = \text{ Net Profit}$$

Cost of Goods Sold

The determination of the cost of goods sold is relatively easy for a retailer of fine jewelry or a furrier, who sells only a few items a day. They have merely to total the purchase invoices of the goods that were sold. Now consider a supermarket or a large department store. To find the purchase invoice and total the cost of every item sold during the day is obviously an impossible task. Accountants handle it this way: To the cost of the merchandise on hand at the beginning of the period, they add the cost of the purchases made during the period. This total is the merchandise available to be sold during the period. From this total, they deduct the cost of the merchandise still on hand at the end of the period. The difference, the amount of the merchandise missing, is the cost of the goods sold. In other words, if we know the amount of goods we began with and the amount of goods that came in, by deducting the amount of goods still on hand, we can determine the amount of goods sold. An accountant expresses it this way:

Opening inventory (on hand beginning of period)	$40,000
Purchases (amount that came in during period)	50,000
Merchandise available for sale	$90,000
Closing inventory (on hand at end of period)	30,000
Cost of goods sold	$60,000

All the figures required for the preparation of an income statement, with the exception of the closing inventory, are readily available to the accountant. The sales are available from the cash registers, the purchases from the purchase invoices, the operating expenses from the check stubs that paid those bills, and the opening inventory from the physical inventory taken at the beginning of the period. Only the closing inventory presents a problem (the opening inventory has already been taken). Taking a physical inventory is costly and time-consuming and disrupts the store's regular procedures; therefore, it is rarely done more than twice a year. On the other hand, management, for effective control, must have income statements much more frequently. Obviously, a method of accurately estimating the closing inventory at cost is needed. The retail inventory method of estimating inventory presents such an estimate.

Retail Inventory Method

The retail method of estimating inventory at cost can be accomplished in three steps. (It must be borne in mind that it is the *cost* of the closing inventory that we are trying to determine.)

1. *Determine the relationship (percent) of the cost of the merchandise to the selling price of the merchandise.* This can be done by keeping records in a manner that will indicate both the cost and selling price of the goods. To do this, all purchases are recorded at cost as well as at selling price. Similarly, all inventories, physical and otherwise, must also be kept at cost and selling price. When this is done, our books of account yield the following information:

	Cost	Retail
Opening inventory	$20,000	$30,000
Purchases	40,000	50,000
Merchandise available for sale	$60,000	$80,000

In other words, we had goods that cost $20,000 on hand at the beginning of the period. We bought additional goods during the period for $40,000. In all, we offered our customers goods costing $60,000 during the period. Figured the same way, the goods that cost $60,000 during the period had a retail value of $80,000. To determine the percentage of the cost of the merchandise to its selling price we divide

$$\frac{\text{Cost}}{\text{Selling Price}} \quad \frac{\$60,000}{\$80,000} = 75\%$$

We have now determined that, on the average, our cost is 75 percent of selling price. Now, we can determine the cost of any lot of merchandise by taking 75 percent of its retail price.

2. *Determine the inventory at retail.* Since we know the value of the merchandise available for sale at retail (from step one), by deducting the sales actually made, we can determine the amount unsold (the inventory) at retail. In other words, if we assume sales of $50,000, we can do the following:

Merchandise available at retail	$80,000
Less: sales	50,000
Inventory at retail	$30,000

If we had $80,000 at retail available to be sold, and we sold $50,000, we must have $30,000 left (inventory) at retail.

3. *Convert inventory at retail to inventory at cost.* Having determined the closing inventory at selling price (retail) and the percent that cost bears to selling price, we can convert the inventory from selling price to cost by applying the percent.

Inventory at retail	$30,000
Percent cost bears to retail	× 75%
Estimated inventory at cost	$22,500

Illustrative Problem

During its first year of operation, the Acme Hardware Store bought merchandise costing $300,000 that was marked to sell for $500,000. The year's sales totaled $200,000. Find the estimated cost of the inventory at the end of the year.

Solution

1. To determine the percentage of the cost of the merchandise to its selling price:

$$\frac{\text{Cost}}{\text{Selling Price}} \quad \frac{\$300,000}{\$500,000} = 60\%$$

We have found that the cost is 60 percent of the selling price. Now if we can find the inventory at selling price, we can convert it to cost by taking 60 percent of it.

2. To determine the inventory at selling price:

The total amount of merchandise available for sale had a selling price of	$500,000
Of this, the amount sold was	200,000
The amount left on hand (inventory) at selling price	$300,000

3. To convert the inventory at selling price to inventory at cost: We have already determined that cost is 60 percent of selling price. Therefore if the inventory at selling price is $300,000,

$$\$300,000 \times 60\% = \$180,000 - \text{Inventory at cost}$$

While some large retailers with extensive computer systems might have their closing inventory at cost readily available to them at all times, the vast majority use the retail inventory method described above. Without this method, and the income statements that are dependent upon it, retail management would have to operate under severe handicaps.

It should be understood that the problems presented were somewhat simplified. Sales returns, purchase returns, additional markups, markdowns, and so forth would have to be taken into account in estimating the cost of the inventory under the retail method.

The reasons for the wide acceptance of the retail inventory method include the following:

1. *Provides frequent income statements.* Since the closing inventory at cost can be estimated by a relatively simple calculation, income statements (by department as well as for the total store) can be prepared when required. This is usually done monthly. By contrast, a store depending on physical inventory taking to determine the cost of the closing inventory is limited to one or, at most, two income statements a year. Efficient managerial control, both for top and middle management, is severely handicapped if income statements are not produced promptly and frequently.

2. *Simplifies physical inventories.* The retail inventory method permits the prices to be taken as they are ticketed on the merchandise. Retailers not using the retail inventory method take physical inventories by style number. The cost of each individual style must then be found to determine the cost of the merchandise on hand, a costly and time-consuming job.

3. *Turns up shortages.* When a physical inventory is taken, the estimated inventory (calculated by using the retail method) can be compared with the actual inventory (inventory determined by actual physical count). Where the physical inventory is less than the estimated inventory, the difference may be due to shortages. This may indicate ineffective control over the merchandise.

4. *Assists with insurance coverage and claim adjustment.* Insurance on inventories is based upon the value of the inventory. The bigger the inventory, the higher the coverage, and the larger the premium. Since insurance is expensive, it is vital to have the proper coverage at all times. Retailers because of the seasonal nature of their businesses, have constantly fluctuating inventories. Using the retail inventory method, they are able to adjust their insurance coverage to their actual needs on a monthly basis. Moreover, insurance companies accept the records of the retail method in settling claims. For example, in the case of a complete inventory loss due to fire, it is often impossible to determine the amount of the loss any other way.

5. *Furnishes basis for dollar control.* If dollar control is to be employed, as it must for any efficient retailing operation, the retail method of estimating inventory must be employed. There can be no effective dollar control without it.

6. *Ensures accurately valued inventory.* Merchandise inventory is an asset. That is to say, it represents a value that the retailer owns. The amount of that value is sometimes lower than its cost. Take, for example, a situation in which goods are marked down. This usually indicates that they can be replaced at a value less than their cost. To include such goods at cost would overstate the inventory, since the goods are worth less than their cost. Under the retail inventory method the goods are listed at retail prices that take markdowns into account. When the cost percent is applied to this marked down amount,

the result is an amount less than cost for marked down merchandise. This accurately represents the true value of such goods.

Some disadvantages of the retail inventory method are as follows:

1. *Averaging.* A serious disadvantage is that it depends upon an average cost percent. When the total merchandise available for sale at retail is divided into the total merchandise available for sale at cost, the resulting percent is the average throughout the store. Since not all sales of merchandise follow the same average, errors occur. In fact, low markup goods generally sell better than the higher markup variety. This results in an actual markup on sales that is different from the cost percent. Retailers who use different markups and special sales have these problems magnified.

2. *Not for all departments.* In some departments, it is impossible to estimate the selling price of goods in advance. These generally are departments in which the merchandise is bought as raw materials and changed before sales can be made. Restaurants, pharmacies, and bakeries are typical of such departments. Department stores that insist upon uniformity among all departments find this a disadvantage. It would seem that insistence upon uniformity under these conditions is a high price to pay for disregarding so beneficial a system.

3. *High operating cost.* The additional records required by the operation of the retail inventory method are considerable. As a result, the cost of the system is high. In addition, accuracy is vital, and expensive checks and counterchecks are necessary.

The determination of whether or not to use the retail method requires the careful comparison of the advantages versus the disadvantages. On balance, the advantages of the system seem to outweigh its disadvantages, as evidenced by the fact that the vast majority of large and medium-sized retailers employ these methods. Many large organizations that use other accounting methods for their income tax return and reports to stockholders use the retail method for the efficiency of managerial control that it provides.

Cost Methods of Determining Inventory

Most retailers (including those using the retail method for managerial control) use the lower-of-cost-or-market method for determining the value of their inventories. This requires the periodic physical count of each item on hand and the identification of the cost of each item. The cost to replace each item is then determined, and the lower-of-cost-or-market (replacement value) is used to determine the value of the inventory. Failure to use the replacement value would result in an overstatement of the inventory, an overstatement of the profits, and an overstatement of the income tax liability. Since the value of the inventory is important, the calculation of its worth is critical. There are several methods of determining the cost per unit of inventory, as will be shown in the following illustrative problem:

Illustrative Problem

During the year, a furniture store made the following purchases of molded folding chairs.

| Feb. 10 | 100 chairs @ $10 | Sept. 14 | 60 chairs @ $ 8 |
| June 20 | 200 chairs @ $12 | Dec. 12 | 100 chairs @ $14 |

On December 31, the date on which the inventory must be determined, there were found to be 120 molded folding chairs on hand. Since it is the policy of the store to stock all such chairs together, it was impossible to ascertain the specific purchase lots from which the 120 chairs came. Calculate the value of the 120 chairs in the merchandise inventory.

Solution

To solve this problem, we must first make certain assumptions concerning the merchandising policy of the store. If the store is operated in such fashion that the first merchandise to come in is the first to be sold, then the inventory at December 31 must be valued at the cost of the last purchases. If the reverse is true, and the last goods to come in are the first to be sold, then the merchandise remaining on hand at December 31 must be valued at the cost of the earliest purchases. Another method of valuing the inventory would be to use an average cost per chair. We shall solve the above problem using all three of these methods.

1. *FIFO.* FIFO is an abbreviation for the first-in-first-out method of pricing inventories. It assumes that the first chairs purchased by the store were the first that were sold. That is, the first chairs to be sold were those purchased on February 10, the second group sold were those purchased on June 20, and so on. Therefore, the 120 chairs remaining on hand on December 31 consisted of the last chairs purchased and the inventory should be valued as follows:

$$
\begin{array}{lll}
100 \text{ chairs @ } \$14 & = & \$1,400 \\
\underline{20} \text{ chairs @ } \$8 & = & \underline{\$160} \\
120 & & \$1,560 \text{ FIFO inventory value}
\end{array}
$$

2. *LIFO.* LIFO is an abbreviation for last-in-last-out. It is the opposite of the first-in-first-out method. That is, it assumes that the last chairs purchased were the first to be sold. Therefore, the first chairs sold were those bought December 12, the next sales were the chairs purchased on September 14, and so on. Using the LIFO method, the chairs left on hand on December 31 were from the earliest purchased, thus

$$
\begin{array}{lll}
100 \text{ chairs @ } \$10 & = & \$1,000 \\
\underline{20} \text{ chairs @ } \$12 & = & \underline{\$240} \\
120 & & \$1,240 \text{ LIFO inventory value}
\end{array}
$$

3. *Weighted average.* Another method of determining the value of the inventory is the weighted average method. This method assigns the average of all of the costs of all of the purchases to the units remaining in the inventory. It is necessary to use a weighted average, one which takes the number of units of each purchase into account, since in a simple average the purchase of one unit would have as important an effect as the purchase of 1,000 units. The 120 chairs in the above problem would be valued as follows:

a. Find the weighted average cost per unit.

$$
\begin{array}{lll}
\text{Feb. 10} & 100 \text{ chairs @ } \$10 & = \$1,000 \\
\text{June 20} & 200 \text{ chairs @ } \$12 & = \$2,400 \\
\text{Sept. 14} & 60 \text{ chairs @ } \$8 & = \$480 \\
\text{Dec. 12} & \underline{100} \text{ chairs @ } \$14 & = \underline{\$1,400} \\
& 460 & \$5,280
\end{array}
$$

$$
\frac{\$5,280}{460} = \$11.48 \text{ Weighted average cost per unit}
$$

b. Multiply the weighted average cost per unit by the number of units in the inventory.

Units on hand on December 31	120
Weighted average cost per unit	× $ 11.48
Weighted average inventory value	$1,377.60

A comparison of the three inventory methods discloses the following:

FIFO inventory	$1,560.00
LIFO inventory	1,240.00
Weighted average inventory	1,377.60

Since such important business considerations as the amount of net profit and the amount of income taxes are directly related to the value of the inventory, it is easy to understand that the method of evaluating inventory is of great importance to business-people.

The preceding problem has been oversimplified for teaching purposes. Regardless of the order in which the goods are sold, retailers are entitled to choose any of the above methods for evaluating their inventories. They are all acceptable to the accounting profession as well as the taxing authorities, as long as the method chosen is used consistently for all years. Since a comparison of the three methods results in different inventory values, the amount of profits and taxes will be affected by the method chosen.

Most retailers attempt to sell their oldest goods first. This is particularly true in the case of goods that are perishable or subject to style changes. FIFO is a logical method for valuing inventories since it most perfectly fits the actual flow of goods from the receiving department to the customer.

During an inflationary period, when purchase prices are constantly rising, the FIFO method results in a high markup. The assumption that the first goods in (the cheapest during an inflationary period) are the first sold results in a low cost of goods sold, and high profits and taxes. Since these goods will have to be replaced at higher costs, FIFO causes problems in a period of rising prices.

In recent years there has been a trend among large retailers to offset the high taxes resulting from FIFO, and by so doing, have funds available for the increased cost of maintaining inventory. LIFO offers such a solution. It became available as the result of a Bureau of Internal Revenue ruling in 1947 and has been growing in use since then.

By assuming that the most recent purchases (most expensive in an inflationary period) are the first sold, LIFO results in a high cost of goods sold and low profits and taxes. Similarly, LIFO provides that the inventory be priced at the oldest (cheapest) prices. The resulting tax savings help provide funds for the increased cost of purchases.

While most large retailers are presently taking advantage of the tax savings available through LIFO, smaller stores are slow to make the change. Among the reasons for the hesitancy on the part of the small store are

1. A complicated accounting system is required to operate the LIFO system.
2. Once LIFO is chosen, it must be used continuously. In times of a declining price level, its effect would be high profits and taxes.

The weighted average method of inventory valuation is essentially a compromise between LIFO and FIFO. The effect of price level changes (inflation) is averaged in the determination of inventory value and profits. Since the records and calculations required to determine the inventory value using this method are considerable, it is less frequently used than LIFO or FIFO. It is likely that the growing use of computers to minimize calculation and record keeping problems will result in an increase in the use of the weighted average method.

Sales and Profit per Square Foot

A method of financial control used by department stores and chain organizations is to calculate volume and profits per square foot of allocated space. Calculation of sales or profits per square foot is simple. It is found by dividing the profits or sales by the number of square feet of the space.

The per square foot figures are used by management in several ways:

1. In the allocation of floor space among departments. When one department has significantly higher figures than its neighbors, consideration must be given to the idea of transferring space from the weaker departments to the stronger.
2. To set standards of what each department should yield. By comparing results to the previously set standards, weak spots among the departments can be determined.
3. To compare the square foot figures with those of competitors.

Per square foot figures have the advantage over simple volume or profit information since they take into account the amount of space used by the particular department or chain store unit. For example, the sporting goods department in a particular store in an organization may make $1,000,000 while another unit in the company may make $800,000. If the better profit maker has twice the amount of square feet, that would be an important piece of information when comparing the two departments. This concept enables the retailer to get a better picture of the situation than if profitability or volume alone were used.

OPERATIONAL CONTROL

For any retail business to be successful, management must exercise careful control in the areas of inventory and expenses. Unless the proper systems are in place the store is likely to run in a less profitable manner.

In the following discussion, the controls used for the inventory and expenses will be addressed separately.

Inventory Control

In most retail enterprises, the amount of money invested in merchandise inventory represents a large part of the organization's total capital. Both the profitability of a store and the capability of its upper and middle management can be judged, in large part, by its inventory. Inventory must be large enough to ensure a high level of sales, but not so large as to result in excessive losses or expenses. It is relatively simple to carry a large enough inventory to satisfy every customer. However, the markdowns, handling costs, rental expense, insurance expense, and so on that go with a large inventory make it uneconomical. To find the proper balance of inventory requires careful control that can be achieved only through a careful analysis of purchases and sales.

Generally, the necessity for inventory control can be summarized as follows:

1. *Matching the stock on hand to customer needs.* A well-run store must have in stock the item that the customer has in mind. While no store can please every customer, any store that expects future traffic must please a substantial number of customers. This can be achieved only through a careful study of the needs and preferences of the store's clientele.

2. *Minimizing markdowns.* The prompt reporting that is a principal feature of a sound merchandise control system brings attention to situations in which there are goods in excess of customer needs. By carefully analyzing sales, a relationship between stock on hand and estimated customer demand can be determined. Conditions in which the stock is in excess of the expected demand may indicate the necessity for immediate markdowns. The timeliness of markdowns is important, since the earlier the markdown, the higher the selling price.

3. *Controlling shortages.* Effective merchandise control indicates the amount of merchandise that should be on hand. When the actual amount on hand is less than the amount predicted, shrinkage has occurred. Sound merchandising control can quickly pinpoint the specific area of shortage. Once the location of the shortage is know, effective security procedures can frequently be initiated.

4. *Controlling the investment in inventory.* The inventory carried by a retail store represents a considerable portion of the store's net worth. When the inventory on hand exceeds the amount required to satisfy customers, money is unnecessarily tied up. Merchandise control, by keeping the investment in inventory in check, frees money for expansion, improvements, and so on.

5. *Reducing stock carrying expenses.* There are many expenses involved in carrying inventory. These include the retail cost of floor space, personnel for handling, insurance premiums, and other overhead costs. Carrying unnecessary stock results in an increase of these expenses. The careful control of merchandise minimizes these expenses. In most retail stores, a reduction in the size of the stockroom, which results from carrying a small inventory, increases the available selling space, a vital factor in a store's success.

6. *Improving purchasing procedures.* The buyer's decisions about what to buy, when to buy, and how much to buy can spell the difference between the success or failure of an operation. It is important that these decisions be based on up-to-date, efficient information about the sizes, styles, and colors the customers require. The best source of such information is a history of past customer requirements. The end product of merchandise control includes detailed analyses of stock, sales, and merchandise on hand and on order. While this does not free the buyer from decision making, it offers vital data upon which the decisions must be based.

Merchandise may be controlled in two ways. The first, dollar control, requires an analysis of all sales and purchase transactions and yields information in terms of dollars. In other words, it produces merchandise information in terms of dollars, or "how much." The second method, unit control, analyzes merchandise transactions in terms of units. The output of unit control is in terms of specific pieces of merchandise, or "what." Both types of information are important, and many stores control merchandise by using both methods.

Dollar Control

The method of accounting for merchandise in terms of dollars may be accomplished by using the cost of the merchandise or, in most cases, its selling price. Dollar control may be used for determining inventory at cost, or the method may be extended to a complete system of merchandise control.

Classification of Merchandise

Since merchandise control in a small store may be nothing more than the proprietor looking over the stockroom and shelves, dollar control for the store as a whole may be adequate. In such a case, dollar control will indicate the total inventory picture. As stores grow in size and become departmentalized, merchandise control in terms of totals becomes ineffective. The very purposes of merchandise control require specific information concerning specific merchandise. For example, it is of little value to the menswear buyer in Macy's to know the total sales, purchases, and inventory of the total R.H. Macy operation.

Departmental Classification. When merchandise transactions are analyzed by departments rather than totals, the information given by a merchandise control system becomes far more useful to top management and to buyers. Classification by departments does not, however, give the buyers information about the individual items of merchandise that make up their departments. For example, a menswear buyer must make a decision about buying dress shirts for next season. Departmental dollar control indicates that the department was very successful last year. However, since the control figures are for the total department, including suits, ties, and sportswear as well as dress shirts, the information is not specific enough for making decisions about individual items.

Price Line Classification. As the classification of merchandise narrows down and becomes more specific, the value of the system's informational output becomes more useful. Buyers who are given merchandise information by price line are able to spot the relative importance of the various categories of merchandise in their departments. The menswear buyer mentioned above is now able to use the merchandise information concerning the effectiveness of the various price lines of dress shirts the store carries, and the buying decision becomes more scientific. It should be pointed out that the buyer still knows nothing of colors and sizes.

Computerized Classification. As the classification of merchandise used for dollar control narrows down and becomes more valuable, the system becomes more detailed, more prone to error, and more expensive to operate. While there is some question about whether or not the computer can actually save money in the operation of a merchandise control system, it is the perfect tool for this sort of application. The computer is designed to deal with the mass of repetitive data that is the raw material for merchandise control. In addition to all of the previously mentioned classifications, computerized merchandise control is capable of producing information about size, color, vendor, and other merchandise characteristics.

Procedures

Two methods may be used to analyze merchandise by the dollar method. These are the perpetual inventory method and the periodic inventory system.

Perpetual Inventory Method.   The perpetual inventory method is used to calculate the amount of merchandise on hand at selling price without physically counting the actual stock on the shelves. By adding the selling price of the goods that came in during the day (purchases) to the selling price of the goods on hand in the morning (opening inventory), the selling price of total goods that were handled (available for sale) can be determined. Deducting the sales from this figure will leave the selling price of the unsold goods (closing inventory). An accountant presents this information as follows:

Opening inventory (goods on hand in the morning)	$ 9,000
Purchases	18,000
Merchandise available for sale (total goods handled)	$27,000
Less: sales	15,000
Closing inventory (goods on hand at closing)	$12,000

The illustration was based on one day's transactions, but the procedure may be used for any period up to one year. In addition, the illustration may be taken to be for one specific price line or, in a sophisticated data processing system, for one particular style, size, and color. When markdowns occur, they must be added to the sales. Failure to do this would result in an overstated closing inventory. In addition, the closing inventory must be reduced by any estimated shrinkage of stock.

The advantage of the perpetual inventory method is that it yields information quickly. As a result, not only are reports to buyers prompt, but income statements can be produced frequently.

The weakness of the system is in its accuracy. The classification of the goods must be correctly indicated on the sales slip for the system to work effectively. Life on a hectic sales floor does not lend itself to careful clerical work. Of course, those computerized systems that employ a prepunched or machine readable sales tag that includes classification information are not as subject to clerical error.

Periodic Inventory System.   The perpetual inventory method was used to determine the closing inventory by arithmetic calculation. The periodic inventory system requires the closing inventory to be determined by actual physical count, and it is the sales figure that is arithmetically calculated. By adding the selling price of the goods on hand at the beginning of the period to the selling price of the purchases made during the period, the selling price of the total goods handled may be determined. From this total, the goods on hand at the end of the period (as determined by actual count) is deducted. The remainder, the difference between the amount that was available before sales were made, and the amount after sales were made, is the amount of sales and markdowns. An accountant states this as follows:

Opening inventory (goods on hand in the morning)	$ 9,000
Purchases	18,000
Merchandise available for sale (total goods handled)	$27,000
Less: closing inventory (goods unsold at end of period)	12,000
Total sales and markdowns	$15,000

The total sales and markdowns must be reduced by the amount of the markdowns to determine the sales.

The advantage of the periodic inventory system lies in its simplicity and reduced paperwork. Its principal disadvantage is that an actual physical inventory must be taken. This is costly and time-consuming, and disrupts the normal operation of the business. For this reason, physical inventories are rarely taken more than twice a year. This severely limits the number of income statements and other informational reports that are made available under the physical inventory method.

Unit Control

As is the case with dollar control, unit control is a system of analyzing merchandise transactions and producing informational reports. The difference between the two methods is that unit control information is kept in units rather than in dollars. In other words, instead of reporting the sales of a particular price line as $1,000, the report would read that 100 units were sold. The advantages of this method of record keeping, particularly to middle management, are considerable. The following information, unavailable under dollar control systems, may be found in unit control reports:

1. *Vendor information.* Unit control systems can be designed to include information on vendors. In such cases the buyer is given information on the salability of the vendor's products, the number of sales returns for each vendor, the vendor's success in meeting delivery dates, the markdowns taken on a particular vendor's goods, and other vendor information of value to middle management.

2. *More accurate information.* The stock-on-hand items listed in unit control reports are easily spot-checked. That is, a salesperson can easily check the inventory report of six pieces of a certain style on hand by going to the shelf and counting the units. This sort of checking should be done constantly and results in more accurate reporting.

3. *Better control of shortages.* The ease with which a unit control inventory may be checked not only turns up shortages easily, but also reveals the specific area in which the shortage occurred. This is helpful in designing security procedures.

4. *Time-in-store information.* Since the merchandise is accounted for by units rather than dollars, specific information concerning the units may be kept. The date of arrival is one such bit of information. Dating provides a buyer with information on slow-moving goods that should be marked down or placed on sale.

5. *Size and color information.* Of great value to the buyer for future ordering and reordering is data on customer preferences in colors and sizes. Armed with this information, the buyer is more likely to make correct decisions, which will minimize future broken-lot markdowns.

6. *Model stock information.* The determination of the ideal model stock requires constant evaluation and updating. An analysis of sales by units sold provides the information for such checking.

7. *Automatic reordering information.* Once the model stock has been determined, reorder levels can be established for staple merchandise. For example, the buyer can decide that one dozen pairs of men's black socks should be ordered whenever the stock falls below two dozen. This becomes an automatic procedure that can be done by a computer or a buying assistant. In this way, the buyer may be relieved of a time-consuming task.

8. *Other buying information.* Data on out-of-stock conditions, the timing of purchases, promotions, and markdowns are quickly and readily available under a unit control situation.

Operating a Unit Control System

The operation of a unit control system is simple. Whether it is hand recorded, as is the case with some small retailers, or computerized as in larger stores, the concept is the same. The following is typical of a unit-control inventory sheet:

Shirts—Style 127

Date	On Hand	Received	Sold	Balance
1	10	—	2	8
2	8	—	3	5
3	5	12	2	15
4	15	—	4	11
5	11	12	6	17

Physical Inventories

The most important feature of any system of merchandise control is the inventory. The stock on hand is the heart of the system, and the effectiveness of a retailer's merchandise control can be checked by comparing the inventory predicted by the system with the inventory found to be on hand by actual count. The taking of a physical inventory—that is, the counting and tabulation of the value of the goods on hand—serves functions other than checking the merchandise control system.

1. Firms with no systems of merchandise control can only determine the value of the merchandise on hand by actually counting the stock.
2. Shortages may be determined by comparing the inventory shown by the merchandise control system with the amount indicated by physical count.
3. The financial statements prepared by accountants require the high degree of accuracy that is the result of actually counting the inventory.
4. The taking of a physical inventory requires looking into corners and calling attention to slow-moving and neglected stocks, which might otherwise go unnoticed.

Frequency of Physical Inventories

Physical inventories should be taken as frequently as possible. However, the problems involved with inventory taking are so great that an inventory count is rarely done more than twice a year, and frequently only once a year. The efforts involved in taking an inventory, in terms of time, expenses, and interference with regular procedures, are so great that many stores take inventory only when required for the accountant's financial statements.

Physical Inventory Procedures

There are probably as many procedures for taking a physical inventory as there are businesses. These methods vary from the proprietor of a small store listing the store's merchandise on a sheet of paper, to the carefully planned large store method, which includes an instruction booklet. The system to be used must be designed to ensure absolute accuracy. A map of the entire store may be made, to ensure that each bin, shelf, and counter is included. Care must be taken to include the goods in the receiving department, shipping department, stockrooms, and window displays. Most inventory procedures include the use of two-person teams that count the stock, check the count, and make entries of the count on specially designed forms. After the counts have been entered on inventory sheets, the costs of each item of stock must be looked up and multiplied by the number of items on hand. The value of each of the items is then added, and the total cost of the inventory is determined.

Computerized Inventory Systems

Inventory taking may be greatly simplified with computerized systems. Such systems include a duplicate of the sales tag, which is affixed to each item in the store. These tags are prepunched with all of the information required for inventory purposes. They are removed from each item by the inventory taker and are then fed into the computer, where they are sorted and tabulated. The computer's output consists of a detailed listing of the merchandise on hand.

Stock Turnover

The function of inventory is to generate sales. Ideally the amount and makeup of the inventory carried should be matched to the maximum amount of sales planned. When more inventory is carried than is necessary for sales, markdowns and excessive capital investment result. Too little inventory results in loss of sales. The most important test to determine the effectiveness of the stock on hand is the stock turnover rate. This test indicates, for a specific period of time (usually one year), the number of times the inventory has been completely sold out and repurchased.

Calculation of Stock Turnover Rate

Stock turnover rate may be calculated at cost, at retail, or in units. Given the following information, turnover rates may be determined as follows:

	Units	Cost	Retail	
Sales 1,400 units				$14,000
Opening inventory	800	$ 6,000	$ 8,000	
Purchases	1,600	12,000	16,000	
Merchandise available for sale	2,400	$18,000	$24,000	
Less: closing inventory	1,000	7,500	10,000	
Cost of goods sold	1,400	$10,500	$14,000	

1. To find the stock turnover rate at retail:

Opening inventory at retail $ 8,000
Closing inventory at retail   10,000
                                              $18,000 ÷ 2 = $9,000 Average inventory at retail

$$\frac{\text{Net sales}}{\text{Average inventory at retail}} = \frac{14,000}{9,000} = 1.56 \text{ Stock turnover rate at retail}$$

2. To find the stock turnover rate at cost:

Opening inventory at cost $ 6,000
Closing inventory at cost   7,500
                                            $13,500 ÷ 2 = $6,750 Average inventory at cost

$$\frac{\text{Cost of goods sold}}{\text{Average inventory}} = \frac{10,500}{6,750} = 1.56 \text{ Stock turnover rate at cost}$$

3. To find the stock turnover rate in units:

Opening inventory in units	800
Closing inventory in units	1,000
	1,800 ÷ 2 = 900 Average inventory in units

$$\frac{\text{Net sales in units}}{\text{Average inventory in units}} = \frac{1,400}{900} = 1.56 \text{ Stock turnover rate in units}$$

As can be seen in the preceding illustrations, when the markup is consistent throughout the period, all of the methods result in the same turnover rate.

A more exact turnover rate can be determined by improving the accuracy of the average inventory. This could be done by adding the beginning inventory for each of the 12 months in a year, plus the closing inventory for the twelfth month, and dividing by 13.

Turnover by Merchandise Classifications

Different classifications of merchandise will have different turnover rates. For example, food stores generally have a turnover rate of about 16, while shoe stores rarely go above 4. Since turnover rates are used for comparison purposes, there is little to be learned by calculating the storewide rate. This is to say, a large department store might achieve the excellent turnover rate of 4, while its toy department has the poor turnover rate of 1.5. For maximum use, the turnover rate should be calculated by merchandise classifications or, at the very least, by departments. Some typical turnover rates are listed in Figure 17– 1.

The Use of Stock Turnover Rates

The effectiveness of a store's or department's inventory management can be determined in part by comparing its turnover rate with that of similar stores, industrywide averages, and the turnover rates of the same store in prior periods. It must be emphasized that a store's turnover rate is only part of the story. Turnover rates can be improved by reducing prices, carrying only fast-moving merchandise, and devising promotions. In other words, a higher-than-average turnover rate does not necessarily guarantee higher-than-average profits.

Grocery stores	16
Gasoline stations	11
Women's ready-to-wear	7
Department stores	6
Discount stores	5
Variety stores	4
Jewelry stores	3

Figure 17–1 Typical turnover rates for certain types of retailers

EXPENSE CONTROL

When the amount for which goods are sold is greater than the cost of the goods and the operating expenses, a profit results. Of the three factors—sales, cost of goods, and expenses—the first two are more subject to control by competition than by the management of a retail establishment. Even in the most carefully controlled buying and selling system, prices are in large part set by vendors and customers. The control of expenses is another matter. In this area the retailer is in full command, and it is this extremely important area that frequently spells the difference between retailing success and failure.

It should be understood that expense control does not mean expense reduction. Frequently, careful expense control can indicate the advantage of increasing some expenses, such as advertising, in order to improve the profit position. Expense control is the process by which expenses are analyzed and set at a level that will maximize profits.

Classification of Expenses

In part, expenses are controlled by comparing the expenses of one retailer with those of a similar store, an industrywide average, or prior periods within the same store. Such comparisons are used to indicate weaknesses, which are then subjected to further study. For example, if a competitor with a similar operation is able to make more sales with lower sales salaries, expense control would point out this fact and provide a basis for further study.

Obviously, if comparisons are to be made, it is important that they be made between exactly the same expenses. It would be impossible to compare the sales salaries expense of two stores if one included fringe benefits and the other did not. To assist in the uniformity of expenses classification, the National Retail Federation suggests the following titles, which it calls Natural Classification:

1. Payroll
2. Fringe benefits
3. Advertising
4. Taxes
5. Supplies
6. Services purchased
7. Unclassified
8. Traveling
9. Communications
10. Pensions
11. Insurance
12. Depreciation
13. Professional service
14. Donations
15. Bad debts
16. Equipment costs
17. Real property rentals

Expense Allocations

Once a sound system of expense classification has been established, the next step in expense control is to distribute these expenses to the various selling departments. This will enable management to check the effectiveness of each of the departments. Expense allocation can be relatively simple, as in the case of selling salaries, which are charged to the department in which the salesperson worked. The case of rent expense or heating expense is more difficult.

The distribution of expenses is facilitated by dividing the expenditures into two broad classifications: the direct expenses, those that occurred only because the department was in existence (sales salaries); and indirect expenses, those that occur whether or not the department exists (officers' salaries). The allocation of direct expenses is simple. There are several theories as to how indirect expenses should be divided.

Methods of Allocation

All methods of allocation agree that direct expenses should be allocated to the department receiving the benefit of such expenses. The methods differ in the manner in which indirect expenses are to be allocated, or if they should be allocated at all.

Net Profit Method

The net profit method requires that all expenses, direct or indirect, be allocated to selling departments so that a net profit may be determined for each department. The distribution of direct expenses should be made according to the department receiving the benefit of the expense. The indirect expenses should be allocated in a logical manner. For example, rent expense may be allocated by floor space.

The prime advantage of the net profit method is that, by showing the net profit of each selling department, it permits judgments to be made as to the department (and department head's) effectiveness. In addition, by taking indirect expenses into account, it indicates to the department head the importance of providing profits to cover these expenses. Finally, the total departmental operating statement is an aid in setting selling prices, since the retail price must be high enough to cover the direct and indirect expenses.

The problem with the net profit method is that the allocation of the indirect expenses is not only expensive, but so complicated that it cannot be accurate. If rent expense is to be allocated on the basis of the feet of floor space used by each department, should main floor front be considered as valuable as fifth floor rear? What is an accurate way for dividing the store president's salary among the various departments? Holding a department head responsible for indirect expenses, which are likely to be inaccurate, and over which the department head had no control, is a serious disadvantage.

Contribution Method

The contribution method attempts to overcome the disadvantages of the net profit method by limiting expense allocation to direct expenses. The final result from this method is controllable profit (only those expenses that the department head controls are deducted). Controllable profit is the department's contribution to the amount required to cover the indirect expenses and net profit.

This method does, in fact, answer the most serious objections of the net profit method. What it does not do is help in price setting, or involve the buyer with indirect expenses.

The Expense Budget

A common and effective method of controlling expenses is by means of an expense budget. This may be defined as a carefully planned estimate of future expenses for a specific period of time. Expense budgeting offers these advantages:

1. *Makes financial provision for future expenses.* By knowing the financial requirements of future expenses, management may make provision for such expenses and be prepared for them when they arise.

2. *Enables planned expenses to be balanced against planned sales.* To achieve a planned net profit, it is necessary to estimate expenses as well as sales and costs. Successful planning requires careful estimates of expenses, sales, and costs.

3. *Provides standard against which to measure performance.* Upon completion of the period for which the expense budget was prepared, a comparison is made between the actual expenses and the estimated (budgeted) expenses. Any significant differences may then be analyzed to determine the reasons for such variations. In this way, weak spots are frequently uncovered.

4. *Fixes responsibilities.* By identifying specific expenses which specific departments, a particular person may be held responsible for seeing to it that the amounts expended are within the budget. It is important that the person held responsible has the authority to approve or disapprove expenditures.

Preparing the Expense Budget

Typically, the expense budget is prepared as part of the overall planning. By adjusting past periods' information with the coming period's expectations, estimated sales, costs, and expenses may be determined. For example, if last year's sales of $100,000 is expected to be increased by 10 percent, then the budgeted sales will be $110,000. Should no change be expected in last year's 30 percent gross margin, the budgeted gross margin will be $110,000 × 30%, or $33,000. If the only change expected in last year's total expenses of $20,000 will be an additional $1,000 for salaries, then the budgeted expenses will be $21,000. The budgeted net profit is $12,000. This can be stated in income statement form as follows:

	Prior Period	Future Period Budget
Sales (to be increased by 10%)	$100,000	$110,000
Gross margin (30% both periods)	30,000	33,000
Less: expenses (to be increased by $1,000)	20,000	21,000
Net profit	$ 10,000	$ 12,000

After the total estimated expenses have been determined, the total is broken down into the various types of expenses such as rent, advertising, utilities, and so forth. Then the various types of expenses are split up among the departments. Department heads are involved in this procedure. The final step in preparing an expense budget is to break down the department budget into short-period budgets.

TRENDS

Better record-keeping leads to tighter operational control and more efficient accounting. The following trend has made a greater impact on retailers to improve their profits.

Software

In its infancy, computer use was limited to few applications. Those retailers who knew the value of computerization for record-keeping and took advantage of it were the giants in the industry. On staff were programmers who created their own packages at considerable expense to the company.

Today a wealth of software is available to fit the needs of every merchant. The programs do everything from keeping unit control records, analyzing stock turnover, recording merchandise by classification and price, and so forth. The availability of these "canned" programs, has led to the elimination of programmers jobs in stores, thus cutting employee expenses.

ACTION FOR THE INDEPENDENT RETAILER

To the small retailer, particularly one who is just beginning a business and is anxious to keep expenses down, the cost of an accountant's services seems like an unnecessary luxury. That an accountant provides a necessary service rather than a luxury is evidenced by United States Department of Commerce records indicating that 84 percent of the retailers who fail do not have adequate accounting records.

Much of the work an accountant does is clerical and can easily be done by anyone who has been given a brief explanation of the requirements. In small firms, where the expense of an accountant may be a burden, many of the simpler accounting functions can be handled by the proprietor, or a part-time bookkeeper whose time is considerably less costly than that of an accountant. It is important, however, that only a trained accountant perform the part of the work that cannot be delegated to an untrained individual.

Many small retailers who employ accountants get far less than the full service available to them. Using an accountant solely for keeping records and preparing tax returns is a serious mistake. The accountant should also be called upon to arrange credit, advise on expansion, forecast sales, and perform a host of other chores. The financial area is complicated and important. Few small business owners and managers are trained for it, and they should lean heavily on their accountants for advice.

Through the keeping of inventory and expense control records, the retailer will be able to get a better picture of his or her operation and turn a greater profit. With the little expense associated with computerization, the road to more sophisticated record-keeping is within reach of the smallest retailer.

IMPORTANT POINTS IN THE CHAPTER

1. The function of accounting is recording business transactions, interpreting the results of the transactions, and giving advice based upon the interpretation.

2. The accountant provides systems of recording and summarizing financial information. These systems involve the use of bookkeeping records, such as ledgers and journals, which are tailored to the individual needs of each retailer.

3. The most important report supplied by the accountant is the income statement. It is a summary of the results of doing business for a specific period of time, which indicates the profit or loss of the business for that period.

4. When a physical count of the merchandise inventory is taken, it is necessary to determine the cost of each unit counted. This can be difficult since similar goods are bought at various costs. First-in-first-out, last-in-first-out, and weighted average are methods of determining the cost of the inventory.

5. In order to ensure high profits and minimize losses, it is vital that management keep careful control of merchandise inventory and expenses.

6. Control of inventory requires an exact knowledge of the various items that make up the total inventory at any specific time. This information can be determined in dollars or units.

7. When dollar control is used as the method of accounting for inventories at retail price, for maximum effectiveness, information on merchandise should be broken down by departments. This enables management to make judgments concerning the operations of each individual department.

8. The inventory of a large retailer is so large and varied that inventory control is enormously complicated. To overcome this difficulty, most large retailers use computers. This enables them to get prompt information on the specific items that make up their inventory.

9. Whatever the method of inventory control used, a periodic physical inventory must be taken at least once a year to check the accuracy of the control inventory.

10. Stock turnover, by indicating the number of times the inventory has been completely sold out and repurchased during a period, is another means of determining departmental effectiveness.

11. Expense control requires that judgments be made on the amount of expenses by comparing the amount of expense a department had in two separate periods, or comparing its expenses within a period with those of a similar department in another store. For comparisons to be effective, expenses must be classified in the same way for all periods. The National Retail Federation has published a list of expense titles that are widely used among retailers.

12. The expense budget is a means of controlling expenses by predicting future expenses for a specific period and then comparing the actual expenses with the predicted expenses.

REVIEW QUESTIONS

1. What benefits can a department store buyer of highly styled merchandise get from the store's accounting department?

2. Prepare an income statement in good form from the following information: Operating expenses $4,000, Sales $12,000, Cost of goods sold $6,000.

3. Why is the computer considered "the perfect accounting tool"?

4. Determine the cost of goods sold from the following information: Closing inventory $60,000, Opening inventory $80,000, Purchases $100,000.

5. Why is managerial control improved when the retail inventory method is used?

6. Explain how the retail inventory method simplifies the taking of a physical inventory.

7. How are shortages discovered by the retail inventory method?

8. A serious disadvantage of the retail method is that it is based on an averaging of markups. Explain.

9. Discuss other disadvantages of the retail inventory method.

10. Given the following information, calculate the inventory value using the FIFO method. There are 19 units in stock.

Opening inventory	14 units @ $ 8
1st purchase	8 units @ $ 9
2nd purchase	12 units @ $10
3rd purchase	6 units @ $12

11. Using the data given in Question 10, calculate the inventory using the LIFO method.

12. Using the data given in Question 10, calculate the inventory using the weighted average method.

13. Discuss the advantages of balancing inventory and customer needs.

14. How does inventory control assist in reducing shortages?

15. Dollar control becomes more valuable as the classification of merchandise narrows. Discuss.

16. How does the periodic inventory system differ from the perpetual inventory method?

17. What are the advantages and disadvantages of the perpetual inventory method?

18. Discuss the advantages to middle management of unit control over dollar control.

19. Discuss the control of shortages under unit control and dollar control. Which is the better method?

20. What are the advantages and disadvantages of a physical inventory?

CASE PROBLEMS

Case Problem 1

The Evans Dress Shop, a moderate-priced specialty store, had a serious fire in September. As a result of the fire, a large portion of the merchandise was completely destroyed. Merchandise with a retail value of $12,000 was undamaged by the fire and considered completely salable. The balance of the goods was completely destroyed, with the individual garments unidentifiable.

The accounting records were kept in a fireproof safe and were available after the fire. A study of these records indicated the following facts:

	Month	Cost	Retail	Actual Sales
Opening inventory	January 1	$25,000	$45,000	—
Purchases	January 31	12,000	18,000	$15,000
Purchases	February	12,000	25,000	15,000
Purchases	March	16,000	30,000	25,000
Purchases	April	14,000	20,000	26,000
Purchases	May	6,000	10,000	25,000
Purchases	June	12,000	16,000	14,000
Purchases	July	4,000	8,000	6,000
Purchases	August	6,000	12,000	4,000
Purchases	September	12,000	16,000	20,000

The insurance company agrees that they have a financial responsibility, but since the garments cannot be identified, the cost of the destroyed goods cannot be determined. They have offered $10,000 in full settlement of the claim.

Questions

1. Is the $10,000 acceptable?
2. How much should Evans get?

Case Problem 2

Trueman's Inc. showed a profit of $46,312 for the fiscal year just ended. Since its overall tax rate is about 50 percent, its tax liability will be considerable. The inventory used in determining its profit was valued, by the FIFO method, at $44,840. The accountant claims that a tax savings would result from a change to the LIFO method of evaluating inventories.

The details of the inventory and purchases are as follows:

Style	Opening Inventory	First Purchase	Second Purchase	Third Purchase	Closing Inventory
127	50 @ $ 74	50 @ $ 80	100 @ $ 81	—	40
216	30 @ 90	100 @ 90	60 @ 93	50 @ $ 96	60
318	30 @ 160	40 @ 170	50 @ 170	30 @ 180	20
426	—	100 @ 250	50 @ 265	30 @ 267	50
731	60 @ 200	40 @ 210	60 @ 210	50 @ 222	30
812	10 @ 180	30 @ 188	40 @ 190	—	30
914	50 @ 300	60 @ 300	50 @ 320	40 @ 330	20

Note: As the inventory increases or decreases, the profit increases or decreases by the same amount.

Questions

1. Calculate the profit using the LIFO method of inventory valuation.
2. Determine the tax savings if the LIFO method is used.
3. Do you feel a change to LIFO is warranted? Why?

Case Problem 3

Prell's, Inc., is a large department store in a metropolitan southeastern city. It is a very successful high-image store blessed with alert, aggressive management and the latest in computer equipment. The merchandising committee of top management meets monthly to survey the inventory situation of the various departments. It uses dollar control to compare the inventory and sales of each department with the inventory and sales position of the same department during the corresponding period of the prior year. At such meetings, any department with an inventory that is out of line is ordered to reduce its stock. The January meeting resulted in an order to the men's haberdashery department to reduce its stock by 15 percent.

The men's harberdashery department of Prell's controls inventory by unit control. Upon receipt of the inventory directive from the merchandising committee, the buyer and the two assistants made a careful study of their unit control system to determine the specific areas in which they were overstocked. The study indicated an excess of inventory in white shirts, socks, underwear, and handkerchiefs, all staple items, that did not meet Christmas selling expectations. The buyer suggests that the only way inventory can be reduced is by a special promotional sale of overstocked items.

A high-image store such as Prell's does not have promotional sales.

Questions

1. As a member of the merchandising committee, what would you suggest?
2. What would be the attitude of the men's haberdashery buyer?

Chapter 18
Credit and Customer Services

Photograph by Ellen Diamond

LEARNING OBJECTIVES

Upon completion of this chapter, the student should be able to:

1. Write a brief essay on consumer motives for owning credit cards.
2. Discuss three methods of credit extended by retail operations.
3. Describe the major responsibilities of the credit department.
4. List the steps in a collection system.
5. Define the federal laws of Truth-in-Lending and Regulation Z.
6. Discuss the various types of services found in stores.

PRIVATE-LABEL IS NOT ONLY FOR MERCHANDISE . . .

Today's consumer who makes purchases with a credit card, most often uses one that is generally referred to as a third-party card. That is, groups like VISA, MasterCard, American Express, and Discover offer plastic cards to those who meet their initial requirements for membership. These credit cards provide relative simplicity by allowing consumers to charge their purchases with one card. The third-party cards caught fire because the consumer is no longer required to carry a bag full of plastic and to pay numerous bills at the end of the billing cycle. Not every retailer was immediately taken with the third party credit concept, because it cut severely into their own credit card operations. Ultimately, however, the vast majority accepted third party cards, not by choice but by necessity, and saw the demise of their own charge programs.

In 1983, Paul Harris, a 224-store moderately priced women's clothing chain, went out of the private-label card business and succumbed to the pressures of the third party cards. After an absence of ten years, the company resurrected its own card, banking on the idea that it would eventually bring more business to them. When, for example, customers receive their monthly statements, the store would be able to market merchandise to them in the same mailing. Since the store is a private-label merchandise emporium, the only place where specific goods are available, Paul Harris believed that the private-label merchandise in itself would motivate shoppers who wanted those items to use the store's cards. Customers would regularly be reminded of the name Paul Harris, and would buy with greater regularity.

In a change from how they initially ran their credit card program, the company decided to go to an outside group, SPS Transaction Services, to run the program and sell them their receivables. That is, once the merchandise was charged on the Paul Harris card, the money was owed to SPS, which regularly pays the store the money owed, less a percentage. In this way, Paul Harris eliminates the need to run a collections department and hound customers who do not pay their bills.

In order to motivate shoppers to get on the private-label credit card program, the company has set-up counters in the stores where instant accounts are opened and customers receive a 10 percent discount on the first purchase for the sign-up. Those interested, if approved by way of direct telephone checks to SPS, may use their new cards at once. The hope is that the system will return a following of loyal consumers to the store.

Consumers are motivated to make their purchases at particular stores for a variety of reasons. While for many, the chief factor is price, a significant number of shoppers head for particular retail establishments because of the services offered.

With price very often the same at many competing operations, and similar merchandise available in more than one store, customers may be appealed to via attractive services. The most widely offered service is customer credit, a variety of others are also offered depending upon the store. Some services are widely available, whereas others are less apt to be found in many stores.

CREDIT

Many American families use at least one type of credit card. This increase in the use of credit has been one of the prime factors in the success of our economic system. It has had the effect of making goods available to consumers that they would not otherwise have been able to purchase: merchandise that they can afford but for which they are unable to save. for most of us, it has acted as a kind of forced savings. The economic result has been an enormous demand for goods and services, which has kept our industrial activity at a high level.

Of the total amount of credit purchases, retail credit accounts for a major share. It is likely that more than 50 percent of our retail purchases are on credit. Naturally, this varies with the type of store. About 70 percent of all department and specialty stores' sales are to credit customers. Even supermarkets now accept credit cards.

Owning Credit Cards

Successful retailing depends upon an understanding of customer motives for credit card use.

Convenience

A credit card identifies the buyer as a good store customer. This improves service, makes it easier to exchange and return items, and facilitates mail and telephone shopping. In addition, charge customers get advance notice of special sales.

Cash is Unnecessary

Many people dislike carrying the large amounts of cash required for big ticket sales. A credit card eliminates fear of theft or loss.

Customers without charge accounts who lack immediate funds frequently request C.O.D. shipments. This requires the payment of C.O.D. charges and waiting at home for deliveries.

Credit Rating

Because we live in a largely noncash business environment, establishing a credit rating is important. Having a charge account with one store is an aid in securing other credit. Similarly, a credit card is a good identification for check cashing.

Why Retailers Give Credit

The vast majority of retailers give credit because they have to. Of course, they would prefer cash transactions, because they bring immediate capital to the store. However, a variety of reasons necessitate credit. Included are the possibility of larger sales, development of a mailing list that could be used for direct mail sales, and unanticipated purchases that might not come about if cash was needed.

Customer Preferences

As we have seen, customers have many valid reasons for demanding credit. Many will simply not patronize a store that does not offer charge accounts. Some years ago, discount retailers were enormously successful. Their operation included reduced selling prices in return for a cutback in customer services. For a while they were very successful, but with the increase in customer demand for charge accounts, they have been forced to offer this service also. This necessitated an increase in selling prices, which narrowed the difference between their offerings and those of their more conventional competitors. At present, many discounters are being forced, to some extent, to change their operations. In other words, competitive pressures are such that a store that does not offer credit will have difficulty maintaining its share of the market.

Customer Relationships

Although it would be difficult to prove, most retailers believe that a charge customer is a loyal one. Tests have shown that charge customers are more likely to read the advertising of stores with which they have accounts. Other research indicates that the charge account buyer is a better customer, in terms of volume, than the cash buyer. It is likely that this "customer loyalty" view of charge accounts is an exaggeration. Given the present wide use of credit, most buyers carry credit cards for competing stores and are hardly loyal to any individual retailer.

Direct Mail Selling

An important benefit that charge accounts bring to a store is a mailing list consisting of persons who have shown a fondness for the store's specific type of operation. This type of list is valuable and difficult to come by. (Most commercial lists include many names of totally disinterested people.) These lists, when carefully used, may be an important source of mail order business. This can be accomplished either as direct mail or, more frequently, with enclosures that are inserted with the monthly charge account statement. When the latter method is used, there is no additional mailing cost and the expense of printing the enclosure is frequently borne by the supplier rather than the retailer.

Salespeople and Credit

To salespeople, the use of credit offers an excellent means of closing sales. An important feature in any sales training program should be the use of credit and the encouragement of customers to open charge accounts. Credit customers are in a position to buy impulsively, add accessories, and buy larger amounts than originally intended. Armed with this information, the salesperson should try to increase both unit sales and higher-priced items. One expert has estimated that most stores lose hundreds of sales each day for lack of a timely credit suggestion. The shoe salesperson who has not suggested a matching handbag, the appliance salesperson who has not pointed out the advantages of the more expensive model, and the white goods salesperson who does not suggest a dozen towels instead of six are all guilty of not using credit as a selling tool.

Kinds of Retail Credit

An important portion of the expansion of consumer credit is that offered by retail stores to their customers. There are four major types of retail credit, and individual retailers offer many variations of these basic kinds.

Charge Accounts

Charge account credit is one type of credit offered by retailers. Customers receive their merchandise at the time of purchase without being required to give a down payment or a pledge of collateral. Upon receipt of a monthly statement, the customer is expected to pay within 30 days. There is no charge for this kind of credit, although customers who fail to pay within the 30-day period are charged interest or a service charge.

Installment Accounts

Installment credit is much more formal than charge account credit. It has the following characteristics:

1. *Down payment.* At the time of purchase, the customer is required to make an immediate payment of a percentage of the total sale. The amount of down payment varies with the type of merchandise and the particular store.
2. *Periodic payments.* Installment account customers agree to make a specified number of equal payments over the life of the loan.
3. *Finance charges.* Unlike charge account customers, installment customers are required to pay interest and other finance charges for the extended life of their loan.
4. *Repossession rights.* Installment sellers retain, as security for their loan, the right to take back the merchandise sold, in the event of nonpayment of an installment when it comes due.
5. *Formal contract.* The installment purchaser must sign a formal contract setting forth the conditions of the sale and the rights of both parties at the time of purchase.

Revolving Credit

Revolving credit is a combination of charge account and installment credit. Installment credit is usually reserved for such expensive items as jewelry, furniture, and appliances. Revolving credit permits installment paying for small purchases. It works this way: A customer is given a credit limit by the store—for example, $500. In addition, the customer has to pay $50 per month whenever there is an outstanding balance to the store until the debt is wiped out. At the same time, more merchandise may be purchased whenever the debt to the store is less than $500. Like that of the installment buyer, this buyer's monthly payment is $50 (unless less is owed), and like the charge customer, this customer can freely buy on credit up to the credit limit. Revolving credit usually carries a service charge (about 1.5 percent per month).

Option Terms

Revolving credit requires a fixed monthly payment. A variation of this permits the customer the choice of paying in full or making some minimum payment (usually $\frac{1}{12}$). Most charge customers are automatically given option terms. their monthly statement indicates the full amount due, and the minimum option payment that will be acceptable if the customer prefers it. Because the option payment is a fixed fraction of the amount owed, it will vary with the size of the balance. Customers who prefer the option payment are billed service charges for the unpaid balance (usually 1.5 percent per month).

Revolving credit with option terms is growing in use. Stores like it because it increases interest income while reducing customer resistance to service charges. Customers like the method because they are given a choice of payments, which they can vary depending upon their budget for each month.

The Retailer's Credit Department

As we have seen, the proper use of credit has become a necessary ingredient in successful retailing. The responsibility for managing credit lies with the credit department, under the supervision of the controller. This department is charged with the following:

1. Opening new accounts
2. Keeping credit records
3. Authorization
4. Billing
5. Collections

Opening New Accounts

Credit card customers are the store's best customers because they are responsible for a major portion of the store's sales volume. Consequently, every effort is made to have noncharge customers open accounts. This may be done by telephone solicitation, and radio, newspaper, and direct mail advertising. Sales personnel are the most important source of new accounts and they are trained to suggest a credit card whenever possible. For new accounts, most stores use the following procedures:

Interview.   The customer interested in receiving a credit card is sent to the credit department, where an interview with a member of the department takes place. During the interview a credit application is filled out. Through the questions on the application and others that the interviewer directs to the customer, the three "C's" of credit are determined: these are character, capacity, and capital.

Approval.   The decision about whether an applicant should be granted credit is the responsibility of the credit manager. With today's easy credit, the vast majority of applications are approved immediately. Upon approval (the interview and approval rarely take longer than 20 minutes), many stores permit the applicant to make credit purchases at once. Other stores postpone the use of credit for a few days while checking outside sources such as TRW. It should be noted that outside sources of credit information are used even when immediate credit is granted. At Lord & Taylor, customers who already have a major credit card are quickly given a Lord &

Taylor credit card for immediate use. The store's decision is based upon the existing credit card.

Setting Credit Limits.   After credit has been approved, a credit limit must be decided upon. That is, a decision must be made about the total amount a customer may be permitted to owe the store at any one time. Such information as general business conditions, unemployment prospects in the area, the credit bureau's report, and weekly earnings are taken into account. Many stores set a credit limit at twice weekly earnings. It should be understood that the limit set can be increased at the customer's request upon further investigation.

For example, Hudson's, Detroit uses a point-scoring system that enables it to raise or lower each customer's credit limit every month. Each account is updated according to the purchases and payments made during that particular month.

Keeping Credit Record

Record keeping for charge customers is one of the responsibilities of the credit department. This is more than a mere bookkeeping chore because customers' credit ratings change, and a careful study of the payment records can frequently indicate the necessity of a reduction in credit limit. Some stores subscribe to rating books that are published by private credit bureaus. These periodicals indicate changes in ratings of consumer credit buyers.

Authorization

Each charge customer is given an identification number that is displayed on a recognition device such as a credit card. This card is presented at a sales cash register. In some stores further identification, such as a driver's license, is required to prove that the buyer is the true owner of the card. In other stores, the charge card must be signed in advance by the customer. This signature is then compared with the signature on the sales slip for discrepancies before the sale is recorded.

Authorization, for the most part, is accomplished through a scanning device which checks the status of the account. When the authorization does not come through because of late payments or purchases in excess of the credit limit, the customer is requested to visit the credit department to try to work things out.

Billing

The last step in credit sales transactions is sending the monthly statement to the customer. This is a list of the month's transactions showing the balance due the store.

Setting a Credit Policy

The three factors that must be considered in setting a credit policy are capital, competition, and kinds of goods.

Capital.   Of great importance in determining the strictness of the credit policy is the financial condition of the store granting the credit. All retailers need their customers' money to pay their own debts. How quickly these funds are needed depends upon their working capital position, their ability to borrow from banks to carry their customers, and their willingness to pay the cost of such loans. Naturally, under-financed stores must have a strict credit policy.

Competition.   The force of competition is probably the deciding factor in determining credit policy. American buying habits would drastically limit the volume of any store that grants significantly less credit than its competitors.

Kinds of Goods.   Perishable goods require stricter collection policies than hard goods. Customers are less willing to pay for goods that are no longer in use. In addition, hard goods can often be repossessed, and continued use by the customer requires timely payments of his or her account.

Collections

Unlike most other services provided by the store, credit can have adverse effects. No matter how carefully the credit manager screens customers, there is little to prevent a proportion of people from not paying their bills. If the store operates its own credit system (credit card organizations will be discussed separately), it is the store which bears the responsibility not only for the collection of bad debts, but also for the alienation of those who are upset by the store's actions.

A sensitive area in the system is how to collect what is owed without offending the customer. Contrary to common belief, the culprits are not always those who have real financial problems. Often, it is the store's better customers who are delinquent payers of their bills. Much caution must be exercised not to offend those people. Although the retailer has every right to collect, the value of the individual's future business must be weighed before the unpleasant task of collection begins. Most retailers would be quick to relate stories concerning good customers who severed their relationships with a store because of overdue bills.

Yes, credit is a service, but often it poses problems.

Collection Policy

Any competent credit manager could cut collection problems drastically by allowing credit only to those accounts whose applications are credit perfect. But such a policy will not do in today's retail market. The forces of competition (everybody offers liberal credit) and the fact that mediocre credit risks are an important source of sales volume force stores to extend credit freely. A store's credit policy is usually set by top management, and is almost invariably liberal. The collection problems caused by the credit policy chosen are the responsibility of the credit department.

Collection Systems

Large organizations have collection systems, consisting of routines that are in all cases followed in prescribed patterns. Customers have a wide variety of payment habits that range from prompt payment to no intention of payment. Because these customer classifications are impossible to determine in advance, a good collection system sifts out the various types with each step in the process.

Impersonal.   People who have failed to receive their statements on time, overlooked the payment, are in temporary financial straits, or are careless are generally sent an insert with the statement, a sticker or a form letter. Good payers usually respond to these impersonal reminders, which are intended to retain customers by maximizing good will.

Impersonal Appeal.   The second step is still devoted to a major effort of retaining good will. Form letters appealing to a sense of fair play, asking for details of any disagreement, and the like are mailed. If there is no response at this time, many stores send telegrams, special delivery letters, or use the telephone.

Personalization.   If there has been no response to any of the prior steps, telephones and letters take on a more threatening tone. At this point, the customer is not one the store is anxious to keep and goodwill is less important. Moreover, those credit customers whom the store wants to keep have already been sifted out, and those that are left are poor credit risks. This does not mean that no attempt is made to retain goodwill. To the contrary, the store needs cash as well as credit customers. However, some goodwill may have to be gambled when a customer has failed to respond to the first attempts at collection.

Legal Action.   When all else has failed, long-past-due accounts are turned over to collection agencies or attorneys. This may result in wage garnishment or repossession.

Credit Card Organizations

Independent third party credit card organizations have become a major source of retail credit. Some, such as American Express, Diner's Club, and Carte Blanche were once generally restricted in use to hotels and restaurants, but are now accepted by many retailers. Bank credit card systems, on the other hand, are widely used in retail stores. These are systems in which banks offer credit to their consumer customers. The two principal bank credit cards are MasterCard and VISA. Their growth as a factor in retail credit has been phenomenal.

Bank credit card operations begin with the customer applying to the bank for a card. (This is sometimes done at a retail store.) After a credit check, a card is issued that is acceptable in almost all retail stores. After making a sale, the store forwards the sales slip to the credit card organization, which remits the amount of the sale to the store after deducting from 4 to 6 percent, depending, upon the store's volume.

The charge customer, under these plans, is the bank's customer. All of the responsibilities for credit decisions and collections belong to the bank. Banks usually allow small sales to be made without authorization. Large amounts are authorized by special telephone lines.

Bank credit is a boon to small retailers who lack the financial strength and know-how to engage in a credit business in any other way. It is widely used among large retailers also. With the growth in use of credit cards, customers prefer to carry a single card that may be used in many situations.

Retailers using bank credit card systems find that they have several disadvantages:

1. The cost of the system is considerable. If it cannot be added to the selling price (usually set by competition), it reduces profits.
2. The illegal use of lost or stolen cards is the store's responsibility. This is a serious factor in high-crime areas, and careful identification is required.

3. The close relationship between the store's credit card holder and the store is destroyed. The various advantages of store credit, such as mail order selling and special sales, are lost, along with customer loyalty.

Government Regulations on Credit

The granting of consumer credit is regulated by a variety of state and federal laws. These regulations are restrictive, and penalties may be severe. All retailers that grant consumer credit should be aware of the laws that affect their operations.

State Laws

State laws controlling installment and other credit sales vary from state to state. Generally, they require written credit contracts that specify the cash price, length of payment, down payment, fees and other credit charges, and so forth. In many states maximum interest rates are set. Some states permit the buyer to cancel the already signed contract within a few days.

Truth-in-Lending Law

In 1968 the Federal Consumer Credit Act (Truth-in-Lending Law) was passed. This law, along with Regulation Z, which was issued under the provisions of the act, required that lenders provide a great deal of information to their installment and charge customers. Among the information given is the time before finance charges are made, the amount of finance charge, and the method of computing the finance charge. Another disclosure must be the annual rate of the finance charge. Thus, a store charging interest at a rate of 1.5 percent per month must notify its customers that the annual interest rate is 18 percent.

CUSTOMER SERVICES

The past decade has witnessed significant changes in retailing. As we have seen, innovative merchants have challenged the traditionalists with merchandising techniques that have captured the attention as well as the dollars of people across the United States. The greatest impact in the race for the consumer's money has been made by the off-pricers. Whether their clout will continue to be felt by the conventional retailer or their methods of doing business will fade as quickly as they have appeared on the scene is not yet known. It is generally agreed that there is a substantial segment of the market that will continue to be motivated by price. In the 1960s, many consumers abandoned the department store for the discount operations, and today the same group seems to have found happiness at the off-price outlets.

Many retailers have experienced trouble when they tried to compete with the stores that sell for less by also selling at lower prices. To meet competition by reducing their prices, the retailers had to tighten the belt in terms of operational expenses. Some stores cut their sales staffs to such small numbers that it became difficult to find assistance on the selling floor. Others fought by curtailing customer services. Neither approach seemed to be the answer that the department stores needed to regain their place in retailing and recapture what they considered to be their fair share of the market.

Finding it difficult to beat the new wave of off-price retailers at the game they play best, the major department stores and large specialty organizations across the nation seemed to have made a unanimous decision to reestablish themselves. The route being taken involves reemployment of services that no longer were being offered, expansion of those that were still in existence, and development of new ones that have indicated creativity and initiative of management.

The services that make up the retailer's list are either free of charge to the customer or carry an extra cost. It is a commonly held belief that even "free" services are actually built into the cost of the goods. Some merchants believe that it is wiser to include the service in the cost, as in the case of alterations, so that the customer won't have to be presented with an "add-on" at the time of purchase. Others, which follow the route of extra costs to those who want the service, believe it should only be charged to the taker of the service and not to those individuals, in the case of alterations, for example, who don't require any.

Whatever the store's philosophy, the list of services provided varies from company to company.

Personal Shopping

Many merchants, especially those with a fashion orientation that caters to the more affluent, have initiated personal shopping services or expanded those that are already offered by their stores. Marshall Field, Chicago, for example, is reemphasizing the training of personal shoppers, which had been deemphasized for years. Instead of using the self-service approach, which many retailers, including Marshall Field, resorted to, the store instituted a policy that implemented better personal shopping to guide the customer who wants assistance in making a decision. Most stores make the public aware of the personal shopping service through advertising and promotion. In its "White Carnation" campaign, Marshall Field notified newspaper readers of 1,000 executives and managers who will be available as personal shoppers for a period of time. So successful was the campaign that the store, again through advertising, notified customers to seek out hosts and hostesses, who would be wearing white carnations, for regular personal attention. Lord & Taylor regularly advertises its personal fashion advisory shopping service, which features fashion advisor Gail Kittenplan and staff for every shopping need. Most retailers agree it is a service that produces greater sales volume.

Gift Registry

Most people are frequently faced with the problem of gift selection. Take the case of a friend or relative getting married. The gift has to be a fairly expensive one and it's difficult to be certain that the newlyweds will really enjoy it, rather than will keep it in a closet, bringing it out only when you are invited to their home.

Many high-image department stores offer bridal registry services to help with this problem. It works this way: the bride and groom visit the store and pick out things that they would like, such as flatware, table ware, linens, and so on, at a wide assortment of prices. The probable gift givers are made aware of this range, and when the time to make the gift selection comes, they go to the store and receive a list of preselected merchandise, from which they can select the item that fits their desired expenditure with confidence that it will be appreciated and that there will be no duplication. The store keeps track of the purchases and constantly deletes the items purchased

Figure 18–1 Customer assisted by bridal registry salesperson. *Courtesy* Williams-Sonoma

from the list. This works well for certain types of expensive gifts. For example, if the bride has her heart set on service for eight of a particular style of expensive silverware, the gifts can be bought as service for one by eight different friends or relatives. As soon as eight individual purchases of service for one have been bought, silverware is removed from the registry listing. Registry is good for the newlyweds since they get what they want, good for the purchaser since it removes gift selection problems, and good for the store since it can generate a lot of business. Figure 18–1 shows a customer being assisted by a bridal registry salesperson.

Dayton's and other stores have taken registry a step further. Hoping to capitalize on the baby boom, they have begun a registry for newborns. New parents complete a form indicating date of birth, sex of the baby, quantity, color, and size of the newborn baby's layette needs. These range from clothing and bedding to nursery and bath. Dayton's calls its baby register the Stork Club, and prospective buyers are given a listing from which to make selections. After each purchase, the list is changed by deleting the item sold. A list is maintained for two years after the baby's birth, and used for direct mail purposes to announce special events and sales.

Merchandise Alterations

Clothing alterations are often referred to as a necessary evil. Many retailers confess that the service is costly and occasionally leads to complications. For example, a customer might love the garment, be displeased with the alteration, and refuse to pay for it, leaving an altered piece of merchandise that is potentially a complete loss. While some stores play down the alteration service for women's clothing, it is virtually impossible to eliminate it for menswear. Men generally do not buy unless the item can be altered. They simply do not have the time or desire to seek outside assistance in the tailoring of their clothing. Most menswear retailers would agree that, without the alteration shop, sales would dramatically decline. Women, on the other hand, generally are not as demanding about on-premises alterations. Those with more time often seek outside services for their needs. Some stores, particularly those that cater to the working female, find that there is a need for tailoring in the store. Whether to charge extra for tailoring or include it within the price of the garment is a problem retailers must face. Traditionally, in the store that features both men's and women's clothing, the male customer's clothing is altered free of charge while the female must pay.

Gift Wrapping

Gift wrapping is provided by most stores that sell merchandise to be purchased as gifts. Some stores, because of their unique gift wrapping, gain a clientele who could otherwise make the same purchase elsewhere. The smaller retailers of boutique items and small giftware often include the cost of gift wrapping in the price of the merchandise. It is traditional that the larger retail organizations provide a free gift wrapping service, making use of less costly materials, and offering fancy packing for an extra charge that varies with the complexity and cost of the wrappings and decorations used. Gift wrapping is an excellent way to advertise a store's image. It is relatively inexpensive for a large store to operate a giftwrap department or for a small store to provide free giftwrap when weighed against the enthusiasm often generated by beautifully decorated packages.

Giftwrap as a source of income is an area that has been woefully neglected until recently. Lately, however, such stores as Macy's, Bloomingdale's, A&S, and others have been focusing on this area, not only as a customer service but as an important profit source as well. Department store executives think of giftwrap as a growth area with better-than-normal margins. A&S, for example, expects giftwrap to be very profitable, and Woodward & Lothrop expects the same. When you consider that Higbee's averages about a quarter of a million dollars a year, it is easy to see the profit potential.

All of this has had a considerable effect on this long neglected growth area. Macy's, California, has gone into giftwrap in a big way. While most stores treat giftwrap as a customer service with which they hope to break even, Macy's treats it as a profit center and actually merchandises it as it does with any other profit center. Macy's designs its own paper, uses highly styled popular colors, and goes so far as using a layered look when that look is fashionable. Its design picks up other major style themes throughout the store, and a wide assortment of dummy packages are displayed in appropriate departments. To Macy's (and others), giftwrap is a new kind of fashion merchandise and it is treated appropriately. Last year, the giftwrap department did a huge volume at higher-than-normal markup, and it is still growing.

Delivery

There are a variety of methods by which stores may furnish customers with a service to deliver goods. When offered such a service, customers will often purchase gifts to be sent to individuals who live at distances from the purchaser. Some merchandise—such as furniture or appliances—is too cumbersome to purchase and take home. Most retailers, though, in store signs, encourage the taking home of the purchase. Delivery could be costly, especially if included in the price, and unnecessary deliveries are avoided. There are a number of delivery arrangements available to retailers. For small items, parcel post is often used. Other goods may be delivered through a store's own trucks or by means of a private carrier. Unless a store does a sufficient amount of business to warrant operating its own delivery system, an outside company is employed. Many of the large retailers who deal in bulk items and operate from warehouses, such as Levitz, the furniture discounter, offer the customer two prices—one including delivery, and one if the merchandise is carried by the customer. In such a situation, an individual has the option to save money even on the traditionally delivered item. In some cases of bulky merchandise, delivery is required. In other cases, the retailer must weigh the advantages and disadvantages of providing delivery service, and whether the service should carry an extra cost to the customer.

Restaurants

More and more retailers are offering dining services to their customers. A restaurant might not be considered a service, but some retailers offer food a lower-than-usual prices in order to dissuade the customer from leaving the store at meal time. By retaining the customer on the premises, the store increases the chances for additional shopping after the meal. Some stores provide the management of these restaurants, while others lease space to experienced food companies to operate the eating facilities. The service runs the gamut from snack bar to the fanciest of establishments, such as Bloomingdale's gourmet railroad dining car restaurant in its flagship store. If a customer is kept in the store for an extended period, then the use of such space for a dining facility is worthwhile.

Children's Play Areas

More and more retailers are discovering that shoppers are able to spend more productive time in the stores when their children aren't with them. Since it is often impossible to leave the children at home, many parents take their offspring to the stores only to find that they can't concentrate on their purchasing needs. The solution for many retailers has been the establishment of supervised play areas where children can be left while the parents go about the business of shopping.

One company that has developed a very successful play area is IKEA, a Sweden-based home furnishings company with American branches currently located in New Jersey, Virginia, Maryland, California, Pennsylvania, and New York. The supervised play area in each location is called the Ballroom, aptly named for the thousands of colorful balls that fill the arena. A density of approximately two feet fills the entire space for the children to prance through. The balls not only serve as an exciting environment to which kids are quickly drawn, but also act as "buffer" in case of hard falls from the many structures that grace the area. Parents are given the comfort of safety since each child is properly "tagged" for identification and can only be retrieved by someone displaying the proper identification card. By the great number of children often seen in the Ballroom, it seems that the idea has met with enormous success. Not only do parents have freedom to shop, but the bundles that they load into their cars indicate that serious shopping was made available since the children were not hampering their decision making.

Additional Services

The extent and nature of other services are directly related to the store's image, the type of business it conducts, and the clientele served. The following is a list of some of the services offered across the country.

- Free interior design advice with furniture purchases
- Use of strollers for toddlers
- Gift registries
- Foreign-language assistance for non-English-speaking customers
- Personal shoppers to advise on purchases
- Play areas for children
- Special shopping days or hours for particular groups, such as the disabled
- Use of community room for organizations
- Travel service departments
- Expanded shopping hours at peak periods
- Automobile leasing with financing arrangements
- Computerized apartment rental service
- Senior citizen discounts
- Corporate gift service where large organizations make major purchases such as candy and flowers
- Monogramming

What is the Silver Key Club?

For the man or woman whose time is at a premium and for whom shopping must involve a minimum of time and effort. Just think . . . your very own **personal shopping consultant.** An N-M expert to pull selections for you or work with you as a consultant in any department in the store.

The Look of It: Your very own **private, elegant club** with a gracious ambiance and deluxe dressing rooms, housed on the upper level.

The Service: Based on a limited **private membership concept,** the initial 12-month membership is $75.00 with a $50.00 yearly renewal. Exercise your option to join and as a member you will receive:

- Silver Key **Reminder Service** for all important gift-giving dates.
- **Refreshments,** light lunch while you shop.
- We'll help **plan your party menu, suggest wines, arrange for flowers.**
- Our very own **Silver Key gift wrap,** complimentary.
- **Makeup Service,** a consultant can meet you in the Club for a late-day re-do.
- Socially correct **stationery, linen, silver, china coordination,** and your very own **monogram design.**
- On request, **priority alteration** service can be arranged.
- A business guest in town? We will be happy to bring them to the Club and extend our service as a **corporate guest on your membership.**

- Of course, invitations to our **fashion events, fashion videotapes,** and selected **catalogue mailings.**
- **Separate accounts** can be arranged for home and business.
- **The Greenhouse.** We'll schedule your stay and gather the clothes needed.
- Complimentary Silver Key **garment bags** and **travel hat boxes.**
- When needed, complimentary **same day delivery service.**
- Returning home? We will call a **taxi or limousine** which can be billed to your account.

The Silver Key Club membership service is but one aspect of our newly created Silver Key Services. We are also headquarters for international shopping, corporate gift-giving and theatrical assistance. Silver Key is all this, and more!

Figure 18–2   Customer service. *Courtesy:* Neiman Marcus

Neiman Marcus offers a vast roster of customer services that one would expect to find at a store of this caliber. Most impressive is its "Silver Key Club," which is directed toward the individual whose shopping obligations are numerous, but whose time is limited. Figure 18–2 summarizes the service.

Improving Customer Services

The most logical way to begin a program of improving customer services is to find out from customers themselves what it is they would like the stores to offer. Customer surveys usually produce the following results:

1. More, and easily located, restrooms
2. Places for customers to sit
3. Coffee or tea service
4. Package and coat checkrooms
5. Child care centers
6. Telephone shopping
7. Availability of wrapping and shipping
8. Valet parking
9. Information booths
10. Automatic doors at store entrances (see Figure 18-3)

When customers are questioned about services, many respond that they would be willing to pay for the extra services.

Figure 18–3 Automatic doors used by many retailers for easy access.
Courtesy: Stanley Magic-Door, Division of the Stanley Works

TRENDS

The types of credit available to consumers and services offered by stores is undergoing changes.

Emphasis On Private-label Cards

Recognizing the fact that customer loyalty often comes from use of a store's own credit card, more and more retailers are making concentrated efforts to broaden their use. In order to do so, many offer initial discounts when an account is open. A & S, for example, motivates its new account customers with an immediate 10 percent discount.

Using Outside Agencies to Operate Credit Cards

One of the reasons some stores shied away from their own cards was the hassle to collect bad debts and to deal with the everyday problems associated with credit. By assigning the accounts to outside companies, the stores receive their money quickly, improve their cash-flow situations, and eliminate the need to interface with delinquent accounts.

Joint Retailer Service Programs

Many shopping malls have established centers that cater to the needs of their shoppers. Some offer gift-wrapping centers, where purchases from any store in the center may be beautifully packaged, the rental of strollers, and the sale of gift certificates for "universal" use.

Expansion of Personal Shopping Facilities

Although many fashion oriented stores will gladly accompany shoppers throughout the store to make purchases, others have gone the extra mile in providing service. Bergdorf Goodman, the upscale New York fashion emporium, for example, has individual rooms set aside where customers who call in advance are treated to seeing merchandise without leaving their private enclosures and are treated to refreshments during the experience.

ACTION FOR THE INDEPENDENT RETAILER

It is in the area of customer services that many people believe the independent is no match for the giants of the industry. This is not true. In almost every instance, the independent can provide service that , if not precisely the same as that offered by its large retail counterpart, provides as much motivation for the customers to purchase.

Smaller retailers can provide the "personal" service that is so often lacking in the big store. In how many large organizations can a customer get the buyer's advice and attention? In the independent store, the owner is usually available to provide the personalization that makes the customers feel important.

Also, just about every small retailer can provide credit, through "house charges" or credit card organizations such as VISA or MasterCard; deliver merchandise; gift wrap packages; provide extended convenience shopping hours at holiday times; offer alterations that are often better than those provided by the large organization, because of on-premises supervision by the store owner; and present promotions that involve customers, such as fashion shows.

The strength of the small business lies in the service is able to provide only because of its size. Many shoppers find a more palatable atmosphere in the independent store than in the impersonal arena of the giant retail operations. If this were not true, the country would be void of the countless boutiques, small grocers, specialty stores, and restaurants that are found in every town and city throughout the United States.

IMPORTANT POINTS IN THE CHAPTER

1. Since World War II, the expansion of credit selling has been phenomenal. At the present time, most nonfood retailers, as well as some supermarkets, offer some sort of credit.

2. Customers use credit because it is convenient, is prestigious, makes carrying large sums of cash unnecessary, provides a credit rating for more credit, and reduces home bookkeeping.

3. Retailers offer credit because customers prefer it, customer relationships are improved, and it provides the opportunity for direct mail sales.

4. Among the types of retail credit available are charge accounts, installment accounts, and revolving credit and option terms.

5. The credit department is charged with the following responsibilities: opening new accounts, keeping credit records, authorizing credit, and billing and collections.

6. In establishing a collection policy, consideration must be given to the financial condition of the store, competitors' policies, and the kinds of goods involved.

7. Large retailers follow carefully prescribed patterns for the collections of late accounts. These begin with gentle reminders and end with legal action.

8. Credit card organizations such as American Express, VISA, and MasterCard are a major source of retail credit.

9. The granting of consumer credit is regulated by a variety of state and federal laws.

10. The variety of customer services often accounts for the amount of business transacted in retailing.

11. Recognizing the number of women in the workforce, many retailers have added services such as personal shopping to accommodate them.

REVIEW QUESTIONS

1. List six reasons why customers prefer to shop with credit cards.

2. Discuss the argument that too-liberal credit terms will bankrupt most American families.

3. Despite competitive pressures, some very successful stores *do not* give credit. How do they survive?

4. Discuss the relationship between a store and its charge customers.

5. How are credit accounts helpful in direct mail selling?

6. Explain the importance of teaching about credit in a sales training program.

7. Should a salesperson try to talk a customer out of a sale if the salesperson feels the buyer's credit burden will be excessive?

8. What benefits do stores get from a liberal credit policy?
9. List five characteristics of installment accounts.
10. Explain how revolving credit works.
11. What is revolving credit with option terms?
12. Discuss the responsibilities of the credit department.
13. Why is the interview important in opening a charge account.
14. What are retail credit bureaus? How are they organized?
15. Discuss the cash register operator's role in the granting of credit approval.
16. What is the effect of goodwill retention on collection policy?
17. List and define three factors that must be taken into account before a credit policy can be set.
18. Compare credit management in a small retail organization with that of a large store.
19. How do the independent credit card organizations operate?
20. Explain the requirements of the Truth-in-Lending Law and Regulation Z.
21. Should retailers charge for alterations?
22. How can the independent compete, in terms of service, with the giant retailers?
23. List three customer services and describe them.

CASE PROBLEMS

Case Problem 1

Smart Set, Inc., is a ladies' specialty store that started in 1970. The store is situated in a growing middle-class suburb of a large metropolitan area. During most of the organization's history, an influx of new homeowners and a lack of aggressive competition have led to steady growth in sales volume. In that period, the store has grown from a family-sized store to a relatively large and successful operation employing 14 persons.

In recent years, major inner-city department stores have begun following their migrating clientele into the suburbs. This, of course, has increased competition enormously. By tasteful buying and intelligent inventory control, Smart Set has been able to compete with the department stores in the area of merchandising; however, it has been forced to increase such customer services as the extension of credit.

Credit selling has expanded dramatically in recent year. Because the store is too small to afford a credit manager, store charge accounts (the only sort of credit offered) have been issued on a haphazard basis. Since the store is situated in a respectable, fairly affluent area, bad debt losses, although higher than normal, have been bearable. Collections, though, have been slow (customers seem to pay competing stores first). The result has been a fairly serious shortage of working capital.

The owner of Smart Set, Inc., has approached you to prepare a collection system for the store. The system given should include a step-by-step program for all late accounts.

Questions

1. Prepare the necessary collection program.
2. Have you any other suggestions?

Case Problem 2

A problem has come up in one of the largest, most successful department store chains in the country. The organization, Bloomcrest's, has many outlets in many major cities and wealthy suburban areas across the nation. The store's clientele consists of upper- and upper-middle-class patrons who flock to this prestigious organization because of the imagination and taste of the merchandising personnel.

Thanks to the uniqueness of the store's offerings, decor, and service, the markup is well above average, making it one of the most successful retail operations in the country. Currently, the only credit card Bloomcrest's accepts is its own.

As would be expected, top management is highly skilled and aggressive. Rather than rest on its laurels, it is constantly trying to improve the operation. One of management's programs is a periodic (every five years) evaluation of store procedures by a large, independent consulting firm.

One of the suggestions recently proposed by the consultants was that major independent credit cards be accepted. They argue that customers are weighted down by the number of credit cards they are forced to carry and many people have decided to replace their bulging wallets with a single, universally accepted credit card such as MasterCard or VISA.

The corporate controller, responsible for chainwide credits and collections, objects.

Questions

1. Present the controller's arguments.
2. Which decision do you favor? Why?

Chapter 19
Research

Photograph by Ellen Diamond

LEARNING OBJECTIVES

Upon completion of this chapter, the student should be able to:

1. List and discuss six areas of the use of research by retailers.
2. Differentiate between, and give examples of, primary and secondary information sources.
3. List three types of questionnaires and give four advantages and four disadvantages of each.

CAN VALUE PRICING AND CUSTOMER SERVICE CO-EXIST?

In today's retail environment, there is no single type of business that guarantees success for its operators. The operations run the gamut from specialized department stores such as Nordstrom, where the surroundings are elegant and the services unique, to the likes of Filene's Basement, where bargains reign and harried shoppers must sift through the offerings to make their selections without benefit of sales associates. Typically, the companies stress just one concept, be it price, service, selection, or comfortable shopping.

When Today's Man, a chain with sales of more than $150 million, considered entering the market with a wide assortment of men's clothing and furnishings, it had to decide upon a concept that would enable it to compete with the already successful department stores, specialty chains, and off-price stores that merchandised menswear. To break into the marketplace meant offering something that wasn't already out there. Through careful research of the competitors, they discovered not one had a business that combined both value and service. If price was the store's central theme, as in the case of Syms, then service wasn't. Similarly, if service was the key ingredient, as in stores like Bergdorf Goodman and Barney's, then price was never considered a factor. Today's Man's research indicated that a marriage of the two would bring positive results.

When shoppers enter one of the more than twenty stores, each averaging 25,000 square feet, their eyes immediately focus on immaculately displayed merchandise set in attractive fixtures, displays that emphasize impeccable taste, and discreetly placed signage that reveals top quality, value-priced offerings. In addition to the positive visual impression, the services afforded the shoppers are unique for this type of venture. Trained salespeople are in abundance to help with selections, and will move from department to department to assist in accessorizing the suit or sports outfit that has been chosen. A specialist in tie selection is always available to match the appropriate neckwear with the clothing. Tailoring, while available at some value-priced stores at a concession station, is a department owned and operated by the company. In this way, customer satisfaction is guaranteed from selection of the garments until they are taken from the store. Checkout time is reduced to a minimum for today's rushed shopper with the aid of the latest in scanner technology and bar coding.

If its current expansion program continues at its present pace, Today's Man will become one of the leading menswear operations in the country. Proper research, and attention to its findings, certainly has its rewards.

Decision making is probably the most important aspect of a manager's job. The decisions of a top manager can affect the entire retail organization. Middle managers, such as buyers or those in charge of selling departments, are concerned with decision making that affects primarily their own departments. Nonetheless, considering the amount of competition in retailing today, decision making at every level must be sound in order to improve the store's position and make certain it receives its fair share of business. Those who prepare haphazardly or make decisions based upon feeling or whim are apt to be unsuccessful retailers.

Retailers are continually trying to beat yesterday's figures. With the constant increase in costs, merely meeting last year's sales figures will result in smaller profits. In an attempt to achieve new goals, retailers are always involved in some type of research. *Marketing research* is a term that should be familiar to all students of retailing. Broadly, it involves the investigation of marketing problems and those recommendations necessary to solve these problems. Retailing is the last step in the marketing of most consumer goods (goods used for one's own personal satisfaction). Therefore, the problems that face the retail store confronted with purchasing merchandise from vendors and selling it to household consumers are often solved through marketing research.

To some students, the term *research* is associated with the scientific method and is thought of as grand-scale laboratory investigations carried out by scientists in white coats. Needless to say, the research used in retail stores may be as sophisticated or as simple as the size of the store or the problem warrants. Research in retailing is not confined to the giants of the industry. The individual proprietor can also become involved in investigating and solving some areas of the uncertainty without going to great expense. Naturally, the larger the organization, the more complex the problems and the more involved the research will be.

AREAS OF APPLICATION

Research is employed by retailers in a wide range of areas. It is used even before the retailer sets up shop to make certain the store is situated in the right location. Research covers every conceivable area of operation, starting before the goods are purchased by store buyers and ending after the customer has them at home. Following are some areas in which management may find research helpful in solving its problems.

Store Location

Picking the right place to house the retail outlet is of primary concern. Without the proper location, the best merchants in the world cannot run a successful operation.

The Customer

Whether the research is formalized by sending questionnaires to customers or carried on informally by having the salesperson determine customer needs through questioning, successful retailers know that satisfying the requirements of the customer is most important. Catering to the shoppers' demands makes it simpler to sell merchandise. Such areas as income, age, taste, education, and occupation must be studied to make certain that the customers' needs, such as style, color, and price, are being satisfied.

Advertising and Sales Promotion

Advertisements and displays and their creation are the result of much research. Whether a store engages in promotional advertising or institutional advertising is not left to chance. Even after a display is executed or an advertisement appears in one of the available media, its effectiveness should be measured. Another question answered through research is, "In which medium should we spend most of the sales promotion dollars?"; and if newspaper advertising is the answer, "Should we advertise in a daily or Sunday paper?"

Sales Methods

While some departments such as precious jewelry and expensive furs almost demand individualized service, other types of merchandise do not present so clear-cut a picture. Some stores offer both service and self-service. By studying the customers, potential customers, and practices employed by competitors and noncompetitors, decisions regarding sales methods can be made.

Merchandising

Perhaps the most important part of retailing is *merchandising,* broadly defined as the entire buying and selling cycle, including all of the activities involved in the process. In addition to studying customer demands, the retailer is interested in the current market conditions, new sources from which to purchase, prices, sales forecasts, and inventory analysis.

Analysis of Costs

Departments either operate on a standard markup for all merchandise or try to maintain an average markup for their entire inventory. Average markup allows for a department to vary the markup on individual items. Whichever method is employed, the markup needed to show a profit must be decided upon only after carefully studying all the costs involved. Markup cannot be a purely arbitrary amount, because of competition. Keeping this in mind, retailers are always trying to reduce costs and losses without pricing themselves out of their market; to accomplish this necessitates a good deal of research.

Customer Services

The amount and types of service to offer pose a problem to retailers. Some stores afford their shoppers such services as personal shopping (accompanying a customer through the store and making suggestions on what to purchase), baby-sitting, and free delivery. Other retailers may eliminate shopping services entirely. The practice to be followed is best determined by studying the customers through some form of research. Some retailers have found that customers are willing to pay a little more in order to have additional services. We need only to compare today's discount operations with those of ten years ago to see that the addition of delivery service and credit service resulted in higher prices.

Personnel

Finding and hiring the best available personnel, at all levels, is often a problem for the retailer. Which sources of supply produce the best applicants, what type of interview is most successful, whether or not testing is meaningful, are just some questions that need answers. The answers are often the result of research.

Certainly each of the areas briefly discussed opens up an infinite number of categories that are researchable and important to the proper overall functioning of the store.

THE RESEARCH PROCESS

Different problems require different research tools, but the research process, whatever the situation, is usually the following.

Identification of the Problem

A variety of factors might lead to the researching of a problem. One, perhaps, might be a gradual decline in sales for no obvious reason, either storewide or confined to a particular department. The reasons for the decline may not be obvious and therefore might necessitate investigation. Another problem might be whether a retail store should expand the facilities at its present location or move to another location. Still another problem might concern the evaluation of the effectiveness of the store's advertising practices in relation to sales. Whatever the area of concern, it must be identified in order to be effectively researched.

Definition of the Problem

Business executives, unlike market researchers, tend to be rather general in describing the problems confronting their organizations. In order to successfully solve a problem, it must be clearly defined. For example, evaluating the effectiveness of advertising and its relation to sales is too vague a question for investigation. Careful analysis of exactly what sales level is expected to result from advertising and whether or not the advertising program is bringing this response is more specific.

Conducting the Study

After the problem has been defined and is considered practical to solve (sometimes the costs are too prohibitive), a study is undertaken.

Studying Secondary Information

Before an investigator becomes involved in original research, an examination of secondary data (data that has already been compiled) is in order. The secondary data might supply background information that could be helpful in solving the problem. Sometimes so much has been published relating to the problem to be solved that it might not be necessary to engage in "field research." Among the secondary sources of information that may be important to retailers are:

1. *Company's own records.* These may include accounting reports such as the balance sheet and income statement; sales records of employees; unit control records (showing the activity of individual merchandise styles); records of returns, credits, and refunds; buyers' records; and records showing activity of charge customers' accounts.

2. *Libraries.* Just about every desired business publication is available in the public library. Those helpful to retailers include *Advertising Age, Chain Store Age, Women's Wear Daily, Visual Merchandising & Store Design,* and *Stores Magazine.* For a complete listing of pertinent computerized literature searches, most libraries have available a Business Periodicals Index. These publications are extremely important in that they often

publish the results of surveys that might be similar to the one being initiated. In that case, an original research project may be unnecessary since the same type of problem has already been investigated.

3. *Trade organizations.* These groups are composed of businesses with common interests. The largest retail trade association is the National Retail Federation, whose membership includes almost every important retail organization. These groups hold periodic meetings that result in forthcoming publications of interest to retailers. Some even publish their own periodicals.

4. *Government.* Much data is available from the federal government. *The Monthly Catalogue of U.S. Government Publications* contains a comprehensive list of government publications. Of particular interest to retail organizations are publications by the Department of Commerce, of which the Census Bureau is a part. Here all pertinent data, by different classifications, relating to potential business are available. For example, the census of housing, the census of business, and the census of population offer the retailer invaluable data.

5. *Private services.* There are several established agencies that have data that is otherwise unavailable without going into original research. Such companies as Dun and Bradstreet (credit information) and A. C. Nielsen Company (radio and TV measurement of audiences) can provide important information for retail research projects.

6. *Colleges.* Research studies are available at many colleges' business administration, marketing, and retailing departments.

Gathering Primary Information

If after exploration of the secondary data, the problem hasn't been solved (and it usually hasn't at this stage), then primary data must be collected. *Primary data* is defined as data compiled from firsthand sources. In retailing these sources include customers, vendors, advertising agencies, the advertising media, and employees of the organization.

There are several techniques employed by retailers in securing primary information. The nature of the problem generally determines the method to be used.

Counts (Observations).   Traffic counts and fashion counts are frequently used by retailers. As the name implies, this method requires the counting and recording of people or things that may be important to the retailer.

Traffic counts may be used when top management, in trying to evaluate a new location for a branch store, is interested in how much traffic passes the proposed site. The traffic is generally broken down into categories generated by public transportation, automobiles, and pedestrian traffic. A simple form is devised to record the number of people passing the location within a given period. A count of this type might also be used when a retailer is considering billboard advertising. Counting the number of people passing the proposed site is relatively simple.

Middle management often engages in informal traffic counts within its own departments. These counts may be used to determine the peak selling period for that department in the day. This information can be a help in scheduling employees' work periods.

Fashion counts are used to determine the type of clothes customers are wearing. This information can be helpful to buyers of fashion goods, in planning additional purchases for the current season or in planning for a new season. These counts, which are merely recorded observations of people, are also helpful in recognizing trends. A survey of this type might be taken at periodic intervals in places where a store's clientele congregates. Checking a particular kind of merchandise by such a survey might reveal factors that would be of interest in future purchasing. For example, a shirt shop catering to the "Madison Avenue advertising executives" might want to determine the colors that should be replenished in inventory and the amounts to be purchased. First, by taking an informal count at places such as luncheon spots frequented by the advertising crowd, or perhaps the entrances to the buildings that house the advertising agencies, the store owner can quickly learn what the store's clientele is wearing. Tabulation of the number of people observed (the number needed is determined by a statistical formula) will produce figures that can be translated into percentages. If, for example, 20 of 100 men observed wore blue shirts, it might be wise for this retailer to carry 20 percent of the store's inventory in blue shirts.

If it is desirable to determine whether color preferences are increasing or decreasing, additional counts can be taken. A comparison of the data taken on two dates would show the trends in men's colored shirts. High-fashion specialty stores often take fashion counts at social events, such as the opening of the horse show in New York City or the first night of the season at the Metropolitan Opera House. Since these events are frequented by fashion leaders, it is wise to see what these people are wearing.

The fashion count is simple to organize, and, in comparison with other methods used in gathering primary information, it is inexpensive. Stores often employ college students for this task since a great deal of research experience is not necessary. About the only really important point that must be impressed upon those who have not "counted" before is that they must have a perfect understanding of what is to be counted. An example of a form used for a fashion count taken by college students for a retailer's use is pictured in Figure 19–1.

Questionnaire.   The most widely used method of gathering information is the questionnaire. This technique is more involved and more time-consuming than the count. Whereas counts require no cooperation from those being surveyed, the questionnaire must seek out those willing to be involved.

Retailers can select from three methods of collecting data: telephone, mail, and personal interview. Which method is the most appropriate depends upon several factors. Among them are

1. Geographic area to be covered
2. Number of people available to carry out the survey

Style	Furs	Materials	Color (If Fabric)	Length
"A" line	Mink	Brocades	Black	Short coat
Cape	Persian lamb	Flat wool	Blue (Navy)	Mid-calf coat
Chesterfield	Rabbit	Leather	Brown	Floor-length coat
Double breasted	Sable	Mohair	Gold	Jacket
Empire	Fox	Satin	Green	Other _____
Jacket	Chinchilla	Suede	Gray	
Mandarin	Seal	Tweed and plaid	Natural	
Redingote	Beaver	Velvet	Red	
Trenchcoat	Muskrat	Other _____	White	
Wraparound	Other _____		Yellow	
Other _____			Other _____	

Place a check mark next to appropriate item. Place only one check mark in each column.

Figure 19–1   Fashion Count
Item Counted: Ladies' Outer Garments
Location: _____
(Fill in name of theater where count was made)

3. Cost
4. Time available to gather information

Closer analysis of the three methods point up their advantages and disadvantages.

Telephone.   The advantages of gathering data by telephone are that

1. It is the quickest method for researching people.
2. The cost of making the calls is relatively small.
3. Questioning can be carried out from a central point without the need for sending people into the field.

Following are some disadvantages of using the telephone:

1. Only those with telephones can be reached. Stores catering to the lower socioeconomic groups may not be able to contact their customers using this method.
2. Many people are reluctant to respond to interviewers they cannot see.
3. If the store's trading area is out of the normal call zone, those living in toll zones might not be called because of the high cost involved. This would present a limited picture of the store's clientele.
4. Calls might be annoying and resented by the store's customers.

Mail.   Advantages of sending questionnaires through the mail are that

1. Postage is relatively inexpensive.
2. Wide distribution (for trading areas of national chains) still affords the same cost to all persons being questioned. The telephone would require different costs because of toll calls.
3. More time is allotted for studying and answering questions.
4. The interviewer cannot influence the answer, as might happen in a personal interview.
5. A field staff is eliminated.

Some disadvantages of using the mail are the following:

1. The rate of return is small. A 10 percent response is considered to be very good.
2. Since the rate of response is so low, the cost per return is very high; the cost of those not returned must be considered part of the overall cost of the survey.
3. Questions might not be completely understood without an interviewer.
4. The time it takes to receive the responses is longer than either personal interview or telephone.
5. Those responding might not be truly representative of the sample.

Since the number of responses and the time factor involved are generally uncontrollable, retailers, in an effort to overcome these disadvantages, often offer premiums as an inducement for better results. Such inducements as courtesy discounts, special prices on particular items, and even cash are offered to those from whom responses are sought.

Personal Interview.   The interview may take place at the individual's home, in front of the retailer's store entrance, or even in the store. This is the only method employing face-to-face involvement. The questions may be either of the short-answer variety (most commonly used by retailers) or open-ended with the respondent giving a complete reaction to the question.

Advantages of a personal interview are that

1. Trained interviewers have success in getting a high percentage of people to grant interviews.
2. Questions that are not completely clear can be explained.
3. Additional probing can be conducted using the open-ended question. This is not possible via the mail.
4. Observations may also be recorded.

The following are disadvantages of personal interviewing:

1. Responding to an interviewer may cause the respondent to "color" responses because of embarrassment—for example, on such items as age and income.
2. Employment of experienced interviewers is costly.
3. Interviewers' biases might be reflected in the responses.
4. Interviews in the home might come at an inopportune time.

Preparation of the Questionnaire Form.   The amount and type of response received from the questionnaire will be only as good as the questionnaire design. Therefore, great care must be exercised in preparing these forms to guarantee accurate results. Among those factors that must be considered are

1. The occupations of those being questioned
2. Educational level
3. Prejudices of those to be interviewed

In constructing the form to be used, the following should be carefully considered:

1. Questions must be easily understood. The language must be compatible with the intelligence of those to be interviewed. This is particularly true in the case of the mail questionnaire, where there will not be an interviewer available to clarify questions.
2. Avoid generalities by eliminating such words as "usually," "generally," and "occasionally." Such words tend to prohibit a clear-cut response from the respondent. For example, "Do you usually shop at the R & M Department Store?" An answer to this question will not tell how often the customer shops at R & M or the percentage of purchases that are made there.
3. Questions should be arranged in sequential order so that each question makes for a smooth transition to the next one.
4. Questions should be concise and to the point.
5. The questionnaire should not be too long. This might discourage a response. A one-page form is most satisfactory for use by retailers.
6. The design must be organized in such a manner that recording is simple. Caution must be taken to provide enough space for responses, particularly if open-ended questions are used.
7. The questionnaire should be organized in such a manner that tabulation of the results is simplified.

Examples of mail, personal interview, and telephone questionnaires are shown in Figures 19–2 (pp. 403–404), 19–3 (p. 405), and 19–4 (p. 406).

Dear Customer:

In our efforts to serve you better and to provide you with the best in shopping facilities, we periodically ask some of our valued patrons to answer a few simple questions. Your responses and suggestions guide us in some key decisions regarding store operations. Our sole objective is to give you the type of store that you can look forward to shopping in the year round.

Please fill in the form below. After completion, fold and insert the form into the attached self-addressed, stamped envelope.

As a token of our appreciation, on receipt of your questionnaire, we will send you a free premium for an attractive gift that may be redeemed at any of our branch stores. Please hurry since the supply is limited and the cutoff date is _____ .

May we thank you in advance for your answers, your comments and your advice.

(Tear off)

1. Do you find the store layout convenient?
   ☐ Yes   ☐ No   (If no, please suggest some changes you would like to see made. Comment in the space provided below.)

   _____

   _____

   _____

2. Are our salespeople always helpful?
   ☐ Yes   ☐ No   (If no, please mention some ways they can better serve you.)

   _____

   _____

   _____

3. Are you satisfied with our checkout counters, particularly in terms of speed, handling of credit cards and charge accounts, and wrapping?
   ☐ Yes   ☐ No   (Please comment below.)

   _____

   _____

   _____

4. What other merchandise lines or service would you like to see added to our store?

   _____

   _____

   _____

5. Are you satisfied with our adjustment and refund policy?
   ☐ Yes   ☐ No   (If no, please suggest ways we can improve this policy.)

   _____

   _____

   _____

Figure 19–2 Mail questionnaire

Classification Data

6. Please tell us approximately how often you shopped here in the past six months. Check the appropriate box below:

None ☐
1–3 times ☐
4–6 times ☐
7–9 times ☐
10–12 times ☐
15 or more times ☐

7. Of your total purchases what percent is:

Cash	%
Charge Account	%
Credit Card	%
Other (specify)	%
	100%

8. What are the occupations of the members of the household?

_____

9. What is the last grade of school completed by family members?

Grade school or less ☐
Some high school ☐
Completed high school ☐
Some college ☐
Completed college ☐

10. Was your approximate family income last year under $25,000 or over $25,000?

Under $25,000	Over $25,000
Was it -	Was it - under $25,000
$7,500–10,000	or over $25,000
or $10,000–12,500	
or $18,000–25,000	

11. Would you please indicate in which of these age groups you belong? Are you in your . . .

20's . . . .
30's . . . .
40's . . . .
50's . . . .
60 and over

Your Name (Please print) _____

Address (Please print) _____

City _____ State _____ Zip # _____
   (Do not abbreviate)

Figure 19–2 (continued)

Questions Asked of Brant Walk-Outs

Pardon me . . . I am making a consumer survey for Brant's.

1. Did you buy anything at Brant's today? ___ Yes ___ No ___ Just passing through

   If respondent answers "yes," thank her for her patronage and tell her that the study you are making does not involve Brant customers.

   If she is just passing through the store, thank her for this information.

   If her answer is "no," go ahead with the rest of the questionnaire.

2. What departments at Brant's did you visit (indicate department and floor)?

3. Would you mind telling us your reason for not buying anything at Brant's?

Item	Didn't have what I wanted (size, color, brand, style, etc.)	Price too High	Salesperson not helpful	Out of Stock	Just looking	Other, specify
a)						
b)						
c)						
d)						

4. When you think of Brant's what is the first thing that comes to your mind?

Classification data -

What part of town are you from? (Eastland, Riverview, etc.)

Do you work downtown? Yes No

Age (to be estimated by interviewer) Under 30 30–44 45 and over

Man Woman

Date and time

Store entrance (circle one)
Walnut Street Cosmetics | Walnut Street Men's Furnishings | Walnut Street Blouse
Euclid Street Purses | Euclid Street Hosiery | Main Street
Euclid Street Men's clothing

Figure 19–3 Personal interview questionnaire. Robert H. Myers, "Sharpening Your Store Image," *Journal of Retailing,* Vol. 36, No. 3.

Focus Groups and College Boards. Some retailers have had success in organizing groups for guidance in such areas as merchandise selection, advertising evaluation, and customer services. The groups are selected from a cross-section of customers or potential customers, depending upon the information that is desired. The groups are either organized permanently to meet periodically and make recommendations, or are temporarily formed.

Most successful to stores selling back-to-school clothing have been the college boards. This group or panel is generally composed of representatives of those colleges attended by the store's customers. Panels of this nature might have as many as 30 colleges represented. The students (usually young women) advise buyers on the selection of styles most appropriate for their colleges and universities. They also can be found on the selling floors, prior to going back to school, to help those students interested in the appropriate selection of clothing for their particular schools. This panel both advises management and helps to sell the merchandise.

Another example of a focus group is one using potential customers. A newly opened retailer, in an attempt to increase disappointing sales, might organize a cross-

RICHARD MANVILLE RESEARCH INC.
230 PARK AVENUE, NEW YORK, N.Y. 10017

<u>WASHING MACHINE SURVEY</u>

NAME: _____   TIME STARTED: _____

TELEPHONE
NUMBER: _____   DATE: _____

Hello, we're conducting a survey and I'd like to ask you a few questions.

1.   Do you have a washing machine in your home?

      4-1 ☐ Yes

      -2 ☐ No   (IF NO, DISCONTINUE -
                  IF YES, ASK:)

2.   Did you buy it within the last six months?

      5-1 ☐ Yes

      -2 ☐ No   (IF NO, DISCONTINUE)

3.   Is it <u>filled</u> by one hose or by two hoses?

      6-1 ☐ One Hose

      -2 ☐ Two Hoses

      -3 ☐ Don't Know

4.   Where in your home or apartment do you keep the washing machine?

      In what room?

      7-1 ☐ Kitchen

      -2 ☐ Basement

      -3 ☐ Washroom

      -4 ☐ Hallway

      -5 ☐ Other (Specify)_____

5.   Is it on rollers or is it permanently installed?

      8-1 ☐ Rollers

      -2 ☐ Permanently Installed

      -3 ☐ Don't Know

      (IF ON ROLLERS, ASK QUESTION 6)

6.   Do you have to move the washing machine each time you use it?

      9-1 ☐ Yes   -2 ☐ No

7a   Is the washing machine regular size or compact size?

      10-1 ☐ Regular

      -2 ☐ Compact

      -3 ☐ Don't Know

b   (IF A COMPACT WAS PURCHASED, ASK:) Why did you purchase a compact
      machine rather than a regular size model? (PROBE)

11-   _____

      _____

      _____

Figure 19–4   Questionnaire for telephone survey

section of individuals who comprise the store's trading area. The group, led by a trained researcher, discusses customer characteristics and needs. After a careful study of a recording of the discussion, recommendations for adjusting the situation can be made. If the data are still inconclusive, the employment of a questionnaire might be found worthwhile, with the questions to be answered formulated from the panel's responses.

Most important in the use of the group is to make certain the individuals truly represent the group you are trying to learn about. For a very small cost, a marketing research firm can arrange any type of focus group. In this way, proper participation will be guaranteed.

Sampling

After preparing the necessary forms to be used, a determination must be made regarding the number of people to be included for the survey to be meaningful. It is neither necessary nor practical to involve every conceivable individual in a group. For example, a retailer located within a trading area of 500,000 people need only investigate a small part of this population. The segment of the population selected is known as a *sample*. The sample is most effective when its members are truly representative of the group to be studied. The size and selection of the sample are based upon many considerations and should be carefully decided upon with the help of a statistician.

Collection of the Data

The actual collection of data depends upon the method to be used. Whichever technique or combination of techniques is employed, the investigators must be thoroughly trained. Stores employing the services of a professional research organization need not be concerned, but those using college students or their own employees to collect data must make certain that there is a thorough understanding of the investigative methods. A successful method used in training laypersons to conduct personal interviews is role playing. One individual assumes the interviewer's identity and the other the consumer's; in this way an individual trained in the art of questioning can observe, criticize, and make recommendations to improve questioning techniques. In the area of observations, investigators must be familiar with what they are observing and recording. The results of the fashion count in Figure 19–1, concerning women's outer garments, could not have been meaningful unless the observers were able to distinguish between such items as a floor-length coat and a calf-length coat. Similarly, those involved in recording information derived from consumer panels must be thoroughly trained in that procedure.

Processing and Analysis of the Data

After the investigators submit the raw data collected, the data must be processed, that is, arranged in proper form for analysis. All the forms must be first inspected and corrected or modified to guarantee that the information is stated appropriately for tabulation. The data must then be classified into categories. This step is simplified if care was exercised in the preparation of the forms used. Without being classified into homogeneous groupings, the data cannot be analyzed. The next step, particularly if computers are to be used for the purpose of tabulation, is coding. A code must be devised for each possible type of reply. For example, code 6 might mean blue and code 12 might stand for red. These codes can then be fed into the computer for quick processing. Coding can be eliminated if the questionnaire was precoded with each item having a number assigned to it on the original form. Actual tabulation can be done by machine, as mentioned, or by hand. Small retailers often use small samples that can be tabulated by hand. More common is the computer tabulation, which mechanically and more quickly and efficiently performs the steps involved.

After the data have been compiled and summarized, analysis takes place. The amount and kind of analyses depend upon the research project. Some studies, such as the fashion count, might be used only to determine which colors are most popular and in what percentages. Other studies might require more sophisticated statistical analysis and interpretation. This phase of the research project is most important, since future decisions will be based upon it. Knowledgeable research analysts are best used to evaluate all possible courses of action and make final recommendations. If a retailer is conducting its own study, it is advisable for everyone in management connected with the project to review the recommendations of the chief researcher before implementing those suggestions.

Preparation of the Research Project

A written report should be prepared outlining the findings of the investigation. It should include the data, analysis, and recommendations bound in some permanent form. This can serve for future reference and related studies.

Most complete research reports follow the areas covered in this chapter. They are

1. The problem defined
2. Methodology used in the study
3. Analysis
4. Recommendations
5. Appendices, to include data from both secondary and primary sources

TRENDS

Merchandise prices are following two specific routes in today's retail environment. The actual prices charged to customers are based upon the store's method of operation.

Traditional Store Pricing

At department stores and specialty chains, the markups and ultimate prices consumers pay for their goods are on the increase. With attention paid to customer service and an increase in "shrinkage," retailers of this nature need to charge more to cover their expenses and return a profit.

The Discount Operations

Value operations or discounters such as Kmart and Wal-Mart are working on markups that are lower than they once were. With competition coming from the warehouse clubs such as Price and Sam's, they must cut costs to bring the customers in. It should be understood that the shoppers who frequent these types of stores are not in search of unusual services and are motivated strictly by price.

Off-pricers

Although the prices charged the shoppers are comparatively low, it should be understood that the costs to off-price retailers are far below the original costs. Thus, the off-pricers are still working on high markups, even though the shoppers are getting bargains.

Markdowns

More and more retailers are marking down their items faster than they once did. Traditionally, markdowns were taken twice a year, at the end of the summer and after Christmas. Today's merchants recognize the need to dispose of unwanted merchandise as soon as possible, to make room for new items that might better capture the shopper's attention. It is not unusual for retailers to take markdowns as early as three weeks after an item arrives if it fails to sell.

ACTION FOR THE INDEPENDENT RETAILER

Research is often looked upon, especially by smaller retailers, as too time-consuming, complicated, and, above all, too costly for their businesses. Although it is true that many studies that are undertaken require large sums of money as well as trained specialists, there are areas of research that can benefit even the smallest retailer with a minimum of expense.

Some principles for independents to follow are

- Read all of the available literature. Trade associations and periodicals provide a multitude of studies that might parallel even the smallest store's problems.
- Make questionnaires available to customers who could comment on merchandise assortment, price lines, and so forth.
- Prepare a fashion count, if appropriate. College classes could be approached to carry out the research as a class project. This gives the retailer information and the students practice.
- Provide a suggestion box for customers, and tally the suggestions. Those that are most prevalent and appropriate could be used.

Research need not be costly. It provides a variety of pertinent information that could be collected with little or no cost to the retailer.

IMPORTANT POINTS IN THE CHAPTER

1. Retailing research involves the investigation of retailing problems and the recommendations necessary to solve those problems. In practical terms, retailing research is an attempt to take some of the guesswork out of managerial decision making.
2. Research is used by retailers in a wide range of areas. These include determining sites for a store's location; gathering information concerning the tastes and

needs of a store's customers; analyzing the effectiveness of a store's advertising and sales promotion; and studying merchandising policies, including resources, sales forecasts, and size and color analyses.

3. Before the methods of research can be decided upon, it is necessary to clearly identify and define the problem.

4. The necessary information upon which the research will be based may be taken from many sources. These include the company's own records, libraries, trade organizations and publications, government publications, and private research organizations.

5. Much retailing research is based upon counts. This method requires the counting and recording of people or things. Such information as the number of people wearing particular styles or colors is typical of research based upon counts.

6. The questionnaire, either by telephone, by mail, or in person, is essentially an involved, time-consuming method of gathering information needed for some research studies.

7. After the research information has been collected, it must be tabulated, analyzed, and reported. Recommendations based on the report are the final step in a research project.

REVIEW QUESTIONS

1. Define marketing research.

2. Discuss some of the factors that should be researched in the selection of a store location.

3. Is top management or middle management more concerned with research in the area of store location? Defend your position.

4. What are some questions answered through research for the manager of a store's advertising department?

5. Identify those areas of investigation that might be helpful to the personnel manager.

6. Why must a problem be carefully and clearly defined in a research project?

7. Even after a problem is identified and defined, it occasionally is not researched. Why?

8. Define the term *secondary data*.

9. Where might a research investigator find invaluable information for a project without looking outside the company?

10. Which publications might be beneficial for retailers to use when they are conducting a study?

11. How might a trade organization help the retail store involved in a research project?

12. Using which type of research technique might a retailer gather information without permission or direct assistance from those being studied?

13. Describe the technique often used by retailers to assess the amount of traffic at proposed sites for branch stores.

14. Compare the advantages of telephone and mail questionnaires.

15. Why do some consider the personal interview the best questionnaire method?

16. Does the writing of a questionnaire need the expertise of someone seasoned in research? Explain your answer.
17. What is a focus group?
18. Define the term *sample*.
19. How are the data, collected through questionnaires or counts, processed?
20. Discuss the reasons for preparation of a formal, written report to show findings and recommendations.

CASE PROBLEMS

Case Problem 1

Business in general is increasing at a reasonable growth rate at Alan's Department Store, located in a downtown metropolitan area. Alan's has been in operation for 40 years. For the past three years the furniture department, in existence since the store's inception, has shown a decline in sales. Neither the buyer, who has headed the department for the past 12 years, nor the merchandise manager in charge of hard goods has been able to stop the slump. A routine study of the situation shows the following:

1. There have been no significant changes in sales personnel. (Alan's has a very low employee turnover rate.)
2. The same vendors are being used as were used in the past.
3. The population in the trading area has been increasing.
4. No new competition has opened for business.
5. Store policy and service have remained the same.

The store's gross has shown a steady increase of about 6 percent annually (last year's sales for the entire store were $26 million), but the furniture department has been declining at a rate of 5 percent annually for the last three years. Since this department accounts for 15 percent of the store's total sales, top management has approved a research project to discover the causes of the problem.

Question

1. Prepare an outline indicating and explaining the approach you would take to solve the problem. Include all the steps you would employ in your design. Your outline should be prepared as though you were a research consultant.

Case Problem 2

Teen-Rite is a specialty shop catering to teenage girls. It carries a complete line of dresswear, sportswear, and accessories to outfit the teenage customer. The largest part of its operation is devoted to clothing worn for school. This past season Teen-Rite did not realize a profit. Traffic into the store was the same as it had been in past seasons, with the same customers comprising the shopping group. Another profitless season could lead to bankruptcy.

One salesperson suggested to Ms. David, the proprietor, that she contact a marketing research firm to help with the problem. Ms. David explained that her operation, which grosses about $750,000 annually, is unable to afford the expense involved. Instead, she decided to carefully study the situation to determine the causes of the problem. After informal talk with customers, she discovered that the school dress regulations in her community had changed and her merchandising practices would have to be updated. Although she discovered the reasons for poor business, she was still confronted with the problem of proper merchandise selection.

Questions

1. With a minimum of cost involved, what research techniques would you employ to determine Teen-Rite's merchandise needs?
2. Prepare the forms necessary to be used in the project.
3. Whom would you use to conduct the project?

Index